P9-CBB-562

John Cheever

The Hobgoblin Company of Love

George W. Hunt, S.J.

CARNEGIE PUBLIC LIBRARY.
Terrell, Texas

813.52

Accession 84-1150   Book Hun

Date 3/84 NETLS   17.95

Grand Rapids
William B. Eerdmans Publishing Company

For
Bob McCarty

Copyright © 1983 by William B. Eerdmans Publishing Co.
255 Jefferson Ave. S.E., Grand Rapids, Mich. 49503
All right reserved
Printed in the United States of America

Library of Congress Cataloging in Publication Data

Hunt, George W., 1937-
John Cheever, the hobgoblin company of love.

Includes index.
1. Cheever, John—Criticism and interpretation.
I. Title.
PS3505.H6428Z69 1983   813'.52   83-1560
ISBN 0-8028-3576-7

Quotations from *The Wapshot Chronicle* and *The Wapshot Scandal* have been used by permission of International Creative Management on behalf of the Estate of John Cheever. The 1979 reissue of the books by Harper & Row was used in the text. *The Wapshot Chronicle* was originally published by Harper & Row in 1957. Four chapters of this book appeared in a slightly different form in *The New Yorker*. *The Wapshot Scandal* was originally published by Harper & Row in 1963. Six parts of this book appeared in *The New Yorker* and one part in *Esquire*.

Grateful acknowledgment is also made to Alfred A. Knopf, Inc., for permission to quote from the copyrighted works of John Cheever published by their house: *Bullet Park*, *Falconer*, *The Stories of John Cheever*, and *Oh What a Paradise It Seems*.

W. H. Auden's "The Truest Poetry Is the Most Feigning" has been quoted by permission of Edward Mendelson, William Meredith, and Monroe K. Spears, executors of the Estate of W. H. Auden, and by Random House, Inc. The poem is found in *W. H. Auden: Collected Poems*, ed. Edward Mendelson (New York: Random House, 1976). Copyright 1954 by W. H. Auden. It was originally published in W. H. Auden, *The Shield of Achilles* (Faber & Faber, 1955).

Contents

Acknowledgments

In its own way the composition of this book followed the circuitous route of the great Jesuit martyrs and missionaries centuries ago—but without the heroism, only the blood. The book was inspired and begun at Le Moyne College, Syracuse, New York; research and the writing of three chapters were completed over two summers at Boston College, Chestnut Hill, Massachusetts; three more chapters were done at America House in New York City; and the final four chapters were composed at St. Peter's College, Jersey City, New Jersey. I wish to express my sincerest thanks to the many Jesuits living in each of these communities, for their generous moral support was invaluable to me. I would like to single out specifically Rev. J. Donald Monan, S.J., and Miss Margaret Dwyer at Boston College, and Rev. Martin F. Mahoney, S.J., and Rev. Walter J. Malone, S.J., at St. Peter's College for their exceptional kindness in providing room for a scholarly wayfarer.

I would also like to thank the following people especially: Rev. Robert E. McCarty, S.J., whose unenviable lot it was to hear the various versions of the text read aloud to him, and yet who retained sufficient patient composure to make excellent suggestions that I followed; Mrs. Jean Britt, who performed the remarkable feat of transcribing pages upon pages of my handwritten scrawl into an attractive, legible manuscript—no mistake here is hers; and also Miss Mary Hietbrink, my gracious editor at Eerdmans, who ironed out the text's many wrinkles with judicious care. Finally, I would like to thank Mr. John Updike and Mrs. Mary Cheever for giving me permission to quote the whole text of John Updike's eloquent eulogy delivered at the graveside of John Cheever in Norwell, Massachusetts.

Chronology

1912   Born on May 27 in Quincy, Massachusetts, the youngest son of Fred-
            erick Lincoln Cheever (1863-1946), a successful shoe salesman, and
            Mary Deveraux Liley Cheever (1873-1956), born in Sheffield, Eng-
            land. He lives with them and his older brother, Frederick (1905-76),
            through adolescence in Quincy.

1923-26   He attends Thayer Lands, a progressive school, and becomes adept
            in French; he wins a short-story contest sponsored by the Boston
            Herald Traveler.

1926-29   He enters Thayer Academy in Braintree, Massachusetts, but is ex-
            pelled for smoking and poor grades and never graduates from high
            school.

1929-31   He lives with his brother Fred in Boston; *The New Republic* publishes
            his short story, "Expelled," in October 1930; he and Fred take a
            walking tour through Europe.

1932   In mid-decade his father's business had suffered serious reversals—
            now their savings are exhausted, the mortgage on his parents' home
            is foreclosed; his parents separate; he and his brother Fred separate
            as well; he moves to New York City where he becomes protégé of
            Malcolm Cowley and writes story synopses for MGM movie studios.
            A photograph of his barren room on 323 Hudson Street, taken by
            Walker Evans, is still featured in the Museum of Modern Art.

1934   He spends his first summer at Yaddo colony in Saratoga Springs, and
            then receives an assignment from the Works Projects Administration
            (WPA) to work on a guide book for Washington, D.C.

1935   *The New Yorker* publishes "The Brooklyn Rooming House," and his
            long association (120 stories) with the magazine begins.

1937-38   He writes a novel, *The Holly Tree,* but when publishers insist on
            modifications, he destroys it. He is reassigned by the WPA and is
            responsible for the final editing of *The WPA Guide to New York City*
            (reprinted in 1982).

1941   He marries Mary Winternitz, daughter of Dr. Milton Winternitz,
            dean of Yale Medical School, on March 22, 1941. He is drafted into

the infantry rifle company as a mortar gunner (later nearly his entire unit is killed in the Normandy invasion); when the Army discovers he is a professional writer, he is transferred to the Signal Corps to work on public relations movies for the Army and is stationed in Astoria, Long Island.

1943 His first collection of stories, *The Way Some People Live*, is published. His daughter Susan is born.

1944 He goes to the Philippines with the Air Corps to record operations.

1948 A theatre adaptation of his short stories, "Town House," is produced at the National Theatre (12 performances); he continues to write stories as well as television scripts for the next few years. His first son, Benjamin, is born.

1951-52 He and his family move out of New York City to Scarborough, New York, about 25 miles north on the east bank of the Hudson; he receives a Guggenheim Fellowship.

1953 His second collection, *The Enormous Radio and Other Stories*, is published.

1954-55 His short story "The Five-Forty-Eight" wins the Benjamin Franklin Award, and "The Country Husband" wins the O. Henry Award as the year's finest short story.

1957-58 His first novel, *The Wapshot Chronicle* (begun in 1952), is published, and later wins the National Book Award. He is elected to the National Institute of Arts and Letters. He moves to Italy for a year, where his younger son, Federico, is born. His third collection, *The Housebreaker of Shady Hill and Other Stories*, is published.

1961 He and his family move to a new home in Ossining, New York. His fourth collection, *Some People, Places and Things That Will Not Appear in My Next Novel*, is published.

1964 His sequel to *The Wapshot Chronicle*, *The Wapshot Scandal*, is published, and later wins the Howells Medal, presented by the American Academy of Arts and Letters, as the most distinguished novel published in the previous five years. His fifth collection of stories, *The Brigadier and the Golf Widow*, is published.

1969 His third novel, *Bullet Park*, is published.

1973 The story collection *The World of Apples* is published; he is elected to the American Academy of Arts and Letters.

1975-76 After suffering two heart attacks within a short period and succumbing to severe alcoholism, he commits himself to Smithers Clinic and is rehabilitated, never to drink again.

1977 His fourth novel, *Falconer*, appears, and he is featured in all the major American magazines.

1978   *The Stories of John Cheever* is published and wins the Pulitzer Prize and the National Book Critics Circle Award; later its paperbound version will win the American Book Award. Harvard University awards him an Honorary Doctorate of Letters.

1979   He is awarded the Edward MacDowell Medal for "outstanding contribution to the arts."

1980   The Public Broadcasting System presents television adaptations of three Cheever stories: "The Sorrows of Gin," "O Youth and Beauty," and "The Five-Forty-Eight."

1981   He completes an original script, "The Shady Hill Kidnapping," that later appears on public television.

1982   His last novel, *Oh What a Paradise It Seems,* is published. He is awarded the National Medal for Literature in April. On June 18 John Cheever dies in his home in Ossining; he is buried in the Cheever family plot in Norwell, Massachusetts.

[Cheever] is one of the few American writers who have undergone a visible development. Take a writer like Farrell. He wrote *Studs Lonigan* first and he wrote *Studs Lonigan* last. Most of them are that way. But here's Cheever—you read those stories and you see his powers of transformation, his power to take the elements given and work them into something new and far deeper than they were at the outset.

Saul Bellow

Literature is the only continuous and coherent account of our struggle to be illustrious, a monument of aspiration, a vast pilgrimage.

John Cheever

In the coining of images and incidents, John Cheever has no peer among contemporary American fiction writers. His short stories dance, skid, twirl, and soar on the strength of his abundant invention; his novels tend to fly apart under its impact.

John Updike

I do not think it too much to get down on my knees once a week to thank God for the coming wonder and glory of life.

John Cheever

Introduction

John Cheever died at an hour edging toward twilight on June 18, 1982, after waging a valiant battle against cancer and other distressing ailments during the last year and a half of his life. An uncommon tenderness and unadorned eloquence characterized the texture of the many obituaries and memorials written in the days and weeks following his death, as if each writer privately strove to appropriate and so celebrate what Michiko Kakatuni in *The New York Times* noted: "His voice was the voice of a New England gentleman—generous, graceful, at times amused, and always preoccupied with the fundamental decencies of life." Cheever, with his keen ear for language and his nose for cant, would have been delighted with the tone and style of these obituaries, though rather amused by the subject that evoked them.

In an unsigned eulogy for *The New Yorker*, John Updike first addressed his attention to that cluster of qualities now known as the Cheeveresque and so rooted in the personality of the man himself:

> From somewhere—perhaps a strain of sea-yarning in his Yankee blood—
> he had got the authentic archaic story-telling temper, and one could
> not be with John Cheever for more than five minutes without seeing
> stories take shape: past embarrassments worked up with wonderful ra-
> pidity into hilarious fables, present surroundings made to pulse with
> sympathetic magic as he glanced around him and drawled a few star-
> tlingly concentrated words in that mannerly, rapid voice of his. He
> thought fast, saw everything in bright true colors, and was the arena
> of a constant tussle between the bubbling *joie de vivre* of the healthy
> sensitive man and the deep melancholy peculiar to American Protes-
> tant males.

Updike then went on to comment on Cheever the writer: "He was often labelled a writer about suburbia; but many people have written about suburbia, and only Cheever was able to make an archetypal place out of it, a terrain we can recognize within ourselves, wherever we are or have been." Finally, Updike concluded by suggesting that Cheever's uniqueness actually finds its locus in a distinctively spiritual and national sensibility, twin traditions that animated his imagination:

> It took an effortlessly moral nature to imagine fall and redemption in that realm of soft lawns and comfortable homes; Cheever's sense of human adventure lay squarely in the oldest American view. Like Hawthorne's, his characters are moral embodiments, rimmed in a flickering firelight of fantasy. Like Whitman, he sang the common man, the citizen average in his sensuality, restlessness, lovingness, and desperation.

At the time of Cheever's death, I had completed over ninety percent of this study, one which attempts to investigate in an orderly way the many magical properties of his fiction to which Updike and others have more eloquently attested. On finishing it, my great regret is that the tenses in the text had to be changed from the present to the past, and that now I am unable to present Cheever himself with a copy of the final product. Along the way, throughout its many permutations, he had been most generous and supportive, exhibiting a modesty and gratitude that was genuinely humbling for me. To have such support can be inhibiting for a critic, I know, but that was the opposite of Cheever's own courteous intent. Let me cite one characteristic letter that I received almost exactly one year before his death. I will quote it in full, because not only does it display his friendly sense of fun, his candor, and his unerring directness of style, but also its magnanimity and quaint spirit actually manage both to expose and impose special challenges for any Cheever interpreter sanguine enough to think he has the "facts."

> Dear George,
>
> Thank you very much for your prayers; and I'm delighted to know that I have readers in Kansas City, that you have a sabbatical and that we will likely meet. I am still weathering a delayed recovery from surgery. Sickness seems to be no part of the story I hope to tell and when I bleed freely I think only of how little use I have for such an experience. I think often of you because I remember you fondly and deeply regret that I should be such a thankless and murky subject. In reviewing my unfortunate self there are three things that I must mention.
>
> Firstly, there is no bibliography. This matters not at all to me, but from time to time I am shown stories that I have completely forgotten. There must be fifty or more of these. Secondly, there are my erotic adventures. These seem never to have enjoyed any perspective in the dissertations I have read. I would not dream of challenging the authority of Venus but I have always felt that the tenderness and ardor that men and women often feel for their own kind is quite blameless. Lastly, there is the fact that I have been diagnosed as having Grand

Mal or what used to be called Epilepsy. When I am cross-questioned on the "aura" that precedes my seizures or fits I come close to the image of a Bishop walking down the beach in Nantucket, giving his blessing in a language that seems to have been forgotten. This is close to the last thing I see before I chew on grandmother's Oriental rug and regain consciousness in the hospital emergency room. This is not to claim for my insights genius or madness but to point out that they are sometimes unwanted. Here endeth the lesson for today.

Love,

John

The letter is hardly a mandate, but a kindly yet evasive invitation. The book I eventually did write addresses the things he mentioned there, but in some ways only glancingly. Although very early on in my efforts I became aware that no definitive bibliography existed, I did manage, after rooting through many old magazines on microfilm, to discover and read almost every story written from his teenage years onward. But I was never guided by an antiquarian impulse in my study; instead, I intended to concentrate on Cheever's mature fiction, attending to those stories and novels that are easily accessible to the reading public. Since Cheever has been the most neglected of our major writers—neglected, that is, as the subject of serious literary scholarship—I felt that the pressing need at the moment was to introduce him, or in some cases re-introduce him, to the general as well as the academic reader in a fashion that probed more deeply and widely than an introduction generally does.

As for Cheever's own erotic adventures and the authority of Venus, true to my specific intention I chose to bypass the genre of literary biography. I have actually included a good deal of biographical information throughout the study, at those points where I thought such information was warranted or particularly helpful. But even these insertions were made with misgivings, for one of my arguments, perhaps repeated overmuch, is that preoccupation with a writer's biography and the ferreting out of connectives between his life and art often crowd out our appreciation of the fictional magic that is *there,* the very reason for our interest in the first place. Excellent literature consists of the marvels of a final transformation, those distillations that imagination alone brings to the business of life; and so, at its best, fiction is ever a re-creation, a refraction of one's perceptive life, an entry with the author into a new world bracketed by the words "as if." One can be impressed by a biography—owing either to the subject's life or to the biographer's skill—but by excellent fiction, like Cheever's, one is enchanted, not merely impressed.

That said, I admit that I am eagerly awaiting a biography of Cheever. It should be as fascinating and complex as the man himself was. From what he and others have candidly confided to me, he was not so different from a central character in *Bullet Park* who confesses that "the truth of the matter is that I frequently fall suddenly in love with men, women, children and dogs. These attachments are unpredictable, ardent and numerous." Moreover, given his distinguished career of over fifty years and the many famous writers and artists he knew well, a biography of Cheever would inevitably become a history of not one but two or three cultural ages in America. My fervent hope, however, is that any prospective biographer would possess a generous sense of humor and a gracious sort of skepticism, for at one with his many endearing charms Cheever was something of a boyish scamp at heart and an inveterate teller of tall tales.

All of this leads me to the third emphasis in Cheever's letter and to the subject of this study. The title, *The Hobgoblin Company of Love*, might sound at first a bit overly piquant, even precious, instead of merely arresting and possibly accurate. Its inspiration derives from a dramatic crisis that occurs in *The Wapshot Chronicle*. Coverly Wapshot, the youngest of the Wapshot clan, has just undergone a series of emotional unsettlements. His wife, once "a Venus from the sea," has unexpectedly left him, and, like all people suddenly bereft, he has ample room for confusion and self-pity within his soul. Eventually, after a series of contretemps, Coverly begins to suffer doubts about his sexual identity and the very meaning of love, and in desperation he writes a letter to his eccentric father, Leander Wapshot. Leander, a figure of whimsical grandeur, writes him back a letter of quaint consolation, the final paragraph of which includes these words:

> Man is not simple. Hobgoblin company of love always with us. . . . Life has worse trouble. Sinking ships. Houses struck by lightning. Death of innocent children. War. Famine. Runaway horses. Cheer up my son. You think you have trouble. Crack your skull before you weep. All in love is not larky and fractious. Remember.

But it is the sentiment summarized and not the context that drew me to the phrase "the hobgoblin company of love," for it represents better than others might that complex cluster of themes and attitudes which lie at the heart of Cheever's fiction. In English folklore and literary myth, Hobgoblin is a mischievous sprite, a prankish fairy capable of startling shape-shifting. His more familiar name is Robin Goodfellow, and his most winning dramatic embodiment is that of Puck in Shakespeare's *A Midsummer Night's Dream*. In the play Puck is both a figure of mischief and a creator of antic order in a world both mysterious and benevolent, clownish and sophisticated. He is the "pert and nimble spirit of mirth" incarnate who weaves the entangled web of romance and comedy. Puck can boast that "I can put a girdle round about the earth/In forty minutes" and yet admit impishly that "those things do best please me,/ That befall preposterously."

There is definitely something puckish and spritely at the narrative center of most of Cheever's fictions. Like Shakespeare's hobgoblin, he is fascinated by metamorphoses of all kinds and entertained by the farcical, especially when it discloses the whirligigs of love and desire. Furthermore, Cheever's sensibility seems to inhabit comfortably that intermediate realm between dream and reality, and to enjoy easy access to both the normal world of everyday business, of getting and spending, and that moonlit wood where spirits dwell, the lush, remote region Oberon describes to Puck.

> I know a bank where the wild thyme blows,
> Where oxlips and nodding violet grows,
> Quite over-canopied with luscious woodbine,
> With sweet musk-roses and with eglantine.

But Cheever's hobgoblin also confronts a world that he sees is itself a "hobgoblin company of love." Here the word "hobgoblin" is an adjective, modifying something more mysterious still. As I shall argue in subsequent chapters, the meaning of "love" in Cheever's fiction is that of a transcendent force, a positive power—bewitching in its energetic potential—enlivening all that is vital in creation. As transcendent, it surpasses all of its manifestations and yet embraces them, too; it seems like a multifarious fellowship with which we are in league, a mystifying, mutating, seemingly capricious presence with which we are, willy-nilly, allied—a hobgoblin company of love. We might single out perceived instances of this fellowship and give them specific names like ardor, decency, loyalty, fidelity, romance, charity, grace, and piety. No matter what label we apply, each of these refers to something "extra," a companionable giftedness that we sense is both outside us and inside us, supporting our every hope for blessedness.

This is the reason why in Cheever's fiction the opposite of love is not hatred nor aberrant sexuality but *death*, death of that something extra that makes wondrous the created world and the lives of its inhabitants. Our human mortality is but a powerful symbol of this more crushing death. At the end of the story "The Lowboy," the narrator bluntly states: "We can cherish nothing less than our random understanding of death and the earth-shaking love that draws us to one another."

But since love enjoys so many varied manifestations and since our company is of a hobgoblin kind, it is inevitable that our perceptions of it will be ambiguous and our grasp of it elusive. A storyteller like Cheever

knows this better than anyone. At the close of another story, the narrator—a Cheever surrogate—asks aloud, how can any storyteller "hope to
celebrate a world that lies spread around us like a bewildering and stupendous dream?" If he is a writer like Cheever, he does so in puckish
ways.

Earlier I and others employed the word "magic" to describe an elusive
quality in Cheever's work. When William Styron, the eminent novelist,
read his eloquent tribute to Cheever before presenting him with the 1982
Medal of Literature, he returned again and again to the word, presuming
correctly that the audience intuited its appropriateness in praising Cheever.
For in recent literary criticism, the word "magic"—because of rather than
despite its vagueness—has become the highest of compliments, referring
to a *je ne sais qua* that explodes for a reader when imagination and a
radiant configuration wed in fiction or poetry. But, if pressed, could one
precisely define the Cheever magic?

I shall devote a whole book in attempting an answer, but talk of
hobgoblins prompts me to address the issue briefly now. First of all,
Cheever's is a white, not a black, magic. We readers familiar with his
fiction are more comfortable than uneasy, sensing we are in good, dex-
terous hands—and to create such reassurance is an art in itself. We delight
in his endlessly repeatable conjuring tricks, and though the events of a
story are sometimes weirdly eccentric, we never feel that the characters
are too distant from us to be both pathetic and funny, and frequently
both simultaneously. The narrative voice can be either mature and reasonable or mannered and distracted; still, the voice keeps hinting at matters extra-terrestrial that either the characters or we have missed or
momentarily forgotten. Like all conjurors, Cheever in this way is able to
stretch all prosaicness by creating continents of complexity amid the commonplace, for he knows that only the sensuous and the moral provide
sufficient elasticity to put a girdle round about the earth. Throughout his
fiction we meet a creature of contradiction, bipolar in personality, and
we sense a continual collision between anger and a deep-rooted kindness,
between perplexity and a tender hopefulness, between the sordid and the
decent impulse, between frustrating failure and noble intention.

These qualities in contention bestow on Cheever's work a halo of
universality, allowing as they do an earthiness, a rooted humanity to
eventuate in a combination of pathos and comedy, simplicity and cunning, rhetoric and poetry. To appreciate a magician one must be open to
suspense and surprise; in Cheever's case, one must appreciate and share
in the way the particular events and characters also represent the unseen,
the universal, the mythic. As John Updike observed in his eulogy mentioned earlier: "A suburban man infatuated with his baby sitter should

make a sad and squalid story, but in 'The Country Husband' the story ends with a glad shout of kings in golden mail riding their elephants over the mountains."

This study is divided into two distinctive parts. The first three chapters are general in perspective in that they present overviews, points of entry into important aspects of Cheever's fiction. The second part consists of separate chapters devoted to each of his novels and to selected stories within *The Stories of John Cheever* in the sequence in which they became available to or noteworthy for the wider reading public. I made strenuous efforts to compose each chapter in such a way that each ought to stand as a distinctive unit, entertaining a restless independence. I did this because of a lurking suspicion that most readers feel as I do: with the exception of good novels, the fun of reading is to dip in arbitrarily and without fuss, peering for plums (the known) while avoiding the pits (the unknown). If my own attention is arrested, I read back and forth as the spirit so moves, but still I find it reassuring when along the way the author never seems to fault me for misbehaving.

But given these lurking suspicions, and granted my last chance for finger-wagging, I should emphasize that the opening chapters—especially the first half of each one—are crucial to my interpretation. I am continually consternated when I meet intelligent readers, including those who enjoy challenging fiction, and they tell me that they find Cheever's stories depressing and sad. Obviously, they have "gotten" something from his fiction, something important, but hardly all. At such times I feel the frustration that Vladimir Nabokov manifests in his *Lectures on Russian Literature* that he delivered at Cornell University. In them he reminded his students with a hint of admonition that

> Chekhov's books are sad books for humorous people; that is, only a reader with a sense of humor can really appreciate their sadness. There exist writers that sound like something between a titter and a yawn— many of these are professional humorists, for instance. There are others that are something between a chuckle and a sob—Dickens was one of these . . . . Chekhov's humor belonged to none of these types; it was purely Chekhovian. Things for him were funny and sad at the same time, but you would not see their sadness if you did not see their fun, because both were linked up.

Nabokov then went on to observe, "What we see is a continuous stumble through all Chekhov's stories, but it is the stumble of a man who stumbles because he is staring at the stars."

For this reason, I begin this study with a discussion of Cheever's tone, which is a Chekhovian tone in a way, but informed by a Christian sensibility that is distinctively his and one that was aerated as he grew older.

The tone is ironic—what other tone captures humor and sadness simultaneously?—but I find the tone more expansive, gradually inching away from the more generally accepted restrictions of irony.

Discussion of tone, then, ineluctably leads one to discussion of style, the writer's technique in transmitting a complexity of tones. Cheever's mature style is a middle style (neither mandarin nor low-life, tough-guy argot), one easily accessible to a reader. It is ever rhythmic, direct, unbullying, and rarely impersonal though often oratorical, a style so assured that in his later fiction the narrative voice provides not only an atmosphere but becomes as rich and telling a presence as the characters. Moreover, one senses gradually that his style—its economy, restraint, and conviction—corresponds somehow to some moral vision at one with it; that his choice of words and clarity of sentence structure mirror a sincerity and honesty that resist fudging the mysteries of life—in short, Cheever's style seems to be the linguistic equivalent of his conscience.

In the course of Cheever's career his style expanded and became more flexible as his moral vision widened and as he wrestled with broader, more complicated themes. The ambiguities perceived, the tensions honestly faced demanded a style capable of encompassing them. For this reason, I devote the third chapter to a discussion of themes in tension, themes that emerge through stylistic emphases and through the employment of recurring images and symbols.

These themes in tension are many, but all are moral and/or religious in import. Cheever is ever a moral realist in that he is completely uninterested in morality as an abstact consideration. Instead—and here he is most like Hawthorne—his concerns center on the challenges, the paradoxes, even the dangers of living a moral life. A Christian believer, he is also convinced that good and evil are inextricably entangled, and so it is not surprising that many of his stories grow into complex fables on the mystery of original sin. Cheever never lost his reverence for Christianity and for the religiously sensitive disposition, for he felt that only religion forthrightly confronts the mystery of good and evil and through symbolic gestures points farther still toward a reconciliation, a greater mystery. However, he engages these subjects as an artist and not as a pamphleteer, eschewing the explicitly pious and proceeding by way of indirection, drama, and symbolism. Some committed believers might wish that he were more explicitly religious or, if not that, at least less vivid in dramatizing the moral confusions of daily life.

Flannery O'Connor, who was herself a committed believer and a novelist with a religiously informed vision, bluntly addressed such complaints in a letter she wrote to an inquirer who wondered whether she ever worried about scandalizing sensitive souls by not being more edifying in her fiction. O'Connor gently but swiftly dismissed this pseudo-problem by admitting frankly that she wrote only "for adults," and then she made clear her own attitude as a novelist—in words applicable to Cheever's work:

> [Fiction] is something that one experiences alone and for the purpose of realizing in a fresh way, through the senses, the mystery of experience. Part of the mystery of existence is sin. . . . Fiction is supposed to represent life, and the fiction writer has to use as many aspects of life as are necessary to make his total picture convincing. The fiction writer doesn't state, he shows, renders. It's the nature of fiction and it can't be helped. If you're writing about the vulgar, you have to prove that they're vulgar by showing them at it. . . .
>
> What offends my taste in fiction is when right is held up as wrong, or wrong as right. Fiction is the concrete expression of mystery—mystery that is lived. Catholics believe that all creation is good and that evil is the wrong use of good and that without Grace we use it wrong most of the time. It's almost impossible to write about supernatural Grace in fiction. We almost have to approach it negatively. As to natural Grace, we have to take that the way it comes—through nature. In any case, it operates surrounded by evil.

After these general introductory chapters, I devote attention to each of Cheever's novels and to selected short stories. I have called my efforts "Readings" rather than "Literary Analyses" or the like, because I felt that taking a more leisurely and yet more attentive attitude toward the texts themselves—and providing a wealth of citations from them—would elicit specific pleasures and more ample rewards than any thematic approach might. Part of Cheever's magic consists in his marvelous control of language, and its power and richness are accumulative—besides, his prose is much better than mine, and I prefer it. Furthermore, since I have become a Literary/Book Editor myself, I have come to realize that the task of a book review is to tell potential readers what they will find. But a literary critic must do that and more: he must also tell actual readers what they possibly missed. To do this one must provide sufficient room for re-entry into the book to point up its spaciousness.

My inspiration for this approach, one that trusts in a reader's patience and private intelligence, derives from Wayne Booth's two excellent books, A Rhetoric of Fiction and A Rhetoric of Irony, and from Vladimir Nabokov's Lectures on Literature. Nabokov put it this way:

> Curiously enough, one cannot read a book: one can only reread it. A good reader, a major reader, an active and creative reader is a rereader. And I shall tell you why. When we read a book for the first time the very process of laboriously moving our eyes from left to right, line after

line, page after page, this complicated physical work upon the book, the very process of learning in terms of space and time what the book is about, this stands between us and an artistic inspiration. . . . But at a second, or third, or fourth reading we do, in a sense, behave toward a book as we do toward a painting.

Nabokov then described the "authentic instrument" to be used by a good reader:

It is impersonal imagination and artistic delight. What should be established, I think, is an artistic harmonious balance between the reader's mind and the author's mind. We ought to remain a little aloof and take pleasure in this aloofness while at the same time we keenly enjoy—passionately enjoy, enjoy with tears and shivers—the inner weave of a given masterpiece. . . . The reader must know when and where to curb his imagination and this he does by trying to get clear the specific world the author places at his disposal.

In this sense, then, this study attempts to be a series of re-readings of Cheever, offered by a re-reader himself who hopes that other readers will be so entertained and perhaps occasionally enlightened that they too will be inspired to re-read Cheever's fiction with an aloof delight. I think also that this approach is one which Cheever himself would have applauded. He was most grateful to his readers and forthcoming about their great importance to him personally. In a brief essay written for The Washington Post, entitled "In Praise of Readers," he ended by saying this:

It is only in books that we can deal with these imponderables— our shared knowledge of the powers of love and the forces of memory— that drive us. Daguerre's discovery of photography and the continuation of this in film and television is—as I see it from a highly prejudiced point of view—partly a revelation of the fact that the photographic process cannot equal written language in its intimacy, radiance and fire.

Either one is serious about salvation or one is not. And it is well to realize that the maximum amount of seriousness admits the maximum amount of comedy. Only if we are secure in our beliefs can we see the comical side of the universe.

Flannery O'Connor

Mr. X defecated in his wife's top drawer. This is a fact, but I claim that it is not a truth.

John Cheever, "The Jewels of the Cabots"

Christian faith represents the most humorous point of view in the history of the world.

Sören Kierkegaard

Christianity is certainly not melancholy; it is, on the contrary, glad tidings for the melancholy; to the frivolous it is certainly not glad tidings, for it wishes first of all to make them serious.

Sören Kierkegaard

Christianity draws a distinction between what is frivolous and what is serious, but allows the former its place. What it condemns is not frivolity but idolatry, that is, taking the frivolous seriously.

W. H. Auden

1: Irony
and
Beyond Irony

Perhaps the most basic challenge a reader of Cheever faces is that of properly interpreting the tone of his fiction. Of course the reader confronts this challenge in the work of any sophisticated writer, but Cheever presents a rather conspicuous instance of this difficulty. John Leonard has dubbed him "our Chekhov of exurbia," for like Chekhov's plays and stories, Cheever's work hovers in the middle distance between the tragic and the comic, wavering between one and the other. A second reading of any of his stories often reverses our first response: on one reading we attend to the realistic or bizarre circumstances and hear a plaintive tone; on another we listen for the undertones and overtones and laugh. A closer, more patient third reading might yield a simultaneity of response— sadness and smiles—where we hear this mix of tones together and appreciate his remarkable ambiguity. On the other hand, a univocal reading is fraught with critical pitfalls: the isolation of one tone leads to pronouncing Cheever melancholy or sentimental; concentration on another nudges him into the restrictive categories of satire or burlesque and their like.

Indeed, even the employment of the word "tone" to describe such difficulties further complicates the issue, since this designation is not overly precise in literary criticism. Since the ground-breaking analyses of I. A. Richards, "tone" has come to refer to the *attitudes* toward the subject and toward the audience that are implied in the literary work. As readers, we infer the tonal attitude or combination of attitudes from the text itself. Such an inference is inevitably related to the *mood* we discover in the work, a discovery we make through discerning the various devices a writer uses to create a mood. These devices, in turn, are multiple, if not infinitely variable (imagery, symbolism, diction, and so on), and thus our difficulties with definition are compounded. On the theoretical level of discourse, the problems relating to tone become so complicated that one begins to wonder how a reader ever appreciates a literary work in the first place. Fortunately, the evidence is otherwise. In practice, attitudes and mood are, let us say, at least intuited, and not in arbitrary fashion but in response to those artistic techniques a knowledgeable reader appreciates.

Today, however, that knowledgeable reader faces a further web of entanglement. Since Auden's Age of Anxiety, which ended around 1960, readers of American fiction have been plunged into the Age of Irony. The particular irony that pervades the age is not so much verbal irony (saying one thing and meaning another) or dramatic irony (the audience knowing facts of which the characters are unaware), but an irony of *attitude*—irony as a criticism of life, irony as a philosophic stance in interpreting the world. Such an irony of attitude inevitably affects literary structure and thus characterizes the *mood* of the work. In short, "irony" and "tone" have become wedded words in our contemporary culture.

A backward look reveals that this development was not in itself ironic or unexpected but in a way inevitable, perhaps more a difference in degree than in kind. Critical historians have marshalled impressive arguments that the ironic emphasis in fiction can be traced back to its very origins, to *Don Quixote* or *Tristram Shandy*. [1] Some move the date in English fiction to Jonathan Swift or further on to Jane Austen,[2] while others find its most pronounced inspiration in the poets of World War I and in their influence on Eliot and his generation.[3] These are historical questions and, as such, are probably irresoluble, since "history has many cunning passages, contrived corridors/and issues." Perhaps Robert Coles is more correct: he argues that irony is a pre-historical given that exists "in the mind's life" and reflects a post-lapsarian perspective, that complex heritage we share in Adam's fall.[4]

Rather than let the argument evaporate entirely, however, let us assume as a starting point that in contemporary fiction we happen upon an irony that is distinctive and reflects a habit of mind that all "serious" writers share. D. C. Muecke describes well the ironic atmosphere permeating the contemporary literate mind when he notes: "[I] rony is now much less often a rhetorical or dramatic strategy which [writers] may or may not decide to employ, and much more often a mode of thought silently imposed upon them by the general tendency of the times."[5] His

1. See Robert Alter, *Partial Magic: The Novel as a Self-Conscious Genre* (Berkeley: Univ. of California Press, 1975); and Ian Watt, *The Rise of the Novel* (Berkeley: Univ. of California Press, 1957), esp. pp. 291-294.

2. Watt, *The Rise of the Novel*, p. 130; Wayne Booth, *The Rhetoric of Irony* (Chicago: Univ. of Chicago Press, 1974); and Wayne Booth, *The Rhetoric of Fiction* (Chicago: Univ. of Chicago Press, 1961), esp. pp. 316-323.

3. Paul Fussell, *The Great War and Modern Memory* (New York: Oxford Univ. Press, 1975).

4. Robert Coles, *Irony in the Mind's Life* (New York: New Directions, 1974), pp. 1-55.

5. D. C. Muecke, *The Compass of Irony* (London: Methuen, 1969), p. 10.

phrase "general tendency" is slippery; any attempt to specify it further creates new frustrations. Perhaps Reinhold Niebuhr succeeded best in his *The Irony of American History*, in which he addressed the changed human condition since World War II, which created a radically new circumstance that is distinctively contemporary and issues in shared, though unspoken, assumptions about the incongruities dominating the minds of modern men. Niebuhr said:

> Pure tragedy elicits tears of admiration and pity for the hero who is willing to brave death and incur guilt for the sake of some goal. Irony, however, prompts some laughter and a nod of comprehension beyond laughter; for irony involves comic absurdities which cease to be absurd when fully understood. Our age is involved in irony because so many dreams of our nation have been so cruelly refuted by history. Our dreams of pure virtue are dissolved in a situation in which it is possible to exercise the virtue of responsibility toward a community of nations only by courting the prospective guilt of the atomic bomb. And the irony is increased by the frantic efforts of some of our idealists to escape the hard reality by dreaming up schemes of an ideal world order which have no relevance to either our present dangers or our urgent duties.[6]

Niebuhr wrote these words in 1952; though somewhat dated, they are prophetic, and accurately describe the bath of incongruity into which all Americans are immersed. Since 1952 those waters have been muddied further by the roiling absurdities of assassinations, the Vietnam War, Watergate, and their aftermaths. Irony has become our very habitat.

American writers since 1960 have disclosed this ironic ambience from different perspectives. Novelists like John Updike, Saul Bellow, J. D. Salinger, Bernard Malamud, and Philip Roth stress the American's sense of displacement, the dramatic realization that he or she is caught between a sense of virtue and a sense of guilt (in Niebuhr's words), between an innocence lost and an elusive ideal to replace it. Others—like Kurt Vonnegut, Joseph Heller, Thomas Pynchon, and Robert Coover—offer us nightmarish visions and so probe the deepest of our apocalyptic fears, challenging us to face the incongruity between our dreams and our schemes. Still others—like Walker Percy, Joyce Carol Oates, the early John Barth, John Gardner, and Flannery O'Connor—diagnose this historical irony in more personal or psychological terms, highlighting what might be called the modern disease of inauthenticity, the sense the contemporary American sometimes has that he possesses no real self, no true identity, no creative powers to offset the ironic tensions he experiences between his private world and his public world.

6. Reinhold Niebuhr, *The Irony of American History* (New York: Scribner's, 1952), p. 2.

All of these novelists take for granted the ironic perspective; their differences lie in the ironic techniques they employ and the degree to which they exploit them. The ironic extreme is most markedly manifest in those writers labeled "post-modernists." Although all of them can legitimately decry such a label, since it implies that they form a school, "post-modernist" would embrace the works of such diverse novelists as John Barth, Richard Barthelme, Robert Coover, William Gass, and John Hawkes in the forefront.[7] For these writers, the fictional text *itself* becomes an object of irony, at best an objective correlative for the absurdity of the modern world. That is, they create deliberately self-conscious novels that flaunt their artificiality and emphasize their fictiveness. Traditional "realistic" devices like plot, character, and causal continuity are manipulated in ironic fashion, and exposed either through obvious parody or through the explicit renouncement of these conventions. The canons of fictional "truth," i.e., the reader's legitimate expectations regarding the narrator's reliability, are now exploited in reverse: narrators reveal that they are unreliable, the text itself is made deliberately suspect, and readers are alerted to the ironic fact that all stories are arbitrary and contrived.

This post-modernist approach met with great critical success, its popularity in academic circles cresting in the late 1960's and early 1970's. But because it was so extreme it contained within itself the seeds of its own destruction. John Leonard said it well in 1971: "With the exception of Nabokov, there is something febrile about their produce, a parodistic element that turns the book back on its author and consumes him, an irony so hyper-developed it becomes a form of suicide."[8]

The ultimate point of this discussion is to determine Cheever's place within contemporary fiction and to forestall possible misunderstandings of Cheeveresque irony. Cheever shares with his contemporaries a keen perception of the irony of recent American history, and he readily employs the full range of ironic techniques some of them choose to exploit. But in some ways he is unlike the post-modernists: for example, he eschews the extreme flank of ironic discourse; instead, he works the other way, in the direction beyond irony. His fictional concerns are never rigidly aesthetic, nor does he believe that the non-ironic forms of fiction are ex-

---

7. See Robert Scholes, *Fabulation and Metafiction* (Urbana: Univ. of Illinois Press, 1973); William Gass, *Fiction and the Figures of Life* (New York: Knopf, 1970); David Lodge, *The Modes of Modern Writing* (Ithaca: Cornell Univ. Press, 1977), pp. 220ff.; Annie Dillard, *Living by Fiction* (New York: Harper & Row, 1982); and Gerald Graff, "The Myth of the Post-Modern Breakthrough" in his *Literature Against Itself* (Chicago: Univ. of Chicago Press, 1979).

8. John Leonard, *New York Times Book Review*, March 17, 1971, p. 31.

hausted. Like D. H. Lawrence, he remains convinced that fiction is "th
bright book of life," that is, that at its most probing it enjoys the potentia
of revealing man's deepest moral and spiritual aspirations.

Cheever is, admittedly, a child of the Age of Irony, but all the morall
and spiritually laden words the ironic sophisticate would avoid he cele
brates. Throughout his work we hear sonorous paeans to "valor, wisdom
kindness, virtue, glory, and paradise," and happen upon superlative ad
jectives like "supernatural," "extraordinary," and "incandescent" as de
scriptive of sensation and moral aspiration. The vocabulary tha
sophisticates shun is one that only the truly wise can master. John Leonard
said it nicely in his review of The World of Apples, one of Cheever's stor
collections:

> I like these words and the emotions they evoke—love, humor,
> serenity, sweetness, strength, clemency, intelligence, ardor, soul. They
> aren't used much, or they are not used honestly, in books by Cheever's
> peers. Irony has deformed these words; they have become indices of
> simple mindedness, their profession is excused or traduced, as a bleak
> joke. There is, of course, no escaping irony. It is an indispensable tool
> for writers of twentieth-century fiction, part of the surgical bag, like
> sex, ennui, paranoia, and contempt for your readers. . . .
>
> Irony can be used the way Cheever uses it: protectively, on behalf
> of ardor and intelligence and clemency, even while these words, these
> values, really, are inadequate to cope with the world of chance, of
> evil. Inside Cheever's irony, love and humor are preserved, not abused.[9]

Leonard's point is well-taken, but it also raises a more basic and
difficult question. Granted that Cheever, like all serious writers, employs
irony, what precisely is that special quality that separates his brand of
irony from that of others? Since all share in irony, does the difference
reside in something beyond irony? And if so, what?

In his superb series of essays, The Rhetoric of Irony, Wayne Booth
provides an important clue. Booth argues that outstanding writers manage
to appeal to the "two grand fundamental human passions": the conviction
that there is more here than meets the eye, and the suspicion that there
is less:

> The shrewd skeptic that we [readers] all learn to become as we meet
> life's con-men is delighted to find, behind the presented words, a fellow
> skeptic demolishing illusions; and then—marvel of marvels—that
> skeptic turns out to be a great dreamer, a man of passion who can
> multiply implications and proclaim mysteries; here is a soul-mate
> indeed.[10]

---

9. John Leonard, "Cheever to Roth to Malamud," Atlantic Monthly, 231 (June
1973), 114.
10. Booth, The Rhetoric of Irony, p. 178.

Booth's reflection clarifies expertly the reason why, in this Age of Irony, we might cherish some writers more highly than others. The key seems to be that outstanding writers, *after* establishing a skeptical perspective that exposes contradiction, hypocrisy, cliché, or whatever, suddenly take *another* step, and by doing so surprise us. The ironic skepticism remains as a negative background or support, but unexpectedly a fervent or lyric voice intrudes, probing toward mystery, toward affirmation, a voice no longer sotto voce but pitched higher, delighting in its embrace of some aspect of natural creation or of humanity's potential. The artistic effect is such that the ironic focus established earlier manages to temper the fervor and vice-versa; the negative perspective of irony is thus, in a way, itself ironized by the positive probing. This reciprocity of differing tones is what delights us. All irony demands a reconstruction, because irony is a negation, a subtraction from what is presented; in this instance, however, an unexpected alternate reconstruction is offered to us readers above and beyond our own reconstruction, thereby satisfying our "two grand fundamental human passions" simultaneously.

A quick mental review of our finest writers in this century confirms this truth. On reading our finest poets—Yeats, Eliot, Auden, Stevens, Frost—or our finest contemporary novelists—Updike, Bellow, Malamud, Cheever—one discovers that in all of them there is a curious mix of dispassion and passion, a negative "nay" to the world and a reaching out despite it; an effort to qualify their deeply-felt affirmations with a wry twist of irony, together with a concomitant effort to qualify the irony as well. In each case the writer attempts to explore something *more* after denying its possibility, and yet it is his irony that keeps his exploration *honest* and his tentative affirmations unsentimental. Perhaps most mysterious of all, however, is the remarkable difference between good and less good writers thereby established. As Wayne Booth stresses brilliantly, fine writers possess either the instinct or the skill to "know where to stop" the irony and offer that something extra.[11] In handling irony, knowing where to stop is as important as—and, it seems, more difficult than—knowing where to begin.

Various writers use different techniques in their effort to push out beyond irony. In contemporary fiction, for example, Saul Bellow will suddenly insert a sober, unironic reflection or will describe with clarity and affection some fleeting sensation understood as emblematic of man's rich and positive linkage with the world. John Updike makes more poetic exertions: he will elaborately probe the potentiality of metaphor, even

---

11. Booth, *The Rhetoric of Irony*, pp. 91-172. An interesting example is also found in Irving Howe's *Celebrations and Attacks* (New York: Harcourt Brace Jovanovich, 1979), p. 99, where Howe faults Flannery O'Connor for obvious and unrelieved irony.

risking an ornate baroqueness at times, in an attempt to render in language the marvelous concealed within the particular.[12]

Cheever will occasionally use these techniques and others. Prominent among them are those more akin to Fable or Allegory, through which morally-weighted abstract words like "love," "fitness," and "decency" take on an affirmative resonance in the story's context. Many of his stories are fables in the sense that they edge into moral tales—but tales tempered by irony. Cheever himself wryly hinted at the reason for this combination when he said: "I came from a Puritanical family and I had been taught as a child that a moral lies beneath all human conduct and that the moral is always detrimental to man."[13]

In Cheever's hands the structure of Fable is altered slightly: the story starts in irony—some absurdity recognizable in urban or suburban life is described in apparently realistic fashion, or the central character(s) encounter some unexpected disaster or dilemma. Then, imperceptibly, the situation or the character(s) metamorphose into the fabulous. A morally parabolic dimension is introduced, and the characters, once viewed ironically, take on the qualities of vitalized abstractions—archetypes, visitors from our dreams, mythic heroes and heroines—while their situation, so ironically commonplace, now discloses the ethical outlines of classical or biblical myth. (See "The Enormous Radio," "Clancy in the Tower of Babel," "O Youth and Beauty!", "The Country Husband," "The Chimera," "The Angel of the Bridge," and "The Swimmer.")

In addition, Cheever consistently employs another device to inch his readers beyond the restricted perspective of irony. He will suddenly punctuate the middle of a story with universal questions of a metaphysical or moral kind, thus stretching our attention beyond the story's immediate action.

How can a people who do not mean to understand death hope to understand love, and who will sound the alarm?

("The Death of Justina")

Which of us is not suspended by a thread above carnal anarchy, and what is that thread but the light of day?   ("Brimmer")

Did she, mounted in public by a naked stranger, remember any of the places where we had made love—the rented houses close to the sea, where one heard in the sounds of a summer rain the prehistoric promises of love, peacefulness and beauty?   ("The Fourth Alarm")

---

12. See George Hunt, John Updike and the Three Great Secret Things: Sex, Religion and Art (Grand Rapids: Eerdmans, 1980), pp. 103-116.

13. John Cheever, "What Happened," in Understanding Fiction, ed. Cleanth Brooks and Robert Penn Warren (New York: Appleton-Century-Crofts, 1959 ed.), pp. 570-572.

What had made the summer always an island, she thought; what had
made it such a small island? What mistakes had they made? What had
they done wrong? They had loved their neighbors, respected the force
of modesty, held honor above gain. Then where had they lost their
competence, their freedom, their greatness?

("The Day the Pig Fell into the Well")

In these and other stories, the more universal questions interrupt the
narrative. In other hands, these would be distractions merely; in Cheever's
hands they establish a complicity with the reader, at once presuming the
reader's agreement and inviting him to consider the narrative action from
a higher plane. These interruptions also cleverly undercut the ironic viewpoint that has been established, a viewpoint the reader has previously
shared.

Irony, of course, cannot be discussed intelligently in isolation from
discussion of style, subject or theme, and characterization—aspects which
I will address later. But here I should emphasize that a major source of
ironic tension in Cheever's fiction lies in the disparity between the decorous, urbane, sensible narrative voice that typifies much of his work and
the eccentric or absurd episodes it recounts. The narrative style establishes
the tension and reinforces the incongruity. As readers we are rendered
complacent, nourished by that wise, cultured voice, only to be made fat
for the slaughter to follow.

For too long, critics have been concentrating on the slaughter only,
and have been content to pigeonhole Cheever as a social satirist. The
implication is that he is something of a savage sociologist in disguise, a
wry and macabre David Riesman who delights in counting the olives in
drained martini glasses or the soggy shards of charcoal at aborted cook-
outs, all the while dissecting the crabbed personalities mowing the crabgrass.

It is true, of course, that Cheever has an unerring eye for satiric
targets, and he hits almost all of them in his writings: advertising and its
slogans, super-highways, the disorganization of organized religion, psychological tests, town meetings, cocktail parties, undertakers, scientists
and their computer mentality, Congressional hearings, homosexuality,
feminism, suburban adultery, airline clerks, psychoanalysis—the list is
endless. Nonetheless, Cheever uses satire as but one arrow in his well-
stocked quiver, and ultimately he is not a satirist. Satire is militant irony;
Cheever's irony is of a gentler sort. Satire is a mode of rejection, whereas
the tragicomical, Cheever's mode, is one of acceptance. His narrative
efforts are usually designed to establish an amicable relationship with the
reader—an attitude also shared toward his characters—a sense of kinship
about life's contradictions. To "get" his fiction, the reader is invited to

share certain assumptions about how people live: yes, we do make a mess of things, *but* perhaps the motive behind the mess might be misguided decency. That "perhaps" edges Cheever's work away from strict satire, while it retains the irony. Furthermore, his is rarely a mocking voice, nor does it chide—it merely decorously reports. Apparently, Cheever neither expects nor necessarily desires that change in man's moral deportment that is usually the aim of satire. On this point he said:

> Writing must extend itself into a whole new sense of factuality. When you find a woman, for instance, obsessed with her plaid-stamp book, I think you perhaps have something there that would be in the nature of an altogether new truth. It is quite possible that a woman who goes to sleep and dreams of getting a new plaid-stamp book is not quite as undignified as she appears to be. . . . One has to accept these people as adult and useful, and people have had worse dreams.[14]

And yet that reluctance to run the full satirical route has disappointed those critics who equate Cheever's tactic with faint-heartedness, a backing away from that long look into the abyss. Such critics tend toward a social view of literature, convinced that anything short of righteous anger or despair at social cankers lacks high seriousness. Thus an obtuse critic like John Aldridge will castigate Cheever for offering us "the soft sell of disaster"; a more sensitive critic like Alfred Kazin will wonder whether "his marvelous brightness is an effort to cheer himself up," for none of his characters has to "collide with or fight with a society which is actually America in allegory."[15] The somewhat muddled Ihab Hassan goes further, calling Cheever a creator of "affirmative statement" who denies "the disagreeable aspects of reality in order to *create* a metaphor of the excellence and continuity of things."[16]

To appreciate Cheever and his distinctive brand of irony, however, requires insight into his religious and philosophic attitudes, which distinguish his work—attitudes that he talked about:

> The religious experience is very much my concern, as it seems to me it is the legitimate concern of any adult who has experienced love. . . . The whiteness of light. In the Church, you know, that always represents the Holy Spirit. It seems to me that man's inclination toward light, toward brightness, is very nearly botanical—and I mean spiritual

14. "Ovid in Ossining," *Time*, March 27, 1964, p. 72.

15. John W. Aldridge, "John Cheever and the Soft Sell of Disaster" in his *Time to Murder and Create: The Contemporary Novel in Crisis* (New York: McKay, 1966); and Alfred Kazin, *Bright Book of Life: American Storytellers from Hemingway to Mailer* (Boston: Little, Brown, 1973), p. 113.

16. Ihab Hassan, *Radical Innocence: Studies in the Contemporary American Novel* (Princeton: Princeton Univ. Press, 1961), p. 194.

light. One not only needs it, one struggles for it. It seems to me that one's total experience is the drive toward light.[17]

In this and similar statements, Cheever was not shy about his religious sensibility. Nonetheless, religious indirection—through imagery, symbol, and conflict—characterizes his fiction. In a passage from *Falconer*—that he himself pointed out as the key to the novel and to his artistic efforts[18]— he tells us the reason for the necessity of indirection:

> . . . as croyants I'm sure we share the knowledge that to profess exalted religious experience outside the ecclesiastical paradigm is to make of oneself an outcast. . . . I truly believe in One God the Father Almighty but I know that to say so loudly, and at any distance from the chancel—any distance at all—would dangerously jeopardize my ability to ingratiate those men and women with whom I wish to live. I am trying to say—and I'm sure you will agree with me—that while we are available to transcendent experience, we can state this only at the suitable and ordained time and in the suitable and ordained place. I could not live without this knowledge; no more could I live without the thrilling possibility of suddenly encountering the fragrance of skepticism.   (p. 72)

IRONY AND HUMOR

These tensions between the consoling knowledge of faith and the "fragrance of skepticisim," between irony and a probing beyond irony, animate Cheever's stories, betraying a religious-philosophic disposition essential to them. Our more usual *literary* categories of irony or wit or satire or humor are inadequate for capturing the specific qualities of that disposition. One must look elsewhere to find categories appropriate to the irony and "beyond irony" one finds in his work.

Here I personally can find no better guide than Sören Kierkegaard (1813-1855), the Danish philosopher and theologian. As a young man, he wrote the equivalent of a modern doctoral thesis on *The Concept of Irony*, a study of Socratic irony through Hegelian eyes.[19] At this stage of his thought, Kierkegaard was highly critical of irony, faulting it as a negative disposition fundamentally out of touch with reality. But as he ma-

17. "John Hersey: Talk with John Cheever," *New York Times Book Review*, March 6, 1977, p. 28.
18. Private letter to the author, December 14, 1977.
19. See Winfield E. Nagley, "Kierkegaard's Early and Later View of Socratic Irony," pp. 271-282; and John William Elrod, "Climacus, Anti-Climacus and the Problem of Suffering," pp. 306-319, in *Thought*, the Fordham University Quarterly, no. 218 (September 1980).

tured and his religious sensibility deepened, he re-thought the concept and saw in it a reflection of spiritual growth and a mode not only of seeing things but of viewing human existence. His thinking then led him to clarify a concept beyond irony which he called humor, something that looks like and partakes of irony but reveals a different existential attitude entirely. (Like Cheever's work, Kierkegaard's writings are always funny and sad simultaneously; in many ways the two men seem like brothers beneath the skin.) Though Kierkegaard's writings can be devilishly opaque at times, his categories of irony and humor emerge with clarity once one understands the outline of his religious psychology.[20]

No doubt the most famous feature of Kierkegaard's thought is his morphology of the three spheres of existence (often called "stages") to delineate the controlling motivation and subsequent orientation that typifies human behavior. The first sphere, the "aesthetical," is characterized by pursuit of personal satisfaction. By employing that word, Kierkegaard did not intend to identify this sphere with aesthetical beauty or with the artistic impulse. Rather, he used "aesthetical" in its more radical and broad Greek derivation, referring to man's capacity for immediate sensuous enjoyments. The aesthetical person is one who seeks immediate pleasures and identifies happiness with the satisfaction of immediate appetites. Observation reveals the curious fact that humans can make almost any object of experience a source of pleasure, even the most exotic or esoteric. Potential objects of pleasure are innumerable; their common feature, however, is that each is always external to man, each constitutes a definite "given" toward which one is passively related. Consequently, the aesthetical person is always at the mercy of the external givens of the natural world: his happiness depends on them, and so he will make every effort to control the capriciousness of the world outside himself; and yet, since such control is impossible, he often finds himself either the victim or the beneficiary of fortune and fate. Kierkegaard felt that this sphere was the

20. What follows is my own explication of this aspect of Kierkegaard's thought. After many years of teaching and reading about S. K., my own attempts at explication have become indistinguishable for me from those I have absorbed from so many expert readings. What follows is at best a distillation and evidence of a genuine debt. See George E. and George B. Arbaugh, *Kierkegaard's Authorship* (Rock Island: Augustana, 1967); Gregor Malantschuk, *Kierkegaard's Thought* (Princeton: Princeton Univ. Press, 1971); Howard V. and Edna H. Hong, *Soren Kierkegaard's Journals and Papers*, 4 vols. (Bloomington: Indiana Univ. Press, 1967, 1970, 1975); Walter W. Sikes, *On Becoming the Truth* (St. Louis: Bethany Press, 1968); Louis Mackey, *Kierkegaard: A Kind of Poet* (Philadelphia: Univ. of Pennsylvania Press, 1971); David Swenson, *Something About Kierkegaard* (Minneapolis: Augsburg, 1941); Stanley Romaine Hopper, *The Crisis of Faith* (New York: Abingdon-Cokesbury, 1944); and Paul Holmer, "On Understanding Kierkegaard," in *A Kierkegaard Critique*, ed. Howard A. Johnson and Niels Thulstrup (New York: Harper, 1962).

sphere of paganism; one is born into it, and he will remain immersed in a fickle, finite world and be dependent on passing temporal satisfactions unless he makes a radical personal choice to "de-throne the aesthetical" and reach out beyond it.

The impulse to make such a "leap," i.e., the decision to renounce this sphere and embrace the next, is precipitated by a private crisis. According to Kierkegaard, that crisis manifests itself as either a perplexity about one's own enslavement to time and its inevitable passing (despair) or as an awakening of freedom within one, the realization of new possibilities (dread).[21] Kierkegaard described despair as "doubt about the validity of one's own existence." One realizes that his life has been determined by the present tense, and since time is in continual flux, the reality of his very self, so defined by time, is called into question. Despair marks a turning point, therefore, because one is forced to stop and reflect self-critically on two major questions: "Who am I?" and "Is there an eternal element somewhere outside me or within me that prompts me to question my temporal existence in this way?"

Kierkegaard analyzed the second reaction he called dread (or anxiety) in great depth. The experience of dread is not like common instances of fear or emotions of fright because, unlike them, dread has no object. Dread is precisely fear of the unknown, the possible unknown—that is, fear of what can be and what one can become—in short, fear of literally "no-thing" in the specific sense of the word. Man's realization of his freedom issues in dread because he perceives that he does confront possibilities, possibilities which he can make actual through an exercise of choice; he becomes "dizzy" with this new-found freedom because the realm of possibilities both attracts and repels his imagination. This dread-ful situation is inevitably ambiguous, then, because man is simultaneously aware of his finitude, especially the limitations of time upon his opportunities for choice, and of the "infinite" range of possibilities open to his future, a seemingly endless range that captivates his imagination. That experience, whereby awareness of both the temporal and the eternal conjoin in a man, Kierkegaard calls "the Moment" in *The Concept of Dread*; "the moment" is a dramatic instance of convergence that occurs in time but possesses a time-less quality.

For Kierkegaard the experience of despair and the critical "moments" of dread are indispensable signals, prompting a person toward spiritual

---

21. Kierkegaard analyzed the effects of despair in his *Sickness unto Death* (Princeton: Princeton Univ. Press, 1941). This exposition was printed in 1849; six years earlier he published *The Concept of Dread* (Princeton: Princeton Univ. Press, 1944). Although these two categories are quite different in nuance and in their relationship to the "spheres," I unite them here for the sake of clarity.

maturity. As such, these experiences are universal and normal. However, both prod one to go further; to stand still or to revert means that one has chosen, at least implicitly, a pagan existence. But if one chooses other-wise, i.e., makes a "leap," then one enters the ethical sphere. This sphere is so named because, upon entering it, one abandons the passivity of the aesthetical life and chooses to be a committed person, to accept obliga-tions and responsibilities in a most personal way and, as a Kantian might put it, to feel so obliged regarding his moral duties that he feels his own sense of obligation is one that all men *ought* to share. In this latter sense, the ethical represents a universal stage. However, the ethical man per-sonalizes that universal "ought"—or, as Kierkegaard says, "he chooses himself absolutely," meaning that he accepts all the temporal contingen-cies of his life and sees his life as a process of "becoming" fully human, and so, unlike the pagan, actively embraces his future, the unknowns and the "not yets" of his life, in freedom.

Unfortunately, the ethical life is difficult, because moral duties con-flict with each other, and this most admirable of men, the ethical person, often falls short of his own ideals. Thus he eventually experiences again those "moments" of despair and dread, which prompt him to transcend himself once more and seek an Other who will deliver him from the burdens of the ethical. This experience anticipates the third "religious" sphere whereby in humility and selflessness he makes a leap of "faith," committing himself to a God whose existence he cannot prove. For the religious man the Eternal now consciously impinges on each instance of his temporal existence; moreover, he feels constantly "invited," if he is a Christian, to a personal relationship with the suffering Christ, who now becomes his model for imitation.[22] Kierkegaard argued that ascent to the religious sphere does not entail losing the previous spheres but merely deposing them as primary spheres. In fact, the religious man most em-phatically "recovers" the joys and sorrows of the aesthetical life and con-tinues to shoulder his ethical burdens, "repeating" both spheres, but with the aid of a new spiritual perspective on life. The religious man still lives in and loves a pagan world, but he does so *as* a Christian, and so his life and loves are elevated.

This excursion into Kierkegaard's thought is, I think, an important propaedeutic for appreciating the complex configurations of Cheever's

---

22. Kierkegaard develops this aspect of Christian imitation in his *Training in Chris-tianity* (Princeton: Princeton Univ. Press, 1941). See Bradley Dewey, *The New Obedience* (Washington: Corpus, 1968); Paul Sponheim, *Kierkegaard on Christ and Christian Coher-ence* (New York: Harper & Row, 1968); James Gustafson, *Christ and the Moral Life* (New York: Harper & Row, 1968), esp. pp. 164-172; and Vernard Eller, *Kierkegaard and Radical Discipleship* (Princeton: Princeton Univ. Press, 1968), esp. pp. 353-400.

fiction. Those transitions that Kierkegaard describes in conceptual categories are ones that Cheever dramatizes by way of metaphor and narrative action. His work is replete with dread-ful "moments" which are triggered by apparently random, "aesthetically" symbolic objects. For example, Cheever said of "The Brigadier and the Golf Widow" that the building of the bomb shelter in the garden is "just a metaphor for basic anxiety."[23] In "O Youth and Beauty!" the living-room hurdle race is a metaphor for anxiety about the loss of vitality and its prospect, death. Stories of this kind are explorations of the unredeemed aesthetical life; other stories, such as "Clancy in the Tower of Babel," "The Country Husband," and "The Death of Justina," dramatize the conflicts of ethical crisis.

In commenting upon human existence, Kierkegaard observed, "Where there is contradiction, there the comical is also present."[24] In his characteristic way, however, he went further, observing that one's perception of the comical reflected one's own position in relation to the three spheres or styles of life proper to human existence. In delineating the types and principled movements of the subjective life, he designated irony as the *confinium* or boundary line of the leap that separates the aesthetical and the ethical spheres, and humor as the boundary line between the ethical and the religious[25].

Philosophers and literary critics have usually discussed irony as a tool for comedy.[26] Kierkegaard was well aware of the techniques of irony in literature, but his concern was with the "concept" of irony and also with what the uses of irony indicated about the ironist's own moral stance and style of life. Ever the dialectician, he saw that the comic perspective of

23. "John Cheever: The Art of Fiction LXII," *Paris Review*, 17, No. 7 (Fall 1976), 57.
24. Sören Kierkegaard, *Concluding Unscientific Postscript* (Princeton: Princeton Univ. Press, 1941), p. 459.
25. Kierkegaard, *Concluding Unscientific Postscript*, p. 448. Kierkegaard treats irony and humor in the *Postscript*, pp. 447-466; 489-493. He did his Master's thesis (equivalent to our doctoral thesis) on *The Concept of Irony* (Bloomington: Indiana Univ. Press, 1971). For a more detailed explication, see Malantschuk, *Kierkegaard's Thought*, pp. 57ff.; 185-220; Paul Holmer, "Faith in a Tragic World," in *The Tragic Vision and the Christian Faith*, ed. Nathan Scott (New York: Association, 1957), pp. 174-187; and Josiah Thompson's "The Master of Irony" in his edited work, *Kierkegaard: A Collection of Critical Essays* (New York: Doubleday-Anchor, 1972).
26. To my mind the finest literary analyses of irony are found in Wayne Booth, *The Rhetoric of Irony*, and D. C. Muecke, *The Compass of Irony*. Both Booth (positively) and Muecke (negatively) also appraise Kierkegaard's categories. For perceptive philosophical treatments that address Kierkegaardian irony, see Stanley Romaine Hopper, "Irony: The Pathos of the Middle," *Cross Currents*, 12 (Winter 1962), 31-40; and Marie Collins Swabey, *Comic Laughter* (New Haven: Yale Univ. Press, 1961).
For broader, more generalized views of the comic in Cheever, see the following fine articles: Frederick Bracher, "John Cheever and Comedy," *Critique*, 6 (Spring 1963), 66-77; and Richard Rupp's chapter on Cheever in his *Celebrations in Postwar American Fiction (1945-67)* (Miami: Miami Univ. Press, 1972).

Carnegie Public Library
207 N. Frances
Terrell , Tx. 75160

the ironist could express two contrary possibilities. On the one hand, irony could reflect a totally negative disposition toward the world, for the ironist is often a person who has despaired of the varied happinesses promised by the aesthetical sphere but has found no substitute for them. He has reached a boundary line and perceives some ethical requirement (Do something about it!), but he refuses to fulfill it. And so, with a knowing and practiced eye, he comically appraises the vanity and hollowness of the life left behind. The ironist's strength—comic detachment—is also his pitfall. As Kierkegaard observed, "Irony is an abnormal growth; like the abnormally enlarged liver of the Strasbourg goose, it ends by killing the individual."[27] On the other hand, since irony is the boundary line of entry into the ethical sphere, he also saw irony as a possible mask or *incognito* for the ethical individual who has made the leap. "If you wish to be and remain enthusiastic," he said, "then draw the silk curtain of facetiousness (irony), and so hide your enthusiasm."[28] Consequently, irony can be revelatory of a *positive* disposition, though a limited one, for the ethical man sees the human comedy in abstract, universal terms while he remains well aware of the arduousness of a genuinely moral life.

Humor was Kierkegaard's category for the boundary line between the ethical and the religious spheres, and he asserted that the radical difference between irony and humor lies in a person's attitude toward guilt and suffering. The ironist can remain on the sidelines, eternally uncommitted, as he points up the contradictory follies of human life. But the ethical man is one who has chosen to plunge into the midst of things; he has taken the risk of committing *himself* to moral demands and of entering the struggle between good and evil.

Yet in the process of his striving, the ethical man becomes conscious of another, quite different kind of contradiction: that of his own and others' failures in comparison with what they know *ought* to be. When one realizes that he is responsible for falling short of his own moral ideal, he experiences guilt; guilt entails not just the normal regret at aesthetical deprivations but genuine suffering of a most private kind. He had sought a bedrock or moral blueprint within the scheme of human ethical behavior, but he no longer finds his efforts reassuring. Quite the contrary. He yearns for something further, for some power that will make his guilt and suffering intelligible, and thus he is on the threshold of the religious sphere. "Humor," Kierkegaard said, "is the last stage of existential inwardness before faith."

When we examine the main body of Cheever's fiction with the aid

27. *The Journals of Kierkegaard*, ed. Alexander Dru (New York: Harper-Row Torchbook, 1959), p. 58.
28. Robert Bretall, *A Kierkegaard Anthology* (Princeton: Princeton Univ. Press, 1946), p. 134.

of Kierkegaard's categories, its distinctive qualities take on clearer focus. One puzzling aspect of his fiction is that his stories alternate between romantic and anti-romantic postures, e.g., between lyrical and rhapsodic evocations of the past and comic deflations of excessive nostalgia for it. The reason is that Cheever's fiction is always "borderline" in Kierkegaard's sense. And, although Cheever employs a broad range of ironic techniques, his ultimate comic perspective—whether romantic or anti-romantic—is not that of an ironist but that of a humorist.

Those themes that irony handles so well—sex, politics, social manners and mores, the ephemeral enthusiasms of a culture—have been predominant for a generation. However, those other themes that elude irony— the anxieties of the soul, spiritual destiny, death in its crushing existential significance, sincere ethical conflict, religious conviction—have not been so well served. These themes, however, are the province of Kierkegaardian humor—and much of Cheever's fiction. For the humorist's stance is not so much detached as it is transcendent. Also, as we have noted, Kierkegaardian humor is consonant with the speculative, poetic tonalities one finds in Cheever, with his attempt to provide a "singing voice" for the intuitional instincts within man and to probe their mysterious origins.

In his review of The Collected Stories, John Irving noted that Cheever "never chooses easy subjects to love. Rarely do his stories lack inevitable suffering, vulgar and human cravings, troubled people who stand on the brink of some despair—typically unnoticed by their brethren. Cheever writes about characters difficult to forgive, but he usually forgives them."[29]

What Irving observed, Kierkegaard stressed: that the difference between irony and humor lies in one's attitude toward suffering and sympathy. Cheever continually dramatizes this disparity in stances throughout his fiction. For example, almost every story begins with the wry perspective of irony—i.e., the detached, often sardonic viewpoint of an outside observer—but as the story develops, this ironic perspective imperceptibly vanishes, and by the story's end an entirely different focus, that of compassionate understanding, has taken its place. This narrative tension allows Cheever to exploit simultaneously—or, better, consecutively—both the rhetorical resources of irony like wit, parody, and satire, and the more poetically lyrical, universal rhetoric proper to humor. Bullet Park contains an illustrative passage that boldly offers the ironic vantage point—only to undercut it by denying its human adequacy:

> Seen at an improbable distance by some zealous and vengeful adolescent, ranging over the golf links, the piece of plush would seem to be the imprimatur, the guerdon, the accolade and banner of Powder Hill

29. John Irving, "Facts of Living," Saturday Review, September 30, 1978, p. 44.

behind which marched, in tight English shoes, the legions of wife-swapping, Jew-baiting, booze-fighting spiritual bankrupts. Damn the bright lights by which no one reads, damn the continuous music which no one hears, damn the grand pianos that no one can play, damn the white houses mortgaged up to their rain gutters, damn them for plundering the ocean for fish to feed the mink whose skins they wear and damn their shelves on which there rests a single book—a copy of the telephone directory, bound in pink brocade. Damn their hypocrisy, damn their cant, damn their credit cards . . . and damn them above all for having leached from life that strength, malodorousness, color and zeal that give it meaning. Howl, howl, howl.

But the adolescent, as adolescents always are, would be mistaken.

(pp. 5-6)

The story "The Worm in the Apple" also makes comic capital of the frustrations of the negatively ironic stance. It opens with this line: "The Crutchmans were so very, very happy and so temperate in all their habits and so pleased with everything that came their way that one was bound to suspect a worm in their rosy apple and that the extraordinary rosiness of the fruit was only meant to conceal the gravity and the depth of the infection."[30] But alas, our indefatigable investigator ferrets out no such worm, and the result is irony turned in on itself, a twist that ironizes the ironist, thereby giving birth to humor. In "A Vision of the World" we hear recorded a similar perception of reversal:

> Time, I thought, strips us rudely of the privileges of the bystander, and in the end that couple chatting loudly in bad French in the lobby of the Grande Bretagne (Athens) turns out to be us. Someone else has got our post behind the potted palms, our quiet corner in the bar, and, exposed, perforce we cast around for other avenues of observation.
>
> (SJC, p. 515)

Given the extraordinary variety of Cheever's fiction, it is extremely difficult to select any one story as an adequate representative of the many themes and the medley of tones I have suggested. But perhaps his masterful "Goodbye, My Brother" might serve, and I offer it merely as a vest-pocket summary.[31]

The story's setting is a summer cottage at Laud's Head, an island off

---

30. John Cheever, *The Stories of John Cheever* (New York: Knopf, 1978), p. 285. Hereafter references to this, the hard-bound edition, will be included in the text.

31. In my reading of this story I am indebted to several insights into it offered by Robert E. McCarty, S. J., "Augustinian Restlessness in the Fiction of John Cheever," a paper presented at the Symposium on Christianity and Literature at the MLA Convention, December 1977; and by Samuel Coale, *John Cheever* (New York: Ungar, 1977), pp. 61-64.

the Massachusetts coast where the Pommeroy family is celebrating a family
reunion. Each member awaits without eagerness the appearance of Lawrence, the estranged brother. When Lawrence arrives, the narrator observes:

> The arrivals and departures of the summer ferry have all the outward
> signs that suggest a voyage . . . but it is a voyage of no import, and
> when I watched the boat come into the blue harbor that afternoon
> and thought that it was completing a voyage of no import, I realized
> that I had hit on exactly the kind of observation that Lawrence would
> have made.   (SJC, p. 4)

In light of the story's development, these lines are laden with multiple
ironies, since images for an existential "voyage" are forthcoming. Yet their
main purpose is to introduce Lawrence, who is the consummate humorless
ironist. The narrator tells us that "my brother looked to me like a Puritan
cleric" (p. 6), and that he disdains gambling because it is "foolish" and
drinks little, requesting "a little rum" with indifference in his voice; his
dispiriting presence immediately creates family tension. His mother soon
begins quietly sipping quantities of gin, and the narrator notes, "She
seemed sadly to be parting from us; she seemed to be in the throes of
travel" (p. 7). Behind Lawrence's back the other family members begin
to complain bitterly about him, "and the abuse seemed to reach a cres-
cendo, and then, one by one, we went swimming in the solid green water.
But when we came out no one mentioned Lawrence unkindly; the line
of abusive conversation had been cut, as if swimming had the cleansing
force claimed for baptism" (p. 10).

With Lawrence present, everyone begins to swim more often, and the
narrator comments,

> If Lawrence noticed this change—this illusion of purification—I sup-
> pose that he would have found in the vocabulary of psychiatry, or the
> mythology of the Atlantic, some circumspect name for it, but I don't
> think he noticed the change. He neglected to name the curative pow-
> ers of the open sea, but it was one of the few chances for diminution
> that he missed.   (p. 10)

It is significant that Lawrence alone refuses to swim, to commit himself
to the "illusion of purification." In fact, we are told that "if he heard the
waves, he must hear them only as a dark answer to all his dark questions;
. . . he would think that the tide had expunged the embers of our picnic
fires" (p. 13).

Lawrence's sour sensibility eventually dampens the satisfaction of every
single appetite. He patronizes the cook and scorns the family backgammon
games, seeing them, no doubt, "as a symbol for more vital forfeits" (p. 12),
but he cannot resist, nonetheless, being a critical observer of every activ-

ity. For the costume ball at the boat club, the narrator wears a football uniform, his wife wears her wedding dress, and his mother dresses as Jenny Lind; when they arrive they discover that other party-goers have duplicated their outfits, and they all laugh in genuine hilarity at the coincidence. But Lawrence, *sans* costume and ever censorious, stares bleakly at their antics "as if in wanting to be brides and football players we exposed the fact that, the lights of youth having been put out in us, we had been unable to find other lights to go by and, destitute of faith and principle, had become foolish and sad" (p. 16).

On the day following the dance, Lawrence and the narrator walk the beach. Lawrence then confesses that he came to the reunion only to say goodbye (typical of a life punctuated only be gestures of leave-taking):

> It was elegiac and it was bigoted and narrow, it mistook circumspection for character, and I wanted to help him. "Come out of it," I said. "Come out of it, Tifty."
> "Come out of what?"
> "Come out of this gloominess. . . . You think that your pessimism is an advantage, but it's nothing but an unwillingness to grasp realities."
> "What are the realities?" he said.   (p. 19)

As Lawrence recites the "factual" realities obvious to any disinterested observer, the narrator becomes angry and strikes his brother with a root he sees lying on the beach. Lawrence is not seriously injured, but the narrator tells us, "Then I wished that he was dead, dead and about to be buried, not buried but about to be buried, because I did not want to be denied ceremony and decorum in putting him away, in putting him out of my consciousness. . . ." (p. 19).

Lawrence leaves, and with him irony departs. The story's majestic final paragraph opens with the narrator's plaintive questions about the constricting "spheres" of life that inhibit our acknowledgment even of dread, much less of beauty and other mysterious "realities." His questions are unanswerable, of course. A partial answer is granted only by a privileged vision, here fittingly a vision of the sea as *both* iridescent and dark. Thus the narrator's tone abruptly changes from the plangent to the lyrical as he sees his wife and sister, both of whom enjoy the names of pagan goddesses, emerging "full of grace" and primal innocence from the redemptive embrace of the eternal sea:

> Oh, what can you do with a man like that? What can you do? How can you dissuade his eye in a crowd from seeking out the cheek with acne, the infirm hand; how can you teach him to respond to the inestimable greatness of the race, the harsh surface beauty of life; how can you put his finger for him on the obdurate truths before which fear

and horror are powerless? The sea that morning was iridescent and dark. My wife and my sister were swimming—Diana and Helen—and I saw their uncovered heads, black and gold in the dark water. I saw them come out and I saw that they were naked, unshy, beautiful, and full of grace, and I watched the naked women walk out of the sea.

(p. 21)

COMEDY AND TRAGEDY

The categories irony and humor, when understood in Kierkegaard's terms, reflect an existential attitude, religious or non-religious, toward the world. Despite this distinction, however, both the ironist and the humorist will use ironic *techniques*, almost in equal measure. This fact raises another issue that apparently perplexes readers of Cheever: are his works comic or tragic or neither or both? Cheever himself opposed the distinction between tragedy and comedy, feeling that "literature—to be literature—must inevitably combine the two."[32] Since a good deal of great literature does not, it is clear that he was speaking primarily of his own work. Perhaps the reason is that he himself consistently chose the ironic mode, that mode which itself contains the ingredient essential to both tragedy and comedy (and humor as an existential point of view embraces them).

The designation "ironic mode" I borrow from Northrop Frye; in his *Anatomy of Criticism* Frye delineates the "spectrum" of irony as it reveals itself in six phases or modes.[33] Although Frye's distinctions have been castigated by some critics for being overly precious or arbitrary, I believe they are most helpful in appreciating the range of Cheever's irony and the tragicomical effect of his finest stories.

Frye argues that on the extreme end of the ironic spectrum lies satire "of the low norm" like folk humor, that "takes for granted a world which is full of anomalies, injustices, follies and crimes, and yet is permanent and undisplaceable" (p. 226). Here the satirist is a "plain, common-sense, conventional person [and] foil for the various *alazons* of society" (p. 226). The second or quixotic phase is "the comedy of escape, in which the hero runs away to a more congenial society without transforming his own" (p. 229). This kind of satiric irony "may often represent the collision between a selection of standards from experience and the feeling that experience is bigger than any set of beliefs about it" (p. 229). The au-

---

32. Cheever made this comment at the Le Moyne College Forum in Syracuse, New York, on April 26, 1980.
33. Northrop Frye, *Anatomy of Criticism* (Princeton: Princeton Univ. Press, 1957). For the sake of convenience, page references to this text of Frye will be included in the text.

thorial attitude might be one of skepticism about all dogmas or of a genial "humor of doubting plain evidence," but proper to it is the "deliberate rambling digressiveness" of the narrative technique, a tactical defense of the pragmatic over the dogmatic (p. 234).

The third phase of irony is "satire of the high norm," in which even "ordinary common sense as a standard" must be abandoned (p. 234). This is irony at its most militant, as found in Petronius, Swift, and Rabelais. The narrator "will show us society suddenly in a telescope as posturing and dignified pygmies, or in a microscope as hideous and reeking giants, or he will change his hero into an ass and show us how humanity looks from an ass's point of view" (p. 234).

The fourth phase is a transitional one from comedy to tragedy, for with it "we move around to the ironic aspect of tragedy, and satire begins to recede" (p. 236). In this phase ridicule is absent, for "such tragic irony differs from satire in that there is no attempt to make fun of the character, but only to bring out clearly the 'all too human,' as distinct from the heroic, aspects of the tragedy" (p. 237). Frye contends that this phase is generally that of the most sincere, explicit realism, like that found in Tolstoy, Hardy, and Conrad.

The fifth phase corresponds to fatalistic tragedy, that of "irony in which the main emphasis is on the natural cycle, the steady unbroken turning of the wheel of fate or fortune. It sees experience, in our terms, with the point of epiphany closed up, and its motto is Browning's 'there may be heaven; there must be hell' " (p. 237). Consequently, the sixth phase "presents human life in terms of largely unrelieved bondage"; in it the human figures are figures of madness or misery. "This brings us around again to the point of demonic epiphany, the dark tower and prison of endless pain, the city of dreadful night in the desert, or, with a more erudite irony, the tour aboli, the goal of the quest that isn't there" (pp. 238-239).

Frye's distinctions are an indispensable aid in appreciating both Cheever's intentions and his literary effects. Earlier I observed that Cheever is not a strict satirist by definition, and yet he continually exploits satiric techniques. Frye includes satire as but a mode or device of irony; satire is characterized by irony, but irony is less restrictive and is employed for many purposes other than satire. Thus an ironist like Cheever will exploit the full range of the ironic spectrum in its six phases, including satire, with the result that the reader begins to see the conjoining of comedy and tragedy as counterparts in the ironic mode.

Several stories (e.g., "The Sorrows of Gin," "The Country Husband," "The Ocean," "Just Tell Me Who It Was," and "The World of Apples") manifest each of these phases to some degree. But perhaps the brilliant story "The Death of Justina" illustrates best the dramatic range of Frye's spectrum, and so rewards close analysis.

I suspect that most readers of "The Death of Justina" are initially shocked by the horrific vision of hell in a suburban supermarket that occurs near the story's close. It is a fleeting glimpse of Frye's sixth phase of irony. The check-out counters are manned by brutes, and

> in every case the customer, at the sight of what he had chosen, showed all the symptoms of the deepest guilt; that force that brings us to our knees. Once their choice had been opened to their shame they were pushed—in some cases kicked—toward the door and beyond the door I saw dark water and heard a terrible noise of moaning and crying in the air. (SJC, p. 436)

What makes this horrific vision of damnation so telling is that earlier the reader has been rendered fairly comfortable by several alternative uses of irony, those proper to the satiric and comic edges of the ironic spectrum. The story begins with an extended harangue about chaos and absurdity, and our usual, spontaneous reaction to excessive complaints of this kind is skepticism of the "come off it" variety. The sentimental, digressive, and perplexed nostalgia that follows reinforces our ironic suspicions. What is all this fuss about "it"?

> So help me God it gets more and more preposterous, it corresponds less and less to what I remember and what I expect as if the force of life were centrifugal and threw one further and further away from one's purest memories and ambitions; and I can barely recall the old house where I was raised, where in midwinter Parma violets bloomed in a cold frame near the kitchen door, and down the long corridor, past the seven views of Rome—up two steps and down three—one entered the library, where all the books were in order, the lamps were bright, where there was a fire and a dozen bottles of good bourbon locked in a cabinet with a veneer like tortoise shell whose silver key my father wore on his watch chain. Fiction is art and art is the triumph over chaos (no less) and we can accomplish this only by the most vigilant exercise of choice, but in a world that changes more swiftly than we can perceive there is always the danger that our powers of selection will be mistaken and that the vision we serve will come to nothing. (p. 429)

That last sentence distracts us from the harangue and moderates our skepticism, but not entirely. Is fiction "the triumph over chaos (no less)"? "Danger" and "vision" are charged words; do they fit, we wonder, or are they extreme? The paragraph ends with an invitation, anticipating our skeptical reluctance: "Just let me give you one example of chaos and if you disbelieve me look honestly into your own past and see if you can't find a comparable experience. . . ." Hereafter the word "comparable" will carry the ironic freight for the reader, and "chaos" and "belief"—such opposed concepts—will pique his interest.

The narrator prefaces his story with apocalyptic premonitions (with the spread of darkness he feels "the force of some primitive memory") and reflections on the immortality of the soul: "The soul (I thought) does not leave the body but lingers with it through every degrading stage of decomposition and neglect" (p. 429). These are followed by fits of "foolish and terrifying anxieties, a definite impairment of my discretionary poles" (p. 430). He tells us, "I felt as if I were being lowered by ropes into the atmosphere of my childhood" (p. 430). Just as the reader begins to question whether all this is insanity or mere excess, these ominous forebodings culminate in an absurdity—the narrator sees a face in his English muffin at breakfast: "The smile faded off the muffin but it had been there for a second—the sense of a person, a life, a pure force of gentleness and censure—and I am convinced that the muffin had contained the presence of some spirit" (p. 430). Note that chaos and belief collide once more and that the muffin wears a smile, an expression "of gentleness and censure."

The action proper begins with the visit of Justina, the elderly cousin of the narrator's wife: "On Tuesday my wife gave her a lunch party. The last guest left at three and a few minutes later Cousin Justina, sitting on the living-room sofa with a glass of good brandy, breathed her last" (p. 430). The first absurdity occurs when the narrator (Moses), a composer of advertising slogans, is telephoned the news while at work and cannot convince his boss that Justina is dead. The boss insists that Moses must write a commercial for a cure-all product named Elixircol before he leaves. Moses complies, and in his frustration composes a parody of one: "Are you falling out of love with your image in the looking glass? Does your face in the morning seem rucked and seamed with alcohol and sexual excesses and does the rest of you appear to be a grayish-pink lump, covered all over with brindle hair?" (p. 431).

Moses then hurries home, but while on the train his reflections enter Frye's second or quixotic phase of irony, that is, he experiences the traveler's realization of a collision between the restrictiveness of social standards and one's more personal sense of the fuller, less restricted possibilities life offers. Moses tells us:

> I stand, figuratively, with one wet foot on Plymouth Rock, looking with some delicacy, not into a formidable and challenging wilderness but onto a half-finished civilization embracing glass towers, oil der-

ricks, suburban continents, and abandoned movie houses and wondering why, in this most prosperous, equitable, and accomplished
world—where even the cleaning women practice the Chopin preludes
in their spare time—everyone should seem to be disappointed.

(p. 432)

When Moses arrives at the stop for Proxmire Manor (his neighborhood), he waits for his wife, there enjoying "the traveler's fine sense of
crisis" (p. 432). At this point in his narrative we come upon another
characteristic Cheever technique: an ironic juxtaposition that simultaneously ushers in and deflates a romantic onrush of feeling. Moses describes his sensation:

> There was a hint of bliss; romantic and domestic bliss. I seemed to
> hear the jinglebells of the sleigh that would carry me to Grandmother's
> house although in fact Grandmother spent the last years of her life
> working as a hostess on an ocean liner and was lost in the tragic sinking
> of the S.S. *Lorelei* and I was responding to a memory that I had not
> experienced. But the hill of light rose like an answer to some primitive
> dream of homecoming. On one of the highest lawns I saw the remains
> of a snowman who still smoked a pipe and wore a scarf and a cap but
> whose form was wasting away and whose anthracite eyes stared out at
> the view with terrifying bitterness.   (pp. 432-433)

The event of his "actual" homecoming brings us into Frye's third
ironic phase, in which "the standard of ordinary common sense" is abandoned. With the dead Justina still sitting on the sofa, Moses encounters
an even greater absurdity: because of new zoning restrictions, he cannot
have Justina declared officially dead nor can he have her body removed
and buried. A sympathetic Dr. Hunter offers an explanation: " 'It seems
that you not only can't have a funeral home in Zone B—you can't bury
anything there and you can't die there. Of course it's absurd, but we all
make mistakes, don't we?' " (p. 433). The doctor suggests that Moses
could take the old lady over to Zone C and claim she died in his car, or
else call the Mayor and ask for an exception to the zoning law.

After this unsatisfying exchange Moses notices that "Justina seemed
to be waiting for me and to be changing from an inert into a demanding
figure. . . . Dusk seemed to be playing directly into her hands and she
gained power and stature with the dark" (p. 434). This palpable presence
of death edges the narrative toward Frye's fourth and fifth phases of a
tragic dimension, but the comically "all too human" and the fatalistic
merge with them. When Moses contacts the Mayor, he agrees that " 'it's
an awful thing to have happened, but the trouble is that we can't give
you a zoning exception without a majority vote of the Village Council
and all the members of the Council happen to be out of town' " (p. 434).

He remains committed to the ludicrous ordinance even in the face of Moses's challenge:

". . . if I make an exception for you I'll have to make an exception for every one and this kind of morbidity, when it gets out of hand, can be very depressing. People don't like to live in a neighborhood where this sort of thing goes on all the time."

"Listen to me," I said. "You give me an exception and you give it to me now or I'm going home and dig a hole in my garden and bury Justina myself."

"But you can't do that, Moses. You can't bury anything in Zone B. You can't even bury a cat."   (p. 435)

But finally the Mayor relents and grants Moses an exception. That evening Moses has the dream of the hellish supermarket, evident of the most extreme phase of the ironic spectrum. The rest of the story briefly recapitulates in reverse the other phases of the spectrum. For the next day Justina is buried in the rain among the dead, and ". . . in Proxmire Manor their unexalted kingdom is on the outskirts, rather like a dump, where they are transported furtively as knaves and scoundrels . . ." (p. 437).

The priest was a friend and a cheerful sight, but the undertaker and his helpers, hiding behind their limousines, were not; and aren't they at the root of most of our troubles, with their claim that death is a violet-flavored kiss? How can a people who do not mean to understand death hope to understand love, and who will sound the alarm?

                                                                                 (p. 437)

The hint of cheer at the priest's presence prepares us for another ironic phase, though it does not occur immediately. When Moses returns to his office, his boss demands that he re-write his satiric commercial. He does so, but in a more savage, cosmic parody that begins: *"Don't lose your loved ones because of excessive radioactivity. Don't be a wallflower at the dance because of strontium 90 in your bones,"* and ends, *"You have been inhaling lethal atomic waste for the last twenty-five years and only Elixircol can save you"* (p. 437).

Moses's boss rejects this second version, too, and in grease pencil marks it—in language so ironically pertinent to the story's theme—*"Do, or you'll be dead"* (p. 437). Moses complies, but instead of praising Elixircol, he simply types the whole of the Twenty-third Psalm in the King James version and goes home. The story closes:

The Lord is my shepherd; therefore can I lack nothing. He shall feed me in a green pasture and lead me forth beside the waters of comfort. . . . Yea, though I walk through the valley of the shadow of death I will fear no evil for thou art with me; thy rod and thy staff comfort me. . . .   (p. 437)

At first the reader is unprepared for the somewhat shocking insertion of the whole psalm, for its inclusion moves the story toward a totally different ironic level and enjoins a different perspective of the events narrated. Structurally, the psalm provides an ironic balance to the story's prologue, which opens with "So help me God" and shouts complaints about chaos and disorder. The equally personal voice of the Psalmist ("my shepherd") and the consolation he seeks become the prologue's counterpoint. In addition, the prologue, written in the present tense, is linked with recollection: the psalm, written in future tense, is hopeful.

Furthermore, the story has been punctuated throughout by Moses's charge to compose an Elixircol commercial, but Elixircol is a product concerned with ephemeral evil only, evil transposed out of its moral/spiritual category into an aesthetic one, so that the traditionally complex meanings attached to the biblical "fear of the Lord" have been trivialized and cosmeticized into "only Elixircol can save you." Thus, in this context, the words "though I walk through the valley of the shadow of death I will fear no evil" point toward a profundity of existential concern and suggest an outreach toward mystery that Elixircol denies. Consequently, it is clear that Cheever intends that the psalm be the "final" perspective, a perspective that prompts a reinterpretation of the events narrated. This alternate perspective so ironizes the previous irony that in itself it is not ironic—rather, it reaches beyond irony by calling all easier ironies into question and, as it were, enclosing the ironic spectrum.

"The Death of Justina" demonstrates Cheever's religious attitudes more definitely than most of his stories, but it ought to cue readers to be alert to the fact that his religious convictions provide a different coloration to irony itself, and blur the more hardened distinctions between tragedy and comedy. Once again, Northrop Frye in his essay "The Argument of Comedy" offers an important insight:

> From the point of view of Christianity, tragedy is an episode in that larger scheme of redemption and resurrection to which Dante gave the name *commedia*. This conception of *commedia* enters drama with the miracle-play cycles, where such tragedies as the Fall and the Crucifixion are episodes of a dramatic scheme in which the divine comedy has the last word.[34]

Whether Frye's contention is historically accurate or universally applicable is arguable, of course, and a host of critics think otherwise, at least with regard to the conclusions implied within it concerning the very

---

34. Northrop Frye, "The Argument of Comedy," in *Theories of Comedy*, ed. Paul Lauter (Garden City: Doubleday-Anchor, 1964), p. 455. He also returns to this theme, this time from a biblical perspective, in his latest brilliant study; see Northrop Frye, *The Great Code: The Bible and Literature* (New York: Harcourt Brace Jovanovich, 1982).

possibility of a Christian tragedy. But my reason for inserting his observation here is that it does describe well Cheever's own point of view
toward tragedy. For Cheever, a resolute believer in both the Fall and
Redemption, comedy always contains potential tragedy within it, and yet
tragedy will ever remain a version of uncompleted comedy. (This is not
true of *every* story, needless to say, but of his major efforts and his *oeuvre*
when judged in its totality.) The difference is determined not only by
where a writer enters but especially by where he ends.

For example, each of the Wapshot novels contains several tragic incidents, but each also ends with an inspiring corrective to univocally
gloomy thoughts, offered by the patriarch, Leander:

> "Stand up straight. Admire the world. Relish the love of a gentle
> woman. Trust in the Lord."   (*The Wapshot Chronicle*)

> "Let us consider that the soul of man is immortal, able to endure every
> sort of good and every sort of evil."   (*The Wapshot Scandal*)

Bullet Park ends with the words, "everything was as wonderful, wonderful, wonderful, wonderful as it had been." Some critics have interpreted
this line as smugly cynical, but as I hope to show, it need not be—it can
be seen, instead, as articulating surprise at the marvelous, a more consistent Cheever theme. The ending to *Falconer* is less ambiguous. Throughout, this novel taps many of the rich resources of irony, moving from
satiric derision to comedy to tragic fate and circumstance and even into
Frye's sixth ironic phase of "unrelieved bondage," only to end with the
protagonist's escape and the line, "Rejoice, he thought, rejoice."

The last page of Cheever's latest novel, *Oh What a Paradise It Seems*,
contains the most lyrical instance of such an ending; it invites us to enter
the thoughts of the protagonist, the old man Sears:

> What moved him was a sense of those worlds around us, our knowledge
> however imperfect of their nature, our sense of their possessing some
> grain of our past and of our lives to come. It was that most powerful
> sense of our being alive on the planet. It was that most powerful sense
> of how singular, in the vastness of creation, is the richness of our
> opportunity. The sense of that hour was of an exquisite privilege, the
> great benefice of living here and renewing ourselves with love. What
> a paradise it seemed!   (p. 100)

But each of these is a character speaking; let us close this chapter by
quoting directly from their source. In a 1977 interview Cheever himself
spoke eloquently to these issues of mystery and opportunity and love:

That one is in conflict with oneself—that one's erotic nature and one's social nature will everlastingly be at war with one another—is something I am happy to live with on terms as hearty and fleeting as laughter. These conflicts—between love and death, youth and age, war and peace—are simply that vast vocabulary we use for the divisions of life. And it seems to me that literature is the best way to refresh this conflict, to embrace it, to admit it in our lives.[35]

35. "John Hersey Talks with John Cheever," *Yale Alumni Magazine and Journal*, December 1977, p. 24. Perhaps some readers will be consternated if they note footnote 17, which is very similar to this one. Actually, the explanation is simple: Hersey and Cheever spoke for a long time, and part of the interview was published in the *New York Times Book Review* and the rest in the *Yale Alumni Magazine and Journal*.

Narrative is a synonym for life—for a chain of lives. Forms
are evolved by the societies they serve, and narratives should
reflect the exaltations, the discursiveness, the spontaneity and
pratfalls one finds in a day.

John Cheever

As I altered my syntax, I altered my intellect.

William Butler Yeats

Of all the characters that a great artist creates, his readers are
the best.

Vladimir Nabokov

Prose was born yesterday—that is what we must tell ourselves.

Gustave Flaubert

Music heard so deeply
That it is not heard at all, but you are
the music
While the music lasts.

T. S. Eliot

A single line, like a phrase in music, may indicate a writer's
key, his pervading tone, which the trained ear can detect
throughout the writer's fiction—but to appreciate the nature
of his music we need a little more.

Wright Morris

Something that has existed since the beginning, that we have
heard, and we have seen with our own eyes; the Word, who
is life—this is our subject.

Saint John

2: Style

In his lectures on fiction at Cornell, Vladimir Nabokov commented on the elusive category "style" by saying, "Style is not a tool, it is not a method, it is not a choice of words alone. Being much more than all this, style constitutes an intrinsic component or characteristic of the author's personality."[1]

Nabokov's comment points up the difficulty inherent in any critical discussion of a particular writer's style. Note that even the Master himself must resort to negatives and then conclude by stressing something "intrinsic" to the author's "personality." This statement is truthful and accurate but none too helpful, for it actually presumes the many elements that issue in that complex of literate energies labeled style. So it appears that, like pornography, one knows style when he sees it but can never define it. Small wonder, then, that most critics prefer to move on to more tractable problems like theme, point of view, and character analysis.

Unfortunately, any critical investigation of John Cheever's fiction cannot so easily slip by a discussion of style. The reason is that the word "Cheeveresque" involves not only thematic or contextual qualities but radically important stylistic ones. Even reviewers and critics who are not partial to Cheever's fiction inevitably, despite reservations in other areas, praise him highly for his style. If Nabokov is correct, why should they?

This chapter is an attempt to answer this question, which, in Cheever's case, has gone unexamined.[2] Such an examination reveals, first of all, that what we now associate with the Cheeveresque style developed gradually and is not distinctively identifiable until the Shady Hill stories, which began publication in 1953. Readers of *The Stories of John Cheever*

---

1. Vladimir Nabokov, *Lectures on Literature* (New York: Harcourt Brace Jovanovich, 1980), p. 59.
2. There are two unpublished doctoral dissertations that discuss Cheever's style in some depth, and I have found both most helpful in my own analysis. See Dennis Coates, "The Novels of John Cheever," Diss. Duke University 1977, 271 pp.; and John H. Wink, "John Cheever and the Broken World," Diss. University of Arkansas 1974, 237 pp.

are generally disappointed when, after completing the first story in the collection, "Goodbye, My Brother," they note that twelve of the subsequent fifteen stories so evidently lack its rhetorical power and originality. The reasons for this odd disappointment are multiple, no doubt, but when one learns that "Goodbye, My Brother" is actually a later story (published in summer 1951) and that the subsequent eleven stories which follow it were composed years before it, one senses that the absence of that story's beguiling style is the explanation rather than other thematic or contextual qualities.

Consequently, any investigation of Cheever's style must address three matters: the stylistic influences of his apprenticeship years (roughly 1930-1950); the peculiar properties of the mature Cheever style; and finally, the relationship of that later style to the literary tradition, specifically to those writers whom Cheever resembles, in the hope that such comparisons might clarify Cheever's verbal richness—the magic readers respond to.

A few brief observations on style in general should precede this investigation. First of all, it should be noted that in discussing writers it is almost impossible, as Nabokov implies, to speak of a style in isolation. A writer's style is necessarily associated with the subject matter, dramatic structure, and point of view in his work and, as such, is but one manifestation of that complex configuration we call artistic technique. Style has been defined as "a combination of two elements: the idea to be expressed and the individuality of the author."[3] This definition emphasizes the reciprocity between the ideas that the fictional material generates and the author's intentions and success in organizing them. Style will always reflect theme (i.e., the incorporation and shape of the idea or subject) joined with a distinctive gift of expression.

In short, shape and shaping spirit are wedded in the work. These meet in language, whereby through words—to offer an extended metaphor—the author places his own personal "voice-print" on the hitherto indeterminate paper. Like a stylus, which makes impressions as it records vocal vibrations, a writer's style, through his word selection and the shape of his sentences, imprints a pattern on paper that is as uniquely his as his fingerprint. Just as the sensitive stylus will register the more subtle vibrations and tonal shifts in the speaker's voice, a writer's style will generally be described in terms of vocal equivalents. For example, changes in pitch or tonal shifts we call lyricism or the like; overtones or resonance we call

---

3. C. Hugh Holman, *A Handbook to Literature* (New York: Bobbs-Merrill, 1972), p. 514.

connotations; the choice of words, their aptness and precision, we call diction; and so on.

These vocal analogies—now hardened metaphors in literary criticism—are especially pertinent to Cheever's later style. To be fully appreciated, Cheever's fiction *must be read aloud*. We respond to the verbal rhythms of such elegant and versatile stylists as John Updike, Saul Bellow, and John Barth *inside* our heads, but these writers are difficult to read aloud for a sustained period. Cheever's prose, on the other hand, almost demands that it be read aloud[4]—its appeal is audile. It comes as no surprise to us when Cheever admits in his preface to his collected stories that a good number of his sentences and stories were composed and tested as spoken creations, with his family and occasional strangers as critical audience.

For too long, academic criticism has been more intent on thematic concerns, the fictional *what*, so to speak, and has given short shrift to the artistic *how*, the less easily stateable aspects of style that ultimately make for fictional magic. Central to that *how* or artistic effectiveness is the writer's voice, and critics who ignore or downplay it create a greater gulf between the pleasures of literature and life than is, in fact, the case. In our common experience of daily life, the sound of a speaker's voice is generally more inviting or more boring than his subject. We react both intellectually and emotionally to the tempo, emphases, and pitch of another's voice rather than attend closely to intellectual or emotional content. What usually moves us first is the speaker, not what he speaks *about*. In daily life a speaker has other advantages besides the sound of his voice, such as gestures, facial expressions, charming idiosyncracies—resources which writers lack. Instead, they must manipulate words, arrange them with dramatic care, punctuate cues for passion to arrest and maintain our attention.

Cheever's style has been likened to that of a poet, but the "poetic" quality of that style derives less from its lyricism than from his exploitation of the major created resource all poets must command: the poet's voice. No matter how high-minded his theme or brilliant his language, if a poet lacks a beguiling voice, his poetry goes flat.

In commenting on this elusive term "voice" in fiction, Anatole Broyard has said that "voice is the sound of conviction, of the writer finding the truth of his experience. It is not eloquence, but the best personal tone the writer can produce, a tone very close to the one he uses when he is

---

4. Roger Shattuck and others have given a great deal of attention to the importance of the oral aspects of literature. For a very sophisticated treatment, see Walter J. Ong, S. J., *The Presence of the Word* (Minneapolis: Univ. of Minnesota Press, 1981).

alone and talking to himself."[5] Broyard goes further to compare a writer's voice to a distillation, a purification, "the ultimately human, appealing sound we retain when all the impurities or interferences are filtered out, when contrivance, pretension, defensiveness and lying are eliminated." Thus style, an aesthetic category, is a close relative of honesty, a moral category.

A review of Cheever's writing career reveals that early on he found his "song," i.e., the themes, settings, and characters familiar in his later work. But it took him a while longer to discover, as he put it in another context, his "singing voice."[6] During the thirties and forties we find Cheever's fiction imitative of the voices of other writers, perhaps because of the literary conventions then prevailing or the restraints of the magazine story format; but from 1950 on we hear a distinctive sound, highly individual and instantly recognizable, a unique possession shared by both reader and writer from story to story and novel to novel.[7]

What makes Cheever's stylistic achievement so exceptional is that the later voice is non-ethnic, unidiomatic, and rarely eccentric (except for Leander's journal in the Wapshot novels). His dialogues, of course, reflect his unerring ear for distinctive accents, but his narrative voice generally remains neutral, issuing in what one might call "Walter Cronkite or John Chancellor American." What for other writers would be a handicap becomes for him a strength. He is able to achieve a wide range of artistic effects without resorting to the devices other writers must use— ethnic accents (Irish, Jewish, Black, et al.) or regional rhythms and elisions (Southern drawl, New Yorkese, Midwestern twang). Where others achieve a verbal vitality and density by exploiting idiosyncracies of language, he does so by way of exceptional lucidity and gracefulness of sentence structure. How does he do it?

5. Anatole Broyard, "The Right Voice Can't Lie," *New York Times Book Review*, October 11, 1981, p. 51.

6. My demarcations regarding Cheever's stylistic "development" are admittedly arbitrary, and I submit them only for clarity's sake. I realize that knowledgeable critics of the early Cheever will find fault with any easy divisions between early and late, apprentice and artist. My intent here is more general than specific and a blurring of edges is inevitable, for the style of certain early stories is hard to differentiate from the stylistic expertise of the later ones. For example, Cheever's "Homage to Shakespeare," which appeared in *Story*, 11 (November 1937), 73-81, possesses many of the stylistic qualities of his later work, though I like to think that it does so *in embryo*.

7. Once again an exception should be noted. The novel *Falconer*, when it appeared, seemed a radical departure in Cheever's style (owing to the absence of lyricism and especially the unexpected vulgarity and coarseness of the language, so appropriate to the prison context). Nonetheless, despite the alteration in vocabulary and the general absence of an intense lyricism, I believe that *Falconer* still exemplifies the patterns of his later style (though shaved finely) more truly than those of his earlier style.

A Writer's Pilgrim's Progress:
The Apprenticeship Years

But first the historical question: how *did* he do it? A clue is found in one of his masterly late stories, "The World of Apples." Near the close of that story we come upon a hilarious and poignant scene in which the central character, Asa Bascomb, an aged poet famous for his ability to divine "the voice of moral beauty in a rain wind," has recently been beset by startling pornographic visions and obscene dreams; for this reason he has decided to make a pilgrimage of purgation to the sacred angel in the village church of Monte Giordano.

> It was an old, small, poor country church. The angel was in a chapel on the left, which the priest lighted. The image, buried in jewelry, stood in an iron cage with a padlocked door. The priest opened this and Bascomb placed his Lermontov medal at the angel's feet. Then he got to his knees and said loudly: "God bless Walt Whitman. God bless Hart Crane. God bless Dylan Thomas. God bless William Faulkner, Scott Fitzgerald, and especially Ernest Hemingway." The priest locked up the sacred relic and they left the church together. There was a cafe on the square where he got some supper and rented a bed. This was a strange engine of brass with brass angels at the four corners, but they seemed to possess some brassy blessedness since he dreamed of peace and woke in the middle of the night finding in himself that radiance he had known when he was younger.[8]

The scene is replete with the ironic overtones and the ambiguous union of humor and sadness that characterizes Cheever's fiction. Particularly touching, however, is Bascomb's impassioned prayer, a selective plea of benediction for the giants in his native language, all of whom were notorious drunks or reputed homosexuals.

A critical case can be made that the figures in Bascomb's pantheon correspond with the major twentieth century influences on Cheever's own stylistic development. One can detect the robust, rhetorical enthusiasm of Whitman, Crane, and Thomas in his lyric celebration of natural creation and of the vigors of youth and innocence. Faulkner's inspiration appears less evident at first, since Cheever's prose is obviously less lush and complex; and yet one can discern similarities beneath this more obvious surface. The romantic voice of yarn-spinner, the lyricism, the Gothic intrusions (here transposed from the South into city and suburbia), the seemingly random digressiveness of the narrative, and especially the

---

8. John Cheever, *The Stories of John Cheever* (New York: Knopf, 1978), p. 622. Hereafter references to the collection will be included in the text.

nstinct to transmute autobiography and family history into saga wherein
St. Botolphs, Shady Hill, and Bullet Park become Atlantic Yoknapataw-
phas—all these are reminders of Faulkner's unique legacy to American
writers of similar sensibility and talent.

But the last two writers cited as worthy of blessing, Scott Fitzgerald
and "especially" Ernest Hemingway, were without question the major
stylistic influences on Cheever during his apprenticeship. Like almost
every other American writer of the thirties' generation, he first was held
in thrall by Hemingway's style: its syntactical simplicity, its externalization
of mood, its emotional restraint leading to effects brought about mainly
through subtle implications rather than psychological exploration.
Cheever's very first published story, "Expelled," which he wrote at age
seventeen after he was expelled from Thayer Academy, reads like a tale
of a prep-school Nick Adams. The story begins:

> It didn't come all at once. It took a very long time. First I had a
> skirmish with the English department and then all the other depart-
> ments. Pretty soon something had to be done. The first signs were
> cordialities on the part of the headmaster. He was never nice to any-
> body unless he was a football star, or hadn't paid his tuition, or was
> going to be expelled. That's how I knew.[9]

Despite the narrative "I" here, the tone is flat and impersonal, the
syntax artificially simple, and the cadence repetitive; and the ominously
vague "it's" and "sometimes" rely on inference only. This voice maintains
its distance throughout the story.

> Every morning we went up into the black chapel. The brisk head-
> master was there. Sometimes he had a member of the faculty with
> him. Sometimes it was a stranger.
> He introduced the stranger whose speech was always the same. In
> the spring life is like a baseball game. In the fall it is like football.
> That is what the speaker always said. . . .
> If they have a mayor the speech will be longer. He will tell us that
> our country is beautiful and young and strong. That the War is over,
> but that if there is another war we must fight. He will tell us that war
> is a masculine trait that has brought present civilization to its fine
> condition. Then he will leave us and help stout women place lilacs on
> graves. He will tell them the same thing.

The wry eye of the mature Cheever is already peeping out in these
lines, but the voice is not yet distinctively his. Hemingway's influence on
him persisted, with alterations, throughout the thirties; in addition, during

9. John Cheever, "Expelled," *New Republic*, October 1, 1930, p. 371.

this period his lean, spare prose began to take on the brighter colorations of Scott Fitzgerald's style, reflecting what Kenneth Elbe called "Fitzgerald's singular ability to dignify the trivial while remaining faintly ironic toward it."[10] This was a happy development, for although Hemingway's influence encourages extraordinary discipline in a writer, imposing standards of simplicity and directness (qualities the mature Cheever retained), that style too easily degenerates into mannerism and artificiality. Fitzgerald's inspiration liberated Cheever's romantic instincts and his deft talent for rendering dramatic scenes wherein characters stand revealed through their actions and words without explicit narrative comment. The majority of Cheever's pre-war and wartime stories are structured by way of these dramatic vignettes, more specifically through carefully exact verisimilar speech so characteristic of Fitzgerald. Readers familiar with Cheever's later fiction would probably consider these stories "playlets," abbreviations of the more expansive form of his later work rather than "legitimate" Cheever stories.

In his own short biography of Fitzgerald written for *Atlantic Brief Lives*, Cheever offers an eloquent tribute to Fitzgerald and, in doing so, points up those very qualities he assimilated during the thirties and later incorporated into his mature work. He says of Fitzgerald's stories that "in spite of their very uneven quality these were not rueful vignettes or overheard conversations but real stories with characters, invention, scenery and moral conviction. . . . The best of the stories were lived as well as written—an irreversible process that sometimes ends in grief, but he remained astonishingly hopeful."[11]

Real stories, moral conviction, and a somewhat "astonishing hopefulness amidst grief" are the key Fitzgeraldian elements that Cheever appropriated—elements that led him beyond the earlier Hemingway standard. His Fitzgerald biography ends with this appreciation, one worth quoting in full because it is indicative of fictional aims he himself cherished:

> Great writers are profoundly immersed in their time and he was a peerless historian. In Fitzgerald there is a thrilling sense of knowing exactly where one is—the city, the resort, the hotel, the decade and the time of day. His greatest innovation was to use social custom, clothing, overheard music, not as history but as an expression of his acute awareness of the meaning of time: All the girls in their short skirts and those German tangos and the hot nights belong to history, but their finest purpose is to evoke the excitement of being alive. He gives one vividly the sense that the Crash and the Jazz Age were

10. Kenneth Elbe, *F. Scott Fitzgerald* (New York: Twayne, 1963), p. 86.
11. John Cheever, "F. Scott Fitzgerald," in *Atlantic Brief Lives*, ed. Louis Kronenburger (Boston: Little, Brown, 1971), p. 276.

without precedent, but one sees that this is a part of his art and that
while Amory, Dick, Gatsby, Anson—all of them—lived in a temporal
crisis of nostalgia and change, they were deeply involved in the universality of love and suffering. [12]

Fitzgerald's stylistic and thematic influence is pronounced and salutary
during this period. However, on re-reading these earlier stories, one is
surprised to discover that Cheever failed to incorporate that one feature
of Fitzgerald's style that one later associates with Cheever himself: a restrained but elegant lyricism. This curious absence invites two possible
explanations. First, during the period of the Depression and World War
II, lyricism in sophisticated fiction was neither popular nor, it seems,
appropriate. A second and probably related explanation is that in 1935
Cheever began his association with the New Yorker magazine. In the ten-
year period from 1935 to 1945 he published at least forty-five stories in
the New Yorker; and by 1982 he had published over 120 stories there, a
total surpassed only by John O'Hara.

Several critics have charged that this was not a beneficial alliance for
Cheever, and that it stunted his artistic growth at the time (and later on,
some argue). [13] The complaint is that the short-story mode of the New
Yorker encouraged a sophisticated but superficial tidying-up of life's complexities and imposed a "self-limited literary landscape" on its writers.
George Garrett has summarized well those features of what many critics
consider a "typical" New Yorker story in its "vintage" years, i.e., the period
of Cheever's apprenticeship:

> Briefly it was the maximum exploration and exploitation of a single
> dramatically presented incident, more or less strictly observing the
> unities of time and place and rich in implication. . . . Plot, in the
> conventional sense, was largely absent, as were the middle-class moral
> dilemmas of slick fiction. . . . Naturally the stories reflected the gen-
> eral moral views of the magazine and its public—reasonably but not
> ostentatiously well-informed, perhaps a little snobbish, though united
> against the more common forms of snobbery, more or less liberal po-
> litically. It was never, not even in the case of certain religious writers,
> religious. Its moral fibre, its touchstone was a kind of secular humanism
> coupled with a gentle intellectual agnosticism. The virtues it honored
> were all civilized virtues, sedentary, sophisticated, and rational, all
> defended by the curtains (never made of iron) of humor, irony, sen-
> sitivity, the skeptical intelligence, and a form of gentility that was au

12. Cheever, "F. Scott Fitzgerald," p. 276.
13. See Samuel Coale, John Cheever (New York: Ungar, 1977), pp. 6, 11. See also
Samuel Coale, "Beyond The New Yorker: The Vision of John Cheever," Trinity Reporter,
Vol. 7, No. 6 (May 1977), 1-4.

courant. . . . The mortal sins in this universe were, inevitably: vulgarity without the redemption of eccentricity, self-pity, stupidity, hypocrisy, bad manners, complacency, excess of passion. . . .[14]

Whether or not the vintage *New Yorker* format did hinder Cheever's writerly progress is a moot point, endlessly arguable as are most etiological issues. What is undeniable is that a good number of Cheever's pre-1950 stories do, in fact, demonstrate the limitations—both literary and moral—proper to the *New Yorker* that Garrett describes. But it is equally undeniable that it was Cheever himself who was mainly responsible for eventually bending the rigidities of that format and broadening its moral and religious landscape, at first tentatively and then more boldly in his postwar fiction.

Sufficient evidence of Cheever's personal restlessness amid such restrictions is provided by the fact that in the late thirties he began alternate work on a novel, *The Holly Tree* (subtitled *Empty Bed Blues*), that was to be unconventional and avant-garde. *The Holly Tree* was a family portrait, foreshadowing the Wapshot novels, and its structure was to be digressive and elliptical, shaped by shifting points of view, and episodic in design rather than formally unified.[15] The publishers Simon and Schuster accepted the novel but wanted Cheever to alter its structure to make it into a conventionally plotted novel; he refused, and sought out other publishers. When they also requested similar changes, he threw the manuscript into a trash can. Although the novel itself was irretrievable, Cheever did retrieve certain autobiographical memories, themes, and stylistic devices and incorporated them in his later fiction.

In 1943, after Cheever entered the service, Random House published a collection of thirty of his stories under the Fitzgerald-like title, *The Way Some People Live.* It is an uneven collection, more a historical curiosity for students of Cheever than a fully realized work. It is interesting mainly for what it reveals about his conservatism in style and narrative strategy at this stage of his authorship. With the exception of "Survivor," all the stories are recounted in the third person. Most are vignettes rather than stories, shaped either by a Hemingwayesque exchange of laconic dialogue or by the placing of characters within a single scene where, in Fitzgerald's fashion, the *atmosphere* of failure and disillusionment is evoked rather

14. George Garrett, "John Cheever and the Charms of Innocence: The Craft of *The Wapshot Scandal,*" in *The Sounder Few: Essays from the "Hollins Critic,"* ed. R. H. Dillard et al. (Athens: Univ. of Georgia Press, 1971), pp. 21-22.

15. See Dennis Coates's dissertation, "The Novels of John Cheever," pp. 35ff., for an interesting narrative of these events.

than dramatized.[16] The pessimistic mood and pronouncedly cool, imitative style that characterize the collection give its stories a curious repetitiveness lacking fire; the work is redeemed only by the experimental story "Of Love: A Testimony." Whereas most of the other stories look backward—are, one might even say, regressive—in that they are so reminiscent of a combination of literary styles that already were becoming outworn conventions, "Of Love: A Testimony" points forward, not only to later Cheever but to the post-modernist techniques of Barthelme, Barth, Pynchon, and others.

The reviewers of *The Way Some People Live* were unanimous in singling out "Of Love: A Testimony" for praise, but their reactions to the complete collection were less enthusiastic. Weldon Kees in the *New Republic* was quick to raise the *New Yorker* objection, complaining that "as individual magazine stories they seemed better than they are; read one after another, their nearly identical lengths, similarities of tone and situation, and their somehow remote and unambitious style produce an effect of sameness and equally of tedium."[17] William Du Bois took a similar tack, criticizing the stories' "epicene detachment and facile despair," qualities he felt were proper to the magazine.[18] Struthers Burt in the *Saturday Review* was perhaps the most prescient. He praised the young writer's talent but added this personal caution: "John Cheever has only two things to fear; a hardening into an especial style that might become an affectation, and a deliberate casualness and simplicity that might become the same. Otherwise, the world is his."[19]

Subsequent literary history suggests that Cheever took Struthers Burt's cautions to heart—but not immediately. During the war years Cheever wrote eighteen more stories, none too distinguishable from his previous efforts. Immediately after the war, however, he wrote a six-part series for the *New Yorker* entitled "Town House," which centered on the difficulties of post-war adjustment and economic conflict experienced by three couples who decide to share a town house in New York City. The series is technically ambitious: its episodic structure, its interweaving of relation-

16. See William Troy, "Scott Fitzgerald: The Authority of Fiction," in *F. Scott Fitzgerald: A Collection of Essays*, ed. Arthur Mizener (Englewood Cliffs, N. J.: Prentice-Hall, 1963), pp. 20-24.
17. Weldon Kees, "John Cheever's Stories," *New Republic*, April 19, 1943, p. 516. For a listing and a short summary of the reviews of this collection, see the indispensable text edited by Francis J. Boscha, *John Cheever: A Reference Guide* (Boston: G. K. Hall, 1981), pp. 11-12.
18. William DuBois, "Tortured Souls," *New York Times Book Review*, March 28, 1943, p. 10.
19. Struthers Burt, "John Cheever's Sense of Drama," *Saturday Review*, April 24, 1943, p. 9.

ships, and its probing of human psychology and of moral complication make it a forerunner of Updike's *Couples* in an urban setting. These postwar stories soon began to demonstrate a subtle alteration in Cheever's work.

Evidently the responsibilities of marriage and a family, the war years, and his displacement from familiar locales because of army service brought about a maturing of Cheever's moral perception, and with it a broadening and deepening of his artistic sensibility. From the start he had been an intelligent and knowing writer; at this point one senses that he was withering into wisdom and truth. Gertrude Stein once observed of another writer, "He has the syrup, but it doesn't pour." For Cheever, the pouring had commenced.

The novelist Wright Morris has said that the craft of fiction is that branch of the arts "where what the author *perceives* is more important than what he observes."[20] One discovers that in Cheever's case the familiar characters, setting, and themes reminiscent of the *New Yorker* format remained, but a gradual heightening took place—a transformation of the familiar into the fabulous, for example, and especially a movement beyond mere diagnostic observation toward more clement perceptions. As the range of Cheever's perceptions widened and deepened, their number and variety more keenly challenged his artistic intelligence, so that his native talent blossomed like seeds in bright sunshine. The result is that his stories, though still rather parochial in context, begin to grope toward a universality of human feeling and an engagement with moral problems. It seems that he spontaneously realized that he needed a more flexible narrative instrument that would reflect this broader literary and moral consciousness as it developed. That is, he needed a more personalized style that would concomitantly liberate his gifts for humor and compassion and sentiment, and replace the more narrow perceptions of irony and muted pessimism found in his earlier work.

THE CREATION OF THE CHEEVERESQUE STYLE

Cheever *himself*, his personality and his perceptions, had changed. Now his first task (as we shall see, by way of a gradual process) was to create his own specific authorial "second self," one which would correspond with both his maturer perception of the world and his own individual perspective.

The "authorial second self" is a phrase offered by Wayne Booth to describe an author's uniqueness, for "as he writes, he creates not simply

20. Wright Morris, *About Fiction* (New York: Harper & Row, 1975), p. 44.

an ideal, impersonal 'man in general' but an implied version of 'himself' that is different from the implied authors we meet in other men's works."[21] Booth goes on to make this important observation:

> It is a curious fact that we have no terms either for this created "second self" or for our relationship to him. None of our terms for various aspects of the narrator is quite accurate. "Persona," "mask," and "narrator" are sometimes used, but they more commonly refer to the speaker in the work who is after all only one of the elements created by the implied author and who may be separated from him by large ironies. "Narrator" is usually taken to mean the "I" of the work, but the "I" is seldom if ever identified with the implied image of the artist.[22]

Booth defines the implied author as the one "who chooses, consciously or unconsciously, what we read; we infer him as an ideal, literary, created version of the real man; he is the sum of his own choices." The implied author or second self, then, is the writer's distinctive personality *as* author (not necessarily as man). The writer creates this personality, this second self, through his efforts to create an individually distinctive voice; his "style" is the final outcome of his efforts to define this second self in the medium of language. Consequently, when we become familiar with this second self so that we desire to return to that "voice," that personality which ultimately shapes the narrative action, we have been, in effect, beguiled by his *style*. As Pascal put it, "When we encounter a natural style we are always surprised and delighted, for we expected to see an author and found a man." Here Pascal's "man" is in fact the author's second self embodied in language.

Throughout Cheever's apprenticeship years, the authorial ideals of an impersonal and objective narrator—so well represented by Hemingway in particular, and by Fitzgerald to some degree—dominated literary fashion. By the end of the war, however, those very ideals had themselves become stylized conventions, and very talented writers like Salinger, Bellow, Mailer, and others began experimenting with more personalized, less objective styles. Cheever's efforts were more gradual—no doubt because he had achieved success by incorporating the then reigning style—and yet one can trace his progressive groping for an authentic "second self" of his own.

The publishing dates of the earlier stories collected in *The Stories of John Cheever* are themselves revealing. In 1946 he wrote "The Sutton

---

21. Wayne Booth, *The Rhetoric of Fiction* (Chicago: Univ. of Chicago Press, 1961), pp. 70-71.
22. Booth, *The Rhetoric of Fiction*, p. 74.

Place Story"; in 1947, "The Enormous Radio," "The Common Day," and "Torch Song"; in 1948, "O City of Broken Dreams" and "The Summer Farmer"; in 1949, "The Hartleys" and "Christmas Is a Sad Season for the Poor"; in 1950, "The Season of Divorce" and "The Pot of Gold"; in 1951 he made a notable advance in "Goodbye, My Brother" and "Clancy in the Tower of Babel," followed by a slight regression in 1952 with "The Superintendent," "The Cure," "The Chaste Clarissa," and "The Children." All of these stories, except for "The Chaste Clarissa," appeared in his collection *The Enormous Radio* in 1953. In it we discover glimmerings or adumbrations of the later Cheever style, but with the exception of "Goodbye, My Brother," none of these stories fully represents the Cheeveresque style of the later years.

First of all, it is noteworthy that, save for "Goodbye, My Brother," all of these stories are narrated in the *third* person, and the narrative voice is detached and dispassionate. True, the stories of the 1946-47 period are more fully shaped than the earlier stories (even the difference in paragraph length and in more extended narrative material is striking), and yet *stylistically* there is little appreciable difference. The extraordinary story "The Enormous Radio" demonstrates that Cheever was now wrestling with more challenging themes and exploring more deeply the implications, moral and psychological, of "ordinary" American life—later themes, in other words—but the tone of the story is uniform throughout, and its narrative voice is not too distinguishable from the chilly grimness of the tale itself.

But "The Summer Farmer," written in 1948, demonstrates the start of a shift in narrative voice. Hints that the narrator is more than a mere reporter are found in its opening sentence:

> The Nor'easter is a train the railroad christened at a moment when its directors were imbued with the mystery of travel. Memory is often more appealing than fact, and a passenger who had long ridden the train might overlook its noise and dirt each time he entered the Grand Central Station and saw there the name of a northerly three-day rain. This, at least, was the case with Paul Hollis. . . . (*SJC*, p. 79)

The directness and simplicity of the earlier stories has been retained, but the narrative tone has been altered. The wry, offhanded judgment on the railroad's intentions vis-a-vis the actual emotional effect of the name "Nor'easter" on its passengers, the insertion of "often," "might," and "at least," the move from the general observation to the introduction of the particular Paul Hollis in a casual way—all suggest that this narrator is no mere observer but "knows" a good deal more than he is telling. This impression is reinforced later on in the paragraph when we are told of the "tumultuous delays of Springfield," "the balky and malingering stride of an old local," and "the leafy and ingenuous streets of the junction village"

(p. 79). These strong, mildly eccentric adjectives cue the reader to stay alert, that detachment is not the avenue of entry.

The story's penultimate paragraph is more characteristic still of the later Cheever style. It is shaped by a series of balanced conditionals, the presumption being that "if" the observer (or reader, in fact) is alert, his objective stance will render him capable of discerning another's subjective disposition, as "if" the outer and the inner were the same. The slyness of the narrator's introduction to these conditionals, the "fact" that "it is true of even the best of us" that we are so capable (p. 88), disarms us at first. But when we readers actually reflect, after completing the paragraph, on the word "true" and puzzle over those words "even" and "best" and especially "our," we wonder whether we have been taken in, whether in fact this narrator has been as "objective" in his report as he has led us to believe, whether "if's" are what stories are all about. The paragraph in toto reads,

> It is true of even the best of us that if an observer can catch us boarding a train at a way station; if he will mark our faces, stripped by anxiety of their self-possession; if he will appraise our luggage, our clothing, and look out of the window to see who has driven us to the station; if he will listen to the harsh or tender things we say if we are with our families, or notice the way we put our suitcase onto the rack, check the position of our wallet, our key ring, and wipe the sweat off the back of our necks; if he can judge sensibly the self-importance, diffidence, or sadness with which we settle ourselves, he will be given a broader view of our lives than most of us would intend.   (p. 88)

The whole paragraph possesses a harmonious structure comprised of elegantly balanced phrases that accumulate with rhetorical power, but the repetition of those qualifying "if's" effectively inserts not only a shortened sound but an intellectual discord as well. Is a "broader view" more truthful?

During this period Cheever hit upon and developed a related stylistic device that characterized his later fiction: that of the conditional "as if." Unlike most writers, he tends to eschew direct comparisons that follow the blunt "like" or "as." Instead, he employs "as if" in flexible fashion. The effectiveness of "as if" lies in its restraint and indirection, and especially in its potential for ironic contrast. In "The Summer Farmer," for example, he uses it to record a "possible" psychological truth in certain passages:

> [Kasiak] looked anxiously at Paul, as if he were ashamed that Paul should notice the mare's extreme decrepitude and reach a mistaken judgment on an animal he loved.   (p. 86)

> As if the life in Kasiak hid slyly from violence behind cartilage and bone, there was no apparent resistance in him. . . .   (p. 87)

In "O City of Broken Dreams," also published in 1948, Cheever expands its potential. Here the "as if" phrases casually capsulate the story's theme with ironic accuracy.

> They wandered through the marble waiting room, following the noise of traffic and klaxons as if it were the bidding of life. . . . The faces that passed them seemed purposeful and intent, as if they all belonged to people who were pursuing the destinies of great industries.   (SJC, p. 44)

The phrase functions similarly in "The Superintendent":

> [The Superintendent] slept with the percussive noises of the building machinery on his consciousness, as if they were linked to his own well-being.   (SJC, p. 165)

"As if" is also a thematic hinge in "Goodbye, My Brother":

> That night, I dreamed about Lawrence. I saw his plain face magnified into ugliness, and when I woke in the morning, I felt sick, as if I had suffered a great spiritual loss while I slept.   (SJC, p. 14)

> And I knew that Lawrence was looking bleakly at the party as he had looked at the weather-beaten shingles on our house, as if he saw here an abuse and a distortion of time, as if in wanting to be brides and football players we exposed the fact that, the lights of youth having been put out in us, we had been unable to find other lights to go by and, destitute of faith and principle, had become foolish and sad.   (p. 16)

The last example represents the flowering of the "as if" device in Cheever's hands; from this point onward he used it with subtle variety on almost every other page of his fiction. As this paragraph indicates, the power of the "as if" is hard to define, for it introduces neither a conditional clause in the strict sense nor a true comparison. Its usage is at once vague and precise. Yet its success lies in the imaginative demands it places on the *reader*, in the implied invitation to conjure along with the narrator another imaginative viewpoint on the action, to *perceive* and not merely observe the events disclosed.

This deliberate evocation of the reader's involvement in the imaginative effort signals an important step in Cheever's stylistic development. On this very point Wright Morris made this telling observation:

> What we choose to call "style" is the presence in the fiction of the power to choose and mold its readers. The sought-for reader, in this view, is the first of the fictions the writer must create, and it is why, for such a writer, the opening lines of a work are so important. There is a voice that seeks to hold one reader enthralled, turn another away.[23]

23. Morris, *About Fiction*, p. 104.

This is a crucial point in any discussion of Cheever's characteristic mature style. The stories he wrote in the late forties and early fifties disclose a writer intent on fashioning two creations simultaneously: a recognizable "second self" and also a recognizable "reader" who will be responsive to his story. The kind of reader Cheever eventually created was the "secret sharer," one who is deeply concerned with moral values and their consequence—by implication, unlike so many other people; and one who is stimulated, not depressed, by irony of all kinds and by the accumulation of disparate incident. Both writer and reader become joint parts in the single imaginative act of composition.

It is not surprising, then, that after establishing this mutual trust between his twin "creations," Cheever became so comfortable with the relationship that he soon abandoned the artificiality of the third-person point of view and wrote the vast majority of his later stories in the first person. He had reached the point at which he knew the reader, and he knew that the reader "knows," too—knows many things about life, knows practically everything one might say, *except* the details of the story wherein they meet together. This privileged knowledge, in conjunction with the complex process recently described, results in that elusive category of "style" which Wayne Booth defines as the "sometimes broadly used [word] to cover whatever it is that gives us a sense, from word to word and line to line, that the author sees more deeply and judges more profoundly than his presented characters."[24] We might be disappointed in them but never in him; he has won our trust.

Style, then, is not an adornment, but is, at some deeper level, a *cognitive* process in which the reader participates, a mode of knowing in that the way a writer organizes and creates his fictional reality (which includes both his "self" and the reader) reflects and extends the vision of life contained in his fiction. That vision might be narrow or broad, and its animating spirit might be generous or niggardly. In Cheever's case his vision and spirit both presume and reward great expectations on the part of the reader—expectations not so much of grandeur as of magnanimity.

On this very point Cheever made two notable personal remarks in two separate interviews, years apart:

> The proper function of writing, if possible, is to enlarge people, to give them their risk, if possible to give them their divinity, not to cut them down.[25]

And:

24. Booth, *The Rhetoric of Fiction*, p. 74.
25. "John Cheever: The Art of Fiction LXII," *Paris Review*, 17, No. 7 (Fall 1976), 64.

I think one has the choice with imagery, either to enlarge or diminish. At this point I find diminishment deplorable. When I was younger I thought it brilliant.[26]

Enlargement is the key to his later style, enlargement on all fronts. Not only is his audience less restricted, but his fellow feeling toward the reader is more expansive; in turn, his narrative voice grows more relaxed and comfortable, trusting and hopeful of mutual attention and collaboration. These enlargements afforded him far greater freedom to manipulate his fictional material than previously, and to explore the implications of—that is, enlarge—his imagery. He could now employ either a first-person or a third-person narrator, either an ostensibly naive or knowing voice; the point of view could be either one of privileged access (though rarely omniscience) in relation to character motivation, or limited and speculative.

But no matter what technique of tone or point of view Cheever employs, we are ever aware that we are in the presence of a *storyteller* intent on beguiling us, a raconteur who remains the controlling center of the narrative's consciousness and movement. The presence of this story-teller endows Cheever's later fiction with a stability and familiarity of form; in other hands, the excess of incident and anecdote, the digressions and intrusions would make a story fly apart. Furthermore, this storyteller presence shortens the artistic distance between Cheever and his reader and gives his fiction an authoritative boldness that replaces the diffidence one senses in his earlier stories.

The most obvious storyteller's device is the technique of directly addressing the reader. This technique brings to a story a lively dramatic force; the voice is unabashedly personal, and we as readers are encountered, willy-nilly, by someone grabbing us by the lapels. A good number of his later stories begin this way: the narrator announces that he is a writer, and the variations in his tone of voice prepare us (or so we think) for what will follow—but we had better listen or else. The range possible with this technique is remarkably wide, as the openings to the following stories manifest:

[A conspirational voice:] I am keeping this journal because I believe myself to be in some danger and because I have no other way of recording my fears.   ("The Ocean," 1964)

[A plea:] Paint me a wall in Verona, then, a fresco above a door.   ("Another Story," 1967)

26. "John Hersey Talks with John Cheever," *Yale Alumni Magazine and Journal*, December 1977, p. 24.

[A complaint:] I would not want to be one of those writers who begin each morning by exclaiming, "O Gogol, O Chekhov, O Thackeray and Dickens, what would you have made of a bomb shelter ornamented with four plaster-of-Paris ducks, a birdbath, and three composition gnomes with long beards and red mobcaps?" As I say, I wouldn't want to begin a day like this, but I often wonder what the dead would have done.   ("The Brigadier and the Golf Widow," 1961)

[A quaint reflection:] Reminiscence, along with the cheese boards and ugly pottery sometimes given to brides, seems to have a manifest destiny with the sea.   ("Percy," 1968)

A variant on this technique of introducing a self-conscious narrator who is aware of himself as a writer is Cheever's employment of a narrator/agent or observer/surrogate who appears to be unaware that he is composing or, better, "reflecting" a literary work—but in fact his "story" does so. A number of Cheever's stories begin with a sentence that arouses our imaginative curiosity because we sense that the sentence is but a kernel summary of a story, a story we are dying to hear the whole of.

The first time I robbed Tiffany's, it was raining. ("Montraldo," 1964)

Coming back from Europe that year, I was booked on an old DC-7 that burned out an engine in mid-Atlantic.
                                        ("Mene, Mene, Tekel, Upharsin," 1963)

The subject today will be the metaphysics of obesity, and I am the belly of a man named Lawrence Farnsworth. ("Three Stories," 1973)

Marge Littleton would, in the long-gone days of Freudian jargon, have been thought maternal, although she was no more maternal than you or you.   ("Three Stories," 1973)

You may have seen my mother waltzing on ice skates in Rockefeller Center.   ("The Angel of the Bridge," 1961)

My name is Johnny Hake. I'm thirty-six years old, stand five feet eleven in my socks, weigh one hundred and forty-two pounds stripped, and am, so to speak, naked at the moment and talking into the dark.   ("The Housebreaker of Shady Hill," 1956)

These first-person narratives provide rather obvious examples of the storyteller as "second self," but that second self is also not shy about insinuating himself into stories that are ostensibly objective in perspective and written in the third person. In these instances, Cheever uses other means to establish a personal intimacy between reader and writer. One device is that of rhetorical questions that assume our agreement or elicit our desire to agree:

Our ideas of castles, formed in childhood, are inflexible, and why try to reform them? Why point out that in a real castle thistles grow in the courtyard, and the threshold of the ruined throne room is guarded by a nest of green adders?   ("The Golden Age," 1959)

Was Mallory's passionate detestation of squalor fastidious and unmanly? Was he wrong to look for definitions of good and evil, to believe in the inalienable power of remorse, the beauty of shame?   ("The Geometry of Love," 1966)

Besides these questions, Cheever has many other ways to coax out our complicity with him as reader-listeners. He will continually shift from the perspective of the dominant pronoun "I" or "he" in the story to address, with suddenness, "you," or, with more subtlety, "we" or "all of us" or "one" as in the French *on*. In "The Swimmer" (1964), for example, at a pivotal point halfway through the objective, third-person account of Neddy Merrill's journey, we hear this interruption: "Had you gone for a Sunday afternoon ride that day you might have seen him, close to naked, standing on the shoulders of Route 424, waiting for a chance to cross. You might have wondered if he was the victim of foul play, had his car broken down, or was he merely a fool" (*SJC*, p. 607).

In this way we are invited into the narrative action, and we as readers become participants, even collaborators (as the indirect questions posed for us indicate) in the story's development. "The Swimmer" is a fine example of how often Cheever can, by using this device, arouse within the reader a sense of acute inner tension between the "atmosphere" of the story—let us say the emotional background he has fashioned for us—and the character's eccentric action proceeding against this background or within this atmosphere. The reader himself feels that *he* is the keenest participant within this tension, that *he* is the one most aware of being caught between atmosphere and action.

Because of the stylistic control manifest elsewhere, the reader is rarely upset by such direct interruptions of the narrative; rather, the reader is flattered, intuiting in them gestures of companionship. In an important essay, "The Novelist as Meddler," George P. Elliott clarifies the mystery of this delightful sharing, a delight of which all good readers—but few critics, it seems—are aware:

Just as the spectator never really forgets that he is in a theatre watching actors, so the reader of a novel does not really forget that he is being told a story. When the narrator is open about his role as a story-teller . . . the reader happily allows him all sorts of liberties of point of view; everyone recognizes the artifice and enjoys it. Only when consistency is promised must inconsistency disturb. . . .

> In fiction, the point of view that matters most . . . is the author's
> set of values, what he considers important, especially morally; for this
> gets at the heart of the novel, the characters' being and doing.[27]

In 1980 Cheever himself commented on the personal delights such liberties allowed him: "The discursive thing I love. When you have the reader's attention, then you can completely do something else. It's almost like making a change of key in some kind of musical development, which rather has the quality—if you can bring it off—of laughter."[28] This analogy with laughter is an apt one, for a listener's laugh reveals that the glue of attention and compatibility has preceded it, and that the complex reordering, the abrupt shift of perspective has in fact taken place and is mutually shared.

Cheever chose the word "discursive" to describe his delightful digressions, but perhaps "excursive" is more accurate. Almost all of his later stories are punctuated by an occasional side trip or a pleasant interlude interrupting the narrative line—incidents or offhand "recollections" that must generate envy in the hearts of writers of less fertile imagination, since the excursion is often itself a story in microcosm. Examples abound, but two are found in his less distinguished story "The Superintendent." The story concerns the hustle and bustle of the superintendent's day, a day crushing in its ordinariness. Yet, on making his usual rounds in the building, the superintendent arrives at apartment 9-E and finds an unusual notice:

> One of the cheap, part-time maids that Mrs. Bestwick had been hiring
> recently had thumb-tacked a sign onto the back door. "To Whom It
> May Concern," she had printed. "I never play the numbers and I never
> will play the numbers and I never played the numbers." Chester put
> the sign in the waste can and rang the back bell.   (SJC, p. 169)

Later in the day, the superintendent takes his break in a shoeshine parlor. Suddenly, the shoeshine man breaks out in confession:

> "I'm sixty-two years old, Chester, and I got a dirty mind. You think
> it's because I'm around shoes all the time? You think it has some-
> thing to do with the way the polish smells? . . . That's what my old
> lady thinks. She thinks it's got something to do with being around
> shoes all the time. All I think about is love, love, love. It's
> disgusting. . . ."   (p. 173)

27. George P. Elliott, *Conversions: Literature and the Modernist Deviation* (New York: Dutton, 1971), p. 105.
28. "The Darkness and the Light of John Cheever," extended interview with Christina Robb, *Boston Globe Magazine*, July 6, 1980, p. 31.

Excursions like these are miniature tales, stories worthy of elaboration but here encapsulated. Their very brevity accentuates the extra-ordinariness of ordinary life: the contradiction between noble and ignoble impulses, between the desire for dignity and the "fact," the meeting point between confusion and something more grand called the human mystery.

The fact that Cheever is just as excursive in his four novels affected their reception among writers, especially those of academic bent. Narrative digressions, no matter how brilliantly executed, are deemed disruptive in a novel, where the critical watchword is unity of design. Since Henry James and Percy Lubbock, much critical ink has been spilled in the attempt to classify just what a novel is or should be. To defend Cheever— whose interest is quite evidently not in the more obvious fictional unities—in the face of such literary criticism is a hopeless task, and possibly an unnecessary one. The problem lies not so much with Cheever as with the categories.

In this connection, Richard Chase offers an enlightening comment on Saul Bellow's *Henderson the Rain King* that is appropriate to a good deal of Cheever's fiction, and especially to negative criticism of his novels. Chase notes that "for much of its length *Henderson* is a 'romance' rather than a 'novel.' It forfeits some of the virtues of the novel (realism, plausibility, specificity), but it gains some of the virtues of romance (abstraction, freedom of movement, extreme expressions of pathos, beauty, and terror)."[29] The distinction between novel and romance is a slippery one, and Cheever's stories and novels continually exploit the flexibility and interpenetration of both these literary forms. Like the novel form, a Cheever narrative will render reality closely, presenting recognizable characters who possess a distinctive past, and whose psychological and social lives are accurately captured. Initially, the things that happen to them are generally plausible, given their circumstances, but then. . . . Then, as in the romance form, action rather than character comes to the fore, reality seems slightly displaced, and allegorical or moral allusions so intrude that the characters themselves seem momentarily detached from the familiar world, floating free as abstract types in a never-never-land.[30] After this romantic interlude, the stories often end with a kind of coda— so effectively done in "The Country Husand" and "The World of Apples,"

---

29. Richard Chase, "The Adventures of Saul Bellow," in *Saul Bellow and His Critics,* ed. Irving Malin (New York: New York Univ. Press, 1967), p. 25.

30. See F. O. Matthiessen, "The Crucial Definition of Romance," and Richard Chase, "Novel vs. Romance," in *Pastoral and Romance: Modern Essays in Criticism,* ed. Eleanor Terry Lincoln (Englewood Cliffs, N. J.: Prentice-Hall, 1969), pp. 268-274; 282-288.

for example—which marks a return to the "novel-like" reality of the opening.

Cheever's success at exploiting the possibilities inherent in both these forms allows him to combine the realistic with the picaresque. He once said that "it seems to me that writing is always in the nature of an adventure. . . ."[31] The ease with which he establishes rapport with us, his readers, is completely disarming: without knowing it, we are so beguiled by this Prospero and Peter Pan that the possibility of adventures elsewhere does not seem extraordinary at all. John Leonard describes this process very well:

> [Cheever] enters his stories the way the rest of us leave our homes, opening the door, stepping out, getting rained on by the day. The awareness of each story seems random; it is composed of what is noticed. But watch: the noticing begins to fix on discrepancies. What is perceived is out of sync with what is felt. What is said is so often wholly inappropriate to the circumstances . . . that the story itself becomes a mugging. It's as if we had agreed to pretend that politeness is a reality; then rudeness, aggression attack not only our notion of ourselves but our notion of how the universe is supposed to be organized.[32]

George Garrett has accurately described the typical Cheever narrator as "a cultivated and slightly superior museum guide." Leonard reminds us, however, that our museum guide, whether in or out of uniform—no matter—is actually a mugger in our midst.

COMPARISONS IN STYLE

Comparing literary styles is always a tricky business and inevitably smacks of the arbitrary, but Garrett's analogy of the museum guide generates such reflections. The museum guide captures well the urbane, chatty, opinionated, even deferential qualities of Cheever's style. Like the guide, Cheever is the model of outward decorum, a quality he claims he owes to the first *New Yorker* editor, Harold Ross, who taught one "that decorum is a mode of speech, as profound and connotative as any other, differing not in content but in syntax and imagery" (Preface, *SJC*, p. viii). But that he is a guide to a *museum* introduces another important perspective.

One suspects that lovers of Cheever's mature fiction are so devoted because his style is reminiscent of the comfortable stylistic qualities of

31. "The Darkness and the Light of John Cheever," p. 30.
32. John Leonard, "Cheever to Roth to Malamud," *Atlantic Monthly*, 231 (June 1973), 112.

nineteenth-century British fiction. Wendell Harris has called this the "assured style," that found in Dickens, Thackeray, Trollope, and others to whom the ideals were lucidity, conciseness, and balance.[33] According to Harris, this assured style reflects their confidence in their own vision of life, an assurance generally not shared by the self-doubting, tentative sensibilities of the twentieth-century mind.

Cheever's was very much a twentieth-century mind and sensibility, but he was also one well acquainted with things Victorian. Not only had he read *Madame Bovary* twenty times in French and English, but when he was a child his grandmother read aloud to him almost the whole of Dickens' works. For any who doubt the continuing influence of Dickens' techniques on Cheever's work, the comparison offered below should provide sufficient evidence. The first paragraph is taken from Dickens' *Our Mutual Friend*; the second is the opening of Cheever's "The Lowboy."

> Mr. and Mrs. Veneering were bran-new people in a bran-new house in a bran-new quarter of London. Everything about the Veneerings were spick and span new. All their furniture was new, all their servants were new, their plate was new, their carriage was new, their harness was new, their horses were new, their pictures were new, they themselves were new, they were as newly-married as was lawfully compatible with their having a bran-new baby. . . .

> Oh I hate small men and I will write about them no more but in passing I would like to say that's what my brother Richard is: small. He has small hands, small feet, a small waist, small children, a small wife, and when he comes to our cocktail parties he sits in a small chair. If you pick up a book of his, you will find his name, "Richard Norton," on the flyleaf in his very small hand-writing. (*SJC*, p. 404)

Echoes of other writers can also be heard in Cheever's fiction: the opening of *The Wapshot Chronicle* is Trollopean, if anything, and *Bullet Park* starts with a voice reminiscent of Thackeray. Gradually his style moves out, of course, to embrace more modern accents as well, and mirror the self-consciousness and confusion of our age. But Cheever did employ in his fiction the familiar rhythms, repetitions, and balance of the Victorian "assured" style as a sort of conservative ballast—a style that functions as does a tonic center in music. The austerity and economy proper to this style thus became an important component in the comic tension present in his fiction, for he was able to counterbalance effectively this "conservative" cadence with direct description of the wildest extravagances or with the ironic juxtaposition of conversational eccentricities

---

33. Wendell Harris, "Style and the 20th Century Novel," in *Critical Approaches to Fiction*, ed. Shiv Kiemer and Keith McLean (New York: McGraw-Hill, 1968), pp. 131-146.

that counterpoint the staid, stately rhythms. A striking example of this comic tension is found in the opening paragraph of "The Swimmer." Here the Victorian cadence and felicity of word arrangement record perfectly the subtle variations on the repetitiveness of human excuses; moreover, they comically capture not only a specific hangover but a more fundamental and universal misgiving that is beyond all genteel excuse:

> It was one of those midsummer Sundays when everyone sits around saying, "I *drank* too much last night." You might have heard it whispered by the parishioners leaving church, heard it from the lips of the priest himself, struggling with his cassock in the *vestiarium,* heard it from the golf links and the tennis courts, heard it from the wildlife preserve where the leader of the Audubon group was suffering from a terrible hangover. "I *drank* too much," said Donald Westerhazy. "We all *drank* too much," said Lucinda Merrill. "It must have been the wine," said Helen Westerhazy. "I *drank* too much of that claret." (*SJC,* p. 603)

The last excuse, the attribution of an ominous power to "claret," has a Victorian ring to it, but we know it is volunteered in a world of swimming pools. The whole paragraph, with its formal balance of phrase counterpointed by conversational nuance, is reminiscent of Evelyn Waugh's comic technique; in fact, many passages in Cheever remind one of Waugh.[34]

Both writers borrow from the assured style and use it to capitalize on the incongruity between the dreamy sensuousness which nature evokes, i.e., the illusory, and the abrupt awakening into the actual. Compare, for example, a paragraph from Waugh's *Decline and Fall* with a paragraph from Cheever's "Just Tell Me Who It Was"—compare Paul Pennyfeather's nostalgic reveries, inspired by a line of Victorian poetry, with Maria Pym's daydream, inspired by the American version of the Victorian ideal:

> English spring, thought Paul. In the dreaming ancestral beauty of the English country. Surely, he thought, these great chestnuts in the morning sun stood for something enduring and serene in a world that had lost its reason and would so stand when the chaos and confusion were forgotten? And surely it was the spirit of William Morris that whispered to him in Margot Beste-Chetwynde's motor-car about seedtime and the harvest, the superb-succession of the seasons, the harmonious interdependence of rich and poor, of dignity, innocence and

34. For a fine analysis of Waugh's style, see David Lodge, *Evelyn Waugh* (New York: Columbia Univ. Press, 1971), pp. 3-45; and William Cook, *Masks, Modes, and Morals: The Art of Evelyn Waugh* (East Brunswick, N. J.: Fairleigh Dickinson Univ. Press, 1971), pp. 17-59.

tradition? But at a turn in the drive, the cadence of his thought was abruptly transected. They had come into sight of the house.

"Golly," said Beste-Chetwynde. "Mamma has done herself proud again."

The trees of Shady Hill were filled with birds—larks, thrushes, robins, crows—and now the air began to ring with their song. The pristine light and the loud singing reminded her of some ideal—some simple way of life, in which she dried her hands on an apron and Will came home from the sea—that she had betrayed. She did not know where she failed, but the gentle morning light illuminated her failure pitilessly. She began to cry.

Will was asleep, but he woke when she opened the front door, "Mummy?" he asked as she climbed the stairs. "Mummy? . . . Hello, Mummy. Good Morning!" She didn't reply.　　　　(SJC, p. 377)

One major difference between the two writers, however, is that the second self in Waugh generally remains objective—morally, emotionally, and stylistically. As I have argued, this is rarely the case with later Cheever: on the one hand, his narrative style retains a classical or Victorian detachment, lucidity, and poise, and yet, on the other, he avoids the charge of snobbery attributed to Waugh by so often entering and exiting from his narrative in a clubby, personal way. One example for comparison is found in the Cheever story "Percy," in the narrator's summary account of the marriage of his quaintly artistic Aunt Percy. The passage is Waugh-like in that the comical effect results from the summary suddenly being at one point qualified by an unexpected adverbial phrase and then by its ending in a climactic phrase that slyly suggests the "real" reason for Percy's noble devotion to her husband:

Percy and Abbot Tracy met in some such place, and she fell in love. He had already begun a formidable and clinical sexual career, and seemed unacquainted in any way with sentiment, although I recall that he liked to watch children saying their prayers. Percy listened for his footsteps, she languished in his absence, his cigar cough sounded to her like music, and she filled a portfolio with pencil sketches of his face, his eyes, his hands, and, after their marriage, the rest of him.　　　　(SJC, p. 636)

That "although I recall that he liked to watch children saying their prayers" is a Waugh-like touch, but the inserted "I" is the opposite of a Waugh technique. It is precisely the Cheever "I"—whether implicit or explicit matters not, since both are variants of the second self—that converts the museum guide into the mugger. If one were to be fanciful, he might describe Cheever's stylistic structure as an old Victorian house with modern furniture. The house itself is comfortable enough, but our attention is drawn to its restless proprietor. He might greet us sedately sitting in a chair, stand to stir the fire, ramble around in the halls, point out the trees or the stars from the solarium, impersonate the neighbors, rummage in the kitchen (but rarely the bath)—do all these things with consummate courtesy; and yet, though the house and its occupant are charming, our attitude is one of wariness, since something simultaneously sportive and sinister attaches to his presence.

As I noted, a good many critics in attempting to appraise Cheever's style inevitably resort to analogies with poetry. This, too, is a fruitful basis for comparison. Richard Boethe, for example, dubbed him "our premier poet of missed connections,"[35] and John Romano has noted that "in his softer moods he is, like Eliot indeed, or like Robert Lowell, a poet mourning the fallen world in the late afternoon of New England culture."[36]

Although these comparisons are appropriate, the curious fact is that Cheever is that rare exception among creative writers, one who has never written poetry as such. When asked why, he replied that "it seems to me that the discipline is very different . . . another language, another continent from that of fiction. In some cases short stories are more highly disciplined than a lot of poetry we have."[37] Characteristically, Cheever placed his stress on the word "discipline," first in the sense of genre and then in the sense of restraint.

And yet, though not formally a poet, Cheever was a genuine lover of poetry. When his family was growing up, he and his wife and children would recite poems each had memorized on Sunday afternoons. Cheever's own favorites were John Donne and William Butler Yeats, eminent representatives of "discipline" in both senses. For readers of his own work, Cheever's personal choice of poets is not surprising.

Cheever stressed that he considered himself "very lucky to have read Donne when I was very young," and singled out the great poet as a literary voice at its "strongest and most radiant."[38] The affinity between the two writers extends to thematic concerns: the tension and admixture of pagan feeling with Christian sentiment, the preoccupation with death and judgment, the representation of the metaphysical by the physical, and the absorption with the mystery of love in all its manifestations. At times

35. Richard Boethe, "The Poet of Shady Hill," Newsweek, October 30, 1978, p. 96.
36. John Romano, "Redemption According to Cheever," Commentary, 63 (May 1977), 66-69.
37. "John Cheever: The Art of Fiction LXII," p. 54.
38. "John Hersey: Talk with John Cheever," New York Times Book Review, March 6, 1977, p. 26.

Cheever even strives for what T. S. Eliot discovered in Donne: a man for whom "a thought was an experience, it modified his sensibility."

Themes aside, however, one strongly suspects that Cheever was drawn primarily to that "strong and radiant" literary voice. Donne's rhythms are those of a natural speaking voice, a voice that at its best is free and audacious; its mixture of gravity and humor issues in a unique sincerity of tone and reflects the conflict of dramatic passions. Donne's poetry is alternately satiric and religious, often conjoining or substituting one attitude for the other in ambiguous fashion—not unlike a Cheever story. What is more, a young writer would be heartened to learn from Donne's example that any of the disparate elements in experience were grist for heightened language, that no separate order of the sacred, profane, or artistic exists by itself.

Cheever's love for Yeats's poetry is less surprising still, for he and Yeats, in many ways, seem brothers beneath the skin, men who are at once Victorian and anti-Victorian. Cheever's stories, in fact, engage the central Yeatsian themes: the passion for decorum and the ceremonies of innocence in the face of the modern world's drowning in decay and disruption; the contrast of man's urge for the "higher" beauties of the artistic and natural order with his "lower" impulses like the sexually chaotic and the murderous; those emotions of manic desperation that accompany one's realization of aging and its consequence, death. Furthermore, in the light of the present discussion, their writing careers record a similar development from concerns with craft and conventional models to concern with style, and manifest a similar resolution. Richard Ellmann reminds us that, for Yeats, style was that element in literature that corresponded to the *moral* element in life; in other words, style by its emphases mirrored delicate gradations of value and directly indicated the writer's personality:

> For style was a question of vigor with which positions were taken and of the honesty with which qualifications were made. How a man decided when he faced the alternatives of being affirmative, negative, skeptical, or mealy-mouthed, modern or archaistic, cautious or brazen, affected his choice of words, his clarity or obscurity in setting forth his themes, his sentence structure.[39]

Ellmann's statement—with necessary modifications, of course—is equally true of Cheever. Both men, as they matured as writers, found

---

39. Richard Ellmann, *The Identity of Yeats* (New York: Oxford Univ. Press, 1954), p. 116. See also David Lynch, *Yeats: The Poetics of the Self* (Chicago: Univ. of Chicago Press, 1979); Harold Bloom, *Yeats* (New York: Oxford Univ. Press, 1970); and A. Norman Jeffares, *W. B. Yeats: Man and Poet* (New Haven: Yale Univ. Press, 1949).

their vision of the world expanding as they wrestled with broader moral themes: religion, industrialization, sexuality, the loss of tradition, and the staying power of all paganisms. As the themes expanded, so did the need for a style that would encompass the ambiguities perceived, the tensions honestly faced. As Yeats said, "The self-conquest of the writer who is not a man of action is style." Style, then, is the linguistic equivalent of a writer's conscience.

In Yeats's case, he discovered his "masks," those artificial creations of other, often opposite selves, which became his instruments for dramatizing the tensions he experienced and all the conflicts that the conscious and unconscious mind engages.[40] Cheever's discovery of that "second self," who shapes his mature fiction, was a less conscious and more easily realized discovery than Yeats's, but its effect on his fiction was similar. Yet he did not need the symbology of Yeats's "A Vision," for example, because his "second self" *is* that of a storyteller by admission and, as such, that self enjoys unobstructed access to a variety of selves that are his fictional characters.

This raises an important consideration, since so many criticisms (and so many interviews) of Cheever center upon ferreting out the biographical elements in his work. In the light of my argument, I believe that this is at best a fruitless enterprise. Whether the second self is Cheever, the man born in 1912, or not is irretrievable in the fiction. What can be said, however, is that the brother versus brother, father versus son, husband versus wife antinomies that recur in his fiction function much like Yeats's contests between self and soul, youth and age, Crazy Jane and the bishop, in that these conflicts are revelatory of a deeper warfare, a more incessant universal strife that takes place within the most remote recesses of any maturing personality. Such *personal* polarities, whether or not rooted in autobiography, are essentially *symbolic* creations, instruments fashioned for and by the second self.

Other thematic polarities in Cheever's writing function in the same way: mythic hero and mundane victim, the sensual and the spiritual, skepticism and belief, estrangement and love, virility and decay, nature and human consciousness, illusion and fact, imagination and reality. Denis Donoghue has observed of Yeats that "his imagination loves to cause trouble, starting quarrels between one value and another."[41] Cheever's

40. See Richard Ellmann, *Yeats: The Man and His Masks* (New York: Macmillan, 1948); and Robert Longbaum, *The Mysteries of Identity: A Theme in Modern Literature* (New York: Oxford Univ. Press, 1977), pp. 147-250.
41. Denis Donoghue, *William Butler Yeats* (New York: Viking, 1971), p. 5. Donoghue's is an excellent short study; also see his *The Ordinary Universe* (New York: Macmillan, 1968), pp. 108-145.

imagination does the same, and his second self is ever the assessor, evaluating, balancing, alternately laudatory and iconoclastic, always in conflict with itself.

If one keeps a copy of Yeats's *Collected Poetry* at his side while reading Cheever, the similarity in style (as well as theme) at certain points is striking. Both styles are essentially oratorical and expressively direct and personal; being so, both must be read aloud, for what sounds at first like a soliloquy in natural speech edges imperceptibly into story. In both, the style alternately beguiles and intimidates the reader; it possesses a simplicity of syntax and vocabulary; above all, it is blunt about its perceptions of good and evil.

Both writers employ but alter the familiar lyric line by colloquializing it through the use of iambic rhythms. By thus conjoining the "lyrical" with the colloquial, each is able to work from the concrete realistic detail to a romantic assertion in seemingly effortless fashion. The ordinary, if not the vulgar, thus prompts the utterance of the old "high-toned" words. The work of both men contains numerous examples of this style, but one is found in the closing lines of Cheever's "A Vision of the World" (reminiscent of Yeats's different vision):

> I think of some plumber who, waked by the rain, will smile at a vision of the world in which all the drains are miraculously cleansed and free. Right-angle drains, crooked drains, root-choked and rusty drains all gurgle and discharge their waters into the sea. I think that the rain will wake some old lady, who will wonder if she has left her copy of *Dombey and Son* in the garden. Her shawl? Did she cover the chairs? And I know that the sound of the rain will wake some lovers, and that its sound will seem to be a part of that force that has thrust them into one another's arms. Then I sit up in bed and exclaim aloud to myself, "Valor! Love! Virtue! Compassion! Splendor! Kindness! Wisdom! Beauty!" The words seem to have the colors of the earth, and as I recite them I feel my hopefulness mount until I am contented and at peace with the night. (*SJC*, p. 517)

One of Yeats's most characteristic devices is the use of repetitive refrains throughout a poem to achieve a heightened rhetorical and dramatic effect:

> Romantic Ireland's dead and gone,
> It's with O'Leary in the grave.   ("September 1913")

> All changed, changed utterly:
> A terrible beauty is born.   ("Easter 1916")

> Like a long-legged fly upon the stream
> His mind moves upon silence.   ("Long-Legged Fly")

> Day-break and a candle-end.   ("The Wild Wicked Old Man")

Cheever uses the technique continually, but, unlike Yeats, he also employs the repetitive refrain to achieve a comical effect—and yet the very repetition itself hints at a more universal moral understanding. For example, in "The Brigadier and the Golf Widow," after Mr. Pastern and Mrs. Flannagan have sported with Venus upstairs, we hear this:

> "I've never done this before," she said later, when he was arranging himself to leave. Her voice shook with feeling, and he thought it lovely. He didn't doubt her truthfulness, although he had heard the words a hundred times. "I've never done this before," they always said, shaking their dresses down over their white shoulders. "I've never done this before," they always said, waiting for the elevator in the hotel corridor. "I've never done this before," they always said, pouring another whiskey. "I've never done this before," they always said, putting on their stockings. On ships at sea, on railroad trains, in summer hotels with mountain views, they always said, "I've never done this before." (SJC, p. 501)

It is this added comic dimension which edges Cheever away from the serious Yeats and closer to W. H. Auden's later verse. Yeats's recurrent themes are nostalgia and mutability: but in Cheever and the later Auden one also finds something in the tone that reaches beyond irony toward humor and acceptance, something in the texture that is distinctively urban and betrays a modern sensibility.

Auden and Cheever are alike in several significant ways. Both as young men were tentative skeptics, and in their thirties formally joined the Episcopal Church; yet a tension between faith and doubt remains at the center of the work of each. Both are enamored of rites and ceremonies; both are continually interested in the plight of "the lost, the lonely, the unhappy"—all those plunged into a vague malaise; both offer as a central image of Man that of a Wanderer, a Traveler, a Man on a Quest. At issue for both is the problem of civility, i.e., the question of how urban man can live in a faceless megapolis that is no longer truly a "society." And both share a darker vision into the ordinary which each exploits, knowing that

> The glacier knocks in the cupboard,
> The desert sighs in the bed,
> And the crack in the teacup opens
> A lane to the land of the dead.   ("As I Walked Out One Evening")

At a deeper level, Cheever shares with Auden two dominant concerns that transcend the somewhat parochial aesthetic concerns which challenged Yeats's intelligence. Both writers are in search of a spiritual order, one that answers to man's complex religious yearnings, but both are also in search of a *moral* order within this world as well, one which mirrors, though always in a glass darkly, the spiritual order. Auden called that latter aspiration the Just City; Cheever, through the surrogate spokesman of the senator in *The Wapshot Scandal,* calls it "the bond of human warmth" that has been underestimated.

More often for both writers, the operative word for the goal of those twin searches is "love." In Cheever's fiction, "love" is a comprehensive, symbolic term. It embraces romantic and sexual impulses, familial bondings, and the longing for companionable community, but at root it is a positive energy animating all that is vital within creation, a transcendent power that surpasses any of its manifestations. Richard Hoggart has noted in Auden's career a deepening realization about the meaning of the word "love." If one substitutes Cheever's name for Auden's, Hoggart's insight capsulizes the evolution one finds in Cheever's work, from his early stories through *Oh What a Paradise It Seems:*

> "Love" seems to have been an undefined but powerful third force, a quality both inside man and affecting man from outside, which at once offered him hope and indicated the perennial and personal nature of his situation. The history of Auden's earlier journey is, roughly speaking, that of the gradual discovery of the potentialities of this word's meaning for him—from an unresolved assertion to a rich and complex ambiguity which embraces the idea of Christian love, of conscience, of charity and grace.[42]

Yet love is both desirable and difficult: as Leander Wapshot quaintly observes, "Man is not simple. Hobgoblin company of love always with us. . . . All in love is not larky and fractious, remember."

For both men the progressive discovery of the manifold meanings of the word "love" coincided with their progress away from satire, with its narrow negative vision, toward the generous release of those comic, humorous gifts stirred by a positive vision. Of course, both Cheever and Auden have been criticized by those who oddly equate the somber with the truly serious, who see tragedy as the only authentic response to life, who presuppose—erroneously—that writers who are funny are, by some tacit syllogism, therefore trivial. Auden thought otherwise:

> For the funniest mortals and the kindest are those
> who are most aware of the baffle of being, don't
> kid themselves our care is consolable, but
> believe a laugh is less heartless than tears. ("Tonight at Seven-Thirty")

42. Richard Hoggart, "W. H. Auden," in *British Writers and Their Works,* No. 5, ed. Bonamee Dobree (Lincoln: Univ. of Nebraska Press, 1964), p. 88.

Awareness of "the baffle of being" is the crucial issue; the recognition that life is both unconsolable and worthy of laughter and that one might opt to emphasize the second realization is revelatory of a special brand of kindness and the opposite of shallowness.

Of course, comic vision is related to comic style—but one does not always imply the other. As Justin Replogle has observed, "Some writers have a vision of life that can be called comic but no comic style. Others have what is generally considered a comic style but no view of life worth mentioning."[43] In both Cheever and Auden, however, manner and matter unite and reinforce each other. Both have a compassionate understanding of the human comedy with its absurd strivings and low-life urgencies; but this very compassion, which reflects tragic sensibility, forestalls the easy, mocking perspective of satire. The voice of Cheever's second self, like that of Auden's, is every decorous, alternately detached and conspiratorial, urbane and educated, but his tone is not "tsk-tsk"; rather it is "Well, what do we know?" and "Wait, there's even more to tell." Fortunately, in Cheever there is always more to tell.

Like Auden's, Cheever's comic stylistic techniques entail a continually abrupt shifting of gears from realism to fantasy, from the abstract or general statement to the concrete detail and back; a seeming solemnity of tone that suddenly issues into something approximating the mock-heroic, catching us unawares; and the odd juxtaposition of different items in a list with the last detail a comic climax. Examples are many, but a representative sample is found in the opening paragraph of "The Death of Justina." Is not this Audenesque—and Cheeveresque?

> Fiction is art and art is the triumph over chaos (no less) and we can accomplish this only by the most vigilant exercise of choice, but in a world that changes more swiftly than we can perceive there is always the danger that our powers of selection will be mistaken and that the vision we serve will come to nothing. We admire decency and we despise death but even the mountains seem to shift in the space of a night and perhaps the exhibitionist at the corner of Chestnut and Elm streets is more significant than the lovely woman with a bar of sunlight in her hair, putting a fresh piece of cuttlebone in the nightingale's cage. (SJC, p. 429)

43. Justin Replogle, *Auden's Poetry* (Seattle: Univ. of Washington Press, 1969), p. 217. To my mind Replogle's is still the finest study of Auden, containing a wealth of insights on his spiritual and poetic career. For other fine studies, see the two studies by Monroe Spears, *The Poetry of W. H. Auden: The Disenchanted Island* (New York: Oxford Univ. Press, 1966), and *Dionysus in the City* (New York: Oxford Univ. Press, 1970); Richard Ellmann, *Eminent Domain* (New York: Oxford Univ. Press, 1967); and John G. Blair, *The Poetic Art of W. H. Auden* (Princeton: Princeton Univ. Press, 1965).

That word "perhaps" in the paragraph reveals the heart of all fiction-making. In a later story the narrator visits an old writer who is on his death bed. His career had long since crested, and the Audenesque narrator offers a reason: "You might say that he had lost the gift of evoking the perfumes of life: sea water, the smoke of burning hemlock, and the breasts of women. He had damaged, you might say, the ear's innermost chamber, where we hear the heavy noise of the dragon's tail moving over the dead leaves" (SJC, p. 471). However, upon the narrator's arrival, the old writer rallies and begins to tell him a new story—an exotic one wherein three strangers meet in an Alpine station shortly before an avalanche—but his story remains unfinished:

> Then he put his head back on the pillow and died—indeed, these were his dying words, and the dying words, it seemed to me, of generations of storytellers, for how could this snowy and trumped-up pass, with its trio of travelers, hope to celebrate a world that lies spread out around us like a bewildering and stupendous dream?   (p. 472)

How? Only through the magic of style, sensibility, and substance. Perhaps Auden's poem "The Truest Poetry Is the Most Feigning" expresses best the many mysterious hows of Cheever's style, and provides the most able summary of our efforts to define it:

> By all means sing of love but, if you do,
> Please make a rare old proper hullabaloo:
> When ladies ask *How much do you love me?*
> The Christian Answer is *cosi-cosi*;
> But poets are not celibate divines:
> Had Dante said so, who would read his lines?
> Be subtle, various, ornamental, clever,
> And do not listen to those critics ever
> Whose crude provincial gullets crave in books
> Plain cooking made still plainer by plain cooks,
> As though the Muse preferred her half-wit sons;
> Good poets have a weakness for bad puns.
>
>   . . . .
>
> For given Man, by birth, by education,
> Imago Dei who forgot his station,
> The self-made creature who himself unmakes,
> The only creature ever made who fakes. . .
> What but tall tales, the luck of verbal playing,
> Can trick his lying nature into saying
> That love, or truth in any serious sense,
> Like orthodoxy, is a reticence?

Ethics does not treat of the world. Ethics must be a condition of the world, like logic.

Ludwig Wittgenstein

In dreams begin responsibilities; in fiction we find their implications and resolutions.

Wright Morris

The religious experience is very much my concern, as it seems to me it is the legitimate concern of any adult who has experienced love.

John Cheever

What, then, is time? If no one asks me, I know what it is. If I wish to explain it to him who asks me, I do not know.

Saint Augustine

But Time, the domain of Deeds,
calls for a complex Grammar
with many Moods and Tenses,
and prime the Imperative. . . .

W. H. Auden

To be or not to be is not the question. The vital question is: how to be and how not to be.

Abraham Heschel

Must I go on boasting, though there is nothing to be gained by it? But I will move on to the visions and revelations I have had from the Lord.

Saint Paul

3: Themes in Tension

A Philosophic Novelist

In his introduction to Joseph Conrad's *Nostromo*, Robert Penn Warren offered this definition of the "philosophic novelist":

> [one] for whom the documentation of the world is constantly striving to rise to the level of generalization about values, for whom the image strives to rise to symbol, for whom images always fall into a dialectical configuration, for whom the urgency of experience, no matter how vividly and strongly experience may enchant, is the urgency to know the meaning of experience.[1]

Warren's description is especially helpful in any discussion of themes in the work of Cheever, for to label him a "philosophic" novelist appears at first to be a poor predication. When a reader thinks of philosophic novelists on the contemporary scene, writers as diverse as Walker Percy, Saul Bellow, Iris Murdoch, Graham Greene, Warren himself—even Norman Mailer and John Barth—come immediately to mind. These novelists are hardly shy about "ideas," and much of the persuasive power of their fiction resides in the reader's engagement with conceptual considerations, with reflections of a more abstract kind, with intellectual debate.

In Cheever's fiction, however, any wrestling with "ideas" in an abstract way is entirely absent. A reviewer who attempts to summarize in conceptual terms one of his stories or novels, teasing out the "point" of the fiction into statement, is doomed to frustration. Furthermore, Cheever eludes all our more familiar conceptual categories like Existentialist, Freudian, and Marxist; to apply these or other handy ideological words seems not only narrow but inexact.

But Warren's description of the philosophic novelist introduces broader

---

1. Robert Penn Warren in the Introduction to Joseph Conrad's *Nostromo* (New York: Modern Library, 1952); reprinted in Robert Penn Warren, *Selected Essays* (New York: Random House, 1958).

considerations quite pertinent to Cheever's work, and can provide an outline for investigation. This description can be divided into four characteristics: 1) documentation of the world strives toward generalization about values; 2) images strive toward symbol; 3) images fall into a dialectical configuration; 4) the urgency of experience issues in pursuit of meaning and knowledge.

In examining Cheever's tone and style I noted how, through a variety of techniques, he is able to make a sprightly leap from a particular predicament (often an absurd or horrific situation) and suddenly invite the reader's more general cosmic view of that same particular. He does this successfully because he first, in Warren's words, "documents his world" so well, i.e., renders it with psychological and dramatic accuracy. The style, by first creating fellow feeling, effortlessly effects a shock of recognition that is shareable. But this is only the style's start; imperceptibly the events disclosed in the narrative introduce another level for reflection beyond the recognizable, a probing into something less easily documented: the mysteriousness of life.

Such probing enters Warren's level of generalization about values; it also elevates what other writers might interpret as only psychic tension into a more radical confrontation with the whole of reality. This level engages *ontological* issues, not merely psychological ones; it concerns the very nature of reality, not only our perception or misperception of it. As John Leonard put it, Cheever's "fiction has consistently been about a certain failure of reciprocity in our relations with the rest of the universe . . ."[2]—in short, about an ontological disjunction.

At its best, Cheever's fiction will elicit *conjointly* psychological, moral, and ontological reflections. But, as Heraclitus said and all fine novelists know, the way up and the way down are the same. On the one hand, our engagement with these "philosophic" considerations betokens our moving upward toward a more rarefied tier of evaluation and judgment, toward a higher level of consciousness. On the other hand, as Wright Morris has said, fiction "provides that link in the chain of awareness that relates man to the *urmensch* of his subconscious."[3] In fiction the process of moving upward to the level of generalization about value must be preceded or accompanied by a reciprocal plunge downward, a tapping of the wellsprings of the unconscious or subconscious, thereby releasing the emotive component along with the intellectual—in short, a complex process that releases an awareness of the universal, not merely the general.

2. John Leonard, "From Cheever to Roth to Malamud," *Atlantic Monthly*, 231 (June 1973), 112.
3. Wright Morris, *About Fiction* (New York: Harper & Row, 1975), p. 7.

It is here that the techniques proper to the philosopher and the literary artist diverge. Where the philosopher achieves "generalization about values" through conceptual clarity, the arrival at definition through denotation, the composer of fiction succeeds when, as Warren indicates, his use of "image strives to rise to symbol," when he exploits the rich variety of the connotations of an image. Mircea Eliade has stressed the importance of respecting this richness:

> Images by their very structures are *multivalent*. If the mind makes use of things to grasp the ultimate reality of things, it is just because reality manifests itself in contradictory ways, and therefore cannot be expressed in concepts. . . . It is therefore the image as such, as a whole bundle of meanings, that is *true*, and not any *one* of its meanings, nor one alone of its many frames of reference. To translate an image into a concrete terminology by restricting it to any one of its forms of reference is to do worse than mutilate it—it is to annihilate, to annul it as an instrument of cognition.[4]

Eliade's life-long task as a historian of religion and an investigator of religious symbolism has been "to rediscover a whole mythology, if not a theology, concealed in the most ordinary, everyday life of contemporary man."[5] His studies have convinced him that "the unconscious, as it is called, is far more 'poetic' and, let us add, more 'philosophic,' more 'mythic,' than the conscious." Why?

A supporter of Carl Jung's psychology, Eliade argues that the images an artist or religious figure produces are drawn from the collective unconscious of the race, that the persistence and recurrence of these images throughout history demonstrate the existence of archetypes or universal symbols which all humanity shares at its deepest psychic level; and furthermore, that such archetypal images can evoke those very psychic image-laden and spiritual-laden energies that have gone undeveloped in our rationalistic, secular age. In this connection Eliade makes an observation that is especially significant for an appreciation of Cheever's fiction:

> Often [man] is re-entering by means of the images and symbols that then come into play a paradisiac stage of primordial humanity. . . . In escaping from his historicity, man does not escape his status as a human being or abandon himself to "animality": he recovers the language and sometimes the experience of a "lost paradise." Dreams, waking dreams, the images of his nostalgia and his enthusiasms, etc., are so many

4. Mircea Eliade, *Images and Symbols* (New York: Sheed & Ward, 1969), p. 15.
5. Eliade, *Images and Symbols*, p. 18. Also see Mircea Eliade, *Myth and Reality* (New York: Harper, 1963); and Shirley Park Lowry, *Familiar Mysteries* (New York: Oxford Univ. Press, 1982).

forces that may project the historically-conditioned human being into a spiritual world that is infinitely richer than the closed world of his own "historic moment."[6]

Cheever expresses a similar perception in *The Wapshot Scandal*:

> We are born between two states of consciousness; we spend our lives between the darkness and the light, and to climb in the mountains of another country, phrase our thoughts in another language or admire the color of another sky draws us deeper into the mystery of our condition.   (p. 140)

This quotation from Cheever is representative in other ways as well. For in it we come upon the images of light and darkness, mountains, another country, the sky—images that recur throughout his writings. In the particular context of a story or novel, such images will have a concrete referent within a scene or situation. However, as this passage implies, these are not images only, but images striving to rise to symbols; their function is evocative, suggestive of another level of meaning beyond the concrete, objective reality referred to. The function of symbolism—and at this point the artist and most philosophers separate—is precisely that of revealing a whole reality that is inaccessible to the other means of knowledge. As Eliade said, such symbolic images are by their very structure *multivalent*. They contain within themselves clusters of meaning, some of which seem contradictory in the rubric of the logician.

This is the reason why Warren insists that the philosophic novelist is one for whom images always fall into a dialectical configuration. The word "dialectical" comes from the Greek word for dialogue. It is a dialogic method of inquiry that proceeds by way of posing oppositions, of moving from question to answer, leading to further questions, of Yes to No to their qualification. The method presumes that reality is not static but is ever in flux; as a consequence, to describe reality in static or changeless terms is to falsify it. The dialectical mind, then, is at relative peace with a reality full of contradictions, where incompatible forces co-exist and a "unity of opposites" restlessly rules.

On the other hand, professional philosophers who employ the language of discursive thought, which is built upon empirical generalizations or the rules of logic, will eschew all ambiguities of statement. Ambivalence and/or indirection are the bane of all positivists, but the boon of all novelists. The power of dialectics lies in its appeal to another chamber of the mind besides the strictly rational, to more complex, psychic processes than those which common-sense language and "rational" discourse

6. Eliade, *Images and Symbols*, p. 13.

address.[7] The dialectical thinker presumes that man's intelligence pos-sesses *both* ratiocinative and imaginative powers, and so he will proceed accordingly. The great strength of dialectics is that it evokes an intuitive perception about reality—but herein lies its limitation as well. For it resists systematic explanation and eludes strictly conceptual analysis.

Criticism of Cheever's work provides ample evidence of undialectical readers. Critics like Aldridge who are frustrated either by his affirmations (the "soft sell of disaster school") or by his negative depiction and assess-ment of modern society misread the inherently dialectical character of his imagination and mistakenly reify or unduly particularize what are meant to be conflicting perceptions. In Cheever, themes are always *themes in tension* and never univocal. His instrument for the communication of themes in tension is the "image rising to the level of symbol" in a "dia-lectical configuration."

For example, the symbol of the mountain, found throughout his work, is both a symbol of aspiration and of obstruction. In mythological terms, the cosmic mountain represents the "bond between Heaven and Earth," the only place not submerged by the deluge.[8] To ascend it is equivalent to experiencing "the break-through into another state," for the pilgrim "transcends profane space" and enters not only a new region but in fact returns to the Center of the Earth, the original place where "creation began." But, alas—as Cheever reminds us again and again—we are in fact cut off from the mountain; it is less a physically palpable presence than it is a distant vision, a reminder for memory and hope.

Water imagery in Cheever's fiction is equally dialectical. Symboli-cally, the waters of the sea and land represent the spring and origin of all the potentialities within existence; they precede and support every form of creation. The sudden appearance of an island or a shore line—so characteristic in Cheever's fiction—is a dramatic instance of the emerging manifestations of the water's creative potential.[9] Yet the waters, as an emblem of eternity, connote simultaneously both life and death, drowning and rebirth. Immersion in the waters (as in "Brimmer," "Goodbye, My Brother," "The World of Apples," and "The Swimmer") can signify a

---

7. Studies on dialectical thought are innumerable and appear in the serious inves-tigation of nearly every important thinker. The most lucid exposition I have seen re-cently was offered by Robert Heilbroner in a short essay on Karl Marx entitled "The Dialectical Vision," *New Republic*, March 1, 1980, pp. 25ff. For an equally lucid pre-sentation of dialectic in Kierkegaard, see Paul Holmer, "Soren Kierkegaard: Faith in a Tragic World," in *The Tragic Vision and the Christian Faith*, ed. Nathan Scott, Jr. (New York: Association Press, 1957), pp. 174-188.

8. Eliade, *Images and Symbols*, pp. 42-43.

9. Mircea Eliade, *The Sacred and the Profane* (New York: Harcourt Brace Harvest Book, 1959), pp. 129ff.

temporary re-entry into chaos, into the amorphous, where all of creation is indistinct; but by the same token, such re-entry, precisely because it dissolves and abolishes all forms, can be purifying and regenerative as well.[10] Cheever sometimes explicitly associates this aquatic symbolism with Christian baptism and its ritual of purgation and renewal. But he need not be religiously explicit for us readers to grasp a spiritual import; the dialectical symbolism of the water (like that of the mountain) always carries with it a soteriological dimension, suggesting a desire for salvation rooted in religious impulse.

In like manner, the other universal symbols Cheever employs—rain, the sun, the moon, blue sky, light and darkness, trees, bridges, narrow gates—enjoy a similar dialectical configuration and reflect, in an emblematic fashion, complex spiritual yearnings. The various images he uses for confinement, such as chains, shackles, threads (as the question in "Brimmer" puts it: "Which one of us is not suspended by a thread above carnal anarchy?") recall a primordial archetype for man's situation in the world. On the religious plane, he is "bound" by God, by His snares, tethered to an invisible spiritual world; but he is also shackled to carnal existence and "bounded" by death and demonic urgencies and fears.

In addition, Cheever choses more specific, less universal symbols, and explores their dialectical polarity. For example, the mechanical creations of modern society—such as the airplanes, elevators, and bridges in "The Angel of the Bridge"—are elaborate conveniences to allow modern man an opportunity to conquer the former limitations of space and time. These creations are all instruments of ascent and liberation, and yet as this story dramatizes, each also divorces man from contact with the earth and the telluric aspect of his humanity. These machines are both help and hindrance, simultaneous symbols of man's new, accelerating departures from the natural world and his loss of an anchor in his natural past. Other machines, such as the radio in "The Enormous Radio" and the television in *The Wapshot Scandal*, are likewise Janus-faced: items of convenience that can open our enclosed world or else narrow it in demonic fashion.

Another example is the bomb shelter, which is a "metaphor for anxiety" in "The Brigadier and the Golf Widow." The effectiveness of this metaphor lies in its ambivalent meaning. At the story's start the shelter is an ostensible symbol of security, of defense against death and destruction, and therefore enviable. But as the story progresses, an ironic conversion takes place, and the shelter soon represents alienation and insecurity, and by the story's end is no longer a citadel of safety but an empty tomb.

10. Eliade, *Images and Symbols*, pp. 151-154.

MORAL FICTION

These examples show how Cheever is also able to employ images and symbols to dramatize *moral* conflict as well as to depict ontological and psychological contentions. In an interview he commented on the recurring polar images of light and darkness in his work, and offered this revealing remark:

> Light is very important to my moods. Blue sky. I always go to William James, of course. A blue sky is quite mysterious, mysteriously heartening, a source of indescribable joy. Light and dark, very loosely, of course, mean good and evil. And one is always seeking to find how much courage, how much intelligence, or how much comprehension, one can bring to the choice between good and evil.[11]

This statement reminds us that Cheever's symbolic polarities are not only shaped to evoke archetypal images and bring them to consciousness, but also meant to address that moral chamber of consciousness we call conscience. In his preface to the collected stories, he noted that "the constants that I look for in this sometimes dated paraphernalia are a love of light and a determination to trace some moral chain of being."[12]

Those very constants, observed in the light of their variants, must be one basis for any discussion of the thematic tensions found in his fiction. To a more obvious degree than most of his contempories and in a way more reminiscent of Hawthorne and Melville in American letters, Cheever, with his dialectical intelligence and imagination, continually centers on moral concerns. The word "moral" here refers to his engagement with the issues of responsibility, duty, and value judgments, of standards that prompt or dismay one's conscience—and of their opposites. He is well aware that the choice between good and evil is not an easy option, but he does presume the division between them is clear. As he observed, "It seems to be that every person knows from time to time what is craven, what is sinful, and what is joyous, what is courageous."[13]

And yet, despite these assumptions, Cheever resists being a moralizer. His fiction is not welcome to readers who desire moral certitudes; he offers no moral blueprints, and is never preachy or judgmental about his characters. Instead, as Wilfred Sheed observed of him, Cheever "treats his characters as he treats his guests, with consummate courtesy and a touch

11. "John Hersey Talks with John Cheever," *Yale Alumni Magazine and Journal,* December 1977, p. 24.

12. John Cheever, Preface to *The Stories of John Cheever* (New York: Knopf, 1978), p. vii. Hereafter references to the collection will be included in the text.

13. "The Darkness and the Light of John Cheever," extended interview with Christina Robb, *Boston Globe Magazine,* July 6, 1980, p. 28.

of irony."[14] Unlike the moralizer, he apparently believes that the moral quality of a person is revealed not only through his conduct but also through his sympathy and courteous forebearance in passing judgments on others.

In Cheever's hands the moral conflicts which his characters undergo take place at moments of *dramatic crisis*; as readers we are prepared, through the dialectical polarities he has established in the story, for precisely this convergence or, better, collision of opposing moral values. This dramatic crisis, ethical in import, generates a moral debate within the reader, but never does the narrator facilely resolve or clarify the moral issues in contention. When the narrator *seems* to tidy up the conflict for us—almost in parody of the last act of a Shakespearean comedy—we readers remain suspicious and resistant to it. Irony and the dialectical elements that have permeated the rest of the story have done their work too well, and such tidying rings untrue; we are meant to remain on our guard and continue the moral debate in privacy.

The story "Marito in Citta" exemplifies what first appears as a "neat" resolution of moral conflict. The story concerns Mr. Estabrook, a husband who is left alone in the city while his wife and children are away on vacation. Estabrook is an upstanding Christian, a pillar of his church, whose "aspirations were earnest, fresh, and worth observing" (*SJC*, p. 584). He anticipates that this temporary estrangement and solitude promise an opportunity for self-knowledge—and they do, through the instrumentality of Mrs. Zagreb, the tailor, whose job is significantly that of "alterations." Their torrid affair issues in telling moral conflict for Estabrook: he is convinced that his adultery is a mortal sin, but "he could not alter the feeling that Mrs. Zagreb, in her knowledgeableness, represented uncommon purity and virtue" (p. 589). Emotionally he experiences no shame, but intellectually he is abashed. His idea of the world as one "ruled by common sense, legitimate passions, and articles of faith" (p. 588) is challenged by his love-making with Mrs. Zagreb, with whom he goes "once more to the bottom of the sea, into that stupendous timelessness, secured against the pain of living" (p. 593). Estabrook becomes at once Apollo and Dionysus, torn between rational promptings of the higher levels of consciousness and the blind forces and powers which he shares with nature.

The affair ends as quickly and precipitately as it started, at Estabook's request. A coda is added to the story that at first glance reads like a "happy ending" (even a Shakespeare-like marriage is in the offing)—a

14. Wilfred Sheed, "Mr. Sunday, Mr. Monday and Mr. Cheever," *Life*, April 18, 1969, p. 40.

quick wrap-up wherein Estabrook, in a self-congratulatory mood, ration-alizes his motives (all based on social status, not morality) for abandoning Mrs. Zagreb. But for a puckish hobgoblin like Cheever, there is no such thing as a "happy" ending, if understood in its usual sentimental sense. The story concludes with Estabrook tidying up his house in apparent contentment, but the last two lines add another level of irony and suggest that the conflict only seems resolved. It closes with a repeat of the words of a farcical Italian song that opened the story and provides the title. Placed here, the final words "O povero marito!" take on a special poi-gnancy, a hint that the "happy" endings of farce do not in fact admit to the lasting dialectic of loneliness and love:

> Walking through the dismantled house, he felt again the chill and bewilderment of someone who has come back to see time's ruin. Then he went up to bed, singing, "*Marito in citta, la moglie ce ne va, o povero marito!*"   (p. 593)

This story's ending is deliberately ambiguous, subtly maintaining to the end its themes in tension. For this reason, no reader can translate this or any other Cheever story into a moral "lesson" without mutilating it. Years ago, Cheever himself was asked whether fiction ought to provide lessons of any kind, and he replied:

> No. Fiction is meant to illuminate, to explode, to refresh. I don't think there's any consecutive moral philosophy in fiction beyond excellence. Acuteness of feeling and velocity have always seemed to me terribly important. People look for morals in fiction because there has always been a confusion between fiction and philosophy.[15]

Cheever's own words are well-taken, and most critics hesitate to label a fiction writer or his themes "moral" because to do so often uncovers a whole nest of interpretive adders, each one cold to the touch and equipped with a philosophic sting. However, since the publication of John Gard-ner's *On Moral Fiction*, this subject has become unavoidable, and the problems must be faced.

In his series of essays Gardner equates "moral fiction" with its "life-giving," "life-enhancing" effect, and calls for a literature that "presents valid models for imitation, eternal verities worth keeping in mind, and a benevolent vision of the possible which can inspire and incite human beings to virtue."[16] This all sounds well and good until Gardner begins his critique of particular writers, and the reader soon realizes that a uni-

---

15. "John Cheever: The Art of Fiction LXII," *Paris Review*, 17, No. 7 (Fall 1976), 61.

16. John Gardner, *On Moral Fiction* (New York: Basic Books, 1978). Gardner's premises are established on pp. 3-40.

vocal argument is being urged that effectively drives out the abundant "life" that Gardner supposedly champions. He makes strenuous claims that he is for "life-affirmation," but the suspicion lingers that he is more passonately *against* something else—against a contrary, equally univocal philosophic stance, whether it be manifest as a critical formalism, an aesthetic nihilism, or a linguistic relativism.

Cheever is one of the few contemporary writers who are spared Gardner's critical wrath. In fact, he is even awarded this cautious compliment:

> Despite these slips [carelessness in authenticating facts] and others, Cheever's writing is important: since he cares about his characters and cares about his readers, his affirmations are sufficiently hard-won to stand up. He qualifies his optimistic Christian vision with the necessary measure of irony . . . and though he asserts, like any good Christian, that miracles do occur, he does not ask us or his characters to count on them. [17]

It is heartening to hear that despite these slips and others, "Cheever's writing is important," but is what follows precisely its importance? Here Gardner betrays a general blindness to Cheever that many other critics share. Admittedly, Cheever's fictive vision is ultimately affirmative, but does that quality in any illuminating way describe its complex magic, its dialectical intelligence? In actual fact, Cheever's fiction probes the mystery of life's contradictions and attempts to capture the alternating impulses of affirmation and denial that characterize the human moral life. Unlike what seems to be Gardner's moral stance, Cheever's stance is never either/or but always both/and—however, both/and inevitably elicits dramatic tension, thereby upsetting humanity's moral preference for either/or.

It would be unfair, of course, to claim that Gardner is against probing the both/and conflicts in fiction. He decidedly is not, and yet it often seems so because he is after bigger game than mere fiction. But in hunting the bigger game he unfortunately makes greater claims for his gun and his aim than art allows, with the result that the fleeter, more elusive game in the foreground eludes him.

In addition, Gardner raises issues that demand clearer distinctions than he offers. His request for "valid models for imitation, eternal verities worth keeping in mind, a benevolent vision of the possible" transgresses the fundamental difference between Art and Ethics, between artistic and

17. Gardner, *On Moral Fiction*, p. 97. After finishing this chapter, I happened upon a fine study that supports my arguments here from a different perspective, exposing our literary "craving for generality." See D. Z. Phillips, *Through a Darkening Glass: Philosophy, Literature and Cultural Change* (Notre Dame: Univ. of Notre Dame Press, 1982).

moral mimeses. Whenever moral standards for imitation—that is, for moral mimesis—are presented to us, they are meant to evoke within us a desire to change our behavior, to personalize the moral ideals offered us. Moral mimesis, almost by definition, is related to *action*—that is, it slices through ambiguity and is meant to abbreviate contemplation and affect conduct. Aesthetic mimesis does not. The intent of a morally concerned artist like Cheever is non-pragmatic in moral purpose: he is in quest of a different kind of existential truth, so his efforts are directed not toward influencing our behavior but toward engaging our imaginative and emotional response. His techniques are always those of indirection; if we hear a direct moral exhortation, our ears ought to perk up, alert to the sounds of "Beware! Beware! There is more here than meets the ear."

Instead, our only legitimate demand of writers of fiction is that they convey an imaginative truth about our humanity in all its complexity, a complexity that *necessarily* includes *moral* conflict (it is at this point that narrow and broader visions of man diverge in fiction). When we praise a writer for his "honesty" or "integrity" or concern for "truth," we are using words that are analogous to those predicted of a moral agent, but analogy and identity are quite different concepts. Our primary criterion for praising a writer must be artistic: has he adequately represented in an imaginative way some human mystery? If he has, then inevitably he has done so by probing and capturing the alternating pulses of affirmation and denial, those slippages and strengths of moral endeavor that characterize the *living* of human life, precisely those efforts and failures which distinguish us from the "amoral" world of animals.

The broader and deeper a writer's imaginative powers, the more acute his dialectical intelligence and sensibility, then the greater our praise for his artistry. It is true, of course, that sometimes we are fortunate enough to refresh our understanding of a moral truth through art (arrive at or reinforce a moral "lesson" in that limited sense), but the fact is, as Allen Tate put it, that "the simple truth is never commonplace unless it is spoken by a commonplace mind." Tate's remark must be extended to moral truths as well: in the hands of an artist we rediscover their simplicity only through complexity.

It is important to recall again Cheever's own comment on his fiction:

> That one is in conflict with oneself—that one's erotic and one's social nature will everlastingly be at war with one another—is something I am happy to live with on terms as hearty and fleeting as laughter. These conflicts—between love and death, youth and age, war and peace—are simply the vast vocabulary we use for the divisions of life.

And it seems to me that literature is the best way to refresh the conflict, to embrace it, to admit it in our lives.[18]

His own work is replete with that "vast vocabulary" for the divisions of life. Any reader can offer his own list of themes in polar tension throughout it: order and chaos, fidelity and divorce, loneliness and love, spirit and flesh, exaltation and despair, nature and consciousness, abundance and decay, agape and eros, estrangement and union. The list is potentially endless. What follows, therefore, smacks of the arbitrary, and it is. I have chosen the following themes because I believe that they embrace and support these others, and, furthermore, that they reflect best the complex moral and spiritual qualities of Cheever's fiction.

NOSTALGIA AND NEWNESS

On receiving the MacDowell Medal for contribution to the arts in September 1979, Cheever told the audience,

It seems to me that only in literature can we refresh our sense of possibility and nobility. This, I know, sounds pious but since it's Sunday, there's no particular reason today not to be pious. . . . The need to write comes from the need to make sense of one's life and discover one's usefulness. For me, it's the most intimate form of communicating about love and memory and nostalgia.[19]

Readers of Cheever in the audience were hardly surprised that, unlike most writers, he should link the significance of literature with piety and with the effort to communicate about love, memory, and nostalgia. Piety here relates best to its Latin meaning, *pietas*, which was among the noblest of the virtues in both the classical and the Christian tradition, for piety means "dutiful devotion" to God, to the family, to the race.[20] It is a moral disposition that refers both backward and forward in time and imposes obligations from the past onto the future. Many of Cheever's stories and both the Wapshot novels dramatize the exigencies of piety and the fact that the promptings of piety necessarily issue in ceremony. The reason is that ceremony is our human way of rendering homage to our life's passage and to our fellow passengers, of formalizing memory, of consciously

18. "John Hersey Talks with John Cheever," p. 24.
19. Reported in the *New York Times*, September 11, 1979, p. C-7.
20. Alwyn Lee, who wrote the cover story on Cheever entitled "Ovid in Ossining," *Time*, March 27, 1964, pp. 66-70, 72, develops this motif of "piety" very nicely— however, as the title indicates, she does so in terms of the Graeco-Roman classical tradition.

creating a vocabulary and ritual pattern to unite the past with the present in a dutiful way.

The most dramatic example of piety and ceremony occurs at the end of *The Wapshot Chronicle,* when Coverly, the youngest son of Leander Wapshot, returns to St. Botolphs after his father's death, and fulfills the old man's request that Prospero's closing speech in *The Tempest* be read at his graveside. It is an eccentric gesture for an eccentric old man, but as an act of piety it is a symbolic fulfillment of Leander's own "pious" hope for his sons. Earlier in the novel we are told, "It was his feeling that love, death and fornication extracted from the rich green soup of life were no better than half-truths. . . . He would like [his sons] to grasp that the unobserved ceremoniousness of his life was a gesture or sacrament toward the excellence and the continuousness of things."[21] His son Coverly earlier had realized that his life's task was "to create or build some kind of bridge between Leander's world and the world where he sought his fortune" (WC, p. 114), and through this symbolic action in ceremony, he has done so.

In the sequel, *The Wapshot Scandal,* Coverly performs a similar ceremonious gesture after the death of his cousin Honora by continuing her ritual of preparing a Christmas dinner for transients and the poor, those guests who "would know most about the raw material of human kindness."[22] Eight blind guests arrive, and

> they seemed to be advocates for those in pain; for the taste of misery as fulsome as rapture, for the losers, the goners, the flops, for those who dream in terms of missed things—planes, trains, boats and opportunities—who see on waking the empty tamarc, the empty waiting room, the water in the empty slip, rank as Love's Tunnel when the ship is sailed; for all those who fear death.   (WS, pp. 306-307)

The ritual of the Christmas dinner not only links Coverly with Honora in piety, but also, on a spiritual level, fulfills the biblical injunction that extends the radical mystery of the first Christmas:

> When you give a lunch or a dinner, do not ask your friends, brothers, relatives or rich neighbors, for fear they repay your courtesy by inviting you in return. No; when you have a party invite the poor, the crippled, the lame, the blind; that they cannot pay you back means that you

21. John Cheever, *The Wapshot Chronicle* (New York: Harper & Row, 1979 ed.), p. 52. Since it is extremely difficult to secure an original hard-bound copy of *The Wapshot Chronicle,* my references in the text will be to this 1979 reissue (together with *The Wapshot Scandal* as a companion volume) by Harper & Row. Hereafter references to the novel will be included in the text.

22. John Cheever, *The Wapshot Scandal* (New York: Harper & Row, 1964 ed.), p. 306. Hereafter references to the novel will be included in the text.

are fortunate, because repayment will be made to you when the vir-
tuous rise again. (Luke 14:12-14)

The ritual of the Christmas dinner links Coverly with Honora and more
vividly with strangers who, like him, are homeless, lost, and uprooted but
who, because of humanity, can make and keep promises.

In Cheever's fiction, as in the *Odyssey* and the *Aeneid,* the instincts
of piety are conjoined with the longings of nostalgia, which in its literal
Greek sense means "the desire for home." Critics of Cheever are alert to
the nostalgic tone that pervades his work, dramatized as the recognition
of the loss of some "thing" or some place once cherished or desired, or as
the sense of one's estrangement amid alien corn. It would be incorrect,
however, to consider nostalgia here as merely a negative affection, pessimistic and indicative of emptiness. Quite the opposite is true of Cheever's
vision. In an interview he addressed the more radical ambivalence of
nostalgia:

> Nostalgia is the longing for a world we all know, or seem to have
> known, the world we all love, and the people in it we love. Nostalgia
> is also a passion; a longing not only for that which is lost to us, or
> which has been destroyed or burned, or which we've outgrown; it is
> also a force of aspiration. It is finding ourselves not in the world we
> love, but knowing how deeply we love it, enjoying some conviction
> that we will return, or discover it, or the way to it.[23]

Nostalgia functions, therefore, not only as the regressive instinct of
reminiscence or regret but as a positive force toward aspiration, imaginative creativity, and newness. The result, as Cheever noted when he
received the MacDowell medal, is that nostalgia is inevitably linked with
memory and love, and thus his characters are ever imbued with these
twin dynamics of nostalgia.

Newness and nostalgia are not opposites. Since we cannot long for
something we do not know, it follows that, when our longings are fulfilled,
our experience of that fulfillment is at once both familiar and fresh.
Nostalgia does not mean that one wishes to return to the trivialities or
failures of the past or relive a previous life in chronological fashion, so it
is not akin to an antiquarian impulse or a quaint *Our Town*-ism. Rather,
one wants to return to those fulfillments of his longings, fulfillments that
he once imperfectly understood and never wholly experienced. A poignant example is found in *The Wapshot Scandal,* when Melissa Wapshot,
a suburban victim of ennui within the narrow confines of Proxmire Manor,
experiences a pensive moment at the tony dance at the Wishings':

23. "John Hersey Talks with John Cheever," p. 21.

She felt a profound nostalgia, a longing for some emotional island or peninsula that she had not even discerned in her dreams. She seemed to know something about its character—it was not a paradise—but its elevating possibilities of emotional richness and freedom stirred her. It was the stupendous feeling that one could do much better than this; that the reality was not Mrs. Wishing's dance. . . . (WS, pp. 50-51)

To be nostalgic means that one recognizes something permanent and independent of the self, something not so much lost as not yet gained. This is Coverly's realization at the end of The Wapshot Chronicle: "Then, before the rain began, the old place appeared to be, not a lost way of life or one to be imitated, but a vision of life as hearty and fleeting as laughter and something like the terms by which he lived" (WC, p. 295).

As a result, nostalgia conjoins memory with hope and aspiration. As Ralph Harper defines it, "Hope, which is not merely desire, consists in asserting that there is at the heart of being beyond all data, beyond all inventories and calculations, a mysterious principle in connivance with me. . . ."[24] The promptings of hope, which nostalgia stirs, are fixed not on absences or losses but on presences once dreamed of and vaguely known but not yet fully encountered. Hope counterbalances what can be one negative result of nostalgia: namely, despair, the desperate relinquishing of one's self to the vicissitudes of time and change. Hope, instead, urges one to find "a principle of identity and integrity and satisfaction which the restlessness itself tells us we need but do not have."[25]

Inevitably, then, as Cheever remarked, nostalgia is linked with love. It is love that rescues nostalgia from egotism and self-pity; love is the "force of aspiration" which, like nostalgia, is rooted in reciprocity, in fidelity and piety. Finally, love is a homecoming, the "place" where two worlds meet in memory and hope, involving a complex of recognitions, i.e., an acknowledgment of one's past through the recognition of the beloved's current presence. Hammer, when the narrator of Bullet Park, reveals that "I had thought of love as a heady distillate of nostalgia—a force of memory that had resisted analysis by cybernetics. We do not fall in love—I thought—we re-enter love, and I had fallen in love with a memory—a piece of white thread and a thunderstorm."[26] Only in love and nostalgia is time arrested.

In his review of De Rougement's Love Declared, John Updike nicely

24. Ralph Harper, Nostalgia (Cleveland: Western Reserve Press, 1966), p. 49. For his analysis of Augustine and Proust, see Ralph Harper, The Seventh Solitude (Baltimore: Johns Hopkins Univ. Press, 1965), pp. 107-153.

25. Harper, Nostalgia, pp. 29-30.

26. John Cheever, Bullet Park (New York: Knopf, 1969), p. 216. Hereafter references to the novel will be included in the text.

summarizes one aspect of this mysterious relationship of love to nostalgia that characterizes their interplay in Cheever's own fiction:

> A phrase identifies man's Iseult as "the woman . . . of his most intimate nostalgia." This hint is provocative. While nostalgia does not create women, perhaps it does create Iseult. What is it that shines at us from Iseult's face but our own past, with its strange innocence and its strange need to be redeemed? What is nostalgia but love for that part of us which is in Heaven, forever removed from change and corruption? A woman, loved, momentarily eases the pain of time by localizing nostalgia; the vague and irrecoverable objects of nostalgic longing are assimilated, under the pressure of libidinous desire, into the details of her person.[27]

Updike's remarks connecting nostalgia with man's "strange innocence" and his "strange need to be redeemed" suggest a religious dimension to nostalgia that we shall investigate later in the light of other themes. Even apart from its religious potential, however, nostalgia—like piety—enjoys a moral property. As Harper asserts,

> Nostalgia is an involuntary conscience, a moral conscience, positive rather than prohibitory. It reminds a person, by way of giving him the experience, of the good he has known and lost. . . . Through nostalgia we know not only what we hold most dear, but the quality of experiencing that we deny ourselves habitually. This is why nostalgia is a moral sentiment.[28]

But there is an important difference between nostalgia and memory, since memory is but one aspect of nostalgia. Memory might be recollection only, a delving into a particular past; nostalgia relates to memory but is not delimited by it, since nostalgia transcends mere recollection, being as it is a force of aspiration and a stimulus to the imagination.

CONFINEMENT AND TRAVEL

In a 1977 interview Cheever said, "My favorite definition of fiction is Cocteau's: 'Literature is a force of memory that we have not yet understood!' It seems to me that in a book that one finds gratifying, the writer is able to present the reader with a memory he has already possessed, but has not comprehended."[29] He then went on to connect the memory-experience with the novel's concomitant ability to make things new:

27. John Updike, Assorted Prose (New York: Knopf, 1965), pp. 286-287.
28. Harper, Nostalgia, pp. 26-27.
29. "John Hersey Talks with John Cheever," p. 22.

It seems to me that writing is always in the nature of an adventure. . . . A novel means newness. It is a discovery. Every good novel takes the great chance of an explorer. You find out not only how far you can go, but how far your reader can go with you. How far you can go and still give to the experience its universality. One is walking in the dark. And in a sense the reader shares this. No one really knows how it is going to come out. If it is successful, it is that shared memory which, up until this point, none of us comprehended.[30]

Cheever's remarks about literature reflect both different—and similar—aspects of the twin poles of nostalgia. Literature effects a discovery that is, in a sense, a recovery: it is at once a voyage out and a journey inward, a probe in the dark and an exploration of obscure memories. And it is this twin dynamic, which the reader shares, that gives literature "the experience of universality."

A writer's success, then, depends upon his talent for tapping the resources of both memory and imagination. As Wilfred Sheed has observed, memory and imagination are separate faculties for most writers, but in Cheever's case they are "but one mega-faculty." Cheever himself said that "[I have] always taken a militant approach to memory—I don't choose to go into a Proustian swoon . . . [and I find] the most useful stratum, the creative stratum is between consciousness and unconsciousness."[31]

As we have seen, Cheever accomplishes this merger by employing images that develop into symbols and, as such, harden into thematic metaphors which tease our own moral memories and our imagination. One such metaphor is that of confinement. In describing his novel *Falconer*, Cheever pointed out,

All of my work deals with confinement in one shape or another, and the struggle toward freedom. Do I mean freedom? Only as a metaphor for a sense of boundlessness, the possibility of rejoicing. I've used three symbols for confinement in my books: the small New England village [St. Botolphs], the world of affluent exurbia, and now prison. But of course in our living we're also confined in the various emotional and erotic contracts we have formed, which one may regret, but which it is difficult to find one's way out of.[32]

Besides the restrictions of place and convention, there are other recurring metaphors of confinement throughout Cheever's fiction. Ciga-

30. "John Hersey Talks with John Cheever," p. 24.
31. "John Cheever: The Art of Fiction LXII," p. 63.
32. John Firth, "Talking with John Cheever," *Saturday Review*, April 2, 1977, p. 22.

rettes, drugs, and drink function as such, metaphors for the choices one makes within a pleasurable world, choices that can become addictions. When they do, the power of moral choice is anesthetized. A comic, fantastical example occurs in the third part of the story "Metamorphoses," when Mr. Bradish decides to give up smoking. At first, in the throes of withdrawal, "the country through which he traveled seemed mountainous and barren. He seemed to be on a narrow-gauge railroad traveling through a rocky pass" (*SJC*, p. 551). But he reasons that "once they were over the pass they would come onto a fertile plain with trees and water. . . . He felt himself to be gaining some understanding of the poetry of the force of change in life, felt himself involved in one of those intimate, grueling, and unseen contests that make up the story of a man's soul" (p. 551). Bradish at first feels that he alone has been transformed, but as the passage indicates, transformation is not a one-way street: the external world is also transformed, and oddly retains its cruel power of adaptation over him:

> He had changed—he had changed, and so had his world, and watching the population of the city pass him in the dusk, he saw them as Winstons, Chesterfields, Marlboros, Salems, hookahs, meerschaums, cigarillos, Corona-Coronas, Camels, and Players. It was a young woman—really a child—whom he mistook for a Lucky Strike that was his undoing. She screamed when he attacked her. . . .   (p. 553)

Cheever reminds us that we Americans unconsciously use material possessions as metaphors and symbols for our self-value and status. The irony lies in the fact that we can become so possessed by our possessions that, like Gertrude Lockhart in *The Wapshot Scandal*, whose downfall "began not with immortal longings but with an uncommonly severe winter" (*WS*, pp. 106-107), we are driven to suicide when our possessions of convenience—in her case the oil burner, the septic tank, the electric heater—break down simultaneously, with the ironic result that "the transparent wrapper that imprisoned the bacon" (p. 106) can reverse the subliminal metaphor and our possessions become emblematic of us.

But confinement, like nostalgia, is a dialectical metaphor. In Cheever's hands it is not merely a negative circumstance but the locus of a positive disposition as well. Its dialectical opposite is not simply freedom or escape understood in political or economic or social terms; it is much broader in metaphoric meaning. In his interview with John Hersey, Cheever addressed this point explicitly when he said, " 'Escape' is not the word one means. There doesn't seem to be any word for eliminating confinement. It is the effort to express one's conviction of the boundlessness of possibility."[33] This attempt at definition points toward a more philosophic notion of freedom. Far more important than the "confining" limitations that inhibit mortal man at every level of his life are the very questions raised by his awareness of confinement. What precisely is it that accounts for man's sensing "the boundlessness of possibility" in the midst of confinement? Why should he be both dissatisfied and hopeful? These questions reach beyond cliché or easy answers and touch mystery. How precisely is man stuck if in fact his "stuckness" bothers him?

A like dialectic is found in the apparently opposite metaphor that recurs throughout Cheever's fiction: the metaphor of travel. Cheever's characters are constantly on the move: trips of all kinds—on trains, planes, ocean liners, moving vans, swims—punctuate their stories. They are either commuters or explorers or runaways and, as such, do not appear to be confined at all—and yet. . . . This motif of travel suggests by contrast the awareness that confinement generates.

Both confinement and travel are opposite images of the same truth. As Robert McCarty has pointed out, both are metaphors for a radical "restlessness" within man that transcends time and place and admixes disappointment with expectation.[34] In "The Scarlet Moving Van" we are told that the "gilt and scarlet of the van, bright even in the twilight, was an inspired attempt to disguise the true sorrowfulness of wandering" (SJC, p. 359). In Bullet Park we hear this question: "What is the pathos of men and women who fall asleep on planes and trains; why do they seem so forsaken, poleaxed and lost?" (BP, p. 6).

The answer to that last plaintive question is that travel is the symbolic reminder of man's restless sense of his homelessness. To disguise or deny this realization, many of Cheever's characters will seek out a temporary home, a vacation resort or villa near the sea. This familiar Cheever setting enables him to situate symbolically the dramatic tension between man's realization of his temporality and estrangement and his longing for the permanent, here the eternal sea, which itself is a symbol for man's less private and universal memory. And so we hear in "The Seaside Houses," for example, that "the journey to the sea has its ceremonious excitements . . . and there is the sense that we are, as in our dreams we have always known ourselves to be, migrants and wanderers—travelers, at least, with a traveler's acuteness of feeling" (SJC, p. 482).

33. "John Hersey: Talk with John Cheever," New York Times Book Review, March 6, 1977, p. 26.

34. Robert E. McCarty, S.J., "Augustinian Restlessness in the Fiction of John Cheever," a paper presented at the Symposium on Christianity and Literature at the MLA Convention, December 1977.

THE SELF: TIME AND ETERNITY

When one connects the themes we have investigated thus far—the dialectic of nostalgia; the metaphors of confinement and travel; the motifs of restlessness, of wandering and return; the interplay between temporal estrangement and the search for the permanent Eternal—then one begins to sense that Cheever's fiction is edging toward those religious and philosophical reflections about the nature of time and the self that enjoy a rich heritage in the Western tradition.

At the dawn of Greek philosophy Heraclitus argued that the fundamental reality is change and impermanence, symbolized by fire, which is itself changeless yet ever changing. Parmenides argued otherwise, maintaining the constancy and permanence of reality. Plato found a middle course by distinguishing time from eternity, arguing that time is the world of becoming and is but a moving image of eternity, whereas eternity, the realm of being, is unchanging, fixed and unified. But, because the Greeks insisted on the circularity of time, the issue was not resolved until Saint Augustine, convinced of the Christian view of time as linear, meditated on the mystery of time and eternity and found the merger of time and eternity in the human mind.[35] Augustine acknowledged that the reality of time was an experience eternal to man, yet he argued that the distinctions of time—past, present, and future—are also experiences within man's mind. In the eleventh book of his *Confessions* he concluded:

> It is not properly said that there are three times, past, present, and future. Perhaps it might be said rightly that there are three times: a time present of things past: a time present of things present; and a time present of things future. For these three do co-exist somehow in the soul, for otherwise I could not see them. The time present of things past is memory; the time present of things present is direct experience; the time present of things future is expectation.[36]

These three "presents" co-exist in the human mind; thus they are a reflection in the temporal order of their simultaneous presence in the Eternal Divine Mind.

This is Augustine's *conclusion*, of course; our interest in connection with Cheever's fiction is Augustine's starting point for that meditation: the mystery of the self evoked by the concurrent dynamics of memory, present experience, and hope within the mind of man.

First, for Augustine the questionability of the self and time (since the

35. See C. A. Patrides' introduction, pp. 1-18, to *Aspects of Time*, ed. C. A. Patrides (Toronto: Univ. of Toronto Press, 1976).

36. *The Confessions of St. Augustine*, Book XI, 20.

self is temporal) arises because of the restlessness and disquietude that is rooted in the mystery of human personality. Restlessness and disquietude mirror man's sense of continuity and fragmentation, of nostalgia and homelessness—a realization of stasis and movement. But disquietude and the enigma of the self *can* issue in a dynamic process—as it does in Augustine—whereby the questionability of the self leads to a longing for an answer, and the wanderer becomes a true pilgrim, one on the way toward rather than away from his goal. For the experience of longing makes the quest akin to the dynamics of love. This is why Augustine interjects in his *Confessions* the telling sentence, "Give me a lover and he will know what I am talking about." The homesick and the lovesick are not so different; both undergo the twin dynamics of nostalgia (memory and hope), the desire for union, for possession and being possessed, and the need for cognition and re-cognition.

Secondly, Augustine probes this mystery of the self by exploring the mystery of memory. He wonders why all men should seek happiness, which is not present in one's memory in the same way as Carthage is to him, and yet happiness must be present somehow in memory—otherwise, how could men seek or recognize happiness? The answer, so reminiscent of Socrates' argument in Plato's *Meno,* is that "we could not long for happiness unless we somehow knew it; but knowing it, in this case, means we somehow remember it, and therefore *once* possessed and enjoyed it."[37] Where? In some other life, not here, some other life which we have forgotten, but not entirely; that other life with God persists in memory, though we have fallen from it. God is absent, but not completely; He remains present in our memories, but His presence is not restricted to our memories, for He is present in all of creation and to all the modes of time—past, present, and future:

> Too late have I loved you, O Beauty so ancient and so new, too late have I loved You! Behold, you were within me while I was outside; it was there that I sought you, and a deformed creature, rushed headlong upon these things of beauty which you have made. You were with me, but I was not with you. They kept me far from you, those fair things which, if they were not in you, would not exist at all.[38]

Earlier I quoted Cheever's statement that he takes "a militant approach to memory" and "refuses to go into a Proustian swoon." The reason why is found in an observation about Proust made by Ortega y Gasset:

---

37. For an excellent analysis of this argument in Augustine, see Robert J. O'Connell, S.J., *St. Augustine's Confessions* (Cambridge: Harvard Univ. Press, 1969), pp. 128ff.

38. From O'Connell's translation (above) of *The Confessions,* Book X, 27.

[Proust] does not wish to use his memories as materials for constructing former realities; on the contrary, by using all conceivable methods . . . he wants literally to reconstruct the very memories themselves. Here for the first time memory ceases to be treated as the means of describing other things and becomes itself the very thing described. For this reason Proust does not generally add to what is remembered those parts of reality which have eluded memory.[39]

Augustine, however, does take a "militant" approach to memory, because he explores the mystery of memory not only in and for itself, but also in its connection with the disquietude that is revelatory not just of the disjunction but also of the more mysterious conjunction of past, present, and future within human consciousness. The recognition of the self for Augustine does not entail merely a reconstruction of the past, as in Proust, but a meditation on memory in the light of the present reality and of future expectation.

In this significant sense Cheever's fiction is Augustinian, not Proustian, and the disquietude he dramatizes hints at Augustine's religious restlessness: "our hearts are restless until they rest in Thee." For example, Cheever's most explicitly "religious" novel, *Falconer*, is located in literal confinement (Falconer prison), and the story's development is shaped by significant memories of the protagonist Farragut and the other characters. The key word in the novel is "remember," and the plot records the linkages in Farragut's mind among past, present, and future tenses and the rhythm of fall and redemption.

Cheever, of course, is not a theologian or a religious philosopher, so his themes elude the precision of statement these disciplines desire. He proceeds as artist, subscribing to Augustine's admission of limitation. Augustine said, "This much I know, although at present I am looking at a confused reflection in a mirror, not yet face to face, and therefore, as long as I am away from you, during my pilgrimage, I am more aware of myself than of you."[40] Being both the cause and effect of disquietude, self-awareness—rather than formal religious meditation—is Cheever's concern. He conveys this restless disquietude in dramatic and psychological ways through stylistic devices, such as the violation of time sequences, the swift alteration of voices and tenses, and the accumulation of images in polar tension. He employs controlling images, images reminiscent of those central to Augustine's writings, e.g., light as a dynamic force, journey and return,

39. Jose Ortega y Gasset, "Time, Distance and Form in Proust," in *Aspects of Time*, p. 138.
40. *The Confessions*, Book X, 5.

the prodigal (especially in the Wapshot novels), and the pilgrim in quest of a peaceable city.[41]

Yet because, as Kierkegaard observed, "Life is lived forward, but must be understood backwards," Cheever tempers all dynamic images with the retrospective impulses of memory, for memory is that component which makes a self a true self. He knows that a man without memory can never be a self, can never live forward or understand backward.[42]

MEMORY AND FORGETTING

Cheever has compassion for those characters who have little hope but at least are rich in memories. The only rather villainous characters in his fiction are those who are forgetful or without memories of any kind, without self-awareness as pilgrims. Blake, the central character in "The Five-Forty-Eight," is such a man. As the story starts he is oblivious of his past and cannot remember the name of a former mistress who is slightly or totally insane; however, she has not forgotten him—in fact, she is pursuing him with a gun. On the train the girl quotes from Job the lines, "Where shall wisdom be found? Where is the place of understanding? The depth saith it is not in me; the sea saith it is not with me. Destruction and death say we have heard the force with our ears" (SJC, p. 243).

The imminence of death and destruction at another's hand—here pointedly taking place on a commuter train, thus joining the routine with the bizarre—makes these *existential* questions for Blake, turning them inward, *reminding* him of other modes of wisdom and understanding. It is significant, then, that this terrifying experience prompts two antipodal memories within him. The first is dire: "He remembered the unburied dead he had seen in the war. The memory came in a rush; entrails, eyes, shattered bone, ordure, and other filth" (p. 245). The second memory is more heartening: "He heard from off the dark river the drone of an outboard motor, a sound that drew slowly behind it across the dark water such a burden of clear, sweet memories of gone summers and gone plea-sures that it made his flesh crawl, and he thought of dark in the mountains and the children singing" (pp. 246-247).

These antipodal memories restore Blake briefly to a realization of life's mysteries posed by Job's questions, and yet the story ends with a moving reversal. After the girl humilates him by forcing his face in the dirt, "he

41. For examples of these images throughout Augustine's work, see O'Connell's study already cited; also see his companion volume, St. *Augustine's Early Theory of Man* (Cambridge: Harvard Univ. Press, 1968).

42. For a supportive reading, see John S. Dunne, *A Search for God in Time and Memory* (London: Macmillan, 1969).

raised himself out of the dust—warily at first, until he saw by her attitude, her looks, that she had forgotten him" (p. 247).

The story "The Lowboy," on the other hand, dramatizes the negative power of memory unredeemed, of fixation leading to illusion. The plot involves the fight between two brothers over the possession of a family heirloom, the lowboy of the title. The older brother, Richard, himself an egocentric, selfish "lowboy" all his life, is desperate to possess it, because he desires " 'One object I could point to, that would remind me of how happy we all were, of how we used to live . . .' " (SJC, p. 405).

His narrator-brother suspects otherwise, wondering "if he didn't want it for cachet, as a kind of family crest, something that would vouch for the richness of his past and authenticate his descent from the most aristocratic of the seventeenth-century settlers" (p. 406). But he reluctantly allows Richard to have the lowboy, and initially Richard is ecstatic: he discovers that the lowboy is historically famous, and is pleased "that what he adored and possessed was adored by most of mankind" (p. 408).

This experience generates in Richard a passion to restore with exactitude everything connected with the lowboy: the old rug on which the lowboy stood, the silver pitcher filled with leaves which covered the "dark ring" on its polished surface. At last the past has been revived, recollection and memory objectified for Richard, his former self—now identified with the lowboy—restored.

All of this *has* happened after intense preparation, but the narrator imagines something else, a result quite unexpected. He imagines Richard relaxing on a rainy night, wrapped in recollection, thinking of the lowboy and its associations. As Richard begins to recall all the hands and fingers which have touched the lowboy, he evokes the spirits of the dead and summons forth the memory of his actual, not his idealized, past. Like the Dickensian ghosts in A Christmas Carol, all the obscene, drunken, rancorous members of his family are called forth, for unwittingly he has reconstructed a Christmas dinner, filled with chaos, from his childhood.

The narrator's imaginings issue in fact. Sometime later, at a Thanksgiving dinner, he notices that "once the lowboy took a commanding position in his house, [Richard] seemed driven back upon his wretched childhood" (p. 411). A more terrible reconstruction has thus taken place: his brother has reverted to the nasty, quarreling figure he was as a child. The story ends with the narrator throwing out all the family heirlooms he himself has kept. He realizes that "we can cherish nothing less than our random understanding of death and the earth-shaking love that draws us to one another" (pp. 411-412). Richard's effort at remembrance has distorted the past; by being overly selective, self-centered, and narrow, he has been discontented with such "random understanding" and ironically has forgotten the mysteries of death and love that alone endure.

The story closes with an exhortation. Its florid rhetorical style is deliberate, for it is meant to evoke another kind of past: the knight's chivalric courage to face the future and pursue the transcendence of things temporal:

> Dismiss whatever molests us and challenges our purpose, sleeping or waking. Cleanliness and valor will be our watchwords. Nothing less will get us past the armed sentry and over the mountainous border. (p. 412)

The tensions between memory and forgetting, despair and hope are the central themes of *Bullet Park*. A touching and laughable example is Hammer's narrative about his efforts to overcome his "cafard," a melancholy despair that, significantly, becomes most powerful when he is traveling. He tells us,

> My best defense, my only defense, was to cover my head with a pillow and summon up those images that represented for me the excellence and beauty I had lost. The first of these was a mountain—it was obviously Kilimanjaro. The summit was a perfect, snow-covered cone, lighted by a passing glow. . . . Next in frequency I saw a fortified medieval town. . . . The image of the walled town, like the snow-covered mountain, seemed to represent beauty, enthusiasm and love. I also saw less frequently and less successfully a river with grassy banks. I guessed these were the Elysian Fields. . . . (BP, pp. 174-175)

It is significant that the three images of consolation span the recorded history (i.e., memory) of man. Hammer tells us that "The vision [of the mountain] dated, I guess, from the bronze or the iron age" (p. 175). The third, that of the grassy banks of the Elysian Fields, is for him "difficult to arrive at," for it lies in the future. The second image, that of the medieval walled town, does connect the past with the present and with future aspiration, for Hammer travels to Rome (he stays at the Eden Hotel) and finds such a town in Orvieto. There he comes upon a building with lighted windows and yellow walls, and he tells us, "I seemed, looking up at them from the sidewalk, to be standing at the threshold of a new life. This was not a sanctuary, this was the vortex of things, but this was a place where the cafard could not enter" (p. 183).

Unfortunately, the owner refuses to sell the building, and Hammer realizes that "I had found my yellow rooms and I had lost them" (p. 184), so he flies back to America. Eventually he comes upon a Pennsylvania farmhouse and discovers his yellow room again, "its lemon-yellow walls simply lighted—and I felt that if I could only possess this I would be myself again, industrious and decent" (p. 185). He buys the farmhouse and marries, but soon the yellow walls crack and discolor, his wife repaints them in pink, and his cafard returns.

This brief episode is a touching example of how deftly Cheever can update the Grail legend and yet combine the romantic with the banal in hilarious fashion. Hammer's quest for the yellow room (the color yellow in Cheever's work is symbolic of the beckoning delights of light) unites recollection with aspiration, a personal pilgrimage with a universal one. As Hammer's reflections explicate, possession of the yellow room corresponds with re-possession of the self. Moreover, the episode produces precisely that delightful effect that Cheever strives for. He once said:

> The books that you really love give you a sense, when you first open them, of having been there. It is a creation, almost like a chamber in the memory. Places that one has never been to, things that one has never seen or heard, but their fitness is so sound that you've been there somehow.[43]

Hammer's eccentric mother recounts a similar experience—this time with music, not color. She tells us,

> "My memory . . . seems to perform music continuously. . . . What mystifies me is the variety in quality. Sometimes I wake to the slow movement of the first Razumovsky. You know how I love that. I may have a Vivaldi concerto for breakfast and some Mozart a little later. But sometimes I wake to a frightful Sousa march. . . . Why should my memory torment me by playing music that I loathe? At times my memory seems to reward me; at times it seems vindictive. . . ."
>
> (p. 154)

It is significant that, like her son's experience, the music she remembers, with its alternating rhythms and emotional effects, intensifies for her during travel. She is especially affected by the sounds of airplane motors. She notes that the sounds of a Constellation are more "contrapuntal" and have a " 'driving and processional sense of baroque music but they will never, I know from experience, reach a climax and a resolution' " (p. 155). DC-7's, however, are " 'both more comprehensive and more limited' " (p. 156), and she recounts an experience aboard one that, in its fanciful way, recapitulates the Cheever themes and images in tension that we have investigated:

> "One night on a flight to Frankfurt I distinctly heard the props get halfway through Gounod's vulgar variations of Bach. I have also heard Handel's *Water Music*, the death theme from *Tosca*, the opening of the

43. "John Cheever: The Art of Fiction LXII," p. 59.

Messiah, etc. But boarding a DC-7 one night in Innsbruck . . . I distinctly heard the engines produce some exalting synthesis of all life's
sounds—boats and train whistles and the creaking of iron gates and
bedsprings and drums and rainwinds and thunder and footsteps and
the sounds of singing all seemed woven into a rope or cord of air that
ended when the stewardess asked us to observe the No Smoking sign
(Nicht Rauchen), an announcement that has come to mean to me
that if I am not at home I am at least at my destination."   (p. 156)

Later she reveals that the force of memory is not restricted to mere
personal quirks but is universal in character. In her travels she begins to
notice that the beds she occupies in hotels and pensions generate within
her dreams akin to the actions and morals of their previous occupants.
She observes, " 'It is a simple fact that we impress something of ourselves—our spirits and our desires—on the mattresses where we lie.
. . . Traveling that year I shared the dreams of businessmen, tourists,
married couples, chaste and orderly people as well as whores' "
(pp. 157-158). This recognition of such absent presences, this sharing in
a dream-world of memory and fantasy, leads her to a significant reflection:

"Was I gifted or were these facts known to all travelers and wouldn't
giftedness be a misnomer for a faculty that could not be exploited? I
have finally concluded that the universality of our dreams includes
everything—articles of clothing and theatre ticket stubs—and if we
truly know one another so intimately mightn't we be closer than we
imagine to a peaceable world?"   (p. 159)

This piquant final question, posed in seemingly guileless fashion, represents a recurring theme in Cheever's fiction. In *The Wapshot Scandal* we
hear the explicit assertion that "we leave behind us, in the hotels, motels,
guest rooms, meadows and fields where we discharge this much of ourselves, either the scent of goodness or the odor of evil, to influence those
who come after us" (*WS*, p. 29). The story "The Seaside Houses" referred
to earlier is a dramatic exploration of this reflection and, like *The Scandal,*
combines the travel motif with the odd premonition about a "moral chain
of being" that escapes analysis.

The narrator in "The Seaside Houses" is a gentle and reasonable man
who has rented a summer cottage for his family. Initially content with his
new home, he gradually realizes that the Greenwoods (a symbolic name),
the owners of the cottage, have left ominous moral baggage behind. The
first inkling occurs when the narrator discovers caches of empty whiskey
bottles in the living room. Next he spies a boy's scrawl declaring "My
father is a rat" on a corner baseboard; a few days later a neighbor spills
obscene gossip about the Greenwoods. Soon the narrator begins to have

dreams that he realizes are Mr. Greenwood's dreams, and Greenwood's absent presence begins to infect him, eventually destroying his relationship with his own wife and family.

In a telling scene in a bar near Grand Central Station, he finally sees Greenwood—a lonely, depressed alcoholic—and, without addressing him but knowing him well, he summarizes Greenwood's autobiography. Yet, despite intuiting these biographical "facts," he realizes that Greenwood's discomposure remains a deeper mystery than any facile summary might suggest: "[Greenwood] has lost his daughter, his house, the love of his wife, and his interest in business, but none of these losses would account for his pain and bewilderment. The real cause would remain concealed from him, concealed from me, concealed from us all" (*SJC*, p. 488). By the story's end, Greenwood has become the narrator's counterpart (the narrator, too, divorces), and the last paragraph ends with his reflections and plaintive questions in another seaside house with another wife:

> The lights from the cottage, shining into the fog, give an illusion of substance, and it seems as if I might stumble on a beam of light. The shore is curved, and I can see the lights of other haunted cottages where people are building up an accrual of happiness or misery that will be left for the August tenants or the people who come next year. Are we truly this close to one another? Must we impose our burdens on strangers? And is our sense of the universality of suffering so inescapable? (p. 489)

CONCLUSION

"The Seaside Houses," like "The Enormous Radio," "The Lowboy," "Just Tell Me Who It Was," "The Swimmer," and others, is a fable on the mystery of original sin. In a later chapter I will analyze particular stories, but given the present context of our discussion, I want to emphasize this general point, because original sin provides the religious subtext for the themes in tension we have noted in Cheever.

The mystery of original sin answers to man's sense of the conjunctions and disruptions perceived on every level of his personality: the ontological, the moral, the psychological, the social, the emotional. The dogma, of course, provides no ready answer (original sin concerns a mystery, not a problem), but it does speak to the disparities and odd unities that characterize human life. These include the strange simultaneity of past and present, manifest in memory and nostalgia; the fact that man's moral confusion seems to mirror a more radical metaphysical conflict in the nature of things; then man's sense of being plunged into an ontological riot, since he possesses a "human" nature and is as "real" as anything else in reality; and finally, man's sharing, as a social being, a solidarity with the race and yet remaining a solitary figure, and so as united with and separated from social reality as he is from the rest of reality.

To dramatize these multi-leveled ambivalences is the intent of Cheever's fiction. It is important to emphasize again that, when Cheever employs mythic, fabulist, symbolic devices in his fiction, he does so not merely to elevate his characters or their perceptions, but primarily to personalize imaginatively man's communal memory, that wellspring of images and archetypes Jung calls the collective unconscious. Elevation of the banal is not his intent. Rather, it is first of all descent, the recovery of a universally shared racial memory both emotive and spiritual, a descent into a memory which—as Augustine demonstrates—paradoxically as-cends toward reflections on a "fall" and to longings for deliverance. As usual, Cheever poses the questions more eloquently:

> Is this an infirmity of the genteel or a conviction that there are dis-cernible moral truths?[44]

44. John Cheever, "The Jewels of the Cabots," in *The Stories of John Cheever*, p. 688.

[A reviewer of **Bullet Park**] said that I missed greatness by having left St. Botolphs. Had I stayed as Faulkner did in Oxford, I would probably have been as great as Faulkner. But I made the mistake of leaving this place which, of course, never existed at all. It was odd to be told to go back to a place that was a complete fiction.

John Cheever

Let others complain that the age is wicked; my complaint is that it is paltry, for it lacks passion. . . . This is the reason my soul always turns back to the Old Testament and Shakespeare. I feel that those who speak there are at least human beings: they hate, they love, they murder their enemies . . . they sin.

Sören Kierkegaard

Art arises out of our desire for both beauty and truth and our knowledge that they are not identical.

W. H. Auden

What gives life its value you can find—and lose. But never possess.

Dag Hammarskjöld

My only fear is that I will not be worthy of my sufferings.

Fëdor Dostoevski

my father moved through dooms of love
through sames of am through haves of give,
singing each morning out of each night
my father moved through depths of height

e.e. cummings

4: The Wapshot Chronicle

In 1957 John Cheever published his first novel, *The Wapshot Chronicle*. It later won the (then) prestigious National Book Award for fiction against such strong competitors as Bernard Malamud's *The Assistant*, Vladimir Nabokov's *Pnin*, William Faulkner's *The Town*, as well as the more widely publicized James Agee's *A Death in the Family* and James Gould Cozzens' *By Love Possessed*. In his acceptance speech for the award, Cheever—by then a *bona fide* novelist—expressed his personal feelings about the novel as a distinctive art form: "It remains for me one of the few places—one of the few forms—where we can record man's complexity and the strengths and decencies of his longings; where we can describe, step by step, minute by minute, our not altogether unpleasant struggle to put ourselves into a viable and devout relationship to our beloved and mistaken world."[1]

Cheever's own words, better than those of any reviewer or critic, capsulate *The Chronicle's* peculiar power: its narrative accuracy, its lyricism, and especially its compassionate exploration of man's engagement with and separation from the multiple "worlds" of his experience.[2] To speak of "worlds" in the plural is not an overstatement. The creative challenge for Cheever was to invent both a place (St. Botolphs) and a people (the Wapshots) and root them within an invented history. The very word "chronicle" in the title reveals his intention to provide a recorded account of a narrow world, delimited within the larger world and yet continuous with it.

But the reader is never led to forget that this chronicle is not an annal or biography or family history. Through various narrative techniques Cheever invites us into another dimension of history, another view of the events recorded. This dimension transcends the particular events de-

---

1. John Cheever, quoted in the Editors' Preface to the 1965 re-issue of *The Wapshot Chronicle* by Time-Life Books (New York: Time-Life Books, 1965), p. ix.
2. For other published close readings of *The Wapshot Chronicle*, see Samuel Coale, *John Cheever* (New York: Ungar, 1977), pp. 65-80; Lynne Waldeland, *John Cheever* (Boston: Twayne, 1979), pp. 37-48; and Clinton S. Burhans, Jr., "John Cheever and the Grave of Social Coherence," *Twentieth Century Literature*, 14 (January 1969), 187-209.

scribed, not, as the historian would, by guessing at motivation or proposing a linkage of cause and effect, but by dramatizing the fact that each human's personal history cannot be reduced to reportage of external action, that it necessarily involves memory, imagination, aspiration, self-deception, and estrangement—for each of us dwells simultaneously in multiple worlds, as genuine and real to us living in history as the events of our decade, generation, or century. In *The Wapshot Chronicle* these worlds collide.

Much ink has been blotted in an attempt to establish that this novel and *The Wapshot Scandal* are crypto-autobiography, recording Cheever's own family history in heightened form.[3] Critical detectives are quick to point out the similarities between the facts of Cheever's life and his fiction. That, like Ezekiel Wapshot, Ezekiel Cheever arrived in New England in the 1630's; that through the nineteenth century the Cheevers enjoyed a genteel prosperity there, only to suffer reversals in the twentieth. That Cheever's own father grew up in Newburyport opposite Plum Island and its recreations; that he lost his business during the Depression and became estranged from his wife. That John Cheever was extremely close to his own brother Frederick, as are Coverly and Moses Wapshot; that they separated through misunderstandings and thereafter were on relatively cool terms. That characteristics of both Sarah and Honora Wapshot are distinctly reminiscent of traits of Cheever's own mother, who, in fact, did run a gift shop in her later life. And so on and so on.

This trail seems—and is—endless, and at times certain surmises are so inventive that, in their own way, they edge toward a new genre of fiction. No important American novelist, of course, can be spared such investigation, and its most prominent victims of late have been Hemingway, Fitzgerald, Faulkner, Bellow, Updike, Roth—and Cheever. It appears that those who are not especially eager for the artistic qualities of the fiction—the *what* that is given—still remain curious, as though under a different enchantment, to discover *where* the novelist got his inspiration. This inevitably results in a transposition of literary criticism into source criticism, and the troubling implication is that the "where" provides sufficient explanation for the "what." At its best, this approach, when disciplined, can furnish insights into a literary biography; when less disciplined, it provides a diverting hobby for some readers and elevates what in other circumstances they would castigate as gossip. At its worst, it can divert too much, eventually distracting us from the more genuine mysteries of an intelligence and imagination that transform both the where and the

---

3. This approach pervades much Cheever criticism and is most pronounced in Lynne Waldeland's study, *John Cheever*. and in *Time* magazine's cover story, "Ovid in Ossining," *Time*, March 27, 1964, pp. 66-70.

what and create something freshly "made"—which is what the word "fiction" etymologically means.

I include these rather tired reflections here because Cheever's own remarks about his fiction often manage both to activate and frustrate such a biographical approach. For example, in his introduction to the 1965 reissuing of *The Wapshot Chronicle*, he spoke of its inspiration and composition:

> There was no West River, no *S.S. Topaze*, no St. Botolphs. A boat that looked like *Topaze* used to be moored in the Harlem Ship Canal off Northern Manhattan and could be seen from the trains on the Hudson River line. The cannon on the green is in Bristol, New Hampshire, the sound of the adzes was heard by my father, and the impulse to construct such a village as St. Botolphs occurred to me late one night in a third-string hotel on the Hollywood Strip where the world from my window seemed so desperately barbarous and nomadic that the attractions of a provincial and traditional way of life were irresistible.[4]

The creation of St. Botolphs in all its particularity is thus that delightful outcome of the remembered real and the invented. No one since Marianne Moore has described it better than she did in her poem "Poetry." There she claims that the success of "literalists of the imagination" (and surely Cheever is one of these) occurs for readers when they "can present/ for inspection, imaginary gardens with real toads to them." In fiction the recreation of particularity makes a novel "realistic" or "representational" in that its mimetic exactness offers the reader a recognizable world, one that does not deliberately distort his common-sense perceptions. The reader *feels* that he has seen St. Botolphs or fragments of it elsewhere—or, better, *thinks* he has.

On the other hand, the reader also intuits that St. Botolphs is not merely representational but is representative besides; that is, the town enjoys symbolic status beyond the realistic. St. Botolphs is and yet is not—and the fact that it is curiously both is one of the novel's subliminal themes. In that same introduction Cheever put it this way:

> St. Botolphs was invented more in irony than in nostalgia. The high pastures of New Hampshire, the rich brews of the North Atlantic and the antics of my cousinage were like the widely scattered ruins of a sort of paradise that served me as an image for that incurable idealism with which most of us approach love, friendship and society.[5]

St. Botolphs, then, is a place given a history but not possessed of a

---

4. Cheever, Introduction to the *Time-Life* re-issue of *The Chronicle*, p. xvii.
5. Cheever, Introduction to the *Time-Life* re-issue of *The Chronicle*, p. xix.

history; it is a recognizable New England town so vividly depicted that we know were we are, and yet no maps would find it; it is more properly a state of mind, the narrator's and the reader's, the scattered ruins of paradise and Moore's imaginary garden. It is important, in this context, to note further that the members of the Wapshot family, those "real roads," are ever its residents. Like the town, they too are at times embodied images, at once realistic and symbolic. Just as St. Botolphs and its environs, though described with precise detail, transcend space as we know it, so too the "chronicle" of the Wapshots, though ostensibly a temporal narrative, transcends time according to our usual categories.

To my knowledge, no critic of the novel has noted that the events narrated are in most cases impossible to date, save in the most general way. Not only do we not hear of such things as war or war's alarms, memorable disasters, and economic depressions, which would provide a chronological handhold, but the length of time-lapses in the story are such that by its end we are not sure how much the characters have aged in the interim. Most readers would likely guess five or ten years, but is this so? The story seems to end in the 1950's, but where does it begin? Given Cheever's manifest talents, this absence of specification is deliberate. The fact that the novel begins and ends with Fourth-of-July celebrations suggests that cyclical time, not linear time, is its main focus.

THE PLOT

I risk belaboring these points for two reasons: first, a plot summary of the novel makes it sound both episodic and random; and second, negative criticism of it generally centers on the question of whether it is actually a "novel" at all. At this point of argument, all critics inevitably enter into an abstract realm where the designation "novel" functions like a Platonic Form, a pre-existent standard of unity and perfection in which only certain fictions participate to a greater or lesser degree. The fact that this Platonic Form arrived late on the scene—in the twentieth century, after hundreds of years of novel-writing—and that it represents concerns more proper to the philosophy of aesthetics than to literary criticism, does not make it dismissible as a critical standard. Like Mount Everest, it is there, and remains an imposing challenge for both the novelist and the critic.

Since these issues are inevitably interconnected, let us begin with the first difficulty. The plot of The Wapshot Chronicle is impossible to summarize briefly in a paragraph or two. Too much happens, and there is a sprawl of discrete incident. Why else call it a chronicle? I like to think that what follows sorts out the action but at the same time exemplifies restraint. (I insert this summary as a refresher for those knowledgeable in Cheever's fiction and as a guide for others. From experience I think both need an overview to obviate confusion before a reading can be offered.)

The story is divided into four sections. Part One introduces us to St. Botolphs, a New England seaside town, once prosperous in the seafaring centuries and now settling into a genteel, peaceable decay. It also introduces us to the Wapshot family—the parents Leander and Sarah Wapshot, their two teenage sons, Moses and Coverly, and their eccentric cousin Honora Wapshot. The narrator reminds us that the Wapshot family, like St. Botolphs, is known for its adventuresome tradition linked with the sea, but its vitality is gradually diminishing. Symbolic of this is the fact that the patriarch Leander is reduced to being a captain of the S.S. *Topaze*, an old tub that ferries passengers from the mainland to a recreation island.

The family's serenity is upset by the unexpected appearance of Rosalie Young. Driving home from the beach, she and her lover have an accident near the Wapshots' home at West Farm, and he is killed. The Wapshots take the girl into their home, where she recuperates. While fishing one day, the older son Moses sees the naked Rosalie bathing in the river. Eventually they become lovers, but coincidentally their sexual meeting is overheard by Cousin Honora, who, by odd circumstance, is hiding in the closet. Honora, who possesses both a will of iron and what remains of the family wealth, is appalled, and through a variety of schemes she finally gets her way: she demands that Moses leave St. Botolphs, as did all the previous Wapshot males, and "go out in the world and prove himself." Coverly is devastated at the thought of his brother's departure, so without telling anyone he, too, leaves to prove himself. A few days later Rosalie's parents arrive to retrieve their daughter from St. Botolphs. Thus Part One ends with a triple departure.

Part Two, the lengthiest section, alternates between narration of the adventures of Moses and Coverly as they go their separate ways, and the quotation of Leander's journal, a journal which is a confessional autobiography that oddly parallels at certain points his sons' experiences. Coverly moves to New York. There, after a series of mishaps, he falls in love with Betsey MacCaffery; he also becomes a taper in the field of computers. He is stationed on Island 93 in the South Pacific, and wins release when he receives word that his father is dying. Part Two ends with his return to St. Botolphs and his reunion with Leander.

Moses's career, meanwhile, has been more bizarre. In Washington, D.C., he becomes engaged in work "so secret that it can't be discussed here,"[6] but he loses his security clearance when he has an affair with

---

6. John Cheever, *The Wapshot Chronicle* (New York: Harper & Row, 1979 ed.), p. 125. Hereafter references to the novel will be included in the text. As I mentioned earlier, because of the difficulty of securing the original hard-bound version, I shall refer to the Harper & Row re-issue.

Beatrice, a band-leader's wife, who lies to the authorities, claiming he seduced her. Disconsolate, Moses decides to go on a fishing trip in the Poconos in an effort to recapture the peaceful solace he experienced on boyhood fishing trips with Leander. While he is there, an accident occurs: an elderly woman is thrown from her horse. Moses comes to her rescue and, by so doing, wins the gratitude of her lover, the wealthy Charles Cutter, who offers him a job at the Fiduciary Trust Company Bond School in New York City. With this turn of events Moses finds contentment. Unlike Coverly, he decides not to return to St. Botolphs when he learns that his father is dying, because he suspects Leander of malingering.

Interspersed with the narrative of his sons' escapades, the entries from Leander's journal record his own youthful career as a Wapshot seeking his fortune. Through it we learn of his childhood in St. Botolphs and the big city of Boston, his first sexual experience, and his job as an apprentice for a boss named Whittier. Through threats and cajolery, Whittier induces Leander to marry a young girl named Clarissa, whom Whittier has gotten pregnant. The plan is to have Clarissa deliver her child and give it to strangers in order to avoid scandal. A daughter is born and given up, but Clarissa is so devastated that she drowns herself. The journal records: "Have no wish to dwell on sordid matters, sorrows, etc. Bestiality of grief. Times in life when we can count only on brute will to live. Forget. Forget" (p. 147). Here the themes of loss of childhood, humanity's effort to survive, and memory and forgetting come to a poignant turning point in the narrative.

At this point the narrative moves beyond the contents of the journal and describes the incidents of Leander's present life. His daughter returns to scorn him; the *Topaze* crashes into Gull Rock and is no longer seaworthy, and his wife Sarah converts it into "the only Floating Gift Shoppe in New England" (p. 189). Leander's reaction to this emasculating series of embarrassments is both moving and comical. The climax occurs when in pique and frustration he fires a shot out the window, hoping hearers will think he has committed suicide; unfortunately, no one hears it except Lulu, the maid, to whom he confesses, " 'I only want to be esteemed' " (p. 196). His hopefulness mounts only with Coverly's return.

Part Three continues the tracing of the roller-coaster careers of the two sons, specifically their encounters with the transformations of Venus and the more mystifying allures of Ganymede. Moses falls in love with the beautiful Melissa, a ward of his eccentric Cousin Justina. Justina presides over the Clear Haven estate, an ornate museum of imported artifacts from Europe gone to seed. Justina's imperiousness and repressed sexuality dominate the story at this point, for Clear Haven's motto is "Look away from the Body and into Truth and Life." Initially, in order to satisfy his

erotic desire, Moses is forced to scamper over the booby-trapped roofto
of Clear Haven to be with his lover, but eventually this strenuous ath
lecticism ends when he gains Justina's permission to marry Melissa. Th
couple does marry, but afterward a curious reversal suddenly takes place
The once-willing Melissa metamorphoses into a spinsterish invalid, re
jecting Moses's tender advances as if under the spell of the chilly spirit
of Clear Haven. But a series of events destroys the power of Clear Haven
Melissa's former husband arrives and steals Justina's jewelry; an art curato
examines the castle's paintings and pronounces them forgeries; and a fir
destroys the castle, forcing Justina to move to Athens. Destruction lead
to restoration, however: with Clear Haven in ruins, Moses and Meliss
reunite.

Coverly, meanwhile, has moved with wife Betsey to Remsen Park
a jerry-built suburban development of crushing sameness. The lonely Bet
sey, desperate for friendship, soon finds a seeming friend in Josephine
Tellerman. Sadly, after a series of contretemps, she discovers otherwise
when Josephine lies to avoid attending Betsey's elaborately planned birth
day party. In despair, she undergoes a transformation similar to Melissa's,
and leaves Coverly. Left alone, Coverly suffers a series of emotional un
settlements, culminating in a relationship, never physically realized, with
a homosexual fellow worker. This triggers a crisis of sexual identity for
Coverly, who worries about metamorphosis himself. But Coverly is re
stored, as his brother was, through three events. First, he encounters the
beautiful Melissa, who re-awakens his erotic instincts and reassures him
of his heterosexuality. Second, he receives a consoling letter from his
father (to whom he had written in desperation) in which Leander admits
to a similar sexual confusion during his own youth. The letter ends with
these reflections on homosexuality, which also summarize humorously the
novel's erotic themes:

"Man is not simple. Hobgoblin company of love always with us. . . .
Life has worse trouble. Sinking ships. Houses struck by lightning.
Death of innocent children. War. Famine. Runaway horses. Cheer up
my son. You think you have trouble. Crack your skull before you weep.
All in love is not larky and fractious. Remember." (p. 251)

The third event is Betsey's return; with Eros re-established, Coverly is
content once more—and thus Part Three ends.

Part Four consists of two brief chapters which link it with the manful
challenges of Part Three. We are told that both Moses and Coverly now
have sons, and since Honora's legacy to them was contingent upon their
having male heirs, they now receive their benefices, which she grants
them readily. They tell Leander that they will buy him a boat, and he

announces to all that he is "going back to the sea." He does so, but in
unexpected fashion. After experiencing disturbing Yeatsian-like dreams of
lewdness and decrepitude, Leander surprises everyone by first going to
church, that place where "he was, more than in any other place in the
world, face to face with the bare facts of his humanity" (p. 291). He prays
fervently and notes that on the church carpet there "were a few pine or
fir needles that must have lain there all the months since Advent, and
these cheered him as if this handful of sere needles had been shaken from
the Tree of Life and reminded him of its fragrance and vitality" (p. 291).
The following day, armed with these conflicting sentiments, he takes a
trip to the sea, which throughout the novel has been a multivalent symbol
of vitality, regeneration, erotic potency, purification, and death, of origin
and return. His entry into it is likewise ambiguous:

> . . . the beach was ribbed like a dog's mouth and the movables in the
> surf splintered and crashed like the walls of Jericho. He waded out to
> his knees and wetted his wrists and forehead to prepare his circulation
> for the shock of cold water and thus avoid a heart attack. At a distance
> he seemed to be crossing himself. Then he began to swim—a sidestroke
> with his face half in the water, throwing his right arm up like the spar
> of a windmill—and he was never seen again.   (p. 292)

The final chapter recounts Leander's funeral: a church service that is,
to the family's surprise, packed with villagers; and the rite at the graveside
where Coverly, fulfilling his father's request, recites Prospero's farewell
speech: " 'Our revels now are ended. . . . We are such stuff as dreams are
made on, and our little life is rounded with a sleep' " (p. 294). Months
later Coverly and his family return for the Fourth-of-July celebration in
St. Botolphs, and in the empty house Coverly discovers a copy of Shakespeare containing a note from his father entitled "Advice to my sons."
Like Leander himself, the advice is a mixture of the practical and the
impracticable, the wise and the foolish, the erotic and the religious. It
ends this way:

> "Avoid kneeling in unheated stone churches. Ecclesiastical dampness
> causes prematurely gray hair. Fear tastes like a rusty knife and do not
> let her into your house. Courage tastes of blood. Stand up straight.
> Admire the world. Relish the love of a gentle woman. Trust in the
> Lord."   (p. 296)

CRITICISMS

Even a plot summary as lengthy as this one bears the same relationship
to The Wapshot Chronicle that an inning-by-inning score does to an exciting baseball game—that is, very little. Any summary of the novel is

hard put to capture the rich variety of style and narrative viewpoint, the imaginative resourcefulness, the delightful cast of minor characters, the marvelous ear for dialogue, the dramatic concision of individual scenes and especially the clever interweaving of narrative and dramatic strands. But perhaps most difficult to convey is the tone: no summary can capture the generous spirit of the book, its compassion and robust energy. What Cheever himself said about the book comes as no surprise to the reader:

> Literature as I see it is more a giving than a diminishment and I felt this especially with *The Chronicle*. While I was writing the book I would walk around the streets, staring into the faces of embarrassed strangers and asking myself what glad tidings could one bring them? Would they like to know that their tax returns would never be audited? Would they like some secret of sexual prowess? Would they like to know that their Redeemer liveth, that their sins were forgiven, that their lives would be long? Depending on the weather and my own humors these faces seemed at times inestimably various and beautiful and at times unregenerate and shut and I settled for a book that closed with praise of a gentle woman and The Lord God of Hosts.[7]

Much of this generous spirit is embodied in Leander, who is the novel's central character even when he is off-stage. He is the soul of the book, its animating principle, emblematic of the life force, continuity, and survival that provide its thematic shape. Leander is also the book's heart—heart as seat of erotic and noble passions in conflict—and the fitting center for a tale that traces bloodlines.

His journal counterpoints and fills out the main narrative, functioning as a kind of mirror in microcosm of the chronicle itself. His eccentric style also nicely counterpoints and complements the graceful sentences of the narrative. Being heart and soul, Leander provides entries that are both concrete and abstract, and his choppy, fragmented sentences accumulatively take on a rhetorical and poetic power hard to describe. If comparison with another poet is urged, I would suggest that he most resembles e. e. cummings (a close friend of Cheever's). Leander's style, like cummings', seems eccentric only in page type, not when read aloud. And the seeming simplicity and fragmentation of Leander's writing generate a quirky lyricism reminiscent of cummings, especially when his lines celebrate natural or sexual impulses and sensuous impressions:

> Waves roar, rattle like New York, New Haven & Hartford. Underfoot dead skates. Sea grass shaped like bull whips, flowers, petticoats. Shells, stones, sea tack. All simple things. In the golden light memories of paradise perhaps; youth, surely, innocence. On beaches the joy and

7. Cheever, Introduction to the *Time-Life* re-issue of *The Chronicle*, p. xix.

gall of perpetual youth. Even today. Smell east wind. Hear Neptune's
horn. Always raring to go. (p. 136)

Cheever has written that the inspiration for Leander's quirky journal
came from his own father. When his father died, he left him with an old
copy of Shakespeare and the beginnings of an autobiography, which dwelt
on his youth in Newburyport in the 1870's.

> As a writer I could appreciate his material but the style was antic,
> ungrammatical and I thought vulgar, and I tried again and again to
> recast his memories in an elegant and lucid prose. I was having par-
> ticular difficulties with his description of riding the first horsecar that
> traveled from Newburyport to Amesbury. "Sturgeon on river then," he
> had written. "About three feet long. All covered with knobs. Leap
> straight up in air and fall back in water. Hold the reins and see the
> sturgeon leap. Boyish happiness!" [This entry is quoted verbatim on
> page 97 of the novel.] Having revised these lines as Gide might have
> written them, I realized that my father was a better writer than I, and
> using his style I went on then to invent a character and a life that
> would have gratified him.[8]

Cheever's admission raises again those two issues raised earlier: the
connection between fiction and biography, and the question of whether
The Chronicle can be designated a novel. The first issue I blithely dismissed, but the second I cannot avoid, because it is a constant in Cheever
criticism. The original reviewers and subsequent critics were unanimous
in their praise of Leander and his journal and of the narrative's style, but
because of the episodic plot (its segmentation ironically exacerbated by
Leander's intrusions), their praise for its overall structure was reserved.

One reviewer went so far as to classify it as a prose Spoon River
Anthology that does not "really wind up as a novel."[9] Similarly, Maxwell
Geismar stated that the first and second halves don't hang together, that
"one has the final impression of a series of related 'sketches,' which do
not quite achieve the impact of the short story proper or the inner growth
and development of a novel."[10] Carlos Baker offered equally representative but more thoughtful criticism in his review:

> As readers of his short stories know, [Cheever] is a wonder with the
> limited scene, the separate episode, the overheard conversation, the

8. Cheever, Introduction to the Time-Life re-issue of The Chronicle, p. xvii.
9. Ernest Kirsten, "Twilight in New England," St. Louis Post-Dispatch, April 28,
1957, p. 4. For a listing and fine capsule quotations from this novel's reviews, see
Francis J. Boscha, John Cheever: A Reference Guide (Boston: G. K. Hall, 1981), pp. 18ff.
10. Maxwell Geismar, "End of the Line," New York Times Book Review, March 24,
1957, p. 5.

crucial confrontation. *The Wapshot Chronicle* reflects these powers with immense vitality, largesse, and profusion. But it is held together largely by spit and wire. It shows that while John Cheever's fortes are many, amusing, touching, and admirable, one of them is not architectonics.[11]

These and like criticisms are, frankly, irrefutable on their own terms. The word "architectonics" is itself a descriptive metaphor, of course, but nonetheless its usage subtly betrays the assumption that the structural design of something mechanical and palpable like a building is a legitimate comparison for the desirable shape of a novel. More often critics employ the metaphor of an organism when discrediting a novel for its lack of unity (as Geismar's review exemplifies). This metaphor, popular since Coleridge and canonized by the New Critics, implies that "organic" unity, the interanimation of parts and their relation to the whole, better reflects the aesthetic ideal. The organic metaphor generally issues in more salutary criteria for criticism than does the architectural metaphor—especially in a discussion of poetry. But it is too rigid a model to apply to the sprawl of most lengthy novels (and epic poems as well), and those who champion it inevitably are forced to tiptoe around the evident truth that even the finest "organic" novels have dead spots.

All of this is a tendentious preliminary for saying that few of our critical touchstones, if rigidly and not flexibly applied, offer much help in appreciating an unusual novel like *The Wapshot Chronicle*, tending, as they do, to misdirect us from its richness. That said, Cheever himself provided another model for exploration in the prelude to a story he wrote in 1974. There he said:

> The obsolescence of linear narrative, in a world distinguished by its curvatures, sometimes forces one into discourse. We can all write a storm at sea and that chase through a mountain pass (at dusk), but there is, it seems to me, some inner form that transcends suspense and the furniture of a novel.[12]

Unfortunately, Cheever does not elucidate further, but the phrase "inner form" is piquant. On the face of it the words "inner" and "form" appear contradictory, but in combination they do suggest a more complex intention and process than the more easily observable "furniture" of narrative.

Earlier I argued that the unity of Cheever's later fiction is arrived at through the narrative *voice*, that instrument which reflects the narrative's consciousness and is the controlling center of dramatic, emotional, and

11. Carlos Baker, "Yankee Gallimaufry," *Saturday Review*, March 23, 1957, p. 14.

12. John Cheever, "The Leaves, the Lion-Fish and the Bear," *Esquire*, 82 (November 1974), 110.

moral awareness. As such, the voice provides the "inner form" transcending the narrative (to use Cheever's words), and thus functions as a principle of unity in the way that a poet's voice does in poetry.

For example, anyone reading Eliot's *The Waste Land* for the first time is hard put to summarize it. Ostensibly it lacks unity, being as it is a pastiche of differing voices, allusions, snippets of overheard conversations, scene sketches, and lyric intrusions (all of which is true of *The Wapshot Chronicle*, one might add). Yet on rereading the poem with care and attention, one realizes that "these fragments I have shored against my ruins" are interrelated, but only through the poet's voice, the verbal equivalent for his shifting consciousness and passionate sensibility. It is not the "furniture" of the narrative but the "appraiser's" inflections that are meant to hold our attention. The challenge for a poetic writer is to establish that controlling voice indicative of his consciousness and sensibility; if he succeeds, he is free to beguile us with different accents and tonalities, for then variations on "outer form" become not a distraction but a delight for the reader. If the critic is still anxious to apply an "organic" standard in such an instance, he will emphasize the *vitality* of the voice that pervades the work rather than another aspect of coherence.

In this connection Cheever offered a revealing statement worth reconsidering when he said, "Narrative is a synonym for life—for a chain of lives. Forms are evolved by the societies they serve, and narrative should reflect the exaltations, the discursiveness, the spontaneity and the pratfalls one finds in a day."[13] The implication is clear: since life's events are haphazard, since the chains of lives are often, alas, disconnected through happenstance, then the ideal of narrative coherence is a slippery touchstone for the art of the novel, that genre which purports to record life's abundant truths.

A READING

But example is better than argument. The long opening paragraph is the best place to start:

> St. Botolphs was an *old* place, an old river town. It had been an inland port in the *great* days of the Massachusetts sailing fleets and *now* it was left with a factory that manufactured table silver and a few other *small* industries. The natives did not *consider* that it had diminished much in size *or* importance, *but* the long roster of the Civil War *dead,* bolted to the cannon on the green, was a reminder of how populous the village had been in the 1860's. St. Botolphs *would never* muster as

13. Cheever, Introduction to the *Time-Life* re-issue of *The Chronicle,* p. xix.

many soldiers again. The *green* was shaded by a few great elms and loosely enclosed by a square of store fronts. The Cartwright Block, which made the western wall of the square, had along the front of its second story a row of lancet windows, *as delicate and reproachful as the windows of a church.* Behind these windows were the offices of the Eastern Star, Dr. Bulstrode the dentist, the telephone company and the insurance agent. The *smells* of these offices—the smell of dental preparations, floor oil, spittoons and coal gas—mingled in the downstairs hallway like *an aroma of the past.* In a drilling *autumn* rain, in a *world of much change,* the green at St. Botolphs conveyed an *impression* of *unusual* permanence. On Independence Day in the morning, when the *parade* had begun to form, the place *looked* prosperous and festive.   (p. 5; italics mine)

The novel opens as a chronicle should, for immediately we are provided with information and a historical perspective, established in the first four sentences by way of contrasting the present with the past. The reader is introduced to the town in a casual and cinematic way, as though a camera allied with a voice-over was panning the scene. The narrator's tone, however, is not uniform: it moves subtly from the matter-of-fact to the elegiac, the wistful, the humorous and ironic, and on to a blending of these tones by the paragraph's end.

I have italicized certain words to point up how the narrator's flexible voice is established. The words "old" and "great" suggest a standard opposite to "now" and "small," one which any observer would presumably accept. This "objective" perspective then shifts to the subjective, noting that the "natives" did not "consider" the town to have diminished much in size "or" importance (as if these were identical), "but" the "dead" offer more honest testimony. Suddenly the reader is alerted to the possibility that what is being introduced is an ironic contrast—not merely a factual one—between past and present, objective and subjective. This narrator seems to know more about what he is describing, and the offhand statement that the town "would never" muster as many soldiers again confirms our growing suspicions. Consequently, we gradually find his voice at once reassuring and unsettling, especially the latter when we hear the surprising description of the store windows—"as delicate and reproachful as the windows of a church." Why include this mixed impression unless it adumbrates contrary religious feelings in the story that follows? And why stress that the smells of the offices are "like an aroma of the past" save for a similar reason? Why mention, if not for this purpose, "autumn rain" in summertime, or the fact that only an "impression of unusual permanence" is conveyed by all this? The narrator has us hooked, so he can gracefully conclude with the matter-of-fact and the upbeat, slyly insinuating, how-

ever, that this is merely the way St. Botolphs "looked" years ago on the
Fourth of July.

Our introduction to the Wapshot family is similarly handled. We meet
Coverly, who "was sixteen or seventeen then" (which? does the narrator
know?) and had a long neck "with a ministerial dip to his head and a bad
habit of cracking his knuckles," but we are also pointedly told that he
possessed "an alert and a sentimental mind" (p. 6). His brother Moses,
of college age, "had reached the summit of his physical maturity and had
emerged with the gift of judicious and tranquil self-admiration" (p. 6).
Their mother, Mrs. Sarah Wapshot, founder of the Woman's Club, is
discovered atop a parade float, and we are informed that in her traditional
appearance there she appeared to the townspeople "exactly like those
religious images that are carried through the streets of Boston's north end
in the autumn to quiet great storms at sea" (p. 7). We begin to wonder
whether she might be like a religious icon in more ways than one. Soon
we come upon Leander, father and husband, at the helm of his ferryboat
Topaze. We learn that the "Topaze seemed to be his creation; she seemed
to mirror his taste for romance and nonsense, his love of the seaside girls
and the long, foolish, brine-smelling summer days" (p. 7).

Nimbly the narrator has introduced us to the central characters by
way of concise, ironically perceptive portraits that will later be dramatized
as accurate. In like fashion, he describes the central events of that day,
the parade and the ferry's crossing—a description that contains in kernel
form the significant leitmotifs and mix of symbols proper to the subsequent
narrative.

The narrator first juxtaposes the trip of the *Topaze* with the progress
of the parade float, both ersatz emblems for travel—the novel's major
theme. We are told that the *Topaze* was "an unseaworthy hulk that moved
. . . her bones shaking so wildly at each change of speed that the paint
flaked off her hull. But the voyage seemed to Leander, from his place at
the helm, glorious and sad. The timbers of the old launch seemed held
together by the brilliance and transitoriness of summer and she smelled
of summery refuse . . ." (pp. 7-8). When the boat would near the shore
of the Nangasakit recreation land, we learn that Leander used to shout,
" 'Tie me to the mast, Perimedes,' when he heard the merry-go-round"
(p. 8). We are given only comical information here, but its allusion to
sirens and a passionate Odysseus, prey to erotic torments but equally
smitten with nostalgia, who longs for a faithful Penelope at the voyage's
end, prepares us for the motifs to follow.

Simultaneously, on land "the parade picked up its scattered bones and
moved" (p. 8). This image of bones not only links the parade nicely with
the "shaking bones" of the *Topaze*, but also is an appropriate symbol for

a family chronicle that records the adventures of the dead and the erotic
stirrings of its surviving males: bones suggest well the confluence of vital
movement, arousal, decay, and death. But if the *Topaze* suggests a ship
of fools, the parade is a tableau, a historical pageant complete with a
sweating descendant of Priscilla Aiden in a heavy wig; like the ferry's trip,
its voyage is also glorious and sad. Furthermore, here the romantic references to water and siren-enchantment are upended and domesticated:

> Then came Mrs. Wapshot, standing at her lectern, a woman of forty
> whose fine skin and clear features could be counted among her organ-
> izational gifts. She was beautiful but when she tasted the water from
> the glass on her lectern she smiled sadly as if it were bitter for, in spite
> of her civic zeal, she had a taste for melancholy—for the smell of
> orange rinds and wood smoke—that was extraordinary. She was more
> admired among the ladies than the men and the essence of her beauty
> may have been disenchantment (Leander had deceived her) but she
> had brought all the resources of her sex to his infidelity and had been
> rewarded with such an air of wronged nobility and luminous vision
> that some of her advocates sighed as she passed through the square as
> if they saw in her face a life passing by.   (p. 9)

At this point the narrator intrudes to tell us that amid this celebration
of America's patriotic past, "some hoodlum—it must have been one of
the foreigners who lived across the river—set off a firecracker under the
rump of Mr. Pincher's old mare and she bolted" (p. 9), disrupting the
parade and carrying the float of the Woman's Club off in a different
direction. The later theme of alienation and "strangers" is here comically
introduced, but we are assured that the unexpected is, for the Wapshots,
destiny, and St. Botolphs nurtures a hardy breed. This first chapter ends
with a reflection that characterizes the novel's final chapter as well. What's
more, it contains a variation on the novel's last line, "Trust in the Lord,"
and closes with a hint that leave-taking in the town is continuous and
inevitable:

> . . . none of the ladies of the Woman's Club was cowardly or foolish
> and they took a firm hold on some nonportable part of the wagon and
> trusted in the Lord. Hill Street was then a dirt road and that being a
> dry summer the horse's hoofs beat up such a pillar of dust that in a few
> minutes the float was gone.   (pp. 9-10)

The second chapter begins the chronicle proper, and is written in
parody of the Chronicles in the Old Testament. Throughout we trace the
series of "begats" that generated the Wapshots all the way back to the
Norman Conquest. Unlike the writer of the biblical chronicles, however,
the narrator cannot resist emphatic insertions or offhand comments that

ruefully connect the family tree with its more recent buds. For example, we learn that it was Ezekiel Wapshot, the first emigré from England in 1630, who established "a family tradition of thoughtful regret that would—three hundred years later—chaff Leander and his sons" (p. 10). This casual insertion is portentous, as is the description of Benjamin Wapshot, an early forebear whose "largest propensities were amativeness, excitability and self-esteem," and who "showed no signs of marvelousness, piety and veneration" (p. 11).

Benjamin's story is recorded at length by his son Lorenzo in his journal, a journal that betrays concerns similar to Leander's later on. Lorenzo describes the awaited return of his father on the second *Topaze* (his grandfather was captain of the first), a return from Samoa anticipated sorrowfully by his family because of rumors about Benjamin's "addiction to immoral practices, viz. drinking intemperately and indulging in lewdness with the natives" (p. 14). Lorenzo describes his family's reaction: "Mother and sisters drinking rum punch. . . . It is Marshman's tale of Samoa that has undone them but they should not judge the absent unkindly nor forget that the flesh lusteth contrary to the spirit" (p. 14). Such lofty sentiments are not shared by the ladies, however: they meet the *Topaze* when it docks only to beat Benjamin with their umbrellas as he descends the gangplank. The narrator then informs us that it was Lorenzo who left the family wealth to Leander's Cousin Honora, and this information brings us back to the events of the opening chapter.

After this historic interpolation, which functions on several levels, the third chapter returns to the Woman's Club float subsequent to the events of Chapter One. Here the narrative voice becomes that of a tour guide, who describes a different kind of parade, one in which the landscape and the townspeople, not the paraders, are on display. At one point, however, the narrator artfully inserts a series of reflections that a "visitor" who *was* a resident but is *now* a stranger might make. These observations, posed as throw-away questions, suggest multiple ironies, so that when we hear the narrator assert that "it did not matter" and "it did not change" very much, we suspect otherwise. From the opening sentence, sentiment and irony, romantic nostalgia and anti-romantic actuality are conjoined:

> But it was difficult, from the summit of Wapshot Hill, not to spread over the village the rich, dark varnish of decorum and quaintness—to do this or to lament the decadence of a once boisterous port. . . . There was beauty below them, inarguable and unique—many fine things built for the contentment of hardy men—and there was decadence—more ships in bottles than on the water—but why grieve over this? Looking back at the village we might put ourselves into the shoes

of a native son (with a wife and family in Cleveland) coming home
for some purpose—a legacy or a set of Hawthorne or a football sweater—
and swinging through the streets in good weather. What would it
matter that the blacksmith shop was now an art school? Our friend
from Cleveland might observe, passing through the square at dusk,
that this decline or change in spirit had not altered his own humanity
and that whatever he was . . . it did not matter whether or not his
way was lighted by the twinkling candles in tearooms; it did not change
what he was.

But our friend from Cleveland was only a visitor—he would go
away, and Mr. Pincher and his passengers would not.   (p. 18)

In a most disarming way this paragraph introduces the novel's major
conflicts and its complex of attitudes. The details selected—"more ships
in bottles than on the water," the art school, the tearooms—indicate the
transformation of the old town "built for the contentment of hardy men"
into the seemingly emasculated modern world. This is the world of displacement in which Coverly and Moses must seek their fortunes, and
both on return will be like the stranger from Cleveland, alienated from
the old town and puzzled about their own identities. Thus the question
"Why grieve over this?" is double-edged, at once rhetorical and hinting
at dark answers. These ominous and complex sentiments are re-introduced
at the chapter's close:

The air smelled of brine—the east wind was rising—and would presently give to the place a purpose and a luster and a sadness too, for
while the ladies admired the houses and the elms they knew that their
sons would go away. Why did the young want to go away? Why did
the young want to go away?   (p. 22)

As if in answer to that question, the first two words of Chapter Four
are "Rosalie Young." Critics who complain of the novel's episodic structure
usually cite Rosalie's sudden appearance and rather abrupt departure as an
example of a character being introduced only to further the action, an
arbitrary contrivance at best. But closer examination reveals otherwise.
First of all, Rosalie functions as an emotional counterpart of both Coverly
and Moses and of their wives as well, and her erotic confusions anticipate
theirs. We are told that "it was always difficult for a stranger to guess
Rosalie's destination, she approached each journey with such great expectations," and that "she was never disappointed nor was she ever dis-
abused . . . nor did she ever seem to reach a point where these differences
challenged or altered her expectations" (p. 23). Secondly, Rosalie's experiences introduce, from a female perspective, several of the novel's multivalent symbols. She and her unidentified lover travel to the beach,

where "the Atlantic Ocean . . . seems there, held in the islands of a sinking coast, to be a virile and a sad presence":

> Thousands of half-naked bathers obscured the beach or hesitated knee deep in the ocean as if this water, like the Ganges, were purifying and holy so that these displaced and naked crowds, strung for miles along the coast, gave to this holiday and carnival surface the undercurrents of a pilgrimage. . . .   (p. 24)

In this description and the day's events that follow it, the religious and the sexual are briefly conjoined. Stimulated by the water's coldness, Rosalie makes love on the shore "to take the only marriage of her body to its memories that she knew" (p. 26). As the tide recedes in the twilight, her companion itches for a repetition; but, with the return of the pleasure boats and the imminent darkness of night, she "was weary of trying to separate the power of loneliness from the power of love . . ." (p. 27). By contrast, her boyfriend "was staring out to sea. Lechery sat like worry on his thin face. He saw the leonine reefs in the sea like clavicles and women's knees" (p. 27).

This multivalent water world, reminiscent of the watery chaos in Genesis, seems but an interlude, for we are suddenly introduced in Chapter Five to the garden world of West Farm, the house of the Wapshots, at nightfall. The narrator seems tongue-tied to capture its paradisaical serenity "as we see the Wapshots, spread out in their rose garden above the river, listening to the parrot and feeling the balm of those evening winds that, in New England, smell so of maidenly things . . ." (p. 29). Instead, as if by contrast, he relates what Aunt Adelaide Forbes has to say. The widow Adelaide's tale is typically Cheeveresque: humane and hilarious, bawdy and beatific. To some it might appear a brief sketch unrelated to theme or action, but not so. In fact, it proleptically capsulates in comic fashion the similar erotic discoveries in a "garden" that will effect (and in the past has effected) the transitions that will punctuate the rest of the chronicle.

Aunt Adelaide recounts how the day before, while pulling carrots, she pulled up this "very unusual carrot":

> "Well, this carrot looked like—I don't know how to say it—this carrot was the spit and image of Mr. Forbes' parts." Blood rushed to her face but modesty would not halt nor even delay her progress. Sarah Wapshot smiled seraphically at the twilight. "Well, I took the other carrots into the kitchen for my supper," Aunt Adelaide said, "and I wrapped this unusual carrot up in a piece of paper and took it right over to Reba Heaslip. She's such an old maid I thought she'd be interested. She was in the kitchen so I give her this carrot. That's what it looks like, Reba, I said. That's just what it looks like."   (p. 30)

Shortly thereafter, at the moment (significantly) when the family is discussing "the freshwater inlet," Rosalie's accident occurs nearby, and the serenity of the Wapshots' garden world is forever shattered by a related, though different, discovery.

The next chapter abruptly leaves the scene and introduces us to Cousin Honora. In a sense she is Leander's twin, the most marvelous character in the book, for she, like him, is generous and stubborn, quixotic and hard-headed, foolish and wise. But Chapter Six is not merely a delightful character sketch; it also contains in abbreviated form the narrative shape of the novel and its major motifs. The chapter opens with a chronicle of Honora's own life, within which the narrator inserts the sly apology that "she had never subjected herself to the discipline of continuousness" (p. 36). (Has this chronicle?) Then, sensing that any formal historical approach is inadequate to his purposes, the narrator concedes that "the best way to understand her is to watch her during the course of a day" (p. 37). The words "the best way" are replete with ironic overtones, and the device of the present tense throughout reinforces them.

This mini-chronicle opens with Honora being awakened by the whistle of the 7:18 train, which "she mistakes . . . for the trumpeting of an angel. She is very religious and has joined with enthusiasm and parted with bitterness from nearly every religious organization in Travertine and St. Botolphs" (pp. 37-38). After her breakfast, we follow her into her garden, where she works until mid-morning; then she steals away and takes a bus to Travertine. Once there, she slips into a movie theatre showing *Rose of the West,* and inside "she suffers all the abrasive sensations of someone forced into moral uncleanliness. . . . It is wrong, she knows, to go into a dark place when the world outside shines with light. It is wrong and she is a miserable sinner" (p. 41).

But she sits through the movie twice. As she leaves, feeling "weary and sad like any sinner" (p. 42), she slips and falls in the lobby on her way to the sidewalk. Others rush to the aid of the fallen old woman, but she asks to be left alone and gets to her feet unaided. When she returns home it is twilight, and as she approaches her house in the half-dark she overhears Maggie, her cook, imitating her for the comic delight of Maggie's sister.

> Honora walks past the window on the soft grass but they have not heard her; they are laughing too loudly. Halfway down the house she stops and leans heavily, with both hands, on her cane, engrossed in an emotion so violent and so nameless that she wonders if this feeling of loneliness and bewilderment is not the mysteriousness of life. Poignance seems to drench her until her knees are weak and she yearns so earnestly for understanding that she raises her head and says half a

prayer. Then she gathers her forces, enters the front door and calls cheerfully down the hall, "It's me, Maggie." (p. 44)

This account of Honora's day portends the narrative curve of the entire chronicle (recall Cheever's remark on narrative form, quoted earlier, that it ought to reflect the varied experience of a common day). It begins in a garden world and involves travel linked with the sea (Honora buys lobsters on the bus trip); it reaches a turning point when *Rose of the West*, which triggers Honora's mixed feelings of desire and guilt, is the point of concentration. Throughout the novel, the color rose and the flower rose are symbolic of the sexual and erotic. (Rosalie's name and person in Part One and the symbolic gesture of Coverly's placing the rose on his sleeping wife after their reunion at the end of Part Three frame the rose symbolism in between.) Honora's encounter with a "Rose" from the West precipitates a slip and a fall, a plunge among strangers. Her return home generates the realization that she is an "outsider," and she wonders whether "this feeling of loneliness and bewilderment is not the mysteriousness of life" (p. 44). But she regathers her strength through gestures like half-prayers, and acceptance of herself and her place in the world is a sign of renewal and affirmation in the face of sadness. Thus the chronicle of Honora's day, though it first appears haphazard, is in fact representative, the central thread interweaving the crazy-quilt careers of the surviving Wapshots.

It is fitting, then, that Honora's will provokes the crisis that shapes the rest of the story. It stipulates that Moses and Coverly, as "the last of the Wapshots," would divide her fortune between them, "contingent upon their having male heirs" (p. 51). A restriction like this is hardly inappropriate in a chronicle intent on "begats," but, more significantly, it provides the impetus for an exploration of the modern meaning of the two words "male" and "heir," which, in conjunction, become the thematic concern of the rest of the narrative. In addition, it provokes a collision between the "rights" of Honora and her sex and the "rites" of Leander and his, initiating another major theme.

In the eighth chapter these contests are joined, and the two-fold exploration begins. We are informed that "Leander would never take his sons aside and speak to them about the facts of life" because "it was his feeling that love, death and fornication extracted from the rich green soup of life were no better than half-truths, and his course of instruction was general. He would like them to grasp that the unobserved ceremoniousness of his life was a gesture or sacrament toward the excellence and the continuousness of things" (p. 52).

A fishing trip in remote Canada is the grand sacramental gesture, the rite of initiation that Leander devises for both his sons. Moses, the first to go with him, is exhilarated when they reach the mountains: "Coming up into a pass Moses raised his head cheerfully to the voluptuous line of the mountains, the illusory blue, thunderous and deep, but the loud noise of wind in the bare trees reminded him of the gentle valley they had left that morning . . ." (p. 54). The reason for his emotional ambivalence soon becomes clearer: the mountains represent the male world, and the valley the female; and though drawn to the strenuous claims of the mountains, Moses realizes now "how deep his commitment to the gentle parochialism of the valley was" (p. 56).

Very late in the novel these themes and images recur, recapitulating deftly a woman's similar experience and highlighting the "distances" between the sexes:

> Now Moses knew that if we grant men vestigial sexual rites . . . there must be duplicate rites and ceremonies for the opposite sex. By this Moses did not mean the ability to metamorphose swiftly, but something else, linked perhaps to the power beautiful women have of evoking landscapes—a sense of rueful distance—as if their eyes had come to rest on a horizon that had never been seen by any man. There was some physical evidence for this—their voices softened and the pupils of their eyes dilated, and they seemed to be recollecting some distaff voyage over distaff waters to a walled island where they were committed by the nature of their minds and their organs to some secret rites that would refresh their charming and creative stores of sadness.   (p. 275)

Coverly's trip with his father makes these contrasts starker still. Before he leaves, his mother puts a cookbook into his pack. When they are deep in the mountains, Leander discovers Coverly reading the cookbook and roars, " 'Goddam it to hell,' " and throws it out, "feeling once more—Icarus, Icarus—as if the boy had fallen away from his heart" (p. 59). Coverly realizes that "he had profaned the mysterious rites of virility and had failed whole generations of future Wapshots . . ." (p. 59).

But later Coverly undergoes another rite of initiation when he and his father cross the waters on the *Topaze* to attend the burlesque cootch show at the fair. The pitchman is perceived as the devil, a serpent speaking from a "red pulpit," but both enter the tent where "the rites of Dionysus were proceeding" (p. 62). Inside, biblical rituals are inverted. "A splintered tent post served for the symbol on the plate—that holy of holies—but this salute to the deep well of erotic power was step by step as old as man" (p. 62). Coverly is "rapt" by the sight of the naked girls but walks out of the tent in confusion when one of them does "something very dirty" (p. 62).

Nonetheless, he has crossed the border from innocence to experience, to a different understanding of mountain and valley worlds, for memory of the girl torments his dreams. The next morning he attempts two rituals of purification: after "looking up and down the cold, fog-hung valley" he dives into the river for a swim and emerges "wondering if the joy of life was in him"; and later he attends church, where, though strenuous at prayer, he is battered by erotic desire, aware now that "the literal body of Christ Church was no mighty fortress" (p. 64). Neither ritual has worked, so he resolves to return to the fairground, the place where the girl had gone through her rites, and there pay for her sexual services. But he does so only to discover that the fair is closed.

These incidents foreshadow Coverly's later frustrations in his pursuit of the meaning of "maleness." Ironically, through these efforts, he establishes himself as the true Wapshot "heir," wresting, like a Jacob, the legitimate birthright from his hairier brother Moses, who achieves masculinity early on but inherits little else of the Wapshot's bountiful legacy.

For, meanwhile, his brother Moses has already united the mountain with the valley worlds in ironic fashion. His sexual experience, as it is described, re-enacts and is replete with the religious and biblical overtones of Coverly's adventure. It occurs on the morning that Moses decides to go fishing in a stream below Parson's Pond near his home. As he approaches it he hears "the noise of the water—like the garbled voices of prophets," and "his heart seemed to rise" (p. 69). When he wades deep into the pool, his crotch gets wet—"a blessing, he thought, hoping that the cold water would discourage his mind from ever leaving such simple pleasures" (p. 70).

There follows one of the most magnificent sections in all of Cheever's fiction. The accuracy of detail and of kinesthetic sensation charges the scene with realistic power, an exuberance at the wonder of nature that the reader shares instinctively. But beneath the descriptive surface, the scene also resonates with symbolic sexual allusions (the Edenesque firs and wild apple trees, the mention of "whole families" of wild trout, the banks of wild "roses," the brief "flood of golden light," Moses' fishing rod bent, then taut, his catch of a fish with "rosy" spots). These represent Moses' (and Coverly's) mandated task as male heirs, and resonate with "garbled voices" of prophecies to come:

> The granite around the pool was square, like quarry stone, the water was black and slow-moving, overhung here and there were fir and wild apple, and although Moses knew that it was a pool where he wasted his time he could not convince himself that it was not inhabited by trout—whole families of shrewd two-pounders with undershot jaws. From this dark pool he waded through white water again to a place

with meadowy banks where Turk's-cap lilies and wild roses grew and
where it was easy to cast. While he was fishing this pool the sun came
up and out—a flood of golden light that spread all through the woods
and sank into the water so that every blue stone and white pebble
showed—flooded the water with light until it was as golden as bourbon
whisky—and the instant this happened he got a strike. His footing
was bad. He nearly fell down, swearing loudly, but his rod was bent
and then the trout surfaced with a crash and made for the logs at the
mouth of the pool, but Moses kept him away from these, the fish
zooming this way and that and the thrill of its life shooting up into
Moses' arms and shoulders. Then, as the fish tired and he got out his
landing net, he thought: What a life; what a grand life! He admired
the rosy spots on the fish, broke its back and wrapped it in fern, ready
now for a big day, a day in which he would catch his limit or
over.   (p. 70)

That last sentence becomes ironic in the context, for shortly thereafter, Moses, though "not insensitive to . . . the loud, prophetic noise of
water" (p. 70), looks down to the pool below him (the hint of a valley?)
and sees the naked Rosalie sunning herself (the golden light) on a rock.
Moses' reaction is described in classically pagan and biblical (from the
Prophet Daniel) allusions: "He watched his gleaming Susanna, shame-
faced, his dream of simple pleasure replaced by some sadness, some heav-
iness that seemed to make his mouth taste of blood and his teeth ache"
(p. 71). Reminiscent of Coverly's experience at the cootch show, this
sight betokens pursuit of complex, not simple, pleasures in his future:

His head was confused and the smell of the dead trout in his pocket
seemed like something from his past. He unwrapped the fish and washed
it in the running water, but it looked like a toy.   (p. 71)

In a sense, Moses has at this point already left the mountain world
of Leander forever. What follows confirms this. He invites Rosalie for a
sailboat trip, and her thoughts recapitulate and reunite the imagery thus
far, this time from a woman's perspective:

. . . dependent mostly upon men for her knowledge and guidance, she
had found them all set on some mysterious pilgrimage that often put
her life into danger. She had known a man who liked to climb mountains and as the *Tern* heeled over and shipped another sea she remembered her mountain-climbing lover, the crusts of fatigue in her mouth,
the soreness of her feet, the dry sandwiches and the misty blue view
from the summits that only raised in her mind the question of what
she was doing there.   (p. 72)

An accident then occurs: a line breaks and the *Tern* begins to drift
out to the open sea; Moses swims to shore and returns to rescue Rosalie

in another boat. When they return to West Farm, a second more serious accident befalls them: Cousin Honora, who spent the day hooking a rug with the pattern of "a field of red roses," is waiting in the closet when the two of them mount the stairs to Rosalie's room—when Moses' question to Rosalie, " 'What harm can there be in something that would make us both feel so good?' " (p. 73), is answered.

These opening chapters in Part One thus establish the "inner form" of the subsequent structure to the events recounted throughout the rest of the chronicle. One might say that Cheever's creative challenge hereafter was akin to what the narrator describes as Coverly's task after he arrives in New York to seek his fortune:

> To create or build some kind of bridge between Leander's world and that world where he sought his fortune seemed to Coverly a piece of work that would take strength and perseverance. The difference between the sweet-smelling farmhouse and the room where he lived was abysmal. They seemed to have come from the hands of different creators and to deny one another.   (p. 114)

Perhaps this last sentence would summarize nicely the complaints of those who find The Wapshot Chronicle disjointed, halved, unbridged. I prefer to concentrate instead on the ambiguous word "seemed," convinced that the bridge's supports are in fact secure on either side. To worry the metaphor a bit, let us say that the narrator's voice functions like a swivel bridge, occasionally rotating, stopping traffic at times and then reconnecting the flow, but—though seemingly separate like the swivel section—very much the control center, regulating congestion and movement. The cables and stays that reach out from either bank—St. Botolphs and the suburbs of the modern world—are the mechanisms of symbol and imagery that support the overarching themes.

A reader alert to connectives soon discovers a balance and proportion to the whole novel. Numerous events, for example, recall and reinforce one another. Leander's separation from his brother Hamlet and his father counterpoint the destiny of his sons; Honora's dream-like lewd vision (pp. 74-75) parallels Leander's obscene dream (pp. 290-291); Coverly's genealogical summary for the psychologist (p. 120) is a parody of Chapter Two; Coverly's stay on Island 93 in the South Pacific is the prosaic modern equivalent of the more poetic Wapshot adventures in Samoa a century before; Betsey as "a Venus from the sea" (p. 150) reminds us of Moses' meetings with Rosalie; Cousin Justina, who collects European artifacts, is the counterpart of Cousin Mildred's husband Harry, who " 'doesn't have anything nice to remember and so he borrows other people's memories' " (p. 116); Moses on the roof of Clear Haven recalls a different kind of mountain-climbing in his youth; Coverly, the boy humiliated by a cookbook, finds his wife attacked in the kitchen by a man condemned by his "wandering hands" (p. 231); Coverly's confusion over his homosexual stirrings parallels Melissa's metamorphosis into a spinster, and both are redeemed by rejecting sterility and death and opting for life's continuity; Betsey and Helen Rutherford are orphan-counterparts, the one possessing "the touching qualities of a wanderer" (p. 157), the other that of a "pilgrim" set upon by dogs (pp. 169-170); finally, Coverly's reverie about a "School of Love" (pp. 245-246) is, in fact, a comic resumé of the novel's whole narrative.

Interwoven with these events in balance are the recurring images and symbols—the sea, mountains, paradisaical green, the color and the flower rose, shelters and exposure—which subtly combine the religious and the erotic, the Christian and the pagan throughout. Leander best exemplifies the series of transfigurations the other characters undergo less obviously than he: by turns he is Odysseus, Neptune, an Old-Testament patriarch, Lear, Timon, Hamlet's father, and Prospero. Heroic stature aside, we also learn "what a tender thing, then, is a man. How, for all his crotch-hitching and swagger, a whisper can turn his soul into a cinder" (p. 195).

The entire novel is about the mystery of transformation, and everyone in it undergoes some temporary or permanent metamorphosis. The reader is not so surprised, therefore, that at the novel's end Honora, "with the ardor of a pilgrim" (p. 294), goes to Red Sox games, and that her shouted plea there is " 'Sacrifice, you booby, *sacrifice!*' " (p. 295)—this also capsulates what *The Wapshot Chronicle* is all about. The themes of duty, ceremony, familial piety, and tradition—those steadfast virtues—are precisely those important to pilgrims. Yet, being pilgrims, they must ever remain strangers and aliens at heart, confronting the loneliness of displacement, wandering the mysterious, labyrinthine paths paved by Eros and Thanatos, all the while trusting in the Lord.

Love and scandal are the best sweeteners of tea.

Henry Fielding

I think not that the novel has been overwhelmed by the complexities of contemporary life; I think that the novel is the only art form we possess that has approached any mastery of this storm. . . .

John Cheever

Bring me a handful of dust from a house where no one has died.

Gautama Buddha

There is nothing the matter with Americans, except their ideals.

G. K. Chesterton

I loved not yet, yet I loved to love . . . I sought what I might love, in love with loving.

Saint Augustine

No one has ever seen God; but as long as we love one another God will live in us and His love will be complete in us.

Saint John

Have I not remembered Thee in my bed: and thought upon Thee when I was waking?

The Book of Common Prayer

5: The
Wapshot Scandal

The *Wapshot Scandal*, the sequel to *The Wapshot Chronicle*, was published in 1964, and it brought Cheever considerable notoriety. He found himself on the cover of *Time* magazine, not photographed but drawn like an El Greco figure, and the object of a perceptive essay entitled "Ovid in Ossining." Now a celebrity of sorts, he was sought after as a sage on things literary, a role he assiduously avoided. The novel itself later won the 1965 William Dean Howells Award, presented by the American Academy of Arts and Letters, for the best work of fiction in the 1960-65 period.

Despite these and other encomia, *The Wapshot Scandal* was not unanimously well-received by the tastemakers among critics, and those who did enjoy it often pronounced it inferior to *The Chronicle*. The unhappier critics rehearsed all the familiar objections to a Cheever novel. For example, Hilary Corke in his review for the *New Republic* faulted it for its "carelessness and looseness of construction" and its "bouts of arrant sentimentality," and found it a compilation of "contradictory episodes" connected with "decorative tinsel."[1] Stanley Edgar Hyman, after sounding similar notes, closed his review in exasperation:

> When a highly esteemed short story writer tries a novel and fails at it, in this amazing country, he is rewarded just as though he had succeeded. . . . Cheever's *The Wapshot Chronicle* won the National Book Award. In *The Wapshot Scandal*, Cheever has tried again, and again failed to make short-story material jell as a novel. As a two-time loser, he can probably expect the Pulitzer Prize.[2]

1. Hilary Corke, "Sugary Days in St. Botolphs," *New Republic*, January 25, 1964, pp. 19-21. For summary comments of other reviews, see Francis J. Boscha, *John Cheever: A Reference Guide* (Boston: G. K. Hall, 1981), pp. 34ff. Lest my remarks mislead the reader, I should make clear that the novel was very well received by the reviewers in *Newsweek*, the *Atlantic Monthly*, *Harper's*, *National Review*, *Commonweal*, *Saturday Review*, and the *New York Times Book Review*. Nonetheless, despite this positive reaction, the misgivings mentioned were all at least tentatively raised.

2. Stanley Edgar Hyman, "John Cheever's Golden Egg," *New Leader*, February 3, 1964, pp. 23-24.

It is not surprising that in the face of such heavy critical hitters *The Wapshot Scandal* was not even nominated for the National Book Award—nor, by the way, did it win the Pulitzer Prize.

Without agreeing, one can sympathize with this critical reaction. *The Scandal* is a difficult book—though hardly as difficult as Hyman makes it seem. Perhaps one reason is that it was evidently a difficult book to write. Even though Cheever had conceived the shape of both *The Chronicle* and *The Scandal* years before, the task of completing the Wapshot saga depressed him greatly because he found it so "pessimistic." In the *Paris Review* interview he revealed these feelings:

> When my first novel, *The Wapshot Chronicle*, was finished I was very happy about it. . . . *The Wapshot Scandal* was very difficult. I never much liked the book and when it was done I was in a bad way. I wanted to burn the book. I would wake up in the night and I would hear Hemingway's voice—I've never actually heard Hemingway's voice, but it was conspicuously his—saying, "This is the small agony. The great agony comes later."[3]

Elsewhere he elaborated on this emotional confusion, revealing that, while he was on his way to the building of his publishers, he threw the manuscript into a trash can, then retrieved it and went into a movie theater to compose himself.[4] He sat with the manuscript on his lap throughout the film, walked to Harper and Row, left the package on an editor's desk, and beat a hasty and despondent retreat. Lovers of Cheever will ever after be uncritical of the cinema's therapeutic potential.

Like them, most readers of the novel are puzzled to learn of Cheever's personal dissatisfaction with it. Even though *The Scandal* is in many respects of darker hue than *The Chronicle*, it is filled with many hilarious episodes and exhibits the full range of Cheever's comic talents—slapstick, satire, farce, multi-leveled irony, and humane humor—in such abundance of invention that any one of its vignettes would make another novel richly memorable.

THE PLOT

Like *The Chronicle*, *The Wapshot Scandal* is divided into parts (three) and composed of thirty-two chapters of varying length. Once again the narratives of the adventures of the surviving Wapshots and their spouses are interwoven in alternate patterns, pointing up dramatic parallels and contrasts in their ongoing stories, so that only at the novel's close can the reader decipher its ultimate design. Save for side trips, the action is con-

3. "John Cheever: The Art of Fiction LXII," *Paris Review*, 17, No. 7 (Fall 1976), 42.

4. Private conversation with John Cheever, December 19, 1977.

fined to four locales: St. Botolphs, where Honora lives; the Missile Research and Development site of Talifer, where Coverly's family lives; Proxmire Manor, the home of Moses and Melissa; and Italy, symbolic of a world even older than St. Botolphs, to which Honora and Melissa escape.

Whereas the attention of *The Chronicle* centered on the quest of the three male Wapshots for the meaning of "male heir," *The Scandal* concentrates on the Wapshot women instead, exploring from their perspective the displacement they experience and the subsequent quest they initiate because of the rapid moral and social changes of the modern world. Coverly still remains the central character, but here he is a passive participant, an "I am a camera" figure registering and recording the dislocations of the Wapshots; his life is effectively enclosed by obligation and circumstance throughout. His brother Moses is but a shadowy figure at best, for darkness, not light, is his fate.

If a plot summary restricts attention to the trials of its principals— and, for the moment, disregards the nicely developed minor characters— then the outline of events is quite clear. The novel opens, as did *The Chronicle*, with a description of St. Botolphs sometime ago in its idyllic past as the town prepares for a celebration—in this case, Christmas Eve. Once again, in cinematic fashion, we view the villagers as they decorate their trees and attend the Episcopal Church, while the carolers prepare to serenade their neighbors amidst the falling snow. But at the end of the first chapter an ominous note is sounded when we learn that Mr. Spofford, who has gone to the river to drown some kittens, slips and drowns himself; he cried for help, but "no one heard him, and it would be weeks before he was missed."[5] Chapter Two is a catch-up chapter in which the narrator identifies himself as the composer of *The Chronicle* and as a neighbor of the Wapshots; he also informs us of the events that have occurred in the interim: mother Sarah has died and Coverly and Moses have gotten new jobs and new homes. The novel's final chapter updates and recapitulates the pattern of the opening chapters: in it the narrator describes Christmas Eve years later, and informs us that he is leaving St. Botolphs forever.

Chapter Three is a bridge chapter structurally, morally, and emotionally. Coverly returns to the town at the present time, visits Honora, and learns that the family house is supposedly haunted. Not believing in

5. John Cheever, *The Wapshot Scandal* (New York: Harper & Row, 1964 ed.), p. 17. Unlike *The Chronicle*, hard-back editions of this novel are easy to secure; and so, instead of using Harper & Row's 1979 ed. of both books, I shall refer to the single edition available in most libraries. Hereafter references to the novel will be included in the text.

ghosts, Coverly goes to the house to stay overnight, aware, however, that "we sometimes leave after us, in a room, a stir of love or rancor when we are gone . . . either the scent of goodness or the odor of evil, to influence those who come after us" (p. 29). But Leander's presence is more palpable still, for Coverly thinks he sees the ghost of his father and guesses why, in Leander's prose, his father should want to return: "Spavined, gray, he had wanted no less than any youth to chase the nymphs. Over hill and dale. Now you see them; now you don't. The world a paradise, a paradise! Father, Father, why have you come back?" (p. 31). Frightened, Coverly flees St. Botolphs and returns to Talifer, ironically a more "ghostly" home, since it is a site for missile research and development, one so secret and secure that it "had no public existence" (p. 33).

Coverly's story hereafter is linked with Talifer, a typification of science and the nuclear age. Constructed for destructive purposes, Talifer is haunted by concern with security. None of the townspeople is friendly—no one comes to Betsey's cocktail party—and most of the offices and laboratories lie underground in "another world, buried six stories beneath the cow pasture" (p. 37). In such a world, tempers are short; and Coverly's battle with a neighbor over a stolen garbage can is interrupted by a missile, leaving its pad, which sheds "a light as bright as the light of a mid-summer's day" and which, significantly, reminds Coverly of Leander's departure, ascent, and ghostly return (p. 36).

Betsey, Coverly's wife, becomes increasingly dispirited and irritable, and remains enchained to the television set. One day Coverly, feeling similarly dejected, decides to walk through the farmland above the missile site. The fields are beautiful, but it is "late in the season" (p. 123), and Coverly thinks that "he had failed at everything" (p. 124). As he bends to tie his shoelace, a hunting arrow whistles over his head and sinks into a tree nearby. The symbolism of the tree of life, the demonic archer "all dressed in red" (p. 124), the fortunate "fall"—all effect a renewal for him, a "resolve to do something illustrious" (p. 125). He resolves to feed the poetry of Keats into a computer to determine the words most frequently chosen by the poet in their order of usage. The experiment works and, much to his surprise, Coverly discovers that " 'within the poetry of Keats there is some other poetry' " (p. 132). The banal poetic result ironically signals one of the novel's themes: " 'Silence blendeth grief's awakened fall/The golden realms of death take all/Love's bitterness exceeds its grace/That bestial scar on the angelic face/Marks heaven with gall' " (p. 132).

Coverly's humanistic enterprise is immediately counterpoised by the appearance of Dr. Cameron, the director of the missile site, a man sexually driven and non-spiritually religious, a liar obsessed with "demonstrabl(e) proofs." Coverly attends a scientific convention with Cameron, and when Cameron forgets his briefcase, Coverly retrieves it. He catches a plane which is subsequently hijacked, is robbed of the briefcase, and loses his security clearance. Later Cameron loses his own clearance at a Congressional hearing, where it is revealed that he has been heartless and inhumane toward his son (the opposite of Leander). Coverly then receives a telegram from Honora, returns to St. Botolphs to find her dying, and stays for her funeral. The novel closes with his later return on Christmas Eve, when he fulfills his promise to Honora to continue her custom of feeding Christmas dinner to the lonely and dispossessed.

Thus Honora and Coverly meet again at the novel's end—though earlier, despite the fact that they go their separate ways, their fate is conjoined (unbeknownst to them). We learn that Honora, who has set up a trust fund for Coverly and his brother, has for years failed to pay income taxes. When the IRS comes to call, she flees with the money to Italy. Her adventures on board the ship she takes comically dramatize the novel's modernistic themes: as the ship leaves, Honora, alone and a stranger, waves a tearful good-bye to no one in particular, and at mealtime she is forced to sit with some dreadful tourists who, proud of their drip-dry orlon clothing, recount their trip through the great old cities of Europe solely in terms of whether they found good washing-and-drying weather there; she plugs in her thirty-five-year-old curling iron and blows out the mighty ship's generators, halting it in mid-passage; her kindness to a stowaway in "a pin-striped suit" comes to a bad end when he attempts to rob her money belt, and she is "terrified—not by him but by the possibilities of evil in the world" (p. 155). After blowing out the generators with her curling iron a second time, she at last arrives in the Old World and feels "in her bones the thrill of that voyage her forefathers had made how many hundreds of years ago, coming forth upon another continent to found a new nation" (p. 160).

But Honora is not in Italy long, for the IRS man pursues her with extradition papers. Homesick and very willing to return, she first gives all her money away to the people of Rome, feeling that "money was filth and this was her ablution" (p. 286). Thus absolved, she returns to St. Botolphs and commits gradual suicide by refusing to eat. She telegraphs Coverly to come, and he does.

The fate of Moses and Melissa is aligned with Honora's. Deprived of his legacy, Moses must go on "wild goose chases" to raise money. He and his wife live in Proxmire Manor, a suburban village that seems "to have eliminated, through adroit social pressures, the thorny side of human nature" (p. 47); yet its inhabitants, like those in Talifer, are haunted by insecurity and boredom. Now neglected, Melissa is ridden with fears of darkness and death and is certain she has cancer. In an effort to reassert the possibilities of life, she becomes infatuated with Emile Cranmer, a nineteen-year-old delivery boy, and begins an affair with him. Doting on him in almost a maternal way, she gives Emile an expensive ring; when his mother finds it, she tells Moses of the affair, and Melissa and Moses separate. Eventually, she and Emile travel separately to Europe, she "buys" him at auction in a male beauty contest, and they live together in Rome.

While in Rome, Melissa undergoes a series of transformations: she dyes her hair red, affects girlish ways, and develops extraordinary sexual powers over Emile. She has become the temptress Circe, and Emile, though smitten, fears that should she find another lover, "he would have been transformed into a dog" (p. 283). But the narrator suggests that a more tragicomical metamorphosis is appropriate. We last see Melissa pushing her cart up and down the aisles of an Italian supermarket (an ironic return to Proxmire Manor), and

> it is Ophelia that she most resembles, gathering her fantastic garland not of crowflowers, nettles and long purples, but of salt, pepper, Babo, Kleenix, frozen codfish balls, lamb patties, hamburger, bread, butter, dressing, an American comic book for her son and for herself a bunch of carnations. She chants, like Ophelia, snatches of old tunes. "Winstons taste *good* like a cigarette should. Mr. Clean, Mr. *Clean*," and when her coronet or fantastic garland seems completed she pays her bill and carries her trophies away, no less dignified a figure of grief than any other. (p. 295)

The age of classical heroes and heroines, of heightened poetic sentiment has reached a new stage of transformation.

A READING

George Garrett in a fine essay has asserted that *The Wapshot Scandal*, though related to its predecessor, is not actually a sequel because the characters have so greatly changed and been modified by the modern age:

> The relationship is much like that of *The Rainbow* and *Women in Love* or, closer to home, *The Hamlet* to *The Town*. Which is to say the two books are Cheever's old testament, written of the time of myths, laws and prophets, and his new testament, beginning now on a Christmas Eve and ending, although on Christmas, with a curious last supper to

be followed shortly by the last book of the Bible—the Apocalypse.
The sins of *Chronicle* are original sins. *Scandal* moves inexorably toward
the end of the world.[6]

Although I have reservations about Garrett's interpretation of *The*
Scandal's ending, I believe his comments capture well the spirit and tone
of both books. The choral voice of Leander, that echo from the age of
the patriarchs, is largely absent here, and yet its return (when Honora
attempts suicide and the narrator recalls Leander's note at the book'
close) always rallies its hearers from despair. And though Leander's voice
is seldom heard, his presence is felt throughout the tale, as though his
journal in *The Chronicle* remains the subtext for *The Scandal*, much the
way the Old Testament provides the imagery, symbols, challenges, and
hopes without which the New Testament is unintelligible. In like fashion
his ghost haunts Coverly, who still employs Leander's principle of interpretation and evaluation: "Oh, Father, Father, why have you come back.
What, he wondered, would Leander have made of Talifer?" (p. 32).

The Age of the Patriarchs is succeeded by the Age of the Prophets.
No one is "begotten" here. Leander's "natural" world, sensuously rich,
alive with savory smells, has been replaced by an aseptic world that, as
Garrett points out, is "practically odorless." The prophetic cast of mind
is disposed toward moral divisions, radical ethical choices, and either/or
dichotomies—an attitude that is reflected in the novel's curious absence
of color and its emphasis on light and shadow, emblematic of the black
and white of moral choice. At the end of the novel we hear a blind old
man shout two prophetic exhortations: " 'Repent, repent, your day is at
hand. Angel voices have told me how to make myself pleasing to the
Lord . . .' " (p. 288); and " 'Have mercy upon us, have mercy upon us,
most merciful Father; grant us Thy peace' " (p. 306).

On both occasions the blind prophet is told to "Hushup, hushup."
The modern world has concerns other than repentance, mercy, and peace,
and seeks different solutions. The New Jerusalem foretold is now the
Missile Site of Talifer, not a city on a hill but a buried citadel with artificial
light and preserved food:

6. George Garrett, "John Cheever and the Charms of Innocence: The Craft of *The*
Wapshot Scandal," *Hollins Critic*, 1 (April 1964), 26. For other admirable readings of the
novel, see Samuel Coale, *John Cheever* (New York: Ungar, 1977), pp. 80-94; Frederick
Bracher, "John Cheever: A Vision of the World," *Claremont Quarterly*, 11 (Winter
1964), 47-57; Clinton Burhans, "John Cheever and the Grave of Social Coherence,"
Twentieth Century Literature, 14 (January 1969), 189-209; and Lynne Waldeland, *John*
Cheever (Boston: Twayne, 1979), pp. 48-62. For an interesting analysis of style in the
Wapshot novels, see Beatrice Greene, "Icarus at St. Botolphs," *Style*, 5 (Spring 1971),
119-137.

They ate frozen meat, frozen fried potatoes and frozen peas. . . .
It was the monotonous fare of the besieged, it would be served everywhere on the site that night, but where were the walls, the battering
rams, where was the enemy that could be accounted for this tasteless
porridge?   (p. 129)

The narrator tells us with pointed wryness that "the concerns of the
site were entirely extraterrestrial" (p. 33), and the language of the scientists and technicians who work there reflects these concerns: "It was
another language and one that seemed to him with the bleakest origins.
You couldn't trace here the elisions and changes worked by a mountain
range, a great river or the nearness of the sea" (p. 177). If the natural
world is the enemy, what, then, is *human* nature?

They were men born of women and subject to all the ravening caprices
of the flesh. They could destroy a great city inexpensively, but had
they made any progress in solving the clash between night and day,
between the head and the groin? Were the persuasions of lust, anger
and pain any less in their case?   (p. 178)

These nagging questions, repeated with variations throughout the
book, pose the terms of the novel's moral debate. At issue is a conflict
between two kinds of knowledge: the knowledge of conquest and manipulation that ignores or denies the mysterious aspects of earthly life, and
the knowledge of humility, in the face of mystery, that issues in reverence
for all things earthly and for man's spiritual aspirations.

The second option is made explicit at a Congressional hearing where
a Leander-like old man rises to address the director of the missile site. He
tells the audience of his reverie about what a man from another planet
would tell his friends after seeing our earth, and he imagines him saying:

"Come, come, let us rush to the earth. It is shaped like an egg,
covered with fertile seas and continents, warmed and lighted by the
sun. It has churches of indescribable beauty raised to gods that have
never been seen, cities whose distant roofs and smokestacks will make
your heart leap, auditoriums in which people listen to music of the
most serious import and thousands of museums where man's drive to
celebrate life is recorded and preserved. Oh, let us rush to see this
world! They have invented musical instruments to stir the finest aspirations. They have invented games to catch the hearts of the young.
They have invented ceremonies to exalt the love of men and women.
Oh, let us rush to see this world!"   (p. 217)

The possible sentimentality of these lines is tempered by the reader's
realization that, ironically, the novel's characters are rushing *away* from
the earth, and that the words are uttered by a frail, feeble old man with

a trickle of saliva running down his chin—a man soon to leave the earth. Once again Cheever underscores the theme of travel, here in a deliberately bizarre way. In *The Chronicle* this motif captures the odyssey-like adventures of the Wapshot males: a pattern of leave-taking, combat, nostalgia, temptations, and homecoming. In *The Scandal*, however, travel is movement without exact destination or is subject to interruption (Coverly's plane is hijacked; Honora's curling iron blows out the ocean liner's generators). It is symbolic of rootlessness or evasion or flight—not from the past but from the present.

By contrast, Honora, a figure from the older, stable, non-synthetic world, is reluctant to leave her home because it gives her a sense of rootedness:

> She had lived out her life there, and each act was a variation on some other act, each sensation she experienced was linked to a similar sensation, reaching in a chain back through the years of her long life to when she had been a fair and intractable child. . . . She did not want to leave her home and move on into an element where her sensations would seem rootless. . . .   (p. 141)

We are not surprised, then, when she flees a homeless death in Italy and returns to St. Botolphs to die.

This contrast is also effectively drawn in the narrator's comparison between the railroad station at St. Botolphs and a modern international airport:

> There was, on one hand, the railroad station in St. Botolphs, with its rich aura of arrivals and departures, its smells of coal gas, floor oil and toilets, and its dark waiting room, where some force of magnification seemed brought to bear on the lives of passengers waiting for their train to arrive; and on the other hand, this loft or palace, its glass walls open to the overcast sky, where spaciousness, efficiency and the smell of artificial leather seemed not to magnify but to diminish the knowledge the passengers had of one another.   (pp. 184-185)

These experiences of disconnection and diminishment are reinforced when Coverly enters the airport cocktail lounge.

> The dark bar had the authority of a creation, but it was a creation evolved independently from the iconography of the universe. . . . There was not even a truncated piece of driftwood or a coaster shaped like a leaf to remind him of the world outside. That beauty of sameness that makes the star and the shell, the sea and the clouds all seem to have come from the same hand was lost.   (p. 186)

As these contrasting images demonstrate, Cheever's dialectical intelligence is at the forefront in this novel. The unity of *The Chronicle* lies in the interweaving of parallel action, recurring symbols, and imagery; *The Scandal* is unified instead by thematic polarities, dialogic questions, and negative and positive reflections. Where *The Chronicle* is robust and celebratory, this novel is frail and sibylline in tone. The reason is that in it Cheever was not addressing the past but the present and the future. A clue to his attitude at the time is found in the comment he offered to Herbert Gold for his story collection, *Fiction of the Fifties*. Gold posed this question: "In what way—if any—do you feel the problem of writing for the Fifties has differed from the problems of writing in other times?" Cheever answered:

> The decade began for me with more promise than I can remember from my earliest youth. . . . However, halfway through the decade, something went terribly wrong. The most useful image I have today is of a man in a quagmire, looking into a tear in the sky. I am not speaking here of despair, but of confusion. I fully expected the trout streams of my youth to fill up with beer cans and the meadows to be covered with houses; I may even have expected to be separated from most of my moral and ethical heritage; but the forceful absurdities of life today find me unprepared.[7]

A tear in the sky, not despair but confusion, loss, separation, and lack of preparation—these are the themes of *The Scandal*. Occasionally, they are effectively posed as questions:

> Who did have the power of penetration? Was it the priest who saw how their hands trembled when they reached for the chalice, the doctor who had seen them stripped of their clothing, or the psychiatrist who had seen them stripped of their obdurate pride, and who was now dancing with a fat woman in a red dress? And what was penetration worth? What did it matter that the drunken and unhappy woman in the corner dreamed frequently that she was being chased through a grove of trees by a score of naked lyric poets? . . . Loneliness was one thing, and [Melissa] knew herself how sweet it could make lights and company seem, but boredom was something else, and why, in this most prosperous and equitable world, should everyone seem so bored and disappointed?   (pp. 49-50)

These questions contain implicit dichotomies: power and malaise, insight (penetration) and ignorance; dreams and reality. Elsewhere, they are stated in modified declaratives like this one:

> In her own youth [Mrs. Cranmer] had seen some wildness but the world had seemed more commodious and forgiving. She had never

---

7. John Cheever in Herbert Gold's *Fiction of the Fifties* (Garden City: Doubleday, 1959), p. 22.

been able to settle on who was to blame. She feared that the world
might have changed too swiftly for her intelligence and intuition. She
had no one to help her sift out the good from the evil.   (p. 239)

Here the themes are stated rather starkly. More often they are dramatized
in events of disjunction or embodied in the fate or intuitions of the
characters, especially minor characters whose experiences, briefly recorded, capsulate those of the central figures. This device universalizes
the perceptions and tempers all moralizing and sentimentality, providing
the novel with a two-tiered synoptic glimpse of the modern world reminiscent of *Upstairs, Downstairs.*

For example, when Betsey feels most despondent and isolated because
no one has come to her birthday party, the delivery man from the dry-
cleaner's arrives and confides, " 'I'm so alone that I talk with the flies' "
(pp. 40-41). Meanwhile, the maid is reading an erotic paperback and
protests, " 'I don't know. I been married three times but right here in this
book they're doing something and I don't know what it is' " (p. 41).

Melissa's counterpart is an ignored neighbor, Gertrude Lockhart.
"[Melissa] was afraid of the dark, like a primitive or a child, but why?
What was there about darkness that threatened her? She was afraid of the
dark as she was afraid of the unknown, and what was the unknown but
the force of evil, and why should she be afraid of this?" (p. 90). Melissa
flees her fear of physical death and commits moral suicide instead. Not
unlike her, Gertrude is undone by her husband's priapic urgencies and the
collapse of all her home's mechanical conveniences, whose operation is
the modern equivalent of the mysterious unknown:

> She cried for her discomforts but she cried more bitterly for their
> ephemeralness, for the mysterious harm a transparent bacon wrapper
> and an oil burner could do to the finest part of her spirit; cried for a
> world that seemed to be without laws and prophets. . . . It was this
> feeling of obsolescence that pushed her into drunkenness and prom-
> iscuity and she was both.   (p. 107)

She commits suicide when the winter cold and actual darkness overtake
her and her house; trapped by them, she takes the only flight available.

Laws and prophets do exist in such a world, however. The roles once
proper to religious figures now belong to men like Dr. Cameron, whose
laws are those of physics, whose prophecies concern the materialistic and
the tangible, and whose vocation is to make the unknown known. The
concerns of the missile site he directs are pointedly described as "entirely
extraterrestrial" (quite different from transcendental), and we are informed
with evident irony that "common sense would scotch any sentimental and

ransparent ironies about the vastness of scientific research undertaken at
'alifer and the capacity for irrational forlornness, loneliness and ecstasy
mong the scientists . . ." (p. 33).

Those readers who are disconcerted by the obviously contradictory
ehavior of Dr. Cameron might well ponder this offhand sentence.
^hroughout the novel, Cameron is a symbolic character; hardly realistic,
e is precisely a challenge to common sense, a figure of sentimental and
ransparent ironies. Cheever is quite capable of creating characters of
onsistency; here, Cameron's radical inconsistency is meant to strain our
redulity. We are told in subsequent paragraphs that he "classified as
bsolete his own sexual drives," and yet that he "was one of those blame-
ess old men who had found that lasciviousness was his best means of
linging to life . . . his best sense of forgetfulness, his best way of grappling
vith the unhappy facts of time" (p. 164). When he flies to Italy in
assionate quest of his prostitute-mistress, a boy in a seat nearby gets sick,
nd Cameron is "shocked out of his venereal reverie by this ugly fact of
fe" (p. 168). Tormented soon after by pornographic reflections accom-
anied by desires for decency, he visits the restaurant where he had ar-
anged to meet his lover only to find it closed; immediately he feels "an
xalting surge of deliverance, a return to himself"; he is "convinced that
here was some blessedness in the nature of things" (p. 176).

Cameron's behavior at the Senate hearings is equally contradictory.
Despite his own mixed experience, he states, " 'Men and women . . . are
hemical entities, easily assessable, easily altered . . . much more pre-
lictable, much more malleable, than some plant life and in many cases
nuch less interesting' " (p. 216). His lack of feeling for humankind is
lemonstrated when his son, an invalid hospitalized for insanity, appears.
The senators ask him about his son and his vicious treatment of him as
 boy. To each of these questions, Cameron answers, " 'I can't recall,' "
ut when his son cries out, " 'Oh, Daddy. It's raining,' " we hear: " 'Yes,
lear.' It was the most eloquent thing he had said. He no longer saw the
earing room or his persecutors. He seemed immersed in some human,
ome intensely human balance of love and misgiving as if the feelings
vere a storm with a circumference and an eye and he was in the stillness
of the eye" (p. 222).

That "as if" description is pointedly "extra-terrestrial," contrasting
ronically with the all-too-human emotions it specifies. Cameron thus is
 representative, rather than a realistically realized, character: he embodies
he detached rationalism of modern science at its most extreme, and so
s a symbol of the forgetfulness of the modern world. Scientists like him
ften assume the perspective of the scientific community and speak with
ts voice; as a result, they often "forget" the human, existential problems

they as *individuals* are heir to.[8] Like him, many tend to see life's evolution in cosmic, collective terms and so "forget" that any one moment, any unique relationship can have decisive significance. These verities are dramatized in sequence here at the Senate hearing: only the voice of Cameron's son "reminds" him back into human existence, into subjective concerns.

In the earlier discussion of themes in tension, I noted that forgetting and remembering are consistent polarities in Cheever's work. This is especially so throughout *The Scandal*, as the incident involving Cameron, and other events, demonstrate. Early in the novel, for example, Coverly flees what is "his and his brother's house, by contract, inheritance and memory" (p. 27) because he is frightened of his father's ghostly presence. When personal problems arise, he assumes a detached stance of denial: "He would decide cheerfully and hopefully that what had happened had not happened although he never went so far as to claim that what had not happened had happened" (p. 69). Later, at a scientific convention, he hears a lecture about experiments that involve sending a man into space in a fluid-filled sack:

> The difficulty presented was that men immersed in fluid suffered a grave and sometimes incurable loss of memory. Coverly wanted to approach the scene with his best seriousness—with a complete absence of humor—but how could he square the image of a man in a sack with the small New England village where he had been raised and where his character had been formed? (p. 178)

Coverly's reluctance to forget—owing to his humor and his human compassion—will finally redeem him by the novel's end. By contrast, his brother and sister-in-law are not so fortunate, for their forgetfulness at the end is absolute: "Like Melissa, [Moses] had developed an adroitness at believing that what had happened had not happened, that what was happening was not happening and that which might happen was impossible" (p. 244). Both, as a result, lapse into nihilism and despair, and are transformed into pagan caricatures: a Circe and a Satyr.

One reason why the death of Honora is so poignant is that her last scenes with Coverly are marked by invitations to "remember." To remember the Christmas dinner, the tomato fights, to remember her reading *David Copperfield* to him when he was sick, and their shared feelings about the book—" 'Remember how we used to cry, Coverly, you and I?' " (p. 294). Her final gift to his memory is her attempt to describe her vision

8. For a fine philosophic analysis of this process within the scientific mind, one analyzed in terms of Kierkegaard's thought, see Ralph Henry Johnson, *The Concept of Existence in the Concluding Unscientific Postscript* (Martinus Mijhoof: The Hague, 1972).

f the gates of Heaven: " 'Oh, they were so beautiful. There were the ates and hosts of angels with colored wings and I saw them. Wasn't that ice?' " (p. 296). Thus she and Coverly are yoked together in a memory /orld more mysterious than Talifer, more continuous and real than Cam- ron's abstract cosmos, intent only on the future and amnesic of all else:

> She would stop breathing and be buried in the family lot but the greenness of her image, in [Coverly's] memory, would not change and she would be among them always in their decisions. She would, long after she was dust, move freely through his dreams, she would punish his and his brother's wickedness with guilt, reward their good works with lightness of heart. . . . The goodness and evil in the old woman were imperishable.   (p. 296)

The realization of the intermixture (and the permanence!) of good nd evil becomes the dramatic theme of the final chapter. In the context t is especially important to note that Coverly joins in two symbolic ctions of meal-sharing after Honora's death. The first is the Eucharistic eremony in Christ Church on Christmas Eve, and the second, on Christ- nas day, is a dinner for the destitute and lonely. Both are *agape* meals, Christian love feasts, and the drabness of the circumstances is meant to ighlight, through contrast, their spiritual significance. In Christian the- •logy the *agape* meal concentrates, in one symbolic action, all the para- loxical truths about the mystery of Christ's coming; in the novel it lramatically concentrates Coverly's many complex and ambivalent real- zations. For the *agape* meal is first of all a memorial, a reminder, lest we orget, of the human commingling of good and evil, of salvation and sin hat prompts its celebration; more subtly, it is (or attempts to be) a sign •f both reconciliation and atonement, and its symbolic beneficence is also acrificial in character. Not only do the human and the divine meet in enewal and commemoration of the Incarnation, the event of the first Christmas, but the humans present, by acknowledging their communal veakness, demonstrate their need-filled desire for union with the divine, or strength to embrace decency and more permanent loves, for assistance n remembering the joys and challenges that have been offered them.

At first glance this is not so apparent. When Betsey joins Coverly in St. Botolphs on Christmas Eve, she complains with repetitious poignancy, ' 'I'm just so tired I could *die*' " (p. 299). Coverly leaves her to attend he Mass at Christ Church with only four other worshippers. The church's nterior is gloomy, and the service itself a travesty. Pastor Applegate, naughty and scornful, mixes up the liturgical order of the ceremony be- :ause he is obviously drunk. But suddenly a Cheeveresque transformation :akes place, and the scene switches from blasphemy to hilarious but heart-

felt prayer, from nonsensical mumbling to an impassioned plea for th
alleviation of modern man's more easily observed miseries:

> [Applegate] lurched around the altar, got the general confession
> mixed up with the order for morning prayer and kept saying: "Christ
> have mercy upon us. Let us pray," until it seemed that he was stuck.
> There is no point in the formalities of Holy Communion where, in the
> case of such a disaster, the communicants can intervene and there was
> nothing to do but watch him flounder through to the end. Suddenly
> he threw his arms wide, fell to his knees and exclaimed: "Let us pray
> for all those killed or cruelly wounded on thruways, expressways, free-
> ways and turnpikes. Let us pray for all those burned to death in faulty
> plane-landings, mid-air collisions and mountainside crashes. Let us
> pray for all those wounded by rotary lawn mowers, chain saws, electric
> hedge clippers and other power tools. Let us pray for all alcoholics
> measuring out the days that the Lord hath made in ounces, pints and
> fifths." Here he sobbed loudly. "Let us pray for the lecherous and the
> impure. . . ." Led by the woman with the flashing hat, the other
> worshipers left before this prayer was finished and Coverly was left
> alone to support Mr. Applegate with his Amen.   (pp. 301-302)

Not only is this passage wonderful in itself, but it contrasts with wha
follows: Coverly's visit to Moses at the Viaduct House. Thus we first hea
a prayerful litany for the communality of misery and a confession of weak
ness, then view a scene of isolation; first hear a prayer of mercy for "the
lecherous and impure" to which Coverly adds "Amen," then a different
ending, an emptier Amen:

> It was Christmas Eve at the Viaduct House but the scene upstairs
> was flagrantly pagan. This was no sacred grove and the only sound of
> running water came from a leaky tap but Moses the satyr leered through
> the smoky air at his bacchante. Mrs. Wilston's curls were disheveled,
> her face was red, her smile was the rapt and wanton smile of forget-
> fulness. . . .   (p. 302)

These contrasts continue through Christmas morning:

> Moses woke in a crushing paroxysm of anxiety, the keenest mel-
> ancholy. The brilliance of light, the birth of Christ, all seemed to him
> like some fatuous shell game invented to dupe a fool like his brother
> while he saw straight through into the nothingness of things. The
> damage he had done to his nerves and his memory was less painful
> than a sense he suffered of approaching disaster. . . . This was the
> agony of death, with the difference that he knew the way to life ev-
> erlasting. It was in the bottles of bourbon Honora had left in the jelly
> closet.   (pp. 303-304)

Thus the second *agape* meal for the blind and destitute, this time a less formal rite than Applegate's, recapitulates and embraces all these themes in tension through the presence of symbolic characters participating in a symbolic act:

> [These blind] seemed to bring with them a landscape whose darkness exceeded in intensity the brilliance of that day. A blow had been leveled at their sight but this seemed not to be an infirmity but a heightened insight, as if aboriginal man had been blind and this was some part of an ancient, human condition; and they brought with them into the parlor the mysteries of the night. They seemed to be advocates for those in pain; for the taste of misery as fulsome as rapture, for the losers, the goners, the flops, for those who dream in terms of missed things. . . .   (pp. 306-307)

This is the novel's climax, and, as such, it ought to convince any doubters that the tilt of the narrative throughout finds its balance in the Christian perspective that controls it. At root it is an exploration of the mystery of the word "love." This dramatic investigation is itself informed by the Christian tradition's distinction between two aspects of love, designated by *eros* and *agape*.

In paganism the Greek word *eros* was generally associated with passion, orgiastic ecstasy, and madness. Because of this, those who translated the Old Testament into the Greek Septuagint preferred the word *agape* instead, for it connoted a more rational love, one aligned with the virtues of fidelity and loyalty proper to covenant obligations. The New Testament writers also avoided *eros* and generally used *agape* to describe the central mystery and virtue of Christianity: love of God and of neighbor. Scriptural exegetes admit that often it is difficult to differentiate whether its usage in various New Testament texts refers formally to the love of God for man or to the mutual love of Christians. Despite imprecision, however, it is clear that, as John McKenzie says, *agape* "becomes a kind of atmosphere in which God and Christians live together; communicated from God, *agape* permeates the Christian community and the individual Christian."[9] In other words, the accent in *agape* is always on divine love as a creative and created grace men share; because God loves man, His love creates the possibility for men to love Him and also love others, the creatures of His love.

After the biblical period, the writers of the early age of the Church were influenced by Platonic and especially neo-Platonic philosophy. Plato's notion of *eros* had elevated the more obvious sensual connotations of the word in Greek usage and instead described the soul's desire for ideal

9. John L. McKenzie, S.J., *Dictionary of the Bible* (Milwaukee: Bruce, 1965), p. 522.

beauty. Early Christian theologians, Neo-Platonists in education, elevated *eros* further to characterize the desire for union with God, for them the equivalent of the gospel's phrase "eternal life." *Agape* referred correctly to a divine or divinized love, but what of man's perspective, such as his "thirst" for God that the Psalmist spoke of? Was not this eros? Augustine's genius in his *Confessions* addressed precisely this subjective question and, in doing so, forged a synthesis between *eros* and *agape*. [10] His reflections led him to realize that the restless longing for God in the human heart—a taste of the eternal in temporal human events—was a longing implanted by God Himself. This restless longing and spiritual desire for a selfless love was man's finite participation in the realization of that selfless love which is a definition of God.

Subsequent controversies about the meaning of Christian love, especially those that concern misinterpretations or misemphases in Augustine, provide a fascinating history in Christian theology. [11] (Augustine wrote in Latin and used the words *amor, caritas,* and *cupiditas* instead of the Greek distinctions of *eros* and *agape*, thereby muddying conceptual waters.) I have no intention of making a longer trot through the history of theology here. Most readers of Cheever are either unaware of or not especially delighted by such fine points in definition, though begrudgingly they might admit its importance. What is important in this study, however, is not whether any or all distinctions are adequate or especially correct, but that Cheever's religious (and romantic) sensibility is biblical with an Augustinian coloration. In other words, "love" for him is an atmosphere permeating the world, a unifying force that energizes everything in creation and one which humans can, if they so choose, participate in and extend. But because his sensibility on this issue is reverential, his fiction also demonstrates that the word "love" should not be used carelessly, that many distinctions are needed to get at its root, that its predication is not only easily abused but is applied with odd reverence to the basest encounters. If love is the energizer of man's noblest instincts, as history claims, how is such random predication possible? If erotic attachments can both build and destroy, what is the meaning of such an exalted word like "love" in the first place? Cheever's fiction meditates on and dramatizes such questions.

10. See Robert J. O'Connell's two studies: *St. Augustine's Early Theory of Man* (Cambridge: Harvard Univ. Press, 1968); and *St. Augustine's Confessions* (Cambridge: Harvard Univ. Press, 1969). O'Connell lucidly presents Augustine's deepening understanding of Eros, Affection, and Love. (See the index for topical guidance.)

11. See Anders Nygren, *Agape and Eros* (Philadelphia: Westminster Press, 1953); Martin D'Arcy, *The Mind and Heart of Love* (New York: Holt, 1947), especially chapter 2; and Karl Barth, *Church Dogmatics*, IV, 2 (Edinburgh: T. & T. Clark, 1969).

So to the point: over the centuries, for reasons many and complex, the vocabulary in the Western world has recovered, though often vaguely, a distinction between *eros* and *agape*. [12] *Eros* is self-evident. We can describe it as romantic love, the selfish desire for the possession of the object, an instinctual impulse (libido) toward union with a biological base, or, more narrowly, the sexual impulse which, we know, is notably both discriminating and indiscriminate. *Eros* is a given, one not especially laudatory, but it is there and always will be. *Agape* is less self-evident and continually a challenge. In English we sometimes call it "charity," a word now debased by its association with alms-giving or judgmental restraint, and it is generally the concern of the religious or the pseudo religious-minded. Charity is selfless; it seeks not to possess but to better the other; its object is goodness, not beauty; and so forth. *Agape* is a very good thing, whereas, *eros* is less good; the former is pure, the latter, at best, mixed; the former is a grace, the latter a given—so the comparisons go.

Most of us know these distinctions, of course, to some extent. The strength of Cheever's fiction is that he challenges our complacent assumptions about them, about their distinctiveness and about their casual intermingling as well. But Cheever is the opposite of a Puritan: at the risk of sentimentality, he celebrates romantic love, even when oddly manifest, as redemptive and humanly genuine. *Eros* is not a mere pointer but the worthiest of possessions, meriting a record of memory and desire, the starting point, at least, and likely our keenest perception of our most generous spiritual instincts. That *eros* is not enough, that its human demonstration in action inevitably yields reflective discontent, reinforces its significance. Augustine's "Our hearts are restless until they rest in Thee" sounds pessimistic only to those ears anxious to translate the words into the singular; the plural "our" expresses the universal truth that is the wellspring of all morality and all theology, both Eastern and Western.

The word "love" in Cheever's fiction (as I noted in discussing Cheever's resemblance to Auden) is a transcendent force, a positive power animating all that is vital in creation. As transcendent, it surpasses all of its manifestations and yet embraces them, too. These manifestations we might

12. Perhaps a clarification is needed. In using the Eros-Agape distinction, I am not intending to discount Freud's analysis of Eros. In his *Outline of Psychoanalysis* and elsewhere, Freud addresses Eros as a basic instinct (opposing it to Thanatos, the destructive instinct). Freud's biological, materialistic insights into the subject of Eros are most enlightening, needless to say, and most people are more familiar with his usage today, understood as psychological and biological concepts. However, my accent is not that; rather, it is on the moral and spiritual distinctions about Eros that derive from a rich and equally sophisticated religious tradition. For a lucid, not overly academic exposition of that tradition, see C. S. Lewis, *The Four Loves* (New York: Harcourt Brace, 1971 ed.).

call Christian love, fidelity, conscience, charity, grace, and human virtues of courage, honesty, and decency, familial commitment—no matter what designation we apply, each of these words refers to something "extra" about human conduct, a difference in quality or kind rather than degree, something beyond the merely natural or expected. Love lasts—it is the spur toward continuity; all else passes away.

Therefore, in Cheever's work the opposite of love is not hatred (and certainly not sexuality) but *death*, death of that extra something that vitalizes and makes wondrous the created world and the lives of its inhabitants. In *The Scandal* this theme is made explicit at the story's close during Coverly's conversation with the dying Honora:

> "I'm dying, Coverly, and I know it and I want to die."
> "You shouldn't say that, Honora."
> "And why shouldn't I?"
> "Because life is a gift, a mysterious gift," he said feebly in spite of the weight the words had for him.
> "Well," she exclaimed, "you must be going to church a great deal these days."
> "I sometimes do," he said.   (p. 290)

This dialogue is pivotal, because Coverly is the sole survivor in an atmosphere of physical and moral suicide. Honora and Gertrude Lockhart are literal suicides; Moses, Melissa, Emile, Cameron, and Betsey, all of whom both fear and desire death, symbolically are suicides. In this light these characters can be viewed as almost abstract types, figures in a morality play embodying the Seven Deadly Sins: Lust (Melissa), Covetousness (Gertrude Lockhart), Pride (Cameron), Envy (Betsey), Gluttony (Emile), Sloth (Moses), and Anger (Norman Johnson). These sins were called deadly because each is fatal to a love relationship, destroying its possible progress.

But compassion, not condemnation, characterizes Cheever's treatment of the distortions of love. Ideally, love to be love means a conjoining of *eros* and *agape* in Augustine's sense, the one a hint of an explanation for the other; in this union *eros* reveals the moral and spiritual properties of the *agape* that animates it. Unfortunately, of course, ours is not an ideal world; hints can lead to misdirection or blind alleys, and *eros* can be forgetful of *agape*. Cheever's genius lies in his ability to move easily—sometimes simultaneously, sometimes not—between this conjoining and disjunction.

Throughout Cheever's fiction the word "love" connotes this ambiguity. When Cheever wishes to distinguish *eros*, i.e., *eros* shorn of moral or spiritual qualities, he will generally use the words "venery" or "carnality" or variants on "forgetfulness" or images from paganism as its equivalent.

Eros in this sense is non-unitive, isolating those smitten by it and offering nothing else extra. It is the limiting bond that draws Moses and Melissa together:

> This volcanic area that Moses shared with Melissa was immense, but it was the only one. They agreed on almost nothing else. They drank different brands of whisky, read different books and papers. Outside the dark circle of love they seemed almost like strangers, and glimpsing Melissa down a long dinner table he had once wondered who was that pretty woman with light hair. (p. 52)

This vision of love ("the dark circle") is inevitably linked with loneliness, which is both its cause and effect. The minor character, the IRS agent Norman Johnson, exemplifies this theme and its primitive or primordial character:

> He was a traveler, familiar with the miseries of loneliness, with the violence of its sexuality, with its half-conscious imagery of highways and thruways like the projections of a bewildered spirit; with that forlorn and venereal limbo that must have flowed over the world before the invention of Venus, unknown to good and evil, ruled by pain. (p. 55)

But Johnson remains a sympathetic figure, because Cheever invites us into his dream-life, one populated, not isolated, one responsive to memory, not amnesic, one filled with inklings of spiritual aspirations sadly irrecoverable in his waking life:

> It seemed like a poor fare for a lonely man [in a hotel] and he felt from the hard mattress where he lay an accrual of loneliness from the thousands like himself who had lain there, hankering not to be alone. He turned off the light, slept and dreamed of swans, a lost suitcase, a snow-covered mountain. He saw his mother lifting the ornaments off the Christmas tree with trembling hands. He woke in the morning feeling natural, boisterous and even loving, but the stranger with a hidden face is always waiting by the lake, there is always a viper in the garden, a dark cloud in the west. (p. 60)

If venery issues in endless amoral wandering, dreams betoken a purposive travel, admixing memory and desire, toward an indefinite but benign destination. The images for venery are those of darkness, violence, estrangement, and confusion; by contrast, the dream images of love are imbued with light, gentleness, sharing, and renewal.

Before her plunge into debauchery, Melissa has two such dreams, followed by a third, which foreshadows her fate. The first dream is of a romantic landscape of "a winding stream with alders, and on the farther banks the ruins of a castle" (p. 88). She picnics on the grass and meets a man swimming in a pool who "spoke to her in French, and it was part of the dream's lightness that it all transpired in another country, another time" (p. 89). Her second dream is equally romantic but this time in the religious sense:

> The imagery of her fever was similar to the imagery of love. Her reveries were spacious, and she seemed to be promised the revelation of some truth that lay at the center of the labyrinthine and palatial structures where she wandered. . . . She was standing at the head of a broad staircase with red walls. Many people were climbing the stairs. They had the attitudes of pilgrims. The climb was grueling and lengthy, and when she reached the summit she found herself in a grove of lemon trees and lay down on the grass to rest.   (p. 91)

These two dreams are about ascent and transport and human contact; the trees and the grass in both suggest a paradisaical garden. Melissa's third dream is brief and different, for she sees "a circle of barbaric dancers" (p. 92). This image, the enclosed circle, effectively suggests the consequent transpositions in her character. The story of her infatuation with Emile is one of enclosure and encirclement, and it subtly records the capacity of the human heart to convert love's most powerful symbols. Soon after Melissa meets Emile she blurts out, " 'You know, you're divine' " (p. 102). Later he remembers this and, puzzled, says, " 'But you speak differently, you know—people like you. . . . Now, you say divine— you say lots of things are divine, but, you know, my mother, she wouldn't ever use that word, except when she was speaking of God' " (p. 120).

Later, after their affair has progressed, Melissa is circumscribed by her desire for this "golden Adam." She wonders, "How could anyone who lives in such a decorous environment be sinful? How could anyone who has so much Hepplewhite—so much Hepplewhite in good condition— be shaken by unruly lusts?" (p. 230). She is anxious to forgive Emile and also find forgiveness for herself and recover her Eve-like innocence. Eventually she seeks out her minister, and is struck by "the antiquity of his devotions": "No runner would ever come to his door with the news that the head of the vestry had been martyred by the local police and had she used the name of Jesus Christ, out of its liturgical context, she felt that he would have been terribly embarrassed" (pp. 236-237). The minister is a good man but "he was not alone in having been overwhelmed at the task of giving the passion of Our Lord ardor and reality" (p. 236). His sense of passion is also directed elsewhere, as one of the next observations indicates: "[Melissa] felt how passionately he would have liked to avoid her troubles" (p. 236). Being a man of the modern world, he recommends she see a psychiatrist, the only one ordained to analyze contemporary passions, or so it seems.

This one very short scene is an excellent example of how deftly Cheever can juxtapose the "ardor and reality" of the lovers' passions with the ardor and reality of the Christian message in a casual, humorous, and compassionate way. The Christian dimension is unobtrusive but very much there; its challenges and values provide the thematic background for dramatic tension. Elsewhere in the novel there are three protracted scenes that critics who are unaware of their thematic and symbolic importance in relation to the novel dismiss as vignettes, if not distractions or purple patches. They are not; each reveals the wedding of the pagan and the Christian, pathos and comedy, ardor and reality in collision, and elucidates the novel's central themes.

The first scene of this kind is Chapter Twelve, a description of Emile and his young friends at the Moonlite Drive-In, "where thousands of darkened cars were arranged in the form of an ancient arena, spread out beneath the tree of night" (p. 113). But this quaint replication of a pagan coliseum lies hard by the most modern of constructs, the Northern Expressway. The narrator remarks, "It was some touching part of the autumn night and the hazards of the road that so many of these travelers pleaded for the special protection of gentle St. Christopher and the blessings of the Holy Virgin" (p. 113). (Recall Apocalypse 12:1, the vision of the woman, adorned with the sun, standing on the moon and wearing a twelve-star crown, the figure on a miraculous medal.)

But at the Moonlite Drive-In a different, non-virginal rite is in progress, for "here was everything a man might need . . . a place to perform the rites of spring—or, in this case, the rites of autumn. It was an autumn night, and the air was full of pollen and decay" (p. 114). Compounding these ironies, the actress on the screen exclaims, " 'I want to put on innocence, like a bright, new dress. I want to feel clean again!' " (p. 114).

Emile, though at the moment undressed in the back seat of a car, blushes at the words. But that blush seems inappropriate to his generation, for "the music he danced to and the movies he watched dealt less and less with the heart and more and more with overt sexuality, as if the rose gardens and playing fields buried under the Expressway were enjoying a revenge" (p. 114):

> The times were venereal, and Emile was a child of the times. . . . When the lilac under his bedroom window bloomed in the spring and he could smell its fragrance as he lay in bed, some feeling, as strong as ambition but without a name, moved him. Oh, I want—I want to do so well, he thought, sitting naked at the Moonlite. . . . Whatever it was, he wanted something that would correspond to his

sense that life was imposing; something that would confirm his feeling
that, as he stood at the window of Narobi's grocery store watching the
men and women on the sidewalk and the stream of clouds in the sky,
the procession he saw was a majestic one.   (p. 115)

Throughout the scene, the contrast between autumn and spring, differing rituals, the stress on the words "under" and "beneath" in contrast
with perceptions "overhead," the fragrance of the lilac, a flower mixing
purple and pure white—all heighten the dramatic juxtaposition of burial
and aspiration, of earthiness and the ethereal.

The second scene is possibly the funniest extended narrative in
Cheever's fiction: Emile's hiding of the Easter eggs. It is delicious farce,
so admirably paced and structured and so cinematic that Mel Brooks or
Woody Allen could never better it. And yet throughout the scene Cheever
insinuates the Christian motif of Easter in a masterly way with the more
pagan updating of the contest of the golden apple. Note, for example,
Cheever's sly, repetitious play on the word "redeemable," here mercantile
in meaning, though preparatory for an Easter event:

> On Easter Eve a thousand plastic eggs were to be hidden in the
> grass of the village. All of them contained certificates redeemable at
> the store for a dozen country-fresh eggs. Twenty of them contained
> certificates redeemable for a two-ounce bottle of costly French perfume.
> Ten of them contained certificates redeemable for an outboard motor
> and five of them—golden ones—were good for a three-week, all-ex-
> pense vacation for two at a luxury hotel in Madrid, Paris, London,
> Venice or Rome.   (p. 248)

Emile is designated the modern Paris, deputed to distribute the prize(s)
created by Eris, the goddess of discord. Early Easter morning he begins
his rounds, and the atmosphere suggests both Christian renewal and pagan
Dionysian vitality: "The world seemed fine in the street light and the
starlight and young, too, even in its shabbiness, as if the fate of the place
had only just begun to be told. The earth . . . was waiting for his treasure"
(p. 254).

Emile's first contretemps occurs because Mrs. Hazzard is awake,
"thinking about the eggs—about those that contained warrants for travel.
. . . Travel was linked in her mind to the magnificence and pathos of
love; it would be like a revelation of the affections" (pp. 255-256). She
shouts from the window, " 'I have to have one of the gold ones, Emile!
Give me one of the gold ones' " (p. 257).

Mrs. Hazzard's voice wakens her next-door neighbor, Mrs. Kramer,
who calls her daughter with the news; her daughter, alerted, rushes from
her house, a strange vision: "Her nightgown was transparent and the

curlers in her hair looked like a crown" (p. 258). She catches up with Emile and demands one of the golden eggs: " 'I want the one for Paris, Emile' " (p. 258). Suddenly a dozen or more women appear, looking as if they are wearing crowns like her; Emile flees to another section of town, only to run into thirty or forty more women, "most of them wearing long robes and what appeared to be massive crowns" (p. 259). Panicked, he drives into an empty lot nearby and pitches the eggs into the deep grass to divert their attention. "He disposed of all but one [of the crates of eggs] before the women reached him and straightened up to see them, so like angels in their nightclothes, and hear their soft cries of longing and excitement" (p. 259).

The scene is hilariously apocalyptic. But the beneficent description of the saints, in white robes and crowns, praising the Easter Lamb in the biblical Apocalypse is here altered, indicative of less exalted and more random desires. Still, "most of the doors [of the town's houses] stood open in the dawn as if Gabriel's long trumpet had sounded" (p. 261). These are expectantly hopeful beneficiaries of another second resurrection. Emile senses the significance of the event—"Something had happened. Something had changed" (p. 262)—but ironically, like Paris in the legend, he awards the prize—the golden egg for Rome—to his Aphrodite (the mother of Eros), Melissa. And with that, his world changes indeed, for thereafter he is an enemy of the goddesses of wisdom and rule.

The third scene, that of the male beauty contest in Naples, is not bizarre if one notes that it extends the thematic implications of the first two scenes. Shortly before the event we are told that "Emile was hungry all the time and his hunger took on the scope of some profound misunderstanding between the world and himself" (p. 275). In this scene that hunger is demonstrated and universalized. Emile enters the beauty contest and becomes one of the ten winners—only to discover that the winners are to be auctioned off. At first Emile is disconcerted and abashed because of his memories of his former life:

> Could it be true that his character was partly formed from rooms, streets, chairs and tables? Was his morality influenced by landscapes and kinds of food? Had he been unable to take his personality, his sense of good and evil, across the Bay of Naples? . . . Was this sin, Emile wondered, and if it was, why should it seem so deeply expressive of everyone there? Here was the sale of the utmost delights of the flesh, its racking forgetfulness. Here were the caves and the fine skies of venery, the palaces and stairways, the thunder and the lightning, the great king and the drowned sailor, and from the voices of the bidders it seemed that they had never wanted anything else.
>
> (pp. 278-279)

The direct and indirect questions tease us as readers into reflection about the multi-layered mysteries of transformation. In a sense the queries are stark, but they are also subtly framed, since they ironically transform images (skies, palaces, stairways) that in other contexts were spiritual emblems. (Note also the allusions to T. S. Eliot's *The Waste Land* in "the thunder and the lightning, the great king and drowned sailor.") At any rate, just when a sophisticate might complain that Cheever here is too explicit, a scene follows that shocks us with its perceptive realism, its dramatization of ambiguity. Another contestant named Pierre climbs onto the block before the bidding for Emile begins:

> His slip was cut scant enough to show his pubic hair and his pose was vaguely classical—the hips canted and one hand curved against his thigh—classical and immemorial as if he had appeared repeatedly in the nightmares of men. Here was the face of love without a face, a voice, a scent, a memory, here was a rub and a tumble without the sandy grain of a personality, here was a reminder of all the foolishness, vengefulness and lewdness in love and he seemed to excite, in the depraved crowd, a stubborn love of decency. . . . It seemed more shameful and more sinful that Pierre, who was willing to perform the sacred and mysterious rites for the least sacred rewards, was wanted by no one and that for all his readiness to sin he might, in the end, have to spend a quiet night in the dormitory counting sheep. Something was wrong, some promise, however obscene, was broken and Emile sweated in shame for his companion, for to lust and to be unwanted seemed to be the grossest indecency.   (p. 280)

The impersonality of venery shocks Emile, but "in an intoxication of pride, a determination to prove that what had happened to Pierre could not happen to him" (p. 280), he mounts the auction block. Melissa, it turns out, is the highest bidder, and she wins him for herself and takes him home. As the two enter the gates of her villa,

> [Emile] could hear the loud noise of a fountain and nightingales singing in the trees and . . . he discovered that he had not brought his sense of good and evil across the bay. . . . He seemed violently to destroy and renew himself, demolish and rebuild his spirit on some high sensual plane that was unbound from the earth and its calendar.   (p. 280)

These Christian symbols of the nightingale (an image for the soul's flight and freedom) and the fountain (an image of Christ, the "living water" and the model of chastity) contrast with Emile's life, which is hereafter transformed: even the "flowers in the garden seemed aphrodisiac and even the blue of the sky like some part of love" (p. 281). The words "some part" express an ironic summary. Emile's final transformation into impersonality takes place under the bewitchment of Circe—Melissa—and we last see him fearful that he will be transformed into a dog.

The novel ends with a coda, autumnal and elegiac, that mirrors the bittersweet mood of the story. The narrator asserts himself again, telling us, "So that is all and now it is time to go" (p. 307). Before leaving, however, he records for us the dreams of the residents of St. Botolphs whom he will leave behind. Despite outward appearances, they too are like Coverly's guests on Christmas Day, somewhat blind and lonely, "those who dream in terms of missed things." All else changes, including St. Botolphs—"The sense of life as a migration seems to have reached even into this provincial backwater" (p. 307)—and yet dreams, those emblematic engines of human aspiration and hope, abide. All else in the story has involved unwished-for transformation; in dreams, something different, transport rather than transformation, is sought after. Each of these dreamers reveals a private heart in quest of either love or heaven or order or adventure or triumph, and so each inevitably must dwell in a wider world beyond the confines of St. Botolphs—a leave-taking not unlike the narrator's:

> Mr. Williams, racked by the earth-shaking, back-breaking, binding, grinding need for love, dreams that he holds in his arms the Chinese waitress who works in the Pergola Restaurant in Travertine. Mrs. Williams, sleepless, sends up to heaven a string of winsome prayers like little clouds of colored smoke. Mrs. Bretaigne dreams that she is in a strange village at three in the morning ringing the doorbell of a frame house. She is looking, it seems, for her laundry, but the stranger who opens the door cries suddenly: "Oh, I thought it was Francis, I thought Francis had come home!". . . Mrs. Dummer dreams that she sails down one of the explicit waterways of sleep, while Mr. Dummer, at her side, climbs the Matterhorn. Jack Brattle dreams of a lawn without quack grass, a driveway without weeds, a garden without aphids, cutworm or blackspot and an orchard without tent caterpillars. His mother, in the next room, dreams that she is being crowned by the governor of Massachusetts and the state traffic commissioner for the unprecedented scrupulousness with which she has observed the speed limits, traffic lights and stop signs. She wears long white robes and thousands applaud her virtue. The crown is surprisingly heavy. (p. 308)

This passage, with its detailed comic compassion, reminds the reader once more of the privacy and mystery of the human spirit, both of which have been the novel's central themes. It is not surprising, then, that we find the narrator himself alone at the story's close, looking back on the village of his creation during a thunderstorm in which "lightning plays around the steeple of Christ Church, that symbol of our engulfing struggle with good and evil" (p. 309). As he describes the "cavernous structure of sound" which the thunder makes, the reader realizes that the very existence of St. Botolphs has been entirely dependent on the structure of sound produced by the narrator's voice and imagination. Once he says farewell, the village vanishes forever, for he has given to airy nothing a local habitation and a name. And yet some effective words will endure, especially honest ones like those written by Leander, words that the narrator himself remembers: " 'Let us consider that the soul of man is immortal, able to endure every sort of good and every sort of evil' " (p. 309).

The vocabulary of choice is hammer, nails, fire and water, air, a more elemental vocabulary.

John Cheever

Here we are all by day; by night w'are hurled
By dreams, each into a sev'rall world.

Robert Herrick

Beware. All those who follow me are led
Onto that Glassy Mountain where are no
Footholds for logic. . . .

W. H. Auden

The diagnosis of the death of the novel one leaves to boors. You and I know that the form counts upon irridescence for its vitality. . . . One never, of course, asks is it a novel? One asks is it interesting and interest connotes suspense, emotional involvement and a sustained claim on one's attention.

John Cheever in an Open Letter
to Elizabeth Hardwick

I cannot agree with recent writers who have told us that we are Nothing. We are indeed not what the Golden Age boasted us to be. But we are Something.

Saul Bellow

6: Bullet Park

John Cheever's third novel, *Bullet Park*, was composed and published during one of the darkest and most bitter periods in American history, the years 1968-69. Frank McConnell has called it "the age of the apocalyptic imagination," reflecting "the nightmare politics of the decade— the feeling that the Kennedy and King assassinations and the long national disgrace of Vietnam had finally delivered us [Americans] to a reality that could only be confronted in terms of surrealism and the comedy of the irrational."[1]

A brief summary listing some of the most important novels of the period is sufficient evidence of McConnell's contention. In 1968, they included Jerzy Kosinski, *Steps* (winner of the National Book Award); John Barth, *Lost in the Funhouse* (nominated); Joyce Carol Oates, *Expensive People* (nominated); Robert Coover, *The Universal Baseball Association, Inc.*; William Gass, *In the Heart of the Heart of the Country*; and John Updike, *Couples*. The significant novels of 1969 included Joyce Carol Oates, *Them* (winner of the National Book Award); Leonard Michaels, *Going Places* (nominated); Kurt Vonnegut, *Slaughterhouse-Five* (nominated); John Hawkes, *Lunar Landscapes*: John Leonard, *Crybaby of the Western World*; Philip Roth, *Portnoy's Complaint*; Larry Woiwode, *What I'm Going to Do, I Think*—and John Cheever, *Bullet Park*.

I submit this list not merely to spur recollection but primarily to situate the writing of *Bullet Park* and especially its critical reception. In 1968 Presidential candidate Hubert Humphrey said that "this country is on the verge of a nervous breakdown," and these novels in differing ways reflect that perception. In the late sixties the center could not hold: America's former, rather complacent image of itself was fragmented, and Americans of all ages were undergoing profound emotional and psychic displacement. Even more horrible events had occurred in our century, of course, but at this time the confluence of competing energetic angers and

1. Frank D. McConnell, *Four Postwar American Authors* (Chicago: Univ. of Chicago Press, 1977), pp. xii, xxvi.

their unforeseen acceleration became allied with an intensive and highly publicized national self-analysis (civil and international wars rarely grant a nation the leisure for any self-consciousness of that kind), and so made this era radically different. Everywhere, on every level of American society, the polarities of energy and atrophy, hope and frustration, glory and guilt collided and sometimes even melded in curious fashion. For sensitive people, "unreality" was the watchword in a country gone mad, and our novelists were the articulate messengers of the bad news.

Earlier in the century, despite the patent absurdities of World War I, a modernist writer like D. H. Lawrence could still extol the novel as "the bright book of life," implying that it provided a window on reality and reached the deepest of life's experiences. But in the late sixties many literate people—most notably academics, closer than most others to the more dramatic and deeply felt emotional disarray so evident on university campuses—were not quite so sanguine as Lawrence. For them the common assumption was that the times were out of joint and cursed spites impossible to set aright; as for the "thereness" of reality, no "there" existed. As a result, many writers and even more critics began to despair of the realistic possibilities of the novel form, that is, of the modernist assumption that the novel was capable of directly engaging historical, moral, and social questions. Instead, many turned inward to concentrate on fiction *qua* fiction, on the bright book with life excised, so to speak. As I mentioned earlier, this effort was labeled "post-modernism" or the like, an unhappy term in hindsight but one that attempted to characterize the deliberately unrealistic, extremely self-conscious fictional techniques popular at the time.

A sympathy with these historical, social, and literary factors is necessary to appreciate the negative reception of *Bullet Park*. In many ways this novel is as eccentric and unrealistic as any of its contemporaries, but Cheever—apparently slotted as a social realist of the old school—was not granted the indulgences accorded the post-modernists. This, however, was but one factor among others. At the time the book was published, the emotional circuits of most readers were overloaded: the depiction of psychic chaos had become a commonplace; anything less bold than a grinning skull seemed quaint or "square." In addition, during this period American cities and especially their suburbs were deemed not part of the problem but *the* problem, symbolic of hypocrisy, complacency, and moral rot, enclaves that smothered the human spirit. For a writer to situate his novel in a suburban setting and to do so in a tone less strident than that of excoriation was to risk the charge of smugness, even perversity. Lastly, this was an era of intellectual impatience, fueled by the fires of focused and unfocused anger; if a writer composed a novel that superficially resembled his previous work and yet was in fact an unexpected departure, most reviewers/readers were too tired or distracted to notice.

All this explanation is a roundabout effort to uncover and record the reasons why a fine novel like Bullet Park was not a critical success. Cheever himself was puzzled, because the disenchantment he had experienced while writing The Wapshot Scandal was gone; he was happy with this book upon completing it. In describing the book's reception, he said, "It wasn't so bad after Bullet Park where I'd done precisely what I wanted: a cast of three characters, a simple and resonant prose style and a scene where a man saves his beloved son from fire. The manuscript was received enthusiastically everywhere, but then Benjamin DeMott dumped on it in the Times and everybody picked up their marbles and ran home."[2]

Though this assessment exhibits writerly pique and a trace of overstatement, Cheever was essentially correct on both counts. First, the story is simple in outline, perhaps the tidiest of all his creations. It concerns the Nailles family: husband Eliot, wife Nellie, and their teenage son Tony, who enjoy a pleasant suburban existence in Bullet Park. Conventional and ordinary people to the core, their lives are upset when Tony inexplicably takes to bed and refuses to get up. The whole of Part One narrates the parents' varied efforts to save Tony from this predicament; finally, to their wonderment, he is revived by the ministrations of a crazed swami whose technique involves the ritual repetition of optimistic chants. Part Two is the first-person narrative of a Bullet Park neighbor named Paul Hammer, who recounts the sad rhythms of his life in order to explain to himself and to us the reasons why he plans to sacrifice a suburbanite on the altar of Christ Church; he is convinced that nothing less than a crucifixion can wake up the world. Part Three unites the three male principals in dramatic collision. Hammer kidnaps Tony and brings him to the church, but before he can carry out his mad scheme, Nailles arrives in time to rescue his son. With Tony again miraculously saved, the story ends where it began—in an atmosphere of apparent suburban serenity, although transfers and transformations have occurred.

As for DeMott's front-page review in the New York Times Book Review, entitled "A Grand Gatherum of Some Late 20th Century American Weirdos," his report was not likely to spur enthusiasm or curiosity within the hearts of the reading public. DeMott faulted Bullet Park harshly for its inconsistency in character and its flimsy structure, and pronounced it a

2. "John Cheever: The Art of Fiction LXII," Paris Review, 17, No. 7 (Fall 1976), 42.

novel marked by "carelessness, lax composition and perfunctoriousness."[3] Like him, other reviewers once again raised what might be called "the Cheever short story objection" against it. Pearl Bell in the *New Leader* found its episodes little more than "rough notes for a short story"; Joyce Carol Oates objected to "Cheever's talky, fragmented, at times exasperating method of narrative," and found it more a "series of eerie, sometimes beautiful, sometimes overwrought vignettes" characterized by "real nastiness, a profound nastiness" beneath the whimsy.[4] Anatole Broyard in the *New Republic* pronounced it a Gothic novel in which Cheever "appears to be almost helplessly carried away by the flood tides of his imagination" and his "palette seems to have nothing but screaming colors."[5]

Although they were fewer in number, other equally perceptive reviewers enjoyed the novel immensely, but unfortunately their positive appraisals were couched more tentatively than those of the nay-sayers. For example, John Leonard claimed *Bullet Park* was "Cheever's deepest, most challenging book" and possessed "the tension and luminosity of a vision."[6] He wondered aloud whether the character of Hammer was one intentionally created as an incredible figure in order to reflect "an aspect or fantasy" that Nailles imagines he defeats to achieve self-redemption. Then John Updike admitted that the novel "holds together but barely, by the thinnest of threads" and that the "tender, twinkling prose has an undercurrent of distraction and impatience," but he praised it finally as "a slowly revolving mobile of marvelously poeticized moments" and concluded with the observation that Cheever "maintains his loyalty to the middling and the decent, but increasingly speaks in the accents of a visionary."[7]

As this brief sample of snippets from thoughtful reviews indicates, one

3. Benjamin DeMott, "A Grand Gatherum of Some Late 20th Century American Weirdos," *New York Times Book Review*, April 27, 1969, pp. 1, 40-41. For a fine sampling from the contemporary reviews, see Francis J. Boscha, *John Cheever: A Reference Guide* (Boston: G. K. Hall, 1981), pp. 54ff. For closer critical readings, see Samuel Coale, *John Cheever* (New York: Ungar, 1977), pp. 95-105; and Lynne Waldeland, *John Cheever* (Boston: Twayne, 1979), pp. 104-116. Waldeland's is an enthusiastic reading; Coale's is less so.

4. Pearl K. Bell, "Taker of Notes," *New Leader*, May 26, 1969, pp. 11-13; Joyce Carol Oates, "Cheever's People: The Retreat from Chaos," *Chicago Tribune Book World*, April 20, 1969, pp. 1, 3.

5. Anatole Broyard, "You Wouldn't Believe It," *New Republic*, April 26, 1969, pp. 36-37.

6. John Leonard, "Evil Comes to Suburbia," *New York Times*, April 29, 1969, p. 43.

7. John Updike, "Suburban Man," *Sunday Times* (London), September 14, 1969, p. 62. Updike's review is reprinted in his essay-review collection, *Picked-Up Pieces* (New York: Knopf, 1975).

cannot but come away with the impression that a first encounter with the novel functions much like a Rorschach test for the reader. Where some see ugly blots, nasty or eerie shapes, others find visionary strokes and meaningful contours. Small wonder this is true, because shortly after its publication Cheever remarked in an interview that "I think the sense of form [in *Bullet Park*] is such a figment of the imagination. It's almost like shaping a dream . . . to give it precisely the concord you want . . . the arch, really. It's almost the form of an arch."[8]

In that same interview—as if in contradiction to that elusive allusion to dream and arch—Cheever said,

> What I wanted to do—since *The Wapshot Scandal* was such an extraordinarily complex book built around non sequiturs, really—what I wanted to do was something quite simple. I kept thinking of William Tell: that this was a man who loved his son and was able to protect him or, as a matter of fact, save him. And I wanted to describe a love that could be implemented, that existed in other than dramatic terms. In a sense, all three of my novels are love stories, really. *The Wapshot Chronicle* is my love for Leander; *The Scandal* is, I suppose, Melissa's love for Emile. And this is simply Nailles's love for Tony. Anything else is all in the nature of a variation.[9]

Cheever was notorious for being evasive in an interview, especially on personal subjects or critical judgments, but he can never be faulted for being dishonest in discussing his own work. These latter remarks indicate that he intended the novel to be a story about love and salvation with a fairly simple thematic structure leading to an upbeat ending. To establish whether he failed in execution or his displeased reviewers failed in perception is precisely the function of close critical analysis. I subscribe to the view that most reviewers misread the tone of the novel badly—admitting, however, that it was easy to do so.

Tone, as in all of Cheever's fiction, is especially crucial here. An excellent critic like George Garrett, who is very partial to Cheever's work, said of *Bullet Park*,

> The savagery, the misanthropy of the work might be (and *has been* by casual critics) called Swiftean. But Swift's contempt of the world was of a very different order, being firmly based upon faith and hope and, sometimes explicitly, sometimes by assumed implication, charity. . . . Full of Christian signs and symbols, this story perverts them one

---

8. Christopher Lehmann-Haupt, "Talk with John Cheever," *New York Times Book Review*, April 27, 1969, p. 43.

9. Lehmann-Haupt, "Talk with John Cheever," p. 43.

by one as the author (who else?) ignores the gospel. There are no glad tidings here.[10]

When a reader of generous sympathy and keen sensibility like Garrett describes the novel further as "a bitter book," devoid of a standard of sanity, that ridicules human suffering ("[Cheever] finds most human suffering ridiculous and vulgar"), attention must be paid. Cheever, no doubt aware of this and similar criticism, was asked by his interviewer, years later, whether he had diminished his characters too much in *Bullet Park*. He replied:

> No, I didn't feel that. But I believe that it was understood in those terms. I believe that Hammer and Nailles were thought to be casualties, which isn't what I intended at all. And I thought I made my intentions quite clear. But if you don't communicate, it's not anybody's fault. Neither Hammer nor Nailles were meant to be either psychiatric or social metaphors; they were meant to be two men with their own risks. I think the book was misunderstood on those terms.[11]

Cheever's later statement refutes but does not actually clarify negative objections. At any rate, the reason I have persisted in citing so many varied readings, including his, is to demonstrate that most extrinsic aids available provide meager assistance for a critical reading. The one exception is provided by John Gardner in an article that appeared in the *New York Times Book Review* in October 1971, almost three years after *Bullet Park* was published. The article is notable because the *Times Book Review* rarely publishes lengthy retrospective reviews, and also because Gardner lambasts the original reviewers, contending that "the Wapshot books, though well made, were minor. 'Bullet Park,' illusive, mysteriously built, was major—in fact a magnificent work of fiction."[12]

Although thick with Gardner's characteristically contentious hyperbole, the article is replete with fresh perceptions that stimulate re-entry and re-evaluation of the novel. In Gardner's opinion,

> Cheever's subject is chance—but more than that. Chance is a vehicle that carries the book into darker country. The opening lines present a setting—a train station—designed to suggest the whole human condition in that mysterious chance-riddled universe. A temporary planet

10. George Garrett, "Afterword: John Cheever and the Charms of Innocence," in *The Sounder Few: Essays from the "Hollins Critic,"* ed. R. H. Dillard et al. (Athens: Univ. of Georgia Press, 1971), pp. 36-37.

11. "John Cheever: The Art of Fiction LXII," pp. 64-65.

12. John Gardner, "Witchcraft in Bullet Park," *New York Times Book Review*, October 24, 1971, pp. 2, 24. Since I will be quoting from this article extensively, page references to it will be included in the text.

whose architecture, like that of the station, is "oddly informal, gloomy but unserious"; a place of isolation where chance seems to rule even art.   (p. 2)

Moreover, Gardner credits Cheever with not being content with the fashionable bleak canards about chance and for reconsidering "the idea of chance, remembering psychic and psychological phenomena," and the claims of good and evil. He creates "a world in a way even grimmer than Beckett's because here love and sacrifice are realities, like hope, but realities in flux, perpetually threatening, perishing":

> The novel says yes-and-no to existentialists, who can account for all but the paragnost. Cheever, in other words, sees the mind in its totality—sees not only the fashionable existential darkness but the light older than consciousness, which gives nothingness definition. Partly for the sake of this wholeness of vision, Cheever abandoned the fact-bound novel of verisimilitude which is by nature impotent to dramatize the mind's old secrets and turned to dependence on voice, secret of the willing suspension of disbelief that normally carries the fantasy or tale.   (p. 2)

One might differ with Gardner's emphasis on chance as the central theme (and with his casual dismissal of the flexible potential of the realistic novel), but his arguments do intelligently reinstate the thematic depth and complex shape of the novel. On this interaction between form and thematic content, Gardner also offers this insight:

> As in all first-rate novels, the form of "Bullet Park" grows out of its subject. More here than in his earlier writings, Cheever depends on poetic (which is to say, magical) devices—rhythm, imagistic repetition, echo. Instead of conventional plot, an accretion of accidents. Far below consciousness, the best people in Bullet Park are mirror images of the worst: they live by magic, correspondence.   (p. 2)

Gardner's critical vocabulary here is deliberately elusive, but his accent on "magical" properties in the novel is central to its understanding. Thematically, the word "magic" captures nicely the variants on the mysterious powers both within and without man that the story explores, powers that alternately appear as beneficent and sinister. The narrative is also replete with magic rituals, inexplicable intercessions, irresistible charms, created and/or crippling illusions, cryptic messages that haunt the hearers, and so on. A magical strangeness (hardly the same thing as alienation) seems at the heart of things; efforts to eliminate this strangeness through rational control or "higher" consciousness are doomed to failure or frustration.

Furthermore, *pace* Garrett, the Christian symbolism throughout reinforces and, in fact, elevates this supernatural and preternatural bias in the novel. Although the magical incidents appear disparate and secular, a distinctively biblical pattern provides the novel's final shape. The echoing sequence of the great biblical "mysteries" underlies its magical unfolding: the mystery of the first Creation and the garden world, of an inexplicable fall and alienation from creation, of the potential of love linked with suffering, of reawakening into salvation through first a redemptive word and then a sacrificial action, of apocalypse and restoration. Cheever, of course, is far too sophisticated a novelist to make this biblical pattern unduly explicit (he obviously is doing other things as well), but the artistic sensibility is ultimately reverent rather than bitter in the face of mystery.

As I have noted, many reviewers detected a cynical tone in *Bullet Park*, especially at the novel's close. Some seized upon the final lines, "Tony went back to school on Monday and Nailles—drugged—went off to work and everything was as wonderful, wonderful, wonderful, wonderful as it had been,"[13] as indicative of a skeptical scoffing only. Indeed, these lines are ironical, but they are that on many levels. The fact that the word "wonderful" is repeated four times is no guarantee of a cynical attitude (nor of simple-mindedness). One might better presume that Cheever, a lover of language and a writer of precision and nuance, inserted this seemingly airy, wistful repetition for a more subtle purpose (let us assume that cynicism is inevitably an obvious stance). If one resists the univocal tongue-in-cheek interpretation, then the multivalent connotations of the word "wonderful"—awesome, unique, miraculous, curious, strange, marvelous, extraordinary, fabulous—when read aloud with different inflections, reflect more appropriately the actual form and content of the novel, as well as offer a more fitting summation. Such a reading might disclose that this novel is more "wonderful" than it first appears, for wonder causes surprise, puzzlement, ambivalence, and admiration. As Coleridge put it in an aphorism, "the first wonder is the offspring of ignorance; the last is the parent of adoration."

In his argument Gardner offhandedly equates the magical with the poetic, but this point is especially well-taken. More so than in Cheever's previous novels, the synergism of form and content in *Bullet Park* relies almost entirely upon the interanimation of images and symbols held in tension and controlled by a similar tone and voice (the "objective" narrator and Hammer's personal voice are eerily identical—and deliberately so). Poetic logic rather than plot is the organizing principle, and it addresses mental and emotional chambers less readily accessible to conven-

13. John Cheever, *Bullet Park* (New York: Knopf, 1969), p. 245. Hereafter references to the novel will be included in the text.

tional discourse. In his interview with John Hersey, Cheever put it this way:

> The force of reality in fiction and the force of reality in a dream are very much the same. You find yourself on a sailing boat that you do not know—going along a coast that is totally strange to you, but you're wearing an old suit, and the person beside you is your wife. This is in the nature of a dream. The experience of fiction is similar: one builds as if at random. [14]

I quote these general remarks (note that the "as if," so casually inserted, identifies the essence of his own art), because eight years before, in the interview I cited earlier, Cheever specifically described *Bullet Park* in similar terms that are worth repeating: "I think the sense of form [in *Bullet Park*] is such a figment of the imagination. It's almost like shaping a dream . . . to give it precisely the concord you want . . . the arch, really. It's almost the form of an arch."

The dream ambience and the arch structure are cues toward appreciating the novel, representing, as it were, Coleridge's definition for poetry as "a more than usual state of emotion with more than usual order." An arch, after all, is an ordering of a distinctive kind: it is a curved construct shaped to admit an opening, the stresses on the center of which are transmitted through the vertical supports. The arch image thus captures nicely the dialectical polarity and mutual interdependence, not only of the symbolism and images in the novel but also of the central characters. Nailles and Hammer, at seemingly opposite ends of the opening, are actually conjoined in action and "stress" through Tony, the central wedge, and the three together constitute the novel's characteriological arch.

The arch also reminds us, lest we forget, that when we use the word "symbol" in discussing a work of art we are actually describing a structure of interrelated symbolism. That is, we respond to a particular image or symbol not as an isolated instance, but as a cue that directs us beyond its immediate meaning to the complex symbolic interrelationship—the *whole* structure of which it partakes. All first-rate fiction does this, of course, but the very challenges *Bullet Park* presents reinforce this artistic truth for the reader. It is the arch-like character of this fiction, its contrived "suspension," let us say, that allows us entry within and beneath the arch into a dream world of interconnected imagery that is at once mysterious and recognizable.

Furthermore, the arch image suggests well the religious attitude that supports the novel's framework and texture. Throughout it we witness the

---

14. "John Hersey: Talk with John Cheever," *New York Times Book Review*, March 6, 1977, p. 28.

terplay between good and evil, faith and doubt, love and its opposites
murder, envy, hatred). Cheever subtly reminds us that none of these
ounters ought to be viewed in isolation, for it is their interconnectedness
id mutuality that constitute the human truth and the religious mystery.
his was John Henry Newman's insight into the nature of Christian faith
The Grammar of Assent. Newman was aware that every empirical state-
ient (such as "Britain is an island" or "I shall die") is doubtable if analyzed
isolated fashion. Only when such a proposition is understood in relation
other propositions and other evidence accumulates does our doubt
iminish. Assent (which he describes as that of the experience "as if we
iw"—which has a Cheeveresque ring to it) reflects a leap akin to an
rtistic response wherein our imaginations suddenly integrate all the di-
erse parts, not so much in coherence as in tension; and those very parts
nce gathered discretely and accumulatively are now grasped as an inter-
lationship of modifiers and emphases, a whole greater than any one or
ie sum of its parts.[15]

Newman extends his analysis to religious assent and actually uses the
nage of an arch to describe it. In Christianity the doctrinal propositions
our likeness to and radical difference from God, sin and grace, the co-
xistence of good and evil) as well as the virtues it champions (courage
nd humility, sanctity and admission of sinfulness, charity and honesty)
ppear contradictory if considered independently and not interdepen-
ently. But no doctrine or virtue is the truth by itself; each modifies and
iterprets another, and the truth resides precisely in their equilibrium,
heir lack of independence.

I outline Newman's argument here at the risk of introducing a di-
erting digression, because his analysis reminds us that meaning emerges
radually (i.e., both artistic and religious meaning) only after we have
ncountered the interaction of apparently contradictory claims upon us.
n Cheever's fiction—especially in Bullet Park—tone, metaphor, image,
nd symbol sometimes seem without "support," buttresses thrown in hap-
iazard directions, and "weightless" to boot.

But if my emphasis on the arch image appears overstretched, so to
peak, then I submit another which might better relate to the argument:
he vortex, an image that recurs throughout Bullet Park and is especially
rominent in Hammer's personal confession. To the naked eye and even
hrough instruments the central axis of a vortex is invisible; only the
pirals whirling about it, those spinning atoms or fluids or vapors sucked

15. For a brilliant discussion (to which I am indebted) of this aspect of Newman's
hought and of the relationship of imagination to belief, see John Coulson, Religion and
imagination: 'in aid of a grammar of assent' (New York: Clarendon-Oxford, 1981), especially
op. 3-86.

and drawn to it, force us to infer its existence as the source of the mov
ment's power. The vortex is thus a fitting image for Hammer's emotion
state, but it also represents the texture of the whole novel and compl
ments the arch as a structural image. The events, characters, and image
in Bullet Park are all vortical in the sense that the novel is ever rotatin
whirling, eddying on conelike levels around an invisible center that cor
tinually alters in shape and depth and direction in rapid interchang
Energy is all. An inordinate desire to isolate one element in the proce
would involve, well, evaporation.

A Reading

The opening paragraph of Bullet Park artfully establishes the tone, view
point, and symbolic setting for what follows. The first sentence read
"Paint me a small railroad station then, ten minutes before dark." Th
words "paint me" sound like both an invocation of the Muse and a con
mand to the imagination, an effort at evocation shared by you and "me.
The "then" which follows it sounds tossed off and casual in the contex
as though other evocations might serve as well, but the request become
disconcertingly precise—"ten minutes before dark." Why? Perhaps th
casually inserted "then" does not mean "in that case" at all, but is specifi
and temporal? What follows reinforces our unsettlement about the am
biguous potential of language and seeing. To show how Cheever build
this impression, I have quoted the entire opening paragraph, italicizin
certain key words that merit attention:

> Paint me a small railroad station then, ten minutes before dark.
> Beyond the platform are the waters of the Wekonsett River, reflecting
> a *somber* afterglow. The architecture of the station is *oddly* informal,
> *gloomy* but *unserious*, and *mostly* resembles a *pergola*, cottage or summer
> house *although* this is a climate of *harsh* winters. The lamps along the
> platform burn with a *nearly* palpable plaintiveness. The setting *seems*
> in *some* way to be at the heart of the *matter*. *We* travel by plane, oftener
> than not, *and yet* the *spirit* of our country *seems* to have remained a
> country of railroads. *You* wake in a pullman bedroom at three a.m. in
> a city the name of which you do *not know* and may never *discover*. A
> man stands on the platform with a child on his shoulders. They are
> waving *goodbye* to some traveler, but *what* is the child doing up so late
> and *why* is the man crying? On a siding beyond the platform there is
> a lighted dining car where a waiter sits alone at a table, adding up his
> accounts. *Beyond* this is a water tower and *beyond* this a well-lighted
> and empty street. *Then you think* happily that this is *your country*—
> *unique*, *mysterious* and vast. *One* has no such feelings in airplanes,
> airports and the trains of other nations.   (pp. 3-4)

"The setting seems . . . to be at the heart of the matter." Note that the description of the railroad station and its environs at first appears to be exact, a deft sketch of a specific time and place. But the adjectives suggest otherwise: the words "somber," "gloomy," and "unserious" connote psychological and emotional impressions, i.e., mediated reactions rather than an objective, immediate observation. Then follows a series of tentative adverbs and adverbial phrases, each of which qualifies everything apparently specific: "oddly," "mostly," "although . . . harsh winters," "nearly palpable." The repetition of the muddied verb "seems" reinforces this sense of imprecision. When the direct address shifts suddenly from "me" to "we" and boldly to "you," we realize that this railroad station is less a specific place than it is a state of mind, a more universal perception that is shareable. The blunt stress is on "You wake in a pullman bedroom at three a.m.," so the implicit invitation is to assume imaginatively the intermediate phase between sleep and wakefulness. Furthermore, it is during this phase that we collide with the mysterious: "You do not know and may never discover" the name of the city the train passes through, and yet quirky questions haunt us—"what is the child doing up so late and why is the man crying?" Significantly, it is at this point that the opening emphasis on the word "beyond" comes to the fore again, suggesting that the vague beyond is also at the heart of the matter. Then the paragraph ends with an ironic "you *think*," followed by a rhetorically banal paean to nationalistic feeling. The last sentence is less personal, and the reader wonders: why doesn't "one" get such feelings elsewhere? The answer will be found in the story that follows, but already we are alerted that it lies not in railroad travel as such but in "such feelings."

Thus in fewer than five hundred words Cheever has skillfully introduced the emotional and thematic arch of the novel, its shifting tone and point of view, as well its symbolic motifs and image clusters. The rest of the first chapter (the plot proper starts in Chapter Two) builds on what has been established, doing so by alternating points of view and playing on variations of thematic contrast, such as those of arrival and departure, distance and nearness, stranger and neighbor, order and disorder, light and darkness, and pretense and fact. As the title suggests, Bullet Park is an ambiguous place, a juxtaposition of the deadly and the idyllic.

A stranger arrives at the station and is met by Hazzard, the real-estate agent, whose name "is nailed to the trees in vacant lots" (p. 4). We learn that "the search for shelter seems to [the stranger] to go on at a nearly primordial level" (p. 4). And so the narrator accompanies the stranger on a tour of Bullet Park. (Later we realize that the stranger is Hammer; at this stage the consciousnesses of the narrator and the stranger merge. The narrator, however, qualifies his observations; in Part Two, Hammer, no longer a stranger to us, speaks directly and without qualification—and therein lies his madness.) At first the stranger's quest seems singular, but we hear otherwise:

> The house or the flat that he looks for, he knows, will have had to have appeared at least twice in his dreams. When it is all over, when the gardens are planted and the furniture is settled, the rigors of the journey will have been concealed; but on this evening the blood-memory of travel and migrations courses through his veins. The people of Bullet Park intend not so much to have arrived there as to have been planted and grown there, but this of course was untrue. Disorder, moving vans, bank loans at high interest, tears and desperation had characterized most of their arrivals and departures.   (pp. 4-5)

These contrasts between Edenesque delusions and the more ominous truth, between dreams and blood memories are described from a close vantage point; Hammer's own story will bring these contrasts closer still. Here they are immediately compared with an opposite telescopic vantage point, a view of Bullet Park "seen at an improbable distance by some zealous and vengeful adolescent" (p. 5). At the story's close, Hammer will be the one zealous and vengeful, but who is this second stranger, this young prophet of damnation, and why is his viewpoint called improbable?

> Seen at an improbable distance by some zealous and vengeful adolescent, ranging over the golf links, the piece of plush would seem to be the imprimatur, the guerdon, the accolade and banner of Powder Hill behind which marched, in tight English shoes, the legions of wifeswapping, Jew-baiting, booze-fighting spiritual bankrupts. Oh damn them all, thought the adolescent. Damn the bright lights by which no one reads, damn the continuous music which no one hears, damn the grand pianos that no one can play. . . . Damn their hypocrisy, damn their cant, damn their credit cards, damn their discounting the wilderness of the human spirit, damn their immaculateness, damn their lechery and damn them above all for having leached from life that strength, malodorousness, color and zeal that give it meaning. Howl, howl, howl.
> But the adolescent, as adolescents always are, would be mistaken.
>   (pp. 5-6)

The whole jeremiad is typically Cheeveresque, rising in random indignations to the the Lear-like howls, and then ironically moderated by the dispassionate "but." We worry and are uncertain about the appropriateness of that "but," and then are not allowed to linger, for the tour guide's voice takes over suddenly and introduces us to those exempted from damnation. First we meet the Wickwires, who are "charming," "brilliant," even "incandescent," and who function as "celebrants" in the only meaningful liturgies of the village. Bullet Park is now a society both transformed and in search of transformation, and its rites betray a transmuted imitation of the traditional religious ceremonies of its Christian and Jewish forebears. The cocktail party has replaced the Mass, the evening song, and the Seder; attendance at round-robin parties is now the true pilgrimage, or the stations to Calvary; the draughts now drunk are distillates, and the sacramental signs are olive pits and lemon peels. Because of their altered intent we might think these rites bloodless and benign. But that is not so:

> For a community that had so few altars—four to be exact—and none of them sacrificial, [the Wickwires] seemed, as serious and dedicated celebrants, to have improvised a sacrificial altar on which they had literally given up some flesh and blood. They were always falling downstairs, bumping into sharp-edged furniture and driving their cars into ditches. When they arrived at a party they would be impeccably dressed but her right arm would be in a sling. He would support a game leg with a gold-headed cane and wear dark glasses. (pp. 6-7)

Throughout religious history, God's ministry has exacted a price; the Wickwires, like all those drunk with the Lord, learn well the implications of martyrdom. Monday mornings test their celebratory "ardor" and witness to their sacrificial spirit. Votaries at ceremonies of the dark, they both whimper in pain when the dawn's light streams into their bedroom; seeing himself in the bathroom mirror, Wickwire "possesses for a moment the curious power of being able to frighten himself" (p. 7). Downstairs he comes upon the empty bottles, those hallowed instruments of the evening's ritual, and lets out a cry of pain:

> They are ranged there like the gods in some pantheon of remorse. Their intent seems to be to force him to his knees and to wring from him some prayer. "Empties, oh empties, most merciful empties, have mercy upon me for the sake of Jack Daniels and Seagram Distillers." Their immutable emptiness gives them a look that is cruel and censorious. (p. 8)

Throughout this scene the inversion of religious gesture and ceremony is manipulated for farcical effect, ending in a secular parody of Christ's Agony in the Garden. (Wickwire rises from bed "for the third time" and finally "boards his Gethsemane—the Monday-morning 10:48.") Less obvious and more subtly ironic, however, is the tour's continuation, in which each of the metaphors is recapitulated: religious transposition, emptiness, light, celebration, and subliminal linkages are established.

As the house-hunting jaunt proceeds, the realistic (Hazzard is a *realtor*, after all) and the surrealistic meld, because the stranger and the strangeness itself become our focus; with him we hear the collision between boosterism and despair, the one less audible than the other:

> Mr. Elmsford (6 bedrooms, 3 baths, $53,000) dusts off his tarnished psalter which is something he never mastered. . . ."Oh, why am I so disappointed," he sings, "why does everything seemed to have passed me by". . . . Then there are the affirmative singers: "Bullet Park is growing, growing, Bullet Park is here to stay, Bullet Park shows great improvement, every day in every way. . . ." (p. 10)

The final stop is at the home of Mrs. Heathcup, who says, " 'The only reason I'm selling is because there's nothing here for me, now that he's gone. Nothing at all' " (p. 11). She tells them with pride that her husband painted the whole house each year, painted a separate room each month, and that he "was painting the dining room the day he passed away" (p. 11). Here the repeated emphasis on painting builds to a humorous obsessiveness on the couple's part, and is a comic variant of the novel's opening sentence (as well as a portent of Hammer's fascination with yellow walls). Then we learn how Mr. Heathcup died: " 'While he was painting I heard him talking to himself. "I can't stand it any longer," he said. I still don't know what he meant. Then he went out into the garden and shot himself' " (p. 12). Mrs. Heathcup still keeps her table set because her husband " 'hated to see an empty table and so I always keep it set, sort of in memory. An empty table depressed him' " (p. 12).

The stranger, Hammer, is taken by "the tragic and brightly lighted place" (p. 13) and decides to return with his wife for her evaluation. The tour ends and the chapter closes the way it began—at the railroad station. Only now we see the station close up, and not at twilight but at night. The romantic timelessness to which the opening lines invited us is now upended:

> Broken windows let in the night wind. The clock face was smashed. The hands of the clock were gone. The architect, so many years ago, had designed the building with some sense of the erotic and romantic essence of travel, but all his inventions had been stripped or defaced and Hammer found himself in a warlike ruin. (p. 14)

Chapter Two, where the story effectively begins, is our second welcome to the commuter community and specifically to Hammer's counterpart, Eliot Nailles. Just as the first chapter started within a structure symbolic of spiritual ambiguities, aspiration, and mystery, so, too, does the second, for we discover Nailles in Christ's Church, less attentive than he would be at the Wickwires' celebrations:

> Holy Communion. Sexagesima. Nailles heard a cricket in the chancel and the noise of a tin drum from the rain gutters while he said

his prayers. His sense of the church calendar was much more closely associated with the weather than with the revelations and strictures in Holy Gospel. St. Paul meant blizzards. St. Mathias meant a thaw. . . . For the crucifixion a bobsled stands stranded in a flower bed, its painter coiled among the early violets. The trout streams open for the resurrection. The crimson cloths at Pentecost and the miracle of the tongues meant swimming. . . . The flesh lusteth against the spirit to the smoke of leaf fires as did the raising of the dead. Then one was back again with St. Andrew and the snows of Advent. (pp. 15-16)

Nailles's divided attention and distracted religiosity are established immediately. We are told that "he did not expect to part with his flesh his memory in the narthex" (p. 16), and this casual observation is both a ominous adumbration of his story to follow and also a wry comment n his tepidity during the church calendar's pre-Lenten period. The li- rgical colors are purple, symbolic of sorrow and penitence as well as ve and truth (after the crucifixion Mary wears purple). As the service ntinues, "only the two candles that represent the flesh and the spirit rned" (p. 17), and it is significant that at this moment Hammer, still lled "the stranger," with whose life Nailles's life will be linked, arrives church.

After "the lights of the flesh and the spirit" are extinguished, the two en meet for the first time. When they identify themselves (Hammer d Nailles), Nailles is dismayed; a believer "in the mysterious power of menclature," he realizes vaguely that "for better, for worse, in madness d in saneness they seemed bound together for eternity by the simplicity their names" (p. 19).

The church setting, the symbols of division, and the preternatural, ysterious bond between the two men thus establish the novel's arch; the ory's end will counterbalance all the joists and stays of this initial en- unter. In recounting Nailles's trip home from church, Cheever in hu- orous fashion also introduces two opposite portents of the confusions d horrors to come. First, we are informed that Nailles keeps his wind- ield wiper on, although the rain has stopped, because "society had come so automotive and nomadic that nomadic signals had been es- blished" (p. 21), transmitted by various car signals; the newspapers in- icate the issues involved and the corresponding signals to employ. In is listing each sounds fanciful and absurd, but this is not so later when e plot unfolds:

Hang the child murderer. (Headlights.) Reduce the state income tax. (Parking lights.) Abolish the secret police. (Emergency signal.) The diocesan bishop had suggested that churchgoers turn on their wind- shield wipers to communicate their faith in the resurrection of the dead and the life of the world to come. (p. 21)

The ridiculous and the sublime comically unite again when Nail
arrives home. On the edge of his property, despite a "No Dumping" sig
he discovers "a gutted automobile, three defunct television sets and
soiled mattress" (p. 21). Each becomes emblematic of his later predic
ment, as we shall see, but at the moment he is dispirited most by tl
ubiquity of the mattresses, "rent, stained, human and obscene," and "h
sadness and unease at the human allusions of this intimate and domest
rubbish disturbed him" (p. 22).

This discrepancy is jarring, for Nailles lives a clean, well-ordered lif
He owns a pleasant Dutch Colonial home—"white," we are told. He
kind to his old dog Tessie, who is "afraid of heights and thunderstorms
and has grown deaf and senile and often whimpers in pain: "The cri
were piteous and senile and the only such cries (or the first such crie,
the house had heard since Nailles had bought the place" (p. 23). H
devotion to his wife Nellie is genuine and dog-like, for she is "the keystor
to his love of the visible world" (p. 24), his own emotional arch-suppor
And he is clearly a family man; we are told that "the love Nailles felt fe
his wife and his only son seemed like some limitless discharge of a clea
amber fluid that would surround them . . ." (p. 25). (Here the cok
amber is ironically double-edged: Hammer, demonically driven by th
color yellow, will in fact "surround" them later.)

The narrator steps forward to acknowledge that these people "seeme
to have less dimension than a comic strip, but why was this? They ha
erotic depths, origins, memories, dreams and seizures of melancholy an
enthusiasm" (p. 25). As if to dramatize this truth, the narrator traces
series of memories each of them privately possesses. The first two belon
to Nailles, and both betray the recollection of murderous impulses. H
recalls visiting his mother in a nursing home and "that she should be s
cruelly smitten and left so close to death challenged Nailles's belief in th
fitness of things" (p. 27). He realizes that, as she lies helpless in bed, h
could smother her with a pillow, and only an act of moral imaginatio
stops him: "Suppose, in spite of her pain and her cavernous loss of con
sciousness she still instinctively and tenaciously loved what remained c
her life; suppose she regained consciousness long enough to see that he
son was a matricide" (p. 29). Nailles's other memory is less benevolent
He recalls the time that his father, drunk and boisterous in a hotel ball
room, took the baton from the conductor and led the band, and he admit
that "had he possessed a pistol, [he] would have shot his father in th
back" (p. 28).

Nellie's private memories are not homicidal but venereal, not o
Thanatos but of Eros. We are told that Nellie's "committee work, flowe
arrangements and moral views would have made the raw material for ;

ight-club act" (p. 29), and that she paints canvases by studiously follow-
ng the numbered instructions. It was her sense of aesthetic exactitude
nd artistic interest that prompted her to go to New York's Greenwich
Village to report on a play's performance for her class on the modern
heatre. The experience gravely upsets her previous fascination with flow-
ry patterns. When a male member of the cast strips to the buff at the
nd of the first act, she wonders, "If these were merely the facts of life
vhy should her eyes be riveted on his thick pubic brush from which hung,
ike a discouraged and unwatered flower, his principal member" (p. 30).

These and like questions haunt her after she leaves the theatre and
oards a bus. She "looked around desperately for honest mothers, wives,
vomen who took pride in their houses, their gardens, their flower ar-
angements, their cooking" (p. 31). In a seat ahead two young men are
aughing and suddenly "one of them threw his arm around the other and
cissed him on the ear" (p. 31). Consternated, Nellie becomes a suburban
Diogenes in quest of an honest woman, a counterpart. She discovers one
n the seat beside her who tells her, " 'I've been looking everywhere for
English cretonne. . . . Nubbly, stretchy reps look completely out of place
n my decorating scheme, but nubbly, stretchy reps are all you can get.
I suppose there must be some cretonne somewhere but I haven't been
able to find it' " (p. 31). While the stranger prates on, the actor's "unwatered flower" and dirty words Nellie has seen and heard "burn in her
consciousness with a lingering incandescence," and she "seemed unable
to return to where she had been" (p. 32). By contrast, her counterpart
now appears contemptible (one who sees "virtue incarnate in cretonne
and evil represented by rep"), and she becomes increasingly anxious to
return home where "she would be herself again" (p. 32). Once on the
train she experiences "the symptoms of restoration," and on arriving home
she finds the cook stewing mushrooms (a Freudian touch) in butter, the
smell of which permeates the house. She goes upstairs to "her pleasant
room" and takes "a pleasant bath, but falsehood, confinement, exclusion
and a kind of blindness seemed to be her only means of comprehension"
(p. 33).

The next recorded memory at first reads like a funny vignette, tossed
in and superfluous, but actually it cleverly combines the murderous and
erotic themes of these earlier memories and relates them in comic fashion
to the couple's son, Tony. The event recounted is an incident that occurred the evening before the present action, after Nellie and Nailles had
returned from a party. It begins with Nailles going upstairs to visit his
son's room. We learn that Nailles is especially anxious to preserve the
boy's innocence, and that "there was some preference in the air, some
enjoyable and yet self-conscious sense that they were playing out the roles

written for them as a Father and a Son. Love was definitely what Nailles felt, and where a more demonstrative man in another country would have embraced his son and declared his love, Nailles would not" (p. 34). Thus role-playing and its implications emerge.

Amidst this awkwardness Nailles puts on a record of *Guys and Dolls.* Years before, though a man uninterested in either theatre or music, he saw the show, and "his rapture [seemed] to have begun with the opening fugue and to have mounted, number by number. On the final chorus he got to his feet and began to smash his hands together, roaring, 'Encore, encore' " (p. 35). Thereafter, he "evolved some sentimental theory about the tragedy of the sublime," convinced the experience "had the perfection of a midsummer day whose sublimity hinted at the inevitability of winter and death" (pp. 35-36). (By ironic contrast, his son entertains similar thoughts during their conversation: in the discord of his father's cough, "the boy was reminded unsentimentally of the facts of sickness, age and death"; p. 34). This evening Nailles leaps to his feet when "Luck Be a Lady Tonight" is played, smashes his fist into his palm, and on "the last chorus he made a groping gesture to illustrate a man reaching for stars" (p. 36).

After being taken through these interludes of memory, each a comic foretoken of the emotionally perplexing events to follow, we are returned gradually—as if in stages of reminiscent withdrawal—before the chapter ends where it began: with the unrecorded, plaintive communication of that Sexagesima Sunday. That morning Nailles goes back to his son's room, the scene of their conversation. He remembers his earlier search for a dictionary, and his opening Tony's only to find more than fifty photographs of naked women slipped inside. This discovery had not dismayed him, although what he did not discover would have. For had he turned on his son's tape recorder, he would have heard Tony's voice saying: " 'You dirty old baboon, you dirty old baboon. For as long as I can remember it seems to me that whenever I'm trying to go to sleep I can hear you saying dirty things. You say the dirtiest things in the whole world, you dirty, filthy, horny old baboon' " (p. 38).

This is a characteristic Cheeveresque touch: the poignancy of ignorance in collision with the startling revelation of a rather muddled factuality. Other novelists might rest content with this irony, but Cheever continues to push on, ushering us into a description of a symbolic action that highlights what has gone before and foreshadows what will follow. Nailles doffs his church clothes, dons his work clothes, fuels his chain saw, and begins to fell some trees blighted by the secretive, deadly agency of the elm beetle. We hear that the "trees had preserved no trace of their lachrymose beauty. They had dropped their upper branches and shed their ark and the wood shone like bone in the winter light, half truncated and ngainly, the landscape for some nightmare or battlefield" (p. 38).

Like all the images and symbols and quirky referents that have accumulated, let us say subliminally, for the reader throughout the chapter, nis passage in iconographic language presages what is to come. And the chapter ends where it started, though what was a distraction artfully becomes the point at issue. Earlier we were told that Nailles was inattentive during the service to the "revelations and strictures in Holy Gospel" (p. 15). Now, while sawing, he senses an unease in the atmosphere and ries to recollect:

> Sexagesima. The Epistle? What was it? Then he remembered. "Of the Jews five times received I forty stripes save one. Thrice was I beaten with rods, once was I stoned, thrice I suffered shipwreck, a night and a day I have been in the deep; in journeyings often, in perils of waters, in perils of robbers, in perils by mine own countrymen, in perils by the heathen, in perils in the city, in perils in the wilderness, in perils in the sea, in perils among false brethren; in weariness and painfulness, in watchings often, in hunger and thirst, in fastings often, in cold and nakedness." (p. 39)

The long quotation is from St. Paul's second letter to the Corinthians 11:23ff.), which is the Epistle reading for Sexagesima Sunday in the Book of Common Prayer. As in the close to "The Death of Justina," the lengthy biblical citation is an authorial signal about intended theme and mood. Placed here, it sounds almost whimsical—but it is not. Immediately after the novel's publication Christopher Lehmann-Haupt asked Cheever specifically about this episode, noting that "in a certain sense he chain saw is sanctified by this association [with Paul's suffering]. And in the end of the book, it's the chain saw Nailles uses to save his son's life." Cheever replied, "All of which I intended," and then he typically moved on to other subjects.[16]

But it is not surprising that Cheever would be both direct and diffident about this passage: Paul's description of suffering provides the implicit religious subtext of the novel, yet it is but one of the many subtexts present, part of the arch support, surely, but conjoined with others. (For example, the whole of Part Two is the confession of suffering undergone by another Paul—Paul Hammer.)

The third chapter begins with Tony's refusal to get out of bed. He admits to his mother that he's not sick; " 'I just feel terribly sad, ' " he says. " 'I just don't feel like getting up' " (p. 40). The rest of Part One (a hundred pages) centers on the confusion that Nailles and Nellie suffer

16. Lehmann-Haupt, "Talk with John Cheever," p. 43.

as a result of Tony's immobility. In a sense, the plot proper is Beckett like, with a little Ionesco thrown in: a good deal of hugger-mugger an perplexed hand-wringing in the foreground, while on stage in the back ground the central character is mute and apparently lifeless.

Nothing else is lifeless, however; this section because of its very re strictedness reveals Cheever's remarkable dexterity, what Saul Bellow re fers to as "his power of transformation; his power to take the element given and work them into something new and far deeper than they wer at the outset."[17] The given at the outset seems meager indeed: a youn; adolescent inexplicably refuses to get out of bed. But the transformation the deepening and freshness that Bellow refers to, occurs by way of subtl evolution: themes in tension, like wakefulness and dreaming, rising anc immobility, madness and sanity, and addiction and freedom, graduall unfold on the various narrative levels. In turn, each is linked with mor familiar Cheever themes: travel and stasis, memory and forgetting, suicide and new life. The result is that the reader assimilates the subtle progress of the narrative, so that, on reflection, Hammer's stark journal in Part Two and the cataclysmic ending of the book do not seem so far-fetched.

Furthermore, the linkage among the three main characters, Nailles, Hammer, and Tony—the characteriological arch I referred to—emerges in like fashion. Each becomes a counter-part or doppelgänger of the others, and a merging of consciousness and psychological confusion is revealed incrementally. Consequently, we are not surprised that the major portion of this section in the novel is structured according to a triadic pattern— meetings, memories recorded in groups of three—often followed by a coda that, though unitive, provides an ironic perspective on the previous three strands.

For example, three doctors are invited to diagnose Tony's condition. Nellie thinks of them as "suitors in some myth or legend where a choice of caskets—Gold, Silver and Lead—was offered to the travelers" (p. 40). Here Tony is allied comically with the melancholy Portia in The Merchant of Venice, but it is not the winning of his hand these suitors are after; instead, "One by one they stood over her son trying to divine or guess the force that had stricken him" (p. 40).

The first unrequited "suitor" is the physician, Dr. Mullin, who pronounces, " 'There's absolutely nothing wrong with him' " and prescribes pep pills. The pills so supercharge Tony that he staggers into the kitchen, eats a huge breakfast, and then rushes out and runs six miles until "he didn't seem drunk any more but he seemed to have lost his memory"

17. William Kennedy, "If Saul Bellow Doesn't Have a True Word to Say He Keeps His Mouth Shut," Esquire, February 1982, p. 52.

(pp. 42-43). This brief fit over, he returns to bed. Next, the psychiatrist arrives and pronounces Tony "quite sick." Something of a determinist by profession, he is curious to discover the causes of Tony's malady. It is at this point of the narrative that Cheever, through the most unlikely instrument of a psychiatrist, makes explicit one of the novel's social themes; in typical fashion, however, Cheever tempers this explicitness through humor. The psychiatrist says to Nellie:

> "There is a tendency in your income group to substitute possessions for moral and spiritual norms. A sense of good and evil, even if it is mistaken, is better than none."
> "Eliot goes to church nearly every Sunday," Nellie said.
> How poor and transparent the fact seemed now that she had stated it. She knew the lassitude of Eliot's prayers, the indifference of his devotions, and that it was habit, superstition and sentimentality that got him up for Holy Communion. "We don't tell lies," she went on. . . . "We don't read one another's mail. We don't cheat. We don't gossip. We pay our bills. Eliot loves me. We drink before dinner. I smoke a good deal. . . ." (p. 45)

The poignancy of her protests is heightened by the minimalism of her standards. (Earlier, on her bus trip, she had sought out "an honest and decent woman," and on finding her counterpart was disappointed.) Yet now we hear her thoughts: ". . . what else was expected of her? Prophets with beards, fiery horsemen, thunder and lightning, holy commandments inscribed on tablets in ancient languages?" (p. 45). Note that these lines are phrased in the interrogative mood; the residents of Bullet Park prefer this mood, content with the more sensible virtues and leaving the more strenuous to speculation. By contrast, these frightful biblical allusions refer to the varied instruments of intrusion whereby God starkly revealed, in the declarative mood, man's ethical obligations—intrusions which seem out of place in Bullet Park.

The third suitor is a "specialist on somnambulatory phenomena" (p. 46). A reformed alcoholic, he enjoys telling of his A.A. meetings where, he boasts, " 'We get our kicks out of talking about withdrawal symptoms. . . . It's like talking about a trip to hell' " (p. 47). He also recalls his transposed fervor, saying, " 'I suppose . . . that ministers and priests think about God all the time. . . . It was just like that with me except that I didn't think about God; I thought about the hootch' " (p. 47). This specialist, now expert in a more mechanical way, tricks up Tony's body with wires and electrodes, leaves in exhaustion, and then submits a detailed report on the boy's sleeping positions on five typewritten pages with a bill for five hundred dollars attached to the report. The whole sequence is an excellent example of Cheever's instinct for casual absurdity: here the problem, of course, is that Tony will not get up, but a specialist on sleep is sought out to help him. Consequently, when at the end an eccentric swami (whose ministrations in coda form oddly recapitulate the attentions of the three suitors) performs his cure, we readers do not find it especially *outré*.

A further reason is that our grip on normality has been gradually loosened, finger by finger, as it were, through the accumulation of daffy incidents and recollections in the interim. The fourth chapter opens abruptly with an extended metaphor, comparing Nailles's view of suffering with a distant, inaccessible landscape. Each of the referents in the passage—the mountains, a far country, travel, dreams, snow—will be repeated again in connection with each of the major characters. (Biblical motifs also resonate softly in the lines: the Prodigal Son lost in "a far country" and a Father's compassion for His Beloved Son.)

> Nailles thought of pain and suffering as a principality, lying somewhere beyond the legitimate borders of western Europe. The government would be feudal and the country mountainous but it would never lie on his itinerary and would be unknown to his travel agent. Now and then he received postcards from this distant place. . . . He wrote entertaining letters to the dying and mailed them off to that remote and quaint capital. . . . He was not meant to travel here and he was surprised and frightened to wake from a dream in which he had seen, out of a train window, that terrifying range of mountains. (pp. 50-51)

These lines, which are both fanciful and funny, are a harbinger of things to come. For pain is not so much a place, a principality, as a condition, and a mysterious condition at that. We are told that it "was the image of Tony in bed that broke down [Nailles's] rigid sense of social fitness" (p. 52). That sense is further weakened shortly afterward when he and his wife attend the Hammers' evening party. Three other couples are also present; in each case they are strangers to the Hammers, there only because they have sold something to Mr. Hammer. Hammer's wife becomes drunk and castigates him, shouting, " 'You're a henpecked doormat and don't try and blame me for it. You're the kind of a man who thinks that someday, someday, some slender, well-bred, beautiful, wealthy, passionate and intelligent blonde will fall in love with you' " (p. 55). The party ends in painful embarrassment.

That evening Nailles lies in bed and realizes that at least on one level he and Hammer are inextricably united: "Hammer and Nailles, spaghetti and meatballs, salt and pepper, oil and vinegar, Romeo and Juliet, block and tackle, thunder and lightning . . . war and peace, heaven and hell, good and evil, life and death, love and death, death and taxes . . . He slept and dreamed" (pp. 56-57). Both are now more than nominally allied, however, and their fate will soon be more dramatically joined. What is more, the "and" of their inevitable linkage will be Tony. Nailles's dream is a portent of the triple alliance to come.

> He dreamed that they were in a small country church that they sometimes attended in the summer. The church was cruciform and had a threadbare green carpet. . . . The occasion was a funeral and the coffin stood before the chancel but he could not remember whose soul it was they had come to pray for and he looked around the congregation to discover who was missing. . . . When he saw that the congregation was intact he realized that the funeral must be his own.   (p. 57)

This dream can be interpreted from any number of perspectives, especially one that emphasizes its horrific aspect, i.e., Nailles's present death-in-life, his psychological divorce from the known comforts of his society. But, given its context and the momentum of the narrative (before he dreams, Nailles vaguely acknowledges his inextricable relationship with Hammer), another, perhaps more fruitful interpretation is called for. It is noteworthy that the funeral's location is in a church that is "cruciform" and has a "threadbare green" carpet. Scholars in symbology remind us that the cruciform shape (even considered independently of Christ's crucifixion) is a primordial symbol for the conjunction of opposites, a wedding of contrary principles and forces, representing the point of near-equilibrium amid antagonistic energies (positive and negative, life and death, spiritual and mundane realms).[18] Similarly, the color green, an intermediate, transitional color in the spectral range, is itself representative of antithetical tendencies: the color both of vegetation and life and of corpses and death. Without pressing such an interpretation too specifically, we see that the dream aptly characterizes Nailles's present condition: one conjoined at mid-point between the "life-less" Tony and the energetic Hammer.

This interpretation clarifies what follows, which on first reading must seem arbitrary or bizarre. For, to our surprise, Nailles awakes the morning following the dream "feeling wonderful." The landscape outside looks "like a paradise" (p. 58), although he knows it is not. " 'Oh I feel so wonderful,' " he says. " 'Something seems to have happened while I slept. I feel as though I'd been given something, some kind of a present. I feel that everything's going to be the way it was when it was so wonderful' " (p. 59).

The irony here is obvious, palpably satirical, but as I have urged, whenever one happens upon obvious ironies in Cheever's fiction, it is

---

18. J. E. Ceriot, *Dictionary of Symbols* (New York: Philosophical Library, 1962), pp. 50-57; 65-70.

precisely at that moment one must be especially alert. Other less obvious ironies are also at work, modifying the conspicuous. Here the rather goony ebullience of Nailles is tempered by associations planted earlier in the story. For example, we hear that on this morning "Nailles felt, like some child on a hill, that purpose and order underlay the roofs, trees, river and streets that composed the landscape" (p. 60). (This is a reversal of the earlier impression of the adolescent stranger on the hill.) Eager to arouse his son, to make him "wake up and take a look" (p. 59), he also wonders about "the purpose, the message, the lesson to be learned from his stricken son" (p. 60). Alas, that message comes but is ambiguous. Tony howls:

> "Give me back the mountains."
> "What, Sonny, did you say?"
> "Give me back the mountains."
> "What mountains, Sonny?" Nailles asked. "Do you mean the mountains that we used to climb? The White Mountains. They're not really white, are they? . . . Are those the mountains you mean?"
> "I don't know," Tony said. He got back into bed.   (p. 60)

This exchange is ostensibly a series of misunderstandings, dramatizing what social psychologists would label "a failure to communicate." It is that, certainly, but the mountain imagery, associated before with the terrifying principality of pain and its snow-topped borders, is here associated with an unnameable aspiration steeped in memory. Throughout literature, on the cosmological level, the mountain symbol is twin in meaning, conjoining earth and its painful decay with heaven and spiritual ascent. In the context of the novel's ambivalent symbolism, this brief conversation records this ambivalence (misunderstanding is inevitable) and is a foretoken of the symbolic and psychological mergings to follow.

Immediately after this exchange, Nailles and Hammer meet at the train station, where "the noise and commotion of the express was like being in the vortex of some dirty wind tunnel" (p. 61), and both become allied, sucked in, through a bizarre incident. A third stranger is sucked under the train, leaving only a brown loafer behind and no evidence of his body. We are told that "the casualty had thrust them into an intimate relationship," and that they "rode into the city together, stunned by the mysteriousness of life and death" (p.163).

Coincidentally, once this new linkage is established, Nailles begins to lose control of an important connection in his life. The next morning he finds the train trip to his office intolerable and he wonders, "Why should this link between his home and his office seem torturous?" (p. 64).

> Nailles's sense of being alive was to bridge or link the disparate environments and rhythms of his world, and one of his principal

bridges—that between his white house and his office—had collapsed.
. . . Station by station he made a cruel pilgrimage into the
city. (p. 65)

The rest of Part One records Nailles's heuristic effort to find "connectives" to explain this new-found disjunction in his spiritual and emotional life. Concomitantly, a more sinister connective with Hammer is
developing—one impossible to explain or make intelligible—that, unbeknownst to him, will continue throughout Parts Two and Three.

The evening of his disconcerting pilgrimage, Nailles has a conversation with Tony. During it he defends suburbia against its critics, remarking
that " 'people seem to make some connection between respectability and
moral purity that I don't get. . . . All kinds of scandalous things happen
everywhere but just because they happen to people who have flower gardens doesn't mean that flower gardens are wicked' " (p. 66). His comments here are tentative, his apologia mixed with bewilderment. Then
he goes on to acknowledge a connective that clearly does not make sense
to him:

> "The newspapers are sometimes very confusing. They keep run-
> ning photographs of soldiers dying in jungles and mudholes right beside
> an advertisement for a forty-thousand-dollar emerald ring or a sable
> coat. It would be childish to say that the soldier died for emeralds and
> sables but there it is, day after day, the dying soldier and the emerald
> ring." (p. 68)

These and other troubling juxtapositions remind Nailles of his "mysterious son" and lead him to recall Tony's birth in Rome. This marvelously
told, brief recollection appears at first like a digression, but its place here
and its wealth of allusive symbols are central to the novel's thematic
structure. Tony's birth was difficult; when the doctor attending Nellie
seemed disturbed, Nailles asked whether Nellie was in danger. The doctor
answered yes and added, " 'Life is dangerous. Why do Americans want
to be immortal?' " (p. 69).

This question lingers, and the description that follows is replete with
mysterious images of the admixed confrontation of mortality and immortality. Note first that a common motif in classical symbolism is that of
"the two peacocks symmetrically disposed on either side of the Cosmic
Tree [that] denote the psychic duality of man (related to the myth of the
Gemini) drawing its life-force from the principle of unity [The Cosmic
Tree]."[19] The cosmic tree, of course, is itself an ambivalent symbol: its
roots reach underground to the lower world of hell and hades, while its

19. Ceriot, *Dictionary of Symbols*, p. 239.

branches reach upward to the heavens and immortality, and so on its axis these separate worlds are linked. This ambivalence plays through Nailles's memory:

> There were some peacocks in a park across the street. They began to shriek as the sun rose. This sounded to Nailles portentous. . . . Nailles walked down the hill to St. Peter's and said his prayers. Then he climbed the stairs to the roof where all the gigantic saints and apostles stood with their backs to him. He had liked the city of Rome. Now it seemed sinister; the city of the wolf.   (p. 69)

The symbolic action of ascent by a stairway and of saintly rejection is followed by an equally upsetting descent. Nailles walks a back street and meets "an old man selling phallic symbols and death's heads" (p. 64); he sees beside a cafe a cage of birds "tearing at raw meat" and, on leaving it, a hyena, "then a cage of wolves" (p. 70). Back at the hospital he learns of Tony's birth and howls with relief. Nonetheless, the circumstances of the birth were indeed portentous, and thus Nailles makes further efforts to ferret out "connectives" to explain his son's present malady.

These efforts involve three memories that stand out in their relationship, and each portends Nailles's present condition. First, he recalls Tony as a nine-year-old addicted to television and their quarrel over his school grades. He confronts the boy in the dark living room where "the tube was the only light, shifting and submarine, and with the noise of the rain outside the room seemed like some cavern in the sea" (p. 70). Nailles, repeatedly indignant about the boy's new-found addiction (and defensive about his own love for gin and cigarettes), tosses the television out the door into the darkness.

The second incident is recounted from Tony's point of view. A high-school junior, passionate about football and worse than indifferent about French, he is summoned to the principal's office and then sent off to a meeting with his French teacher. The setting for their encounter, beneath a poster of the medieval fortified town of Carcassonne, is described in imagery that has recurred earlier and is an immediate reminder of the television incident, here transposed:

> The brilliant, fluorescent lights in the ceiling made the place seem to be a cavern of incandescence, authoritative in its independence from the gathering dark of an autumn afternoon; and the power to light the room came from another county, well to the north, where snow had already fallen.   (p. 79)

The French teacher is Miss Hoe, and as her name implies, she sees herself as a tamer and tidier of Nature and is, in fact, as walled-in as Carcassonne. She asks Tony his birthday, and he answers, " 'May twenty-seventh.' " This is an in-joke (Cheever was born on May twenty-seventh), but what follows is significant. She notes that this makes him a Gemini and casually adds, " 'Gemini determines many of your characteristics and one might say your fate . . .' " (p. 80).

Gemini is a zodiacal constellation that represents the two youths of Greek and Roman myth, Castor and Pollux, sitting side by side in the heavens. Two bright stars are situated in the heads of the twins, named for each one—Castor, a greenish star intermediate between the first and second magnitude, and Pollux to the east, a full yellow star of the first magnitude. Throughout Greek and Roman civilizations, the Gemini were in some places worshipped as gods, and in others venerated as mortal heroes who became immortal. A most persistent legend connected with them is that the Twins were assigned different immortal realms and so, in generous spirit, they alternated: on one day, Castor would dwell in Olympus while Pollux spent his day in Hades, and on the following day they would change places.[20]

Consequently, the Gemini as symbolic twins take on pronounced cosmological and pyschological or existential significance. They represent the ontological duality of mortality and immortality, light and darkness, the Olympian mountains and the river of Hades—the dualistic and yet constant nature of the universe. As the Heavenly Twins, they represent opposites fused together and integrated into Oneness; as the Earthly Twins, they are emblems of the break or split of opposites ever in conflict. Their alliance in contradiction is dynamic, each being "existentially" the po-tential inversion of the other, representing the ambiguity of humankind and the interchangeability of dissident contraries.

Throughout his fiction Cheever continually employs the Gemini theme (and that of Cain and Abel) to dramatize the existential divisions within humanity. The creation of Hammer and Nailles is simply the most obvious variant of this theme. But *Bullet Park* differs from his other tales in that a third character, Tony, who is a Gemini born, is the focal point and agent, creating the zone of contradiction, as it were, whereby the other two unite and divide.

Tony's scene with Miss Hoe thus enjoys a symbolic status of its own. She asks him to give up football, and he wonders, "How could they take this naturalness away from him and fill up the breach with French verbs?" (p. 81). Angry, he tells her, " 'You know I could kill you. . . . I could kill you. I could strangle you' " (p. 81). Tony's murderous impulse links him with his father earlier and with Hammer later. Miss Hoe's screams

---

20. See *The New Century Classical Handbook*, ed. Catherine Avery (New York: Appleton-Century-Crofts, 1962), pp. 408ff. on the Dioscuri.

precipitate a hilarious sequence of accusation and misunderstanding, leading to Tony's arrest. But beneath the broad fun is an emphasis on the "unnaturalness" of the sensations Tony feels. While he hears the police sirens, he imagines himself an actor in a television crime drama or a soap opera. At the police station, "Fluorescent tubing shed a soulful, grainy and searching light and an extraordinarily harsh and unnatural voice was coming from a radio" (p. 85). When Nailles arrives to pick up Tony, he is sympathetic, and on their drive home offers a curious confidence to his son. In the immediate context his words seem merely sentimental, but the emphasis on light, the color yellow, and the leaves of nature hint at a more mysterious understanding, impossible to express:

> A little wind was blowing and as they drove, leaves of all colors—but mostly yellow—blew through the shaft of their headlights and what he said was: "I love to see leaves blowing through the headlights. I don't know why. I mean they're just dead leaves, no good for anything, but I love to see them blowing through the light."   (p. 88)

The third memory of the Nailles-Tony relationship further establishes their identification from the perspective of loss and replacement. Tony takes a trip to the city, and when he does not return, a worried Nailles "felt very old, as if while he slept he had put down the dreams of a strong man—snow-covered mountains and beautiful women. . . . He felt frail, wizened, a shade of himself" (p. 90). Moreover, we learn that Nailles's deepest fear is that "he would have no resources to protect [Tony] from the terror of seeing his beloved world—his kingdom—destroyed. Without his son he could not live. He was afraid of his own death" (p. 91).

These sentiments and the regal images in which they are couched are comically transformed by what follows. Tony returns and admits to his father that he spent the night with a war widow, Mrs. Hubbard. Her name suggests a nursery rhyme, and her arrival prompts a transformed version of a fairy tale within Nailles's heart:

> But his strongest and strangest feeling, observing the boy's air of mastery, was one of having been deposed, as if, in some ancient legend where men wore crowns and lived in round towers, the bastard prince, the usurper, was about to seize the throne. The sexual authority that Nailles imagined as springing from his marriage bed and flowing through all the rooms and halls of the house was challenged. There did not seem to be room for two men in this erotic kingdom. . . . He wanted to take Nellie upstairs and prove to himself, like some old rooster, that the scepter was still his and that the young prince was busy with golden apples and impuissant matters.   (p. 96)

The encounter with Mrs. Hubbard is possibly the most richly comic episode in Cheever's fiction; it reaches its climax when Nellie finally

realizes the specialness of the relationship and in a fit of emotional confusion suggests, " 'Let's play I packed my grandmother's trunk. We always
used to play it when Tony was a boy and things weren't going well' "
(p. 98). Each participant's choice of one object to pack is revelatory of
his/her aspiration or fixation. Nellie starts with a grand piano, Nailles
follows with an ashtray, Mrs. Hubbard adds "a copy of Dylan Thomas,"
Tony a football; on her second turn Nellie offers "a handkerchief," and
finally Nailles says, " 'I packed my grandmother's trunk and into it I put
a grand piano, an ashtray, a copy of Dylan Thomas, a football, a handkerchief and a baseball bat. . . .' " (pp. 98-99).

The delightful incongruity of the choices should not distract us from
the fact that the scene comically plants the erotic/murderous ambivalence
that dominates the plot from this moment onward. Here Cheever's wonderful talent for inserting a series of digressions, what seem like red her-
rings, reinforces simultaneously the comic and thematic movement. The
next section is shaped around three memories private to Nailles and Nellie, developed like motifs and counter-motifs. The first two occur when
Nailles stops at a roadside bar, where his ordering a martini "marked him
as a traveler and a stranger" (p. 106). He overhears two stories, both of
which accent the process of remembering and forgetting. The first story
is told by a man who recalls a girl who used to say hello all the time,
even when they were getting ready to make love: " 'When I was getting
undressed she'd kiss my ears and everything and keep saying hello, hello,
hello' " (p. 106). He ends by remarking, " 'I suppose she must have said
something else but I honestly can't remember her saying anything but
hello' " (p. 106).

The second man's story betrays a similar hypnotic repetitiveness. He
admits to the patrons that he is a jealous man and that, when he became
suspicious that his wife was promiscuous, he hit upon an idea. " 'The
Thing. Has she got the Thing on. If she's got the Thing on she's planning
to put it out' " (p. 107). His jealousy issues in a detective's passion. One
evening he checks the medicine cabinet only to discover "the Thing"
gone, so he confronts his wife, " 'and she cried and cried and said she
had the Thing on because we did it in the morning and you know she
had me there because I couldn't remember whether or not we did it in
the morning' " (p. 107). His jealous suspicions increase the night that he
discovers two "Things" in the cabinet. His wife claims she purchased the
second that afternoon " 'because there was a hole in the old Thing' "
(p. 108). Disbelieving, he calls the drug store where she claims to have
bought it, but the druggist protests that "he couldn't remember, it was a
busy afternoon and he couldn't remember . . ." (p. 108). Shortly after,
the man happens upon another "Thing" in his wife's sewing box and is

on the verge of consternated despair. His story ends: " 'About a week after that they put the pill on the market and she threw away all her Things and started taking the pill and so, of course, I never knew' " (p. 109).

As noted earlier, Cheever enjoys exploiting the ironic technique of juxtaposing an overheard, random conversation with a central character's unarticulated confession in order to highlight the bizarre parallels proper to the human comedy. Here Nailles, himself a stranger in the bar, happens upon another stranger's perplexed recollection, and for the first time he becomes conscious of the fragility of fidelity. On hearing the tale, he is disconcerted more than amused, for to him "marriage was not an affair of the heart—it was a matter of life and death" (p. 109). He himself recalls a magical moment of marital oneness with Nellie when she slept in his arms. On waking she asked " 'Did I snore?' " He answered (ominously in the subsequent context), " 'Oh, terribly . . . you sounded like a chain saw' " (p. 109). But, despite this touching remembrance he goes home and almost immediately checks his medicine cabinet "for the same obscene and detestable purpose as had the stranger in the bar. Then he went downstairs and asked Nellie what sort of a day she'd had. 'I went shopping,' she said . . ." (pp. 109-110). An "extremely shabby scene" follows. Thus another metamorphosis has mysteriously taken place: Nailles has become the counterpart of a stranger.

The interlude that follows is narrated in the third person, summarizing Nellie's own narrow escapes from adultery. Her erotic career consists of three incidents, each aborted through circumstance rather than choice, as though hazard alone (remember the realtor Hazzard) determines the moral structure and values of Bullet Park. Chance accidents notwithstanding, we hear: "So her chasteness, preserved by a fire, a runny nose and some spoiled sturgeon eggs was still intact, although she carried herself as if her virtue was a jewel—an emblem—of character, discipline and intelligence" (p. 112).

The third memory, like those of the two strangers, is also recounted in the first person by Nailles. This recollection, set in a thunderstorm between the flickering variants of light and darkness, provides the emotional bridge with the novel's last chapter. Nailles relates the confrontation he had with Tony on a miniature golf course:

> I remember the thunder because I remember thinking how much I liked the noise of thunder. It seems to me a very human sound, much more human than the sound of jet planes, and thunder always reminds me of what it felt like to be young.   (p. 114)

Nailles repeats this sentimental association, and yet when Tony reveals he is quitting school, Nailles tries to appear reasonable "like a character in a play" but cannot empathize with his young son. While they talk at cross-purposes, they are pointedly interrupted: strangers with "spooky voices" and unidentifiable faces—as in a scene from hades—play through on the course. As their heated confrontation continues, Nailles blurts out, " 'I love you, Tony' "; and Tony answers, " 'The only reason you love me, the only reason you think you love me is because you can give me things' " (p. 117). Nailles's anger mounts and he swings at Tony with the golf putter but the boy eludes him. His account ends: " 'So there I was on this ruined miniature golf course having practically murdered my son but what I wanted to do then was to chase after him and take another crack at him with the putter. . . . He's been in bed ever since' " (p. 118).

Thus one transmutation of a character into his counterpart has reached its first climax: the murderously inclined Nailles is now much like his son, repelled by the "unnaturalness" Miss Hoe represents. The second climax occurs with the plotting of the murderous Hammer. Meanwhile, a second transmutation takes place, for Nailles becomes the ambulatory version of his bed-ridden son (later Hammer's narcotized condition will complement their condition). Panic-stricken, he can no longer travel to work without a tranquilizer that gives him "the illusion that he floated upon a cloud like Zeus in some allegorical painting . . . beaming a vast and slightly absentminded smile at poverty, sickness, wealth, the beauty of strange women, the rain and the snow" (p. 121).

Nailles's new-found illusion and abstractedness from the natural world are reflected in a murderous symbolic action. One morning Nellie discovers him in his underpants firing a shotgun at a snapping turtle in their garden, and in "this pure and subtle light the undressed man and the prehistoric turtle seemed engaged in some primordial and comical battle" (p. 122). Man's contest with the reptile in an Edenesque garden is repeated once more, but we learn that "it was Nailles, not the reptile, who seemed out of place in the early light. It was the turtle's lawn, the turtle's sky, the turtle's creation, and Nailles seemed to have wandered mistakenly onto the scene" (p. 122).

This Edenesque motif of a fall and "unnatural separation" accrues, admixed with the contrast between the Zeus-like floating sensation and more mundane perceptions. Eventually, a desperate Nailles must meet a stranger, a drug pusher, in a Catholic cemetery, and this setting itself supports the Gothic aspects of his lapsed condition: "He passed an array of motley angels—some of them life-sized, some of them dwarfs. Some of them stood on the tombs they blessed with half-furled wings, some of them clung with furled wings to the cross" (p. 125).

This is the low point in the cyclical rhythm of Part One, a pattern repeated in briefer fashion in Parts Two and Three. The upswing maintains these biblical motifs by way of understated allusion to Christ's redemptive act on Calvary. Nellie has been informed by her former maid (who stole from her) that a "faith-healer" and "magician" named Swami Rutuola might be able to heal her son. Significantly, she seeks him out on a rainy day, and the "rain that day tasted as salty as blood" (p. 128). She follows the address to Peyton's funeral parlor and there is disturbed by the "strangeness," the "alien reek of the hallway" that "seemed to strip her of any moral reliability" (p. 128). The tensions between life and death, salvation and loss increase, and recapitulate in a crystallized form the novel's previous symbols and themes:

> Her instinct was to turn and go; her duty was to climb the stairs; and the division between these two forces seemed like a broad river without bridges—seemed to give her some insight into the force of separateness in her life. She seemed to be saying goodbye to herself at a railroad station; standing among the mourners at the edge of a grave. Goodbye Nellie.   (pp. 128-129)

Upstairs, waiting outside a door, she hears what sounds like "lewd or alcoholic" giggling, and then smells wood shavings when she steps inside the door, which leads her to wonder: "Which came first, Christ the carpenter or the holy smell of new wood?" (p. 130). But this eccentric question is not as eccentric as the swami himself, whose injured eye, "immovable, was raised to heaven in a permanent attitude of religious hysteria" (p. 130).

Few writers but Cheever would be both reverent and fanciful enough to create a half-mad swami who effects a spiritual release for the troubled. The swami tells Nellie that he discovered his peculiar talent while working as a porter in Grand Central Station. There, in the middle of the night, he met a man, not unlike other Cheever travelers, who was despondent. In the darkened station only the Kodak advertisement was lit brightly, a happy scene of a man and a woman and two children on a beach, and

> "behind them, way off in the distance, were all these mountains covered with snow. . . . So then I told him to look at the mountain to see if he could get his mind off his troubles. So then I said let us pray . . . and I realized that I couldn't remember many prayers myself so I said let's make up a prayer and then I began to say valor, valor, valor, over and over again and in a little while he joined me."   (p. 134)

The swami arrives at the Nailles home to employ his original technique on Tony in the boy's bedroom. Downstairs, an incident takes place so casually that the reader might miss it because of the lively commotion elsewhere. A neighbor stops by and tells Nailles she needs bail money because her son is a draft evader and her husband was arrested for possession of drugs—a bizarre situation resembling that of Tony and Nailles.

Nailles kindly gives her two hundred dollars as a gift. Simultaneously, another gift is being exchanged upstairs. The swami tells Tony that he considers himself "a spiritual cheerleader" (p. 139). He has in his repertoire a variety of cheers but what is required is an effort of imagination, a particularization of time and place: " 'I say that I'm in a house by the sea at four in the afternoon and it's raining and I'm sitting in a ladderback chair with a book in my lap and I'm waiting for a girl I love who has gone on an errand but who will return' " (p. 140). He and Tony try this technique, repeating each phrase one after another. Finally, the swami tells him, " 'Now let's try the love cheer. Repeat Love a hundred times . . .' " (p. 141). Tony does so with vigor and then says, " 'I know it's crazy but I do feel much better. I'd like to try another prayer' " (p. 141).

Part One began with an invitation to imaginative effort ("Paint me a railroad station then, ten minutes before dark"), and so it ends. Throughout, the many symbols and images are repeated endlessly, and the many transferences between characters and incidents effect a similar mode of repetition; it is fitting, then, that it should close with a repetitive chant led by an acknowledged conjurer. Upon recovering, Tony tells his parents, " 'I don't feel sad any more and the house doesn't seem to be made of cards. I feel as though I'd been dead and now I'm alive' " (p. 142). This last line is fitting also, for it recalls the parable of the prodigal son, echoing the father's words when his beloved son returns (Luke 15:24), and answers in complex fashion the curious questions posed in the first paragraph at the railroad station: "what is the child doing up so late and why is the man crying?" The whole of Part One celebrates the collision of many and varied mysteries.

A careful reading of Part Two, Hammer's confession, reveals a similar configuration and a variation on progressive repetitions. Earlier, while describing Cheever's themes, I commented on key parts of this section; here, rather than undertake further close reading, I will explore some of its unifying strands.

First, Part Two begins and ends on a beach with Hammer reading a book (recall the swami's exhortation) in the immediate past. He takes pains to describe this experience on the beach with great accuracy, and his interpretation of the events presage the novel's final confrontation. A man alone, separated from his family, he makes a declaration as though assuming our agreement:

> We traditionally associate nakedness with judgments and eternity and so on those beaches where we are mostly naked the scene seems apocalyptic. Standing at the surf line we seem, quite innocently, to have strayed into a timeless moral vortex.   (p. 146)

Before the reader can demur "do we?" or question "A moral vortex?" we hear of Hammer's encounter with two strangers. The first is a "faggot" who stops nearby; young and "smug" and "comely," he deftly reveals himself. The second stranger is fortyish, neither muscular nor comely, a man with his wife and children trying to fly a kite. Hammer chooses the second man quite arbitrarily, and we hear him say, ". . . the filament of kite line in my fingers, both tough and fine, that had quite succinctly declared my intentions to the faggot seemed for a moment to possess some extraordinary moral force as if the world I had declared to live in was bound together by just such a length of string—cheap, durable and colorless" (p. 147). The kite string thus is an image of a precarious moral force; his success with it here in aiding the stranger is insufficient: "The faggot had vanished but I longed then for a moral creation whose mandates were heftier than the delight of children, the trusting smiles of strangers and a length of kite string" (p. 147).

This brief episode, especially that last sentence, functions like the exposition of the main theme in a sonata: what follows will entail restatement, development, recapitulation, and a coda. Reviewers and critics were consternated by Hammer's switching his murderous goal from Nailles to Tony—to them the choice seemed arbitrary. In a way it is, but it is the subliminal reversal of the equivalent arbitrary choice made on the beach. One might choose to emphasize a homosexual/heterosexual division in Hammer's heart; though this avenue might well bear interpretive fruit, the fact is that "the faggot had vanished," and what follows is more eerily important.

Hammer longs for "a moral creation whose mandates [are] heftier" than a kite string. The rest of his narrative consists first of his pursuit of kite strings, i.e., of connectives and attachments, thin though they be, that might allow him to grasp his identity; and, second, of his pursuit of a moral mandate, which he finds eventually in his mother's crazed purpose when she tells him, " 'I would settle in some place like Bullet Park. . . . I would single out as an example some young man, preferably an advertising executive. . . . I would crucify him on the door of Christ's Church. . . . Nothing less than a crucifixion will wake that world' " (pp. 168-169).

Neither endeavor will bear fruit, of course, but our fascination resides less in action than in the twin quests themselves. Early on, Hammer makes it clear that he has no intrinsic identity. He was born out of wedlock to a woman named Gretchen who as a girl inhabited the world of the Galsworthy novels and who detested her own name—she "claimed at one time or another to be named Grace, Gladys, Gwendolyn, Gertrude, Gabriella, Giselle and Gloria" (p. 148). He was called Paul Oxencroft at birth but that was later "thought unsatisfactory," and a lawyer came to talk to his mother about it. Hammer notes, "While they were discussing what to call me a gardener passed the window, carrying a hammer, and so I was named" (p. 151). Later, while a sophomore at Yale, he wanted to change his name to Robert Levy, aware that Hammer "was no name at all" (p. 173). But the judge refused his petition, and the new notoriety of his bastardy further severed him from polite society.

Hammer's father is a remote, though ever-present, figure in his life. A muscular weightlifter, he posed for the statuary on hotels and opera houses throughout Europe, "one of those male caryatids" supporting these structures (p. 151). In his travels Hammer believes that he glimpses artistic renderings of him everywhere, even "lying in a field of weeds in West Berlin" (p. 152). As a young boy he visits his father at a hotel in Boston and discovers not a god-like Atlas but an inebriated Noah "in a pole-axed, drunken sleep, naked. . . . He looked . . . like the faded figure of some Icarus or Ganymede that you might find painted on the wall of some old-fashioned, second-rate Italian restaurant, fly-specked and badly drawn" (pp. 164-165). Like Nailles earlier, Hammer is tempted to murder him, but he "settled on an uneasy brand of forgiveness and went away" (p. 165). Hammer sums up his bastard's fate by stating that he is "the only son of a male caryatid holding up the three top floors of the Mercedes hotel and a crazy old woman" (p. 170).

Hammer's mother *is* a crazy old woman, but in this novel three peripheral crazies (she, the swami, and the alchemist-chemist) are the spokesmen for the novel's themes. Furthermore, like the journals and letters in the Wapshot novels and *Falconer*, her eccentric letters repeat and explicate the story's recurring themes. For example, she writes Hammer and tells him of three dreams. The first is of " 'an entire movie . . . , not a scenario but a movie in full color about a Japanese painter named Chardin' " (p. 153). This juxtaposition of the exotic Orient with Jean-Baptiste Chardin, that gentle celebrant of Western bourgeois family life, is not quite so bizarre to us readers who have been prepared earlier for curious "painting" parallels. About her second dream she tells Hammer, " 'I dreamed I went back to the garden of the old house in Indiana and found everything the way I'd left it. . . . There it all was, not as I might remember it . . . but as a gift to me from some part of my spirit more profound than my memory' " (p. 153).

Throughout *Bullet Park* a garden is symbolic of the ordered world where chaos or suffering unexpectedly intrudes (cf. pp. 9, 12, 21, 121); here the garden is the point of conjunction between memory and imagination, a gift of the twin aspects of nostalgia. His mother's third dream sustains this theme. She dreams she is on a train and outside she sees "blue water and blue sky"; looking in her handbag, she "finds an invitation to spend a weekend with Robert Frost" (p. 153). She admits that she knows Frost is dead, and that they would not be compatible, but "it seemed like some dispensation or bounty of my imagination to have invented such a visit" (p. 154).

As I have argued, these dream revelations provide the clue to the imaginative shaping of *Bullet Park*: from the novel's opening sentence the appeal is addressed to the reader's memory and imagination, i.e., to a personal exertion akin to an artistic effort. When and if the reader responds, the result is not so different from that experienced by Hammer's slightly unhinged mother, who confides,

> "My memory . . . seems to perform music continuously. . . . What mystifies me is the variety in quality. Sometimes I wake to the slow movement of the first Razumovsky. You know how I love that. . . . But sometimes I wake to a frightful Sousa march followed by a chewing gum commercial and a theme from Chopin. I loathe Chopin. Why should my memory torment me by playing music that I loathe? At times my memory seems to reward me; at times it seems vindictive. . . ." (p. 154)

Her words might well serve as a metaphoric summary of a reader's reaction to *Bullet Park*. Perhaps closer to the mark is her comment about traveling; she claims that the airplane engines sound like " 'some universal music as random and free of reference and time as the makings of a dream' " (p. 155). This signals what the novel attempts to establish: the merger of dream and music, of memory and imagination, of the recognizable and the invented.

This is also the clue—or better, in the context, the thread—to Hammer's errant behavior. He was born by chance (his mother was "dogged by bad luck," including her pregnancy). And though his Grandmother loved him, "delighted by the fact that I had a head of yellow curls," chance intervened once more, and by the time he was eight, he tells us, "my hair was quite dark" (pp. 150-151). Later his passionate quest of the room with yellow walls will be emblematic of his nostalgic desire to retrieve that past and fix, as it were, his true identity now lost. On seeing a room with yellow walls for the first time, he imagines that the occupant "would be a single man like myself but a man with a continent nature, a ruling intelligence, an efficient disposition. The pair of windows filled me with shame" (p. 179). Immediately after, he moves from hotel to hotel in New York; he leaves the Hotel Madison because "there were mirrors on all the walls so that I could not escape my own image" (p. 180). Fleeing to Chicago, he stays at the Palmer House, but the "fact that my room had no uniqueness seemed seriously to threaten my own uniqueness. I suffered an intense emotional vertigo. The fear was not of falling but of vanishing" (p. 181).

At last he finds the room with yellow walls in Orvieto, Italy, and tells us, "I seemed, looking up at [the lighted windows and the yellow walls] from the sidewalk, to be standing at the threshold of a new life. This was not a sanctuary, this was the vortex of things, but this was a place where the cafard could not enter" (p. 183). Not a sanctuary, he tells us, but the vortex—that is, the unseen center controlling contradictory currents, the invisible axis of identity amid rotating energies. This is a telling image, for earlier he had described the cafard as "no more visible than a moving column of thin air" (p. 174)—and the cafard cannot enter here. Previously, his only protection against the cafard had been an imaginative effort, his conjuring of three images: a snow-covered mountain, lighted by a passing glow; a fortified medieval town; and a river with grassy banks. (The snow-covered mountains and the fortified town of Carcassonne we already saw associated with Nailles and Tony.) Now the yellow room has replaced the efforts of imagination, but not for long. When Hammer loses possession of the yellow room, the vortex evaporates, and his identity once again becomes fragmented.

Clues about such a potential transformation are planted in two comic incidents. Earlier Hammer had sought out a psychiatrist named Doheny who "seemed, like some illusion of drunkenness, to have two faces and I found it fascinating to watch one swallow up the other" (p. 177). Doheny diagnoses Hammer as "a repressed transvestite homosexual," and Hammer, angry at this two-faced man, calls him a charlatan because he hangs no diplomas in his office. Insulted, Doheny produces several diplomas, all made out to a Howard Shitz; like Hammer and his mother, Shitz had changed his name, though for reasons more obvious than theirs.

The second incident occurs after Hammer has found the yellow walls "for the third time" (p. 184)—in an old Pennsylvania farmhouse, which he manages to buy. His cat, named Schwartz, leads him to a small frame house nearby whose owner is a chemist who makes perfumes. The chemist is a typical minor character in Cheever; though slightly fatuous, if not balmy, he actually enunciates the novel's major theme and quaintly clarifies Hammer's odd character within it:

> "The concept of man as a microcosm, containing within himself all parts of the universe, is Babylonian. The elements are constant. The distillations and transmutations release their innate power. This not only works in the manufacture of perfume; I think these transmutations can work in the development of character."   (p. 204)

This alchemical gobbledygook is immediately dramatized. The chemist introduces his granddaughter, Marietta Drum, who wears "a cloth coat with a white thread on one shoulder" (p. 204). Hammer reveals that "the white thread had some mysterious power as if it were a catalyst that clarified my susceptibilities. It seemed like magic . . ." (pp. 204-205). He falls in love with Marietta, and soon after they marry; for the wedding she wears "a gray suit with a white thread on the lapel" (p. 215). The marriage disintegrates quickly, because Marietta's disposition varies in ways opposite to the weather: spring-like or clement weather makes her irascible, but blizzards, thunderstorms, and the like sweeten her nature. Hammer confesses that he is non-plussed:

> My fault was that I had thought of love as a heady distillate of nostalgia—a force of memory that had resisted analysis by cybernetics. We do not fall in love—I thought—we re-enter love, and I had fallen in love with a memory—a piece of white thread and a thunderstorm. My own true love was a piece of white thread and that was so. (p. 216)

Scorned now by Marietta, he must abet the powers of memory with those of the imagination. To console himself he begins to invent dream girls. The dream girls fall into three categories: first, he summons up girls he has known, then girls he has spotted on magazine covers, and, finally, "a third group of comforters produced, I suppose, by some chamber in my nature. These were woman I had never seen" (p. 217). It is at this point that Nailles, whose picture Hammer had seen in a magazine, appears for the first time in Hammer's life-narrative. He tells us, "I envied men like Nailles who might, I suppose, looking at Nellie, recall the number and variety of places where he had covered her . . . while I, looking at Marietta, would remember the number of places where I had been rebuffed" (p. 218).

But it is not sexual envy that begets Hammer's murderous impulse. Rather, it is that the yellow paint on the walls of his house has begun to crack and discolor, not unlike his marriage and his self. Not knowing how important yellow walls are to him, his wife has them repainted pink— whereupon Hammer's cafard returns, and with it his moral vortex, which spins errantly until the climax in Part Three.

But Part Three is more than merely a dramatic climax; it is the completion of the book's arch, recapitulating the novel's earlier images and symbols and reorganizing them in a specifically Christian perspective. Each of these images and symbols is ambiguous, if not paradoxical, and to interpret them univocally is to mistake the novel's complex meaning.

Because we know of Hammer's mad scheme to burn someone on the altar of Christ's Church, Part Three begins in irony, narrating Nailles's boyish enthusiasm for fire-fighting in language that is replete with ominous foreboding, as the accent on "seemed" suggests:

> To hell over the hills and dales of Bullet Park late at night, ringing his bell and blowing his siren, seemed to him the climax of his diverse life. Mouthwash, fire trucks, chain saws and touch football! The village seemed upended in the starlight and the only lights that burned burned in bathrooms. It was his finest hour.   (p. 225)

An apocalyptic undertone resonates throughout these lines and grows in intensity throughout what follows. Chapter One began with a description of the Wickwires' cocktail rites; Chapter Sixteen begins with another—that of a meeting of the Volunteer Fire Department. Sobriety and the somber characterize the proceedings; we are told that "had anyone spoken humorously it would have been a misunderstanding of the gravity of these rites" (p. 227). Nailles nominates Hammer for membership and, though Hammer's honesty is called into question, the motion passes. During drinks after the meeting, Nailles invites Hammer to join him in another masculine rite, the fishing trip, and the two set out on Saturday morning.

Outwardly the trip is uneventful. Its dramatic power lies in the ironic juxtaposition of geography with an emotional resonance that is oddly misplaced in the circumstances. The Saturday traffic appears "catastrophic," with trucks "as massive and towering as the land castles of the barbarians" making this "simple journey seem warlike" (p. 229). Warlike it is; but Nailles, unaware that his companion plans to murder him, sees the external modern world as the "anxious wasteland through which one raced the barbarians" (p. 229).

The irony of circumstance and ignorance becomes more pointed when they reach the fishing stream. The sound of the stream "was explicitly the sound of laughter—nothing else. Giddy laughter, the laughter of silly girls and nymphs, rang through the bleak spring woods" (p. 229). The actual absence of women, however, makes "the sound of watery laughter" a muted chorus, a commentary on the natural/unnatural polarities present. We learn that both men "were about the same weight, height and age, and they both wore a size-eight shoe" (p. 230). We learn little else about them physically, nothing to differentiate them except hair color and gesture. Knowing Cheever's formidable powers for description and particularization, we realize that this scantness of depiction is deliberate. So our attention is drawn instead to emotional differences:

> Hammer's face was thin and he frequently touched it with his fingers— a sort of groping gesture as if he were looking for something he had lost. . . . He had a nervous way of shifting his head, setting his teeth

and bracing his shoulders as if his thinking consisted of a series of
resolves and decisions.   (p. 230)

That Cheeveresque "as if" highlights the irony of the scene. We learn
of Nailles's sentimental thoughts about male friendship, a complacent
affection he thinks he shares with Hammer, a generous relationship unlike
love because "it was a contentment in which there was no trace of jealousy, sexuality or nostalgia" (p. 231)—in a word, assuringly "natural"
according to his lights. Hammer, meanwhile, is planning to murder Nailles,
an act that "did not, at this point, strike him in any way as unnatural"
(p. 231). Thus both men are enjoying "natural" thoughts but hardly sharing the same kind.

> The woman who dreamed of a mink coat—Hammer thought—had
> more common sense than the woman who dreamed of heaven. The
> nature of man was terrifying and singular and man's environment was
> chaos. It would be wrong, he thought, to call Nailles's religious ob-
> servances a sham. He guessed they were vague and perhaps sentimental
> but since Christ's Church was the only place in Bullet Park where
> mystery was professed and since there was much that was mysterious
> in Nailles's life (the thighs of Nellie and his love for his son) there
> was nothing delinquent in his getting to his knees once a week. Ham-
> mer had chosen his victim for his excellence.   (p. 232)

Significantly, it is Hammer's crazed perspective that renders most
clearly the ambiguity of the novel's religious impact: the overlapping in
human humility of the supernaturally mysterious (which Christ's Church
represents) and the naturally mysterious (Nailles's twin human loves).
Nailles's "excellence" lies in his bewildered acknowledgment of both these
mysteries, not in anything more obviously heroic. Despite all his faults,
Nailles opts for life, unlike his companion. As their fishing trip ends, he
assists his old setter, Tessie, into the car by picking her up and placing
her on the back seat. Hammer asks, " 'Why don't you do something about
her?' " Nailles, not understanding, answers:

> "Well, I've done everything I can or almost everything. . . . There
> is a kind of serum you can get, a distillate of Novocain. It's supposed
> to prolong a dog's life but it costs fifteen dollars a shot and they have
> to have it once a week."
> "I didn't mean that," Hammer said.
> "What did you mean?"
> "Why don't you shoot her?"
> The contemptible callousness of his new companion . . . provoked
> a rage in Nailles so towering and so pure that for a moment he might
> have killed Hammer.   (pp. 233-234)

All else is mysterious and muddled; only murder is "so towering and so pure." Reflections on the perfection, the flawlessness of the murderous intent open the final chapter, completing a bridge with the emotional reversal on the fishing trip. We are asked, "Have you ever known the homicide's sublime feeling of rightness?" as we follow Hammer's day of preparation (p. 235). Unfortunately, he drinks too much in order "to make the ecstasy of his lawlessness endurable" (p. 236), and, inflamed with his project, he seeks out the Swami Rutuola to inform him of his plan. Again, as at the end of Part One, the Swami becomes the eccentric instrument of salvation.

The scene suddenly shifts to the Lewellens' house, site of the dinner party and the kidnapping. Tommy Lewellen ostensibly represents the complacent soul of Bullet Park, but as we readers enter his thoughts this evening, we are surprised at what we hear. His reflections echo the "improbable" jeremiad of the vengeful adolescent on the hill in Chapter One, but from a jaded vantage point:

> What was wrong with friendly talk and well-dressed men and women eating ham and chicken? Nothing, nothing, nothing at all except that the blandness of the scene would be offensive. No one would get drunk, no one would fight, no one would likely get screwed, nothing would be celebrated, commemorated or advanced. If the gathering he awaited stood at the brink of anything it stood at the brink of licentiousness. Sheer niceness, he thought, might drive a man to greet his guests wearing nothing but a cockwig. Gross and public indecencies would cure the evening of its timelessness and relate it vigorously to death. (p. 238)

The repetition of the words "nothing" and "no one" and the equation of excitement with venery create a stark contrast to Hammer's crazed intention "to wake up the world" through a crucifixion. Though the party is a genuine rite, it is empty of sacrifice and genuine gestures of love and generosity, and thus "nothing would be celebrated, commemorated or advanced." How fitting, then, that the arrival of the "incandescently charming"—albeit maimed—Wickwires, those emblems of the new priesthood, should sanction its commencement. Mrs. Wickwire's ironic pronouncement, " 'What a divine idea to have a tent' " (p. 239), capsulates all their rigorous efforts at religious transmutation.

Cheever then inserts a brief scene back at Nailles's house that subtly reinforces and then coalesces the emotional and symbolic tension established thus far. We discover Nailles standing naked in his bedroom, reluctant to dress. Nakedness, of course, has always been one of the most powerful symbols of human ambiguity, expressive of the tension between purity, innocence, and newness of life—as in Christian baptism—and lasciviousness and the fall in Eden. We watch Nailles undergo this conflict:

> Having, in his experience with trains, learned something about the mysterious polarities that moved him, he wondered what would happen if his unwillingness to dress turned into a phobia. . . . He did not cherish his nakedness but he detested his suit. Spread out on the bed it seemed to claim a rectitude and a uniformity that was repulsively unlike his nature. Did he want to go to the party in a fig leaf, a tiger skin, nothing at all? Something like that. (pp. 239-240)

Nailles's ambivalence is further established most artfully. Immediately after this reflection he thinks of his mother, reminding us of his gentle, though murderous, admixture of feeling in Chapter Two. Then suddenly, "from some part of his mind, deeper than memory, he heard singing" (p. 240). It is the plaintive song of a forsaken lover that so haunts Desdemona in Shakespeare's *Othello* that she sings it while she undresses prior to her murder at her husband's hand:

> "The poor soul sat singing by a sycamore tree,
> Sing all a green willow,
> Her hand on her bosom, her head on her knee,
> Sing willow, willow, willow." (p. 240)

The song is appropriate here, one of ignorance and innocence conjoined with premonition before a cataclysm. A second incident follows, indicative not of memory but of loss and recovery. Nailles looks for his wallet and is disturbed to find his pocket empty: "The empty pocket seemed mysteriously portentous, as if he had asked some grave questions about pain and death and had got no answer; had been told there was none" (p. 240). Frantic, he tries to retrace the rhythm of his life, and along with Nellie, like the resourceful widow in the parable, he roots under and through all the furniture in the house. Their action is symbolic, "mysteriously portentous" in another sense, as the Christian religious metaphors suggest. "To look into their faces you would have thought they had lost their grail, their cross, their anchor" (p. 241). On finding the wallet, Nellie cries out, and we are told, "It was the pure voice of an angel, freed from the mortal bonds of grossness and aspiration" (p. 241). And Nailles elatedly thanks "his deliverer" (p. 241).

The convergence of this mix of symbols continues as Nailles and Nellie leave for the party and hear thunder sounding. As we learned earlier, the sound always reminds Nailles of his youth and is associated with mountain-climbing. He tells Nellie of his memory of climbing in the Tirol, and adds that in " 'the Tirol when there's a thunderstorm they ring all the church bells. All up and down the valley. It's very exciting. I don't

know why I tell you all of this. I guess it must be the storm' " (p. 242).
These images of the higher world mixed with those of alarm, of thunder
and mountains and church bells, connect subliminally with the action
that follows.

Hammer kidnaps Tony and drives to the church, where "ten minutes
earlier Miss Templeton had finished arranging the roses on the altar"
(p. 242). (In Christianity the red rose represents martyrdom—on Sexagesima, chrysanthemums were placed there.) Toting the boy and the gas-
oline with which to immolate him, Hammer enters the church and locks
the narthex door, the only point of entry. The description of his activity
inside plays on variants of light and fire and wind, of a heat exploding to
heighten this mad distortion of Christian allusions:

> The only light that burned was the vigil, and in this faint light he
> dragged Tony down the aisle to the chancel. He found the switch for
> the chancel lights and was about to pour the gasoline onto Tony when
> he thought he would first smoke a cigarette. He was tired and winded.
> He laughed when he noticed how expertly the Lamb of God on the
> altar hooked its hoof around the wooden standard of Christendom. He
> heard a stir from the narthex and he thought his heart would explode
> until he realized that it was nothing. It had begun to rain. That was
> all. (p. 243)

The Lamb of God, representing the effective instrument of the new
Passover, is the Christian symbol of Jesus Christ's innocent sacrificial
death. Here Hammer laughs at "how expertly" the Lamb's hoof hooks
around the Cross. This particular configuration in Christian art represents
not only suffering only but triumphant suffering, that is, the Lamb's conquest in Resurrection, in the release of new life through redemption. In
the symbolic context, it is not surprising that Hammer should sense "a
stir" of wind and that rain should follow—as we have seen throughout
Cheever's fiction, rain and wind are emblematic of Christian baptism and
spiritual regeneration.

These symbolic hints prepare us for the action to follow. At the party
Nailles is cryptically told by the swami—who pointedly is asked whether
he is making a "delivery"—to " 'Go to Christ's Church now,' " and it is
significant that Nailles never loses his composure, which is not characteristic of him. When he arrives at the church he recognizes Hammer's
car, and we are told that "in some way he had expected this" (p. 244).
The reason why is not disclosed, but it need not be, given the multiple
levels of mystery surrounding the episode. When Nailles pounds on the
locked door, Hammer shouts out his intention to kill Tony. Calmly,
Nailles returns to his house, gets his chain saw, and goes back to the

church. He cuts through the front door and enters the church to find Hammer sitting in a front pew, crying; the rescue emphasizes the water and light imagery of the apocalyptic setting:

> Nailles lifted his son off the altar and carried him out into the rain. It was pouring. Water seemed to crowd into the light. The rain fell with such force that it stripped the leaves off the trees and the air smelled of bilge. It was the cold rain that brought Tony around.   (p. 244)

Earlier I cited at some length those reviewers who were captiously dismayed by the implausibility of the ending. If plausibility is the criterion, then of course *Bullet Park* is a failed novel. But if a tale is shaped like a dream, structured as an arch of symbol and images beneath which the reader enters at some risk, then plausibility is one's least likely expectation or desideration. Instead, artful repetition and the nourishment of wonder are all one hopes for.

> Tony went back to school on Monday and Nailles—drugged— went off to work and everything was as wonderful, wonderful, won- derful, wonderful as it had been.   (p. 245)

It seems to me only in literature can we refresh our sense of possibility and nobility.

John Cheever

In the prison of his days
Teach the free man how to praise.

W. H. Auden

Dayadhvam: I have heard the key
Turn in the door once and turn once only
We think of the key, each in his own prison
Thinking of the key, each confirms a prison
Only at nightfall, aethereal rumors
Revive for a moment a broken Coriolanus.

T. S. Eliot

So prophesy. Say to them, "The Lord Yahweh says this:
I am now going to open your graves; I mean to raise you from
your graves, my people, and lead you back to the soil of Israel."

Ezekiel 37:12-13

I was a stranger, and you took me in;
Naked, and you clothed me;
I was sick and you visited me;
I was in prison and you came to me.

Matthew 25:35

Being such an one as Paul the aged, and now also a prisoner
of Jesus Christ.   *Philemon 9*

7 : *Falconer*

The publication of *Falconer* in 1977 was both a literary event and a genuine surprise.[1] Readers who had grown comfortable inhabiting "Cheever Country," that imaginative domain of suburbs abutting Route 95 between New York and Boston, were suddenly ushered elsewhere—into Falconer prison on the Hudson—and told a tale of a man who is both a drug addict and a fratricide.

Falconer is considered the most streamlined of Cheever's novels, perhaps because its basic plot outline is the easiest to summarize. The central character is Ezekiel Farragut, a college professor convicted of murder, who must share cell-block F with a band of killers and thieves. Because he is plunged into loneliness and isolation, his interior story is shaped through his retrieval of memories—about his childhood in New England, his unhappy marriage, his affairs, his hopes and eccentric dreams. Exteriorly, the dramatic events are few: he falls in love with a young inmate named Jody, observes Jody's escape, listens to the recollections of his fellow prisoners, and finally, after ministering to a dying inmate, takes the man's place in a burial shroud and makes his own miraculous escape.

When the novel appeared, reviewers were quick to note the story's parallels with Cheever's own life since *Bullet Park*. In the early 1970's he had volunteered to teach a writing course in Sing Sing Prison near his home in Ossining, New York. In April 1973 he suffered his first heart attack and was forced to give up the prison work; after recovering, he went to the University of Iowa that fall to teach creative writing at the Iowa workshop. On returning home in summer 1974, he began to drink heavily and suffered a second heart attack. He recovered sufficiently once more, and that fall took a post as teacher and lecturer at Boston University, but his depression deepened and his drinking increased. In March 1975 he committed himself to the Smithers Clinic for alcoholics in New York City. Later he confessed that "the turning point, I think, was when

1. For capsulated comments from the contemporary reviews, see Francis J. Boscha, *John Cheever: A Reference Guide* (Boston: G. K. Hall, 1981), pp. 80ff.

196

appeared to be dying. It made me realize that my ardor for life was quite genuine, and anything I could do to continue alive and useful I was quite willing to do."[2] He gave up drinking and returned to his work-in-progress.

I had started to write Falconer when I was in Boston, when I was drunk and drugged much of the time, putting hats on the statuary on Commonwealth Avenue, and so forth. However, I did not complete the novel until I had some rather grueling experiences in both alcohol and drug withdrawal, and I was delighted to be free. That, obviously, is part of the book. I'm very reluctant to admit it because I would not want the novel to be thought an account of Cheever's escape from a rehabilitation center. I wanted to write as dark and as radiant a book as possible. I didn't know that the hero would get out of prison until I was about halfway through. I came running out of the house and shouted, "He's going to get out! Hey! Hey! He's going to get out." I was probably convinced that he was going to escape before I started but it was at some more obscure stratum of my intelligence. I wanted to write about confinement.[3]

Cheever began the book again in the middle of May 1975 and finished it eleven months later. He noted that "I finished, I remember distinctly, on Maundy Thursday" (April 15, 1976), three days before Easter, an appropriate time for a book about renewed life. Yet, despite the rhythmic similarity between Farragut's pilgrim's progress and his own, he emphasized that "this novel was not written out of a singular experience of alcohol or drugs. I like to think it is the sum of my living."[4] Which it is.

Falconer was greeted with impressive critical enthusiasm more pronounced than the reception of any of Cheever's previous works. He was the subject of an excellent cover story in Newsweek magazine, and for the first time in his career he submitted to legions of interviewers on television and in print. Before this, he had been cryptic or evasive or worse with interviewers, and after each publication of his novels he had fled the country rather than face immediate judgments or inquiries. He admitted, "My stores of contempt were much higher then. Now, it's clear to me that I count on this audience of strangers to whom I speak my most intimate thoughts. I'm dependent emotionally on their response—never more so than with Falconer because it deals with controversial matters."[5] The man had mellowed or, as he preferred to say, "maybe matured."

More remarkable than the enthusiasm of reviewers, however, was the

2. Susan Cheever Cowley, "A Duet of Cheevers," Newsweek, March 14, 1977, p. 70.

3. "John Hersey Talks with John Cheever," Yale Alumni Magazine and Journal, December 1977, p. 24.

4. Cowley, "A Duet of Cheevers," p. 70.

5. Cowley, "A Duet of Cheevers," p. 73.

fact that *Falconer,* perhaps because of its specific challenges, spurred some
critics to make special intellectual efforts to evaluate it.[6] The result was
that few of the book's reviews were slipshod or superficial, and most were
genuinely insightful. Janet Groth in *Commonweal* noticed that Cheever
"has incorporated into the novel a symbolic richness usually associated
with deeply imaged poetry" like that admixture of "the sacred and profane
. . . reminiscent of John Donne."[7] The two most intelligent and thoughtful reviews were provided by Walter Clemons in *Newsweek* and Joan
Didion in the *New York Times Book Review.* Clemons pointed out that
the grim and forbidding world of Falconer prison is observed with chilling
exactitude,

> and yet the experience of reading the book is one of elation. We are
> in the hands of a writer in full and secure possession of his powers,
> ready to tell us what he has learned during his lifetime about men and
> women, and men and men, and willing to grant us the freedom of our
> imaginations. "Falconer," without betraying or evading its subject mat-
> ter, moves with a mysterious buoyancy. This is a "prison novel," yet
> it has the grace that recalls "The Great Gatsby"—with particular ref-
> erence to the quality of its prose but also to the presence in the book
> of a characteristic that Nick Carraway noted in his doomed boot-legger
> friend: "some heightened sensitivity to the promises of life . . . an
> extraordinary gift for hope, a romantic readiness."[8]

Joan Didion stressed the spiritual instead of the romantic, and so
agreed with Clemons but from a different perspective. She seized upon
the "note of 'homelessness' that John Cheever strikes with an almost
liturgical intensity," and recognized Cheever as "a writer who seems to be
working out, quite stubbornly and obsessively, allegorical variations on a
single and profoundly unacceptable theme, that of 'nostalgia,' or the particular melancholia induced by long absence from one's country or home."[9]
Unlike some shortsighted reviewers, Didion also grasped the novel's religious dimension, not by noting obvious episodes but by intuiting its
spirit:

> On its surface "Falconer" seems at first to be a conventional novel of
> crime and punishment and redemption . . . and yet the "crime" in this
> novel bears no more relation to the "punishment" than the punishment

6. Outside of reviews, the closest critical readings that have been published (which
I have seen) are those offered by Samuel Coale, *John Cheever* (New York: Ungar, 1977),
pp. 107-113; and Lynne Waldeland, *John Cheever* (Boston: Twayne, 1979), pp. 127-140;
and the article by Robert Morace to which I will refer.
    7. Janet Groth, "Cheers For Cheever," *Commonweal,* June 10, 1977, p. 374.
    8. Walter Clemons, "Cheever's Triumph," *Newsweek,* March 14, 1977, p. 62.
    9. Joan Didion, "Falconer," *New York Times Book Review,* March 6, 1977, p. 22.

bears to the redemption. The surface here glitters and deceives. Causes
and effects run deeper. . . . Of all those Cheever characters who have
suffered nostalgia, Farragut is perhaps the first to apprehend that the
home from which he has been gone too long is not necessarily on the
map. He seems to be undergoing a Dark Night of the Soul, a purification, a period of suffering in order to re-enter the ceremonies of
innocence, and in the context the question of when he will be "clean"
has considerable poignance.[10]

If Didion's tone here sounds tentative, as the words "perhaps" and
"seem" indicate, the conclusion to her review is assured and stark—and,
I think, correct:

> In this way "Falconer" is a kind of contemplation in shorthand, a
> meditation on the abstraction Cheever has always called "home" but
> has never before located so explicitly in the life of the spirit. I have
> every expectation that many people will read "Falconer" as another
> Cheever story about a brainwashed husband who lacked energy for the
> modern world, so he killed his brother and *who cares*, but let me tell
> you: it is not, and Cheever cares.

These and similar reviews alert us as readers to the fact that *Falconer*,
despite its locale, is not so different from *Bullet Park* after all. The realistic
surface not withstanding, it too is "shaped like a dream" and achieves its
fictional unity by way of imagery, symbol, and theme. Some episodes and
characters within it strain our credulity, which is precisely Cheever's intention: he wants to upset our readerly comfort with verisimilitude and
induce us to re-enter the story by way of alternate avenues. For example,
both Jody's and Farragut's escapes *are* implausible; they defy legitimate
expectations and are unabashedly designated as "miracles." Farragut's wife,
Marcia, and his brother, Eben, are likewise less-than-plausible figures, so
inconsistent in behavior and elusive of recognition that the reader *must*
call into question Farragut's interpretation of their personalities.

Cheever himself offered an alternate avenue for entry when he said,
"I used the imaginary prison of Falconer principally as a metaphor for
confinement. It would be the third large metaphor I've used. The first is
St. Botolphs, a New England village which has a confinement of traditional values and nostalgia; the second was the suburban towns, Bullet
Park and Shady Hill, again areas of confinement; and the third is Falconer. *Not* Sing Sing."[11] In another interview he amplified this remark
by saying, " 'All my work deals with confinement in one shape or another,

10. Didion, "Falconer," p. 24.
11. John Hersey: "Talk with John Cheever," *New York Times Book Review*, March
6, 1977, p. 24.

and the struggle toward freedon. Do I mean freedom? Only as a metaphor for'—he picks up the book, turns the pages to a passage where he has struggled to define it—'a sense of boundlessness, the possibility of rejoicing!' "[12]

Cheever's comments here confirm the quality of "abstraction" in the novel that Joan Didion alludes to. The story's abstract properties edge it away from the stricter modes associated with the novel form and inch it more closely toward those fictional categories like parable, allegory, fable, even anagogy, in which the concrete images or incidents are meant to be understood not only in themselves, but as vehicles for a moral or spiritual meaning beyond the text. Unlike the novel, in which the narrative structure itself is so indispensable, these other fictional forms rely on the manipulation of an extended metaphor for their effect. Ultimately, however, *Falconer* eludes the more rigorous structures proper to these categories; it is not a parable or allegory or fable or anagogy but suggests features of each of them. This is a roundabout way of repeating Didion's emphatic close: *Falconer* ought not to be read on the literal level alone, for its odd configuration is meant primarily to appeal to our moral and spiritual imaginations, evoking those distinctive sentiments that lead us *beyond* the text. In the novel Farragut expresses Cheever's intention this way: "The time for banal irony, the voice-over, he thought, is long gone. Give me the chords, the deep rivers, the unchanging profundity of nostalgia, love and death."[13]

The very opening of *Falconer* is deliberately studied, stressing the symbolic ambience of the place and the singularity of its point of entry. Note that each benign figure on the escutcheon of the entrance is armed with a weapon, and that the bas-relief itself, once the product of man's metallurgy, now resembles something even more primal than man and definitely darker—pieces of the blackest substances of earth:

> The main entrance to Falconer—the only entrance for convicts, their visitors and the staff—was crowned by an escutcheon representing Liberty, Justice and, between the two, the sovereign power of government. Liberty wore a mobcap and carried a pike. Government was the federal Eagle holding an olive branch and armed with hunting arrows. Justice was conventional; blinded, vaguely erotic in her clinging robes and armed with a headsman's sword. The bas-relief was bronze, but black these days—as black as unpolished anthracite or onyx. How many hundreds had passed under this, the last emblem

---

12. John Firth, "Talking with John Cheever," *Saturday Review*, April 2, 1977, p. 22.

13. John Cheever, *Falconer* (New York: Knopf, 1977), p. 36. Hereafter references to the novel will be included in the text.

most of them would see of man's endeavor to interpret the mystery of imprisonment in terms of symbols.   (pp. 3-4)

That last line renders explicit Cheever's writerly efforts thereafter: to interpret the mystery of imprisonment in symbols. Significantly, the rest of the chapter will reinforce this meaning, emphasizing "image," "impression," "representation"—all emblematic words. Later still, as the story develops, these are conjoined with the emblems of memory as well. In one remarkable passage later on, we enter Farragut's reverie and the images evoked are archetypal (the impeded light, the impenetrable wilderness, the vast silence and the hint of promise, the collision between newness and nothingness), or else mythically marvelous (the knights and the unicorns and the goat):

> The light in the prison, that late in the day, reminded Farragut of some forest he had skied through on a winter afternoon. The perfect diagonal of the light was cut by bars as trees would cut the light in some wood, and the largeness and mysteriousness of the place was like the largeness of some forest—some tapestry of knights and unicorns— where a succinct message was promised but where nothing was spoken but the vastness. The slanting and broken light, swimming with dust, was also the dolorous light of churches where a bereft woman with a hidden face stood grieving. But in his darling snowy forest there would be an everlasting newness in the air, and here there was nothing but the bestial goat smell of old Farragut and the gall of having been gulled.   (p. 152)

Coming across this passage late in the novel, the reader responds to its force not solely because of the elegant simplicity of a style made effective through the wedding of the concrete image and the abstract expression, but precisely because its address is subliminal, and our readerly threshold of sensitivity has been sculptured so adroitly early on.

The story's opening upsets a reader's realistic expectations almost immediately. The first paragraph is composed from the first-person point of view ("at the time of which I'm writing"), and yet is objective and distanced in tone. Then the second paragraph shifts to the third person, a privileged vantage point—more personal and intimate—where we readers share Farragut's perspective on the action. This point of view characterizes the rest of the novel with the exception of the account of Jody's escape (pp. 130-133); in this passage the sudden shift of perspective is so jarring that we wonder whether or not this event is the product of Farragut's imagination.

We meet Farragut—"fratricide, zip to ten, #734-508-32" (p. 4)—at the moment he is deprived of his name and former identity. We first encounter him, like so many Cheever characters, traveling: "The windows of the van were so high and unclean that he could not see the color of the sky or any of the lights and shapes of the world he was leaving" (p. 4). In the van the man manacled to his right is the first to introduce the subject of "freedom," but his misgivings on the subject are ironically comic: " 'And I never got laid free, never once. I paid anywhere from fifty cents to fifty dollars, but I never once shot a lump for free' " (p. 5). The novel, of course, will meditate on the loftier meanings of the word, but its insertion here comically anticipates those efforts.

When the van arrives at the prison entrance, Farragut sees the escutcheon and is convinced he will die here. The novel's subsequent structure is announced forthwith: "Then he saw the blue sky and nailed his identity to it and to the phrasing of four letters that he had begun to write to his wife, his lawyer, his governor and his bishop" (p. 5). (The first two will not be written, but the latter two will be—cf. pp. 69ff.; pp. 71ff.; pp. 74ff.). Once inside we hear the first of the story's many poignant questions. A stranger asks, " 'What time you got?' " Farragut unstraps his watch and hands it to him, only to have the stranger pocket it. Stripped of his name and now stripped of his connection with time itself, Farragut remains haunted by the question posed. Later he reflects on the mystery of time and understands it in the context of the novel's sacramental and religious imagery: "Time was new bread, time was a sympathetic element, time was water you swam in, time moved through the cellblock with the grace of light" (p. 125).

As I mentioned, Farragut's entry into Falconer records a series of impressions and images (the symbolic ambience), each of which prefigures the accumulative complex of associated meanings that make up the story's final imaginative contour. We hear that "the shabbiness of the place . . . gave the impression, briefly, that this must surely be the twilight and the dying of enforced penance . . ." (p. 6). Unexpectedly, Farragut sees "a man in prison grays feeding bread crusts to a dozen pigeons. This image had for him an extraordinary reality, a promise of saneness. . . . For reasons unknown to Farragut the image of a man sharing his crusts with birds had the resonance of great antiquity" (p. 7).

That resonance is doubly ironic in the context. As Samuel Coale points out, the prison is aptly named, "for the falcon is a bird of prey, capable of being trained to pursue other birds."[14] A falconer trains these hawks for the sport of depredation, and pigeons are an easy quarry. The ironies mount and are tempered simultaneously. Farragut then notices in a building, "high on a water pipe at the ceiling, a tarnished silver Christ-

14. Coale, *John Cheever*, p. 107.

mas garland. The irony was banal but it seemed, like the man feeding birds, to represent a grain of reason" (p. 7).

After taking an even more banally ironic psychological test, Farragut is interviewed, and his interrogator asks the novel's second question: " 'Aren't you ashamed?' " Farragut is then ushered into cellblock F, where an unidentified inmate then asks four brief and brutal questions that will soon comprise the explorations that constitute Farragut's interior journey (involving his family, his addiction, his sexuality, and his guilt):

> While he was making his bed, someone asked, "You rich?" "No," said Farragut. "You clean?" "No," said Farragut. "You suck?" "No," said Farragut. "You innocent?" Farragut didn't reply. Someone at the back of the block struck a guitar and began to sing in a tuneless bluegrass voice: "I got those innocence blues/I'm feeling blue all the time. . . ." (p. 10)

The first chapter ends with Farragut's meeting with Chicken Number Two, the "famous tattooed man" who has forgotten his own name. At the story's close they will make a real and symbolic exchange of their corporeal selves; here Chicken Number Two's words foreshadow that future "conversion" in ironic fashion when he assures Farragut, " 'There has to be something good at the end of every journey and that's why I wanted you to know that it's all a terrible mistake' " (p. 11).

Thus in eight pages Cheever has artfully established the tonic key that will resonate with plaintive or joyous-sounding variation throughout. In addition, he has introduced in equally artful fashion, the many subordinate metaphors that complement the central metaphors of freedom and confinement. The colors black and blue, the concrete images of birds, bread, and water, of height and space, of darkness, twilight, and light, and the metaphoric themes of travel, journey, nakedness, and strangeness will gradually interanimate with each other and, trope-like, will augment the major metaphors.

This subtle imaginative process, in which the reader participates, is in fact described at a climactic point in the novel. Farragut lies in bed and envies the dead, who, unlike the living, do not think or recollect in imaginative fragments. He covets their wholeness of vision and immediacy of apprehension, and in pursuit of these attributes he seeks out a comprehensive metaphor to understand his world. Ironically, the one he uncovers dramatizes his true human condition all the more.

> The dead would at least have panoramic memories and regrets, while he, as a prisoner, found his memories of the shining world to be broken, intermittent and dependent upon chance smells—grass, shoe leather, the odor of piped water in the showers. He possessed some memories,

but they were eclipsed and indisposed. Waking in the morning, he cast wildly and desperately around for a word, a metaphor, a touch or smell that would grant him a bearing. . . . He seemed, in prison, to be a traveler and he had traveled in enough strange countries to recognize this keen alienation. It was the sense that on waking before dawn, everything, beginning with the dream from which he waked, was alien. He had dreamed in another language and felt on waking the texture and smell of strange bedclothes. From the window came the strange smell of strange fuels. He bathed in strange and rusty water, wiped his ass on strange and barbarous toilet paper and climbed down unfamiliar stairs to be served a strange and profoundly offensive breakfast. That was travel. It was the same here. Everything he saw, touched, smelled and dreamed of was cruelly alien, but this continent or nation in which he might spend the rest of his living days had no flag, no anthem, no monarch, president, taxes, boundaries or graves.   (pp. 51-52)

Chapter Two begins with the visit of Farragut's wife, Marcia. Feminists might take offense that her character, an amalgam of Circe, Aphrodite, Sappho, Hera, and Persephone, is absurd and unrealistic. In that assessment they are correct, but offense would be a misguided reaction. John Leonard has said that "women in Cheever's fiction are *supposed* to be mysterious and unfathomable, like God."[15] Leonard's remark is both generically true and specifically true of Marcia. More important in the context, however, Marcia is a metaphoric creation, representing the bifurcation of Farragut's self, an emblem of an alienation he perceives. Her presence here is filtered through Farragut's disrupted memory and imagination, and so inevitably she appears a figure of detachment and displacement—one who embodies the "strangeness" in himself he cannot articulate—and a reader intuits in the subtext of their conversations that she, too, confined as are his fellow inmates, is an emotional counterpart of Farragut himself.

The description of Marcia's initial visit to the prison suggests this with its stress on incongruity amidst the familiar. It begins with Farragut's entering the visitors' room: "Farragut stepped into this no man's land and came on hard, as if he had been catapulated into the visit by mere circumstance. 'Hello darling,' he exclaimed as he had exclaimed 'Hello darling' at trains, boats, airports, the foot of the driveway, journey's end" (p. 14). As they talk, he overhears a banjo and singing "brought into that boarder country," and for an instant he feels himself to be "a man of the world, a world to which his responsiveness was marvelous and absurd" (p. 16). Their scene together fluctuates between the apparently realistic and the surrealistic, between aborted verbal exchange and mem-

15. John Leonard, "Cheever Country," New York Times Book Review, March 7, 1982, p. 25.

ory transformed by imagination—in short, it is acoustically dissonant like some overheard music, marvelous and absurd.

Marcia's quasi-mythic stature is insinuated immediately. As they talk, Farragut recalls something his son told him:

> "You know," his son had said, "I can't talk to Mummy when there's a mirror in the room. She's really balmy about her looks." Narcissus was a man and he couldn't make the switch, but she had, maybe twelve or fourteen times, stood in front of the full-length mirror in their bedroom and asked him, "Is there another woman of my age in this county who is as beautiful as I?"   (p. 18)

In a fine article on *Falconer*, Robert Morace argues that the key to the novel is the confinement of self-love, an egoistic immaturity that Farragut must outgrow in order to achieve salvation.[16] I agree with Morace's stress on the theme of the imprisonment of the self, but the repeated allusions to the myth of Narcissus also suggest a more complex variant. In the classical myth Narcissus falls in love not with himself but with an *image* of himself, a reflection in water that enraptures him. His most famous lover is the nymph Echo, who, punished by Zeus's consort, could no longer use her voice except in foolish repetition of another's speech. In Ovid's *Metamorphoses*, the meeting between Narcissus and Echo is described: he calls, she answers his call by repeating his words, and then, thinking he desires her, she runs to him only to have him spurn her advances. Rejected, Echo pines away for love in solitary grief, and eventually nothing remains of her but her voice. And yet, her voice is present when Narcissus himself, grieved by his inability to possess his own image—an infatuation that ironically parallels her own—dies crying, "Alas! Alas!," a shout she echoes at his death.[17]

The Narcissus-Echo myth and its related modulations (echoes or replications, fascination with images, mirror reflections, metamorphoses) interweave throughout *Falconer* in the stories, memories, and conversations recorded of its characters. In addition, as Robert Graves reminds us, the flower narcissus was so called because of its narcotic, addictive properties, another central theme in the novel. In the scene between Marcia and Farragut we hear this exchange when she asks him, " 'When do you think you'll be clean?' " He answers, " 'I don't know. I find it difficult to imagine cleanliness. I can claim to imagine this, but it would be false. It

16. Robert Morace, "The Religious Experience and 'The Mystery of Imprisonment' in John Cheever's *Falconer*," *Cithara*, pp. 44-53.

17. Robert Graves, *The Greek Myths*, I (New York: Penguin Books, 1955), pp. 286-288. See also *The New Century Classical Handbook*, ed. Catherine Avery (New York: Appleton-Century-Crofts, 1962), p. 735 and *passim*.

would be as though I had claimed to reinstall myself in some afternoon of my youth' " (p. 25). This conversation about efforts of the imagination prompts him to recall their past, oddly mirrored relationship.

> "I don't have to listen to your shit anymore," she had screamed. He was astonished, not at her hysteria, but at the fact that she had taken the words out of his mouth. "You've ruined my life, you've ruined my life, you've ruined my life," she screamed. "There is nothing on earth as cruel as a rotten marriage." This was all on the tip of his tongue. But then, listening for her to continue to anticipate his thinking, he heard her voice, deepened and softened with true grief, begin a variation that was not in his power. (pp. 25-26)

This memory then collides with another, for Farragut recalls, "He had been called a bitch by a woman he deeply loved and he had always kept this possibility in mind" (p. 26). What possibility? What image? These questions become the points for Farragut's subsequent meditation on the mystery of the self and sexuality. Later in the novel, as he waits in erotic longing for the arrival of his male lover Jody, we enter his reflections.

> But why did he so long for Jody when he had often thought that it was his role in life to possess the most beautiful women? Women possessed the greatest and the most rewarding mysteriousness. They were approached in darkness and sometimes, but not always, possessed in darkness. They were an essence, fortified and besieged, worth conquering and, once conquered, flowing with spoils. At his horniest he wanted to reproduce, to populate hamlets, towns, villages and cities. . . . Women were Ali Baba's cave, they were the light of the morning, they were waterfalls, thunderstorms, they were the immensities of the planet, and a vision of this had led him to decide on something better when he rolled naked off his last naked scoutmaster. (p. 100)

All these are images, complex and ambiguous: either exotic images of adventure, secrecy, and conquest, or earthy images of vastness and vision. Farragut tries to imagine himself and Jody in this world he had known with women, specifically in a European pension or boardinghouse: "It was five. They were at the end of the bar. Jody was wearing a white duck suit that Farragut had bought him; but that was as far as he could go. There was no way he could wrench, twist, screw or otherwise force his imagination to continue the scene" (p. 102). This unsuccessful effort at imaginative projection leads him to consider another possibility, "the danger that Farragut might be in love with himself" (p. 103). He recalls a man he knew who was narcissistically obsessed and discounts it in himself, but then remembers Jody complimenting him on his beauty and his reaction (reminiscent of the flower that buds in the Narcissus myth): "in some part of the considerable wilderness that was himself, a flower seemed to bloom and he could not find the blossom and crush it with his heel" (p. 104).

The year that *Falconer* was published, I was present at a private conversation with Cheever. Someone asked him whether he received any negative reactions to the homosexuality in the novel, and Cheever replied, "There's no homosexuality in *Falconer*." When he was reminded of the Jody-Farragut relationship, he answered, "Oh, well, that's not homosexuality." I realized at the time that Cheever was not dissembling or being fanciful but was granting a clue to the novel's symbolic intent. Earlier I quoted Joan Didion's remark that *Falconer* is "a meditation on the abstraction Cheever has always called 'home' . . . located so explicitly in the life of the spirit." The Jody-Farragut relationship, the physicality of which is described so gently and fleetingly, is but one occasion for such a meditation. The tone of the following passage is ruminative, as the words "if," "might," and the like indicate, and the considerations lead us beyond the more narrowly carnal concerns of sexuality:

> But if in loving Jody he loved himself, there was that chance that he might, hell for leather, have become infatuated with his lost youth.
> . . . He missed his youth, missed it as he would miss a friend, a lover, a rented house on one of the great beaches where he had been a young man. To embrace one's self, one's youth, might be easier than to love a fair woman whose nature was rooted in a past that he could never comprehend. . . . To love oneself would be an idle, an impossible, but a delicious pursuit. How simple to love oneself!
> And then there was to think upon the courting of death and death's dark simples, that in covering Jody's body he willingly embraced decay and corruption. (p. 104)

The accent on "simple," on the non-complications of youth and death, contrasts with the more mysterious complexity of love itself; the gradual discovery of this distinction and the spiritual growth it entails mark Farragut's interior journey. Ironically, he learns this truth only by recognizing that he, so singular a self, shares a common lot with humanity.

We find glimmerings of this realization in Chapter Two, when Marcia leaves the prison and Farragut runs upstairs to catch a glimpse from a cell window of the visitors who, like his wife and unlike him, are free of Falconer. "They were free and yet they moved so casually through this precious element that it seemed wasted on them. There was no appreciation of freedom in the way they moved" (p. 29). Farragut notices the protective movements of these visitors: a man pulling up his socks, a woman rooting in her pocketbook for keys, another opening an umbrella. "These were their constraints, the signs of their confinement, but there

was some naturalness, some unself-consciousness about their imprisonment that he, watching them between bars, cruelly lacked" (p. 29).

Falconer prison is Farragut's new "home," and a "family group" of
seven men in cellblock F soon forms. Each of these men is a counterpart
of some aspect of Farragut's own emotional life, and the stories they tell
counterpoint his own. The laconic Ransome killed his father, and he and
Stone, whose eardrums were pierced with an ice pick, are inseparable.
Tennis, once a minor tennis champion, claims, " 'I'm in here because of
a clerical error, an error in banking' " (p. 31). Bumpo, noted as "the
second man to hijack an airplane" (p. 31), wears a large ring, "set with
a diamond or a piece of glass" (p. 32). He protests that he would " 'sell
it tomorrow if somebody'd guarantee me it would save a life. . . . But first
I'd want to see the documents'" (p. 32). The Cuckold, who claims,
" 'I iced my wife by mistake' " (p. 33), runs a prison business making
bracelets out of spoons and spends his time telling lurid stories about his
deceiving wife.

Each of them leads a life that objectivizes guilt and compassion and
is sustained by a denial of some personal truth. Their instincts for compassion and religious gesture are transmuted into their care for cats. One
night at supper Farragut palms three slices of bread for his favorite cat,
Bandit, and as he jogs to his cell with "the illusion of freedom," he smells
the guard Tiny's supper of London broil. This sensory event triggers the
first of many Eucharistic associations that shape the novel:

> Food was a recently revealed truth in his life. He had reasoned
> that the Holy Eucharist was nutritious if you got enough of it. In some
> churches, at some times, they had baked the bread—hot, fragrant and
> crusty—in the chancel. Eat this in memory of me. Food had something
> to do with his beginnings as a Christian and a man.   (p. 35)

The irony of this reflection is compounded by what follows. While
Farragut in his loneliness ("as loneliness can change anything on earth")
talks to Bandit, telling the cat about mountain-climbing in the Abruzzi,
the general alarm bell rings. Tiny has rung it, bent on revenge, because
some cats ate the meat on his plate. A havoc of slaughter ensues: the
guards arrive, and a scene, deliberately surrealistic in its horror, takes
place in which all the less wise cats are murdered. The episode is symbolic
of Falconer itself, and the fact that the fortunate Bandit escapes the
slaughter foreshadows Farragut's happy chance. The horrific scene and the
chapter end with these lines: ". . . Farragut climbed onto his bunk, knelt
there and said: 'Blessed are the meek,' but he couldn't remember what
came next" (p. 41). These lines are poignant in multiple ways: it is Farragut's first prayer; what comes next are the words "for they shall inherit

the earth": and what follows is the story of Farragut's own, even more miraculous survival in this dungeon of death, a renewed inheritance of the earth.

The third chapter begins with an observation about Farragut's addiction as representative of the linkage of humanity with primal nature, thus connecting it with the preceding symbolic slaughter and the abbreviated prayer: "The drug he needed was a distillate of earth, air, water and fire. He was mortal and his addiction was a beautiful illustration of the bounds of his mortality" (p. 43). Then this reflection on the symbolic meaning of addiction as elementary and earth-connected deepens and develops into an elaborate metaphor or conceit that equates addiction with religious sacraments, spiritual fervor, and insight, a common creed:

> The declaration of addiction was in every paper, magazine and airborne voice. Addiction was the law of the prophets. . . . The bridges that he drove across to get to the university [where he would shoot up] were the distillate of engineering computers, a sort of mechanical Holy Ghost. The planes that took him from his university to some other university arced luxuriously into an altitude where men would perish. . . . There were some men of such stupidity that they did not respond to these murderous contradictions and led lives that were without awareness and distinction. His memory of a life without drugs was like a memory of himself as a blond, half-naked youth in good flannels, walking on a white beach between the dark sea and a rank of leonine granite, and to seek out such a memory was contemptible.   (pp. 44-45)

On a first reading this passage sounds like an anti-modernist tirade, confused and regressive. In a sense it is, and therein lies its irony. But the emphasis falls on one's awareness of "murderous contradictions," and the passage is meant primarily to be anticipatory. At this point Farragut mistakenly equates addiction with *both* confinement and liberation; the profounder irony here resides in the fact that his choice of metaphor (of addiction as emblem of both mortal confinement and spiritual exaltation) is a corrupted transposition of religious, sacramental symbolism: "Drugs belonged to all exalted experience, thought Farragut. Drugs belonged in church. Take this in memory of me and be grateful, said the priest, laying an amphetamine on the kneeling man's tongue. Only the opium eater truly understands the pain of death" (p. 45). Only later, when he withdraws from drugs, will Farragut be able to "rejoice" and find liberation by embracing another "contradiction."

As in most of Cheever's fiction, the story proceeds by way of a poetic logic, that is, through an association of themes and images, which generally appear as pairs of contrarieties posed to the characters. Here Farragut meditates on "murderous contradictions" and resolutely refuses to probe the private corridors of his memory. And yet, here intimations of mortality (the murder of the cats, his meditation on addiction) impel him to do unconsciously what he refuses to do consciously: to retrieve "his beginnings as a Christian and a man." The sacramental symbolism of the Eucharist ("Take this in memory of me") that he upends early on becomes a muted thematic presence thereafter. The Eucharist itself is expressive of somewhat "murderous contradictions" (sin and salvation, death and new life, deprivation and food, isolation and community, memory and expectation, cruelty and love, confession of guilt and redemption), and thus it is the fitting subliminal symbol for the religious design of Farragut's story.

The event that releases Farragut's first store of memories is both bizarre and itself symbolic. In bed one night he watches the news on television, which is dominated by the story of a murderess who before her crime lived in an exclusive community. The murderess herself has vanished, so newscasters for the past two weeks have filled air time by questioning closely the memories of her neighbors. " 'Oh, she was so kind,' her neighbors said, 'so clean, so friendly, she loved him so that I can't imagine . . .' What they couldn't imagine was that she had murdered her husband, carefully drained his blood and flushed it down the toilet, washed him clean and begun to rectify and improve his physique" (p. 47). Evidently, memory and imagination themselves fashion a "murderous contradiction" for them. Moreover we learn that the murderess, intent on fashioning a "perfect man," had decapitated her husband and substituted the head of a second victim; still discontent, she gradually removed his other bodily parts and replaced them with those of victims more favorably endowed. "Offers to exploit the remains for commercial purposes were being considered, but nothing had been agreed upon. Night after night the fragments of the tale ended with a draw-away shot of the serene white house, the specimen planting and the velvet lawn" (p. 47).

This minor incident is a foretoken of Farragut's exertions of memory and imagination, and the final lines that cap it reveal its process: "night after night the fragments of [Farragut's] tale" (p. 47) and of his nonphysical self are re-collected and re-fashioned into newness, if not quite the perfection the murderess sought. Farragut's first memories are connected with death and his narrow escape from it (portending the novel's close), and each relates to members of his original family. First, he recalls his mother's tale about his father inviting an abortionist to dinner during her pregnancy in order to snuff out Farragut's life before birth. The threat of death thus existed even before memory. Next, Farragut remembers a time that he and his brother went walking on a beach. His brother suggested that he swim in the choppy surf, and Farragut waded in. But some "stranger, a fisherman," shouted a warning to him about the treacherous rip tide, " 'a well-known deathtrap,' " and Farragut left the water (p. 48). "[He] remembered being happy at the fact that he was alive. The sky was blue" (p. 49).

The next memory involves Farragut's "homecoming" from a drug rehabilitation center. A doctor had diagnosed heart damage and prescribed rest and little exertion. Farragut's wife knew this, and yet she seemed to delight in tormenting him by slamming doors abruptly, thus shocking his fragile heart. One morning, waking up on the couch, his vision blurry and his heart weary, he heard his wife leaving their bedroom and coming down the hall.

> "Is there anything I can get you?" she asked. Her tone was murderous.
> "Some sort of kindness," he said. He was helpless. "A little kindness." (p. 50)

The final memory is of his brother Eben again, this time at a party. While Farragut was standing on a sill at an open window, "someone gave him a swift push" (p. 50). He landed unhurt on the pavement below and never learned who pushed him, but years later his brother recalled the incident and told him, " 'It was that man from Chicago' " (p. 51). Farragut wonders whether by saying so Eben "had incriminated himself" (p. 51).

All four memories of miraculous escape from death reveal a similar pattern: each of them is indefinite, uncertain, and suspect. The agents of his potential murder are identified only through hearsay or through guess, that is, an imaginative interpretation on Farragut's part. Was his a family of murderers in actual fact? We readers are unsure. Cheever thus teases our own imaginations, and we must depart from each of these vividly told accounts and wonder in private. Our puzzlement increases with the incident that follows.

Remember that Farragut recalls these memories on a night when he believes "he would die. He would be murdered" (p. 47). The next morning he pleads for a drug fix, but doesn't get it, and Chisholm, the deputy warden, enters the cellblock with two guards to watch his seizures of withdrawl. Even in the callous climate of the prison, this casual cruelty on the part of authorities seems far-fetched. Nonetheless, eagerness for plausibility should not distract us from what the scene represents: a recapitulation of the four memories of nearness to and escape from death. In his cell Farragut is racked with chilling convulsions. "No longer even on his knees, but moving over the floor like a swimmer, he got to the chair, looped the buckle onto itself for a noose and fastened the belt to a nail on the chair. He was trying to strangle himself when Chisholm said: 'Cut the poor prick down and get his fix' " (p.(53). The borderline between that of murder victim and suicide, especially its psychic vagueness at root, is thus dramatized.

After being hit with a chair, Farragut wakes in the prison infirmary, and as he comes to, he hears Tiny's question that will become the refrain for his own spiritual trip through mind and memory: " 'Farragut, Farragut . . . why is you an addict?' " (p. 54; cf. pp. 62, 63, 190).

"Farragut was not disconcerted by the question, but he was provoked" (p. 54). The provocation then evokes yet another memory: he thinks that it is only "natural" that he is an addict because he had been "raised by people who dealt in contraband" of "unlicensed spiritual, intellectual and erotic stimulants" (p. 54). We learn that he is the product of "a border principality," a "border of sorrow" (pp. 57, 59). The other quaint inhabitants were his parents and his brother, and here the reminiscences are themselves oddly reminiscent of the Wapshot novels. Take, for example, his memory of his mother. "For Farragut the word 'mother' evoked the image of a woman pumping gas, curtsying at the Assemblies and banging a lectern with her gavel" (pp. 56-57). He cannot square this image (note he never says "reality" here) of motherhood with the image in a Degas painting of a woman with a bowl of chrysanthemums. Yet, "the world kept urging him to match his own mother, a famous arsonist, snob, gas pumper and wing shot, against the image of the stranger with her autumnal and bitter-smelling flowers. Why had the universe encouraged this gap?" (p. 57).

The last question sounds cosmic but is more likely fanciful, since Farragut is not so unlike the rest of his family. "[They] were the sort of people who claimed to be sustained by tradition, but who were in fact sustained by the much more robust pursuit of a workable improvisation, uninhibited by consistency" (p. 59). His most dramatically vivid memory is that of his father's plan to drown himself off the island of Nagasakit— a scheme that his mother announced at the dinner table without any apparent interest. Though not quite sixteen at the time, Farragut took the family car, drove to Nagasakit, and ran down to the beach. Seeing nothing but the ocean, he wondered: "How could he tell if it contained his father, with pearls for eyes?" (p. 61), a thought which echoes the lines from The Tempest appropriated by T. S. Eliot in The Waste Land. Crossing the road to the amusement park, he heard laughter, and then spotted his father on the roller coaster, "pretending to drink from an empty bottle and pretending to contemplate suicide from every rise" (p. 62). At Farragut's request, the car operators brought his father to earth. " 'Oh, Daddy,' said Farragut, 'you shouldn't do this to me in my formative years' " (p. 62).

Farragut suggests that all this is sufficient explanation for his drug addiction; a reader notes the repetition on "pretending" suicide and, recalling Farragut's own attempt, wonders about this and other easy explanations.

After assaulting the lawyer who hears his complaint against Chisholm, Farragut is assigned a cell in solitary. He has secreted a pen in his anus and resolves to compose letters by writing rough drafts on his bed sheet and committing the text to memory. When we read the letters he writes we are initially perplexed by their sober, stilted style, so unlike the novel's narrative and dialogue. But their very formality and abstract quality serve a purpose: their intrusion effectively stalls the narrative action and offers, as in a musical counterpoint, a combination of melodic lines that contribute to the novel's final thematic texture.

In the first letter, addressed to the governor, Farragut discusses the subjects of election and justice as these terms are understood in their civic, secular senses. Farragut reminds the governor that he was elected by only " 'a slender majority' " but that he, Farragut, was elected " 'by a much more ancient, exalted and unanimous force, the force of justice' " (p. 69). As a result, he feels that he is " 'a much more representative elected member of society' " than the governor (p. 69). The governor attained his elected office through chicanery, but says Farragut, " 'the elective office that I hold is pure' " (p. 69). Farragut goes on to protest Chisholm's attack on him and the withholding of the drug doctors have prescribed for him as a higher injustice, a breach in the fabric of authority and trust that ethics and the law presume.

This letter to the governor is by turns precious, self-pitying, sentimental, and arbitrary if not cynical in its logic. What it reveals is a perplexed mind puzzling out the true meaning of human innocence and justice. Its significance lies in its placement, for it immediately precedes Farragut's letter to his Bishop, in which he again probes the mystery of justice and election as it is biblically revealed. To appreciate these passages, it is important to recall that in the Bible there is, strictly speaking, no abstract idea of justice; there, justice is allied with the notions of judgment, righteousness, and mercy—all virtues which belong properly to God, who is their bestower. The concept of God's judgment is exceedingly complex, and exegetes advise caution in wrenching any univocal meaning out of context.[18] What can be said, however, is that God's judgment is always viewed in polar tension, containing within its meaning positive and negative significances simultaneously. It entails both punishment and salvation, expressive of either God's anger or His mercy; it

18. See, for example, John L. McKenzie, *Dictionary of the Bible* (Milwaukee: Bruce, 1965) and the articles on Judgment, Faith, Mercy, Righteousness, etc.

is both universal and particular; and it is both realized in contemporary history and is eschatological—that is, men are effectively judged *now* depending on whether they themselves judge for or against God now, and yet the finality and perfection of His judgment is reserved for a future beyond all nows, the biblical Day of Judgment. Farragut's letter, though deficient in theological clarity, expresses each of these ambiguities as he attempts to wrestle with the most cosmic of mysteries.

The letter begins with a statement about Farragut's own ambivalent belief. In Scripture, faith is inevitably linked to God's judgment (which embraces His righteousness and mercy), for faith radically entails a confidence and trust in all of God's activities. But faith always remains a gift; all men are sinners, and no one is judged righteous without God's favorable judgment (grace). Yet, being a gift, faith incorporates a knowledge, an intellectual attitude of acceptance that some individuals do not share. Deprived of such knowledge, these individuals fail to comprehend the language of faith, because this language is specialized, involving the grammar, the rhetoric, the poetry, and the vocabulary of a mother tongue that sounds like gibberish to them. This sad truth about man's inability to communicate is itself a challenge to faith and an invitation to skepticism, because it, too, relates to the mystery of God's judgment. Farragut, now condemned to a literal solitariness, is well aware of these tensions.

> "I was confirmed at the age of eleven by Bishop Evanston in the same church where I was christened. I have continued to take Holy Communion every Sunday of my life, barring those occasions when I was unable to find a church. In the provincial cities and towns of Europe I attend the Roman Mass. I am a croyant . . . and as croyants I'm sure we share the knowledge that to profess exalted religious experience outside the ecclesiastical paradigm is to make of oneself an outcast. . . . I truly believe in One God the Father Almighty but I know that to say so loudly, and at any distance from the chancel—any distance at all—would dangerously jeopardize my ability to ingratiate those men and women with whom I wish to live. I am trying to say—and I'm sure you will agree with me—that while we are available to transcendent experience, we can state this only at the suitable and ordained time and in the suitable and ordained place. I could not live without this knowledge; no more could I live without the thrilling possibility of suddenly encountering the fragrance of skepticism."   (p. 72)

Next, Farragut addresses the subject of imprisonment, a life that ironically " 'follows very closely the traditional lives of the saints' " (p. 72). He says: " 'We prisoners, more than any men, have suffered for our sins. . . . We are in fact the word made flesh; but what I want to do is call your attention to a great blasphemy' " (p. 73). The descriptions of the "blasphemy" might sound unctuous and sentimental unless the reader realizes that Farragut is in fact condemning the one-sided, negative understanding of Judgment Day, a reckoning devoid of compassion, mercy, and love:

"As Your Grace well knows, the most universal image of mankind is not love or death; it is Judgment Day. . . . Here the Divinity sifts out the souls of men, granting to the truly pure infinite serenity and sentencing the sinners to fire, ice and sometimes piss and shit. . . . The Divinity is the flame, the heart of this vision. A queue approaches the Divinity, always from the right. . . . Forfeiture and torment are, even in the earliest reports, much more passionately painted than eternal peace. . . . The presence of God binds the world together. His force, His essence, is Judgment." (pp. 73-74)

The pessimism of this attitude abruptly changes in the next letter Farragut composes. " 'Oh my darling,' he wrote, with no pause at all and to a girl he had lived with for two months when Marcia had abdicated . . ." (p. 74). This swift transition is less stunning than it first appears. Meditation on faith and skepticism, negative judgment and election understood apocalyptically, unconsciously lead him to consider another aspect of God's judgment—namely, love. In what is perhaps the most famous or familiar account of the Last Judgment (Matt. 25:31-46), the sheep and the goats are separated according to their gestures of love and kindness to others. In the scene both groups are challenged to "remember"; they misunderstand and forget, but the point of the apocalyptic parable is that the Judge does not—He remembers, and His memory is itself a judgment on love.

Farragut's third letter is shaped around the refrain "remember," and the word occurs in each of its paragraphs. He states the reason: " 'I do not love, I am unloved, and I can only remember the raptness of love faintly, faintly' " (p. 75). The series of memories consists of re-imagined moments, a constellation of disparate images rather than specific events. The clue to the letter's spirit is Farragut's remark that " 'I suppose I am dealing with romantic and erotic things, but I think I am dealing with much more' " (p. 76). The final memory, that of the two of them skiing together down a mountain on a spring-like winter day with the snow thawing, is symbolic of Farragut's own gradual emotional thaw and descent. " 'The clinicians would say that we were skiing down every slope of our lives back to the instant of our birth; and men of good will and common sense would claim that we were skiing in every possible direction toward some understanding of the triumph of our beginnings and our ends' " (p. 81).

In the next chapter Farragut's love affair with Jody is preceded by his new-found responsiveness to the mysterious beauty of nature. The time is autumn, and the changing leaves of the multi-colored trees "had the power to remind" him of "the enormous and absurd pleasure he had, as a free man, taken in his environment" (pp. 84-85). His reaction is almost evangelical: "The simple phenomenon of light—brightness angling across the air—struck him as a transcendent piece of good news. He thought it fortunate that as the leaves fell, they turned and spun, presenting an illusion of facets to the light" (p. 85).

He then notices the arrival of a flock of red-winged blackbirds whose flight is noted as ambiguously symbolic. "They all had the choppy flight of caged birds . . . all of them flying clumsily but given by their numbers a sense of power—the magnetic stamina of the planet—drawn through the air like embers on a strong draft" (p. 86). Farragut views all this movement in terms of opposite, distinctive images: the birds move "as the air moved, like dust, like pollen, like ashes, like any sign of the invincible potency of nature" (p. 86).

It is in the context of this suggestibility to the transcendent and the "miraculous potency of nature" that Farragut's affair with Jody must be understood. He, too, is a force of nature, and mysterious, yet he also wears around his neck "a simple and elegant gold cross" (p. 87). At their first tryst Jody leads Farragut to the so-called "Millionaire's View" of the prison, where one can see "a two-mile stretch of river with cliffs and mountains on the western shore" (p. 87), reminding us of Farragut's last letter to his lover. During their love-making Jody repeatedly calls Farragut "Chicken," a fitting soubriquet for one who will substitute himself for Chicken Number Two. When we hear of Jody's mad scheme to escape with the cardinal's retinue (the cardinal is coming to hand out diplomas to the graduates of the prison's high-school class), we admit to its implausibility. Jody himself says, " 'What a miracle!' " but explains why such a caper is in fact possible at all:

> "At Mass you don't look at the other acolytes. That's the thing about prayer. You don't look. When you see a stranger on the altar you don't go around asking who's the stranger on the altar. This is holy business and when you're doing holy business you don't see nothing. When you drink the blood of Our Savior you don't look to see if the chalice is tarnished or if there's bugs in the wine. You get to be transfixed, you're like transfixed. Prayer. That's why it is. Prayer is what's going to get me out of this place. The power of prayer." (p. 97)

The night before Jody's planned escape, Farragut himself does utter a selfless prayer. The weather is ominous, and if it rains the next day, the cardinal's visit will be canceled. His unspoken words—"Have pity upon him, then; try to understand his fears"—are ambiguous, including both himself and Jody, for he desires to see "his beloved escape" (p. 123). A baptismal-like rain falls heavily, and when he awakes, he discovers that he "got what he had bargained for: a day of incomparable beauty" (p. 124).

The mechanics of the cardinal's arrival by helicopter is typically Cheeveresque on one level of reading, that is, satiric and mildly fantastic. But the foundations of a second Cheeveresque level have been laid. The cardinal's arrival and descent from another space is a reminder of the apocalyptic imagery used in the New Testament for Judgment Day, based on the descent of the Son of Man from the clouds of heaven in the Book of Daniel (7:13f.). And the cardinal's triumphant arrival at the prison is described in updated allusions to the apocalyptic imagery of the Book of Revelation, including Saint John the Divine's Amen:

> The crimson of the cardinal's robes seemed living and pure and his carriage was admirable and would have quelled a riot. . . . He made a sign of the cross as high and wide as his reach and the great spell of worship fell over that place. *In nomine Patris et Filii et Spiritus Sancti.* Farragut would have liked to pray for the happiness of his son, his wife, the safety of his lover, the soul of his dead brother, would have liked to pray for some enlargement of his wisdom, but the only word he could root out of these massive intentions was his *Amen.*
>
> (p. 127)

There follows a comic insertion to highlight the odd reversals soon to take place. The commissioner of prisons stands to speechify and, moved by his own fatuous eloquence, says that reform " 'begins at home, and where is home? Home is prison!' " (p. 129). Speaking of his efforts and those of other correctional administrators, he says, " 'We might compare [it]—compare only, of course—to a miracle' " (p. 129).

After the distribution of diplomas, the mass begins, and it is noteworthy that Cheever chooses to use only those prayers from the Latin mass that concern mercy, new life, and benediction. We are told that "the raptness of prayer enthralled Farragut as the raptness of love" (pp. 129-130). Eventually, the cardinal leaves, and the apocalyptic imagery, intermingled with the imagery of Christ's ascension at the end of Luke's gospel, returns:

> The props kicked up a cloud of dust and the engine ascended. Someone put a recording of cathedral bells on the public address system and up they went to their glorious clamor. Oh, glory, glory, glory! . . . The sound of the chopper and the bells filled heaven and earth. They all cheered and cheered and cheered and some of them cried. The sound of the bells stopped, but the chopper went on playing its geodetic survey of the surrounding terrain—the shining, lost and beloved world.   (p. 130)

After this climax, the "miraculous" mechanics of Jody's escape do not seem so far-fetched. This judgment day has been not a doomsday but a day of deliverance, blessing, and answered prayers, and we are reminded that the original Good News was a message about such things. Later we learn that Jody had engineered his escape in part by giving another inmate his tiny golden cross (p. 138). This is the first of similar exchanges.

The descent-ascent pattern of the helicopter becomes the pattern of Farragut's life after Jody has gone. During the riot at Amana Prison ("man" with the negative alpha-privative at its beginning and end), the Falconer authorities distract the inmates by calling for "short arm inspection." This confluence of circumstances leads Farragut to contemplate the human condition of his fellows: "They were souls who could not be redeemed, and while penance was a clumsy and a cruel answer, it was some measure of the mysteriousness of their fall. In the white light they seemed to Farragut to be fallen men" (p. 153). When the guard claims the TV is broken, thus cutting them off from news of Amana, Farragut "found himself sinking, with no resistance at all, into a torpor. . . . Down he seemed to go . . . down into a lewd and putrescent nothingness" (p. 153). His descent is compounded hellishly when Chicken Number Two sets fire to his mattress and a pandemonium ensues that is soon checked by water hoses. Farragut's spirits arise only when he begins to build a radio from a toilet-paper roll and some copper wire that he has stolen and hidden in his cell: "How beautiful the wire seemed, a slender, clean, gold-colored tie to the world of the living . . . the splendor of building, out of paper and wire, some bond or lock or shining buckle that could fasten two worlds. When it was done he sighed like a gratified lover and mumbled: 'Praise be to Thee, O Lord' " (pp. 155-156).

The next vivid scene that connects with this one in metaphoric irony occurs when the prisoners are invited to pose for a photograph beside a decorated Christmas tree, a kind gesture sponsored by a woman in memory of her son. The prisoners volunteer their "outside" addresses, and Chicken Number Two writes: "Mr. and Mrs. Santa Claus, Icicle Street, the North Pole" (p. 164). The incongruity of this invention and its poignancy in the prison's circumstances are at one with the multiple meanings of the mystery of Christmas itself.

> The irony of Christmas is always upon the poor in heart; the mystery of the solstice is always upon the rest of us. The inspired metaphor of the Prince of Peace and his countless lights, overwhelming the maddening and the threadbare carols, was somewhere here. . . . Mrs. Spingarn genuinely loved her son and grieved at his cruel and unnatural end. The guards genuinely feared disorder and death. The

inmates would fleetingly feel that they had a foot in the faraway
street.   (p. 163)

The "metaphor of the Prince of Peace," which has gradually become
more dominant, from this moment on displaces the metaphor of confinement, and the Christological associations mount until the novel's close.
Concomitantly, Farragut is gradually freed from his own narcissism through
hearing the echoes of his own plight in the stories of his fellow inmates.
The Cuckold's stories about the homosexual hustler (pp. 110ff.) and his
own wife (pp. 181ff.), Jody's escape (pp. 130ff.), Marshack the guard's
protests (pp. 144ff.), Tennis's pitiful denials (pp. 150ff.), Chicken's rav-
ings (p. 170)—all are mirrored reflections, echoes of Farragut's condition.
Farragut's conversation with Bumpo also prepares us for the salvific transfer
to follow. Farragut pleads with him to sacrifice his diamond so that the
radio he is building, the link with the outside world, might be complete.
He reminds Bumpo: " 'I have heard you speak fluently about your will-
ingness to give your diamond to some starving child or some lonely crone,
by-passed by the thoughtless world. . . . Dear Bumpo, God gave you your
diamond and God means you should give it to me' " (pp. 167-168).
Bumpo's refusal is ambiguous: " 'You didn't know you could save the world,
did you?' he asked the diamond" (p. 169), and that unanswered question
becomes a tantalizing foreshadowing.

Another more dramatic foreshadowing occurs immediately after, when
Farragut has an odd dream. He dreams that he is on a cruise ship, relaxed
and bored by the usual goings-on during such curises. One afternoon,
feeling idle and a bit uneasy, he sees a schooner come up along port-side
with flags flying that he does not recognize. Caution is necessary, of
course, to avoid interpreting dream symbolism too exactly; its power lies
precisely in its symbolic ambivalence. Nonetheless, there are fairly well-
established or recurring symbolic meanings that provide at least limited
entry for understanding this dream in its context.

The cruise ship here seems to represent the Ship of Death, in idle
motion over the amorphous and hostile sea. The arrival of the sailing
ship, the twin-masted schooner, is a deliverance and rescue from it. Ex-
perts in mythology contend that "the attainment of the Great Peace is
depicted in the form of sailing the seas," and that for this reason Christianity uses the ship to represent the Church.[19] Furthermore, the schooner,
unlike other modern ships, encapsulates other important symbolism because of its structure. Its mainmast at the center of the vessel suggests the
Cosmic Tree in mythology. The Cosmic Tree or the Tree of the World

19. See J. E. Ceriot, *Dictionary of Symbols* (New York: Philosophical Library, 1962),
pp. 280-281.

is so called because it is symbolically situated at the center of the Universe, upholding and uniting the three cosmic regions of Heaven, Earth, and Hell on one axis, for its roots are underground and its branches rise to the sky. Mircea Eliade points out that "Christianity has utilized, interpreted, and amplified the symbol. The Cross made of the wood of the tree of good and evil, appears in the place of the Cosmic Tree. . . ."[20] The Cross, then, is both the Tree of Death and the Tree of Life, a simultaneous symbol of life, death, resurrection, and new life. The Sea also incorporates (as does the sacrament of baptism) each of these references.

The images in Farragut's dream are thus multivalent and resonant in multiple ways. As noted, the schooner arrives with flags flying from its mast, but Farragut "does not understand these" (p. 174). In symbolism, flags, because of their high position and movement, represent exaltation, a heightening, victory, and transcendence.[21] Note that Farragut must climb down a rope ladder in order to leave the cruise ship (Ship of Death) and board this Ship of Transcendence, which transports him from danger.

> The schooner has come for him. He goes below, climbs down a rope ladder onto her deck and as they sail away he waves goodbye to his friends on the cruise—men, women and the members of the ship's orchestra. He does not know who owns the schooner and who greets him there. He remembers nothing except that he stands on her deck and watches the cruise ship regain speed. She is a big old-fashioned cruiser, named for a queen, white as a bride, with three canted stacks and a little gold lace, like a toy boat, at her bow. She goes crazily off course, veers to port and heads at full tilt for a nearby island that looks like one of the Atlantic islands, only with palms. She rams the beach, heels to starboard and bursts into flame, and while he sails away he can see, over his shoulder, the pyre and the enormous column of smoke.   (p. 174)

The final chapter opens appropriately with an apocalyptic symbolic action. The prisoners are stripped "naked again" and wait in line for new clothing. We are told: "The new issue was a noncommittal green, scarcely, thought Farragut, a verdant green, scarcely the green of Trinity and the long summer months, but a shade up from the gray of the living dead" (p. 179). (This brief description is rich in meaning. In Christian sym-

20. Mircea Eliade, *Images and Symbols* (New York: Sheed & Ward, 1969), p. 161; also see Shirley Park Lowry, *Familiar Mysteries* (New York: Oxford Univ. Press, 1982), pp. 132-176.
21. Ceriot, *Dictionary of Symbols*, p. 103.

bolism the color green represents hope, regeneration, and victory; hence it is the color worn by the priest on Trinity Sunday and the weeks that follow it.)

An influenza epidemic then makes inoculation of the prisoners necessary. While standing in line for his shot, Farragut asks why he has not been receiving his methadone. The orderly tells him, " 'Some of us have been wondering when you'd notice. You've been on placebos for nearly a month. You're clean, my friend, you're clean' " (p. 186). Farragut is shocked; he "could not congratulate himself on having mastered his addiction, since he had not been aware of it" (p. 187). A second, specifically Christian sign of gratuitous deliverance and freedom occurs shortly thereafter. Farragut is in the throes of a high fever that reminds him of "the bliss of drugs" when "a strange thing" happens:

> He saw, at the open door of his cell, a young man with summery hair and immaculate clericals, holding a little tray with a silver chalice and ciborium. "I've come to celebrate the Holy Eucharist," he said. Farragut got out of bed. The stranger came into the cell. He had a very cleanly smell, Farragut noticed as he approached him and asked, "Shall I kneel?" "Yes, please," said the priest. . . . There was nothing on his mind at all and he entered, completely, into the verbal pavane he had been taught as a youth. "Holy, Holy, Holy," he said in a loud and manly voice. "Heaven and earth are full of Thy Glory. Praise be to Thee, O Lord most high." When he had been blessed with the peace that passes all understanding, he said, "Thank you, Father," and the priest said, "God bless you, my son."   (pp. 187-188)

Jesus Christ's celebration of the Eucharist at the Last Supper was His final sacramental gesture before the start of His Passion, a Passion that ended in death and was followed by new life. Here, Farragut wonders aloud why he alone was chosen to receive the Eucharist: " 'He didn't do his thing for anybody else. Why did he pick on me?' " (p. 188). But he receives no immediate answer.

When Chicken Number Two becomes ill, it is Farragut who washes his tattooed body and places him in clean sheets—details reminiscent of the gospel account following Christ's crucifixion. The dying Chicken tells him, " 'What I'm trying to say is that I ain't learned all I know through experience . . . so I figure I must come into this life with the memories of some other life' "; and his final words are " 'I'd go down [to certain death] a very happy man because I'm intensely interested in what's going to happen next, I'm very interested in what's going to happen next' " (p. 200). Farragut's sense of some spiritual commutation between the two of them arises immediately:

> He seemed to draw from Chicken Number Two's presence a deep sense of freeness; he seemed to take something that Chicken Number Two was lovingly giving to him. He felt some discomfort in the right cheek of his buttocks, and half-standing, he saw that he had been sitting on Chicken's false teeth. "Oh, Chicken," he cried, "you bit me in the ass." His laughter was the laughter of the deepest tenderness and then he began to sob. (pp. 201-202)

This scene is replete with Christian resonances (including the goad), and the themes of death issuing in new life, of the substitution of one in death that others might be redeemed and free, intensify in the action that follows.

After Chicken dies and is put into his burial sack, Farragut finds "the courage to take his rightful place in things as he saw them" (p. 202). He unzips Chicken's sack, the noise of the zipper like "some plainsong" (p. 202), takes out Chicken's body, and climbs into the sack, the interior of which has "the smell of some tent" (p. 203). Men arrive to pick up the sack, and the experience revives a pre-memory within Farragut which is a symbolic foretoken.

> The sensation of being carried belonged to the past, since it gave him an unlikely feeling of innocence and purity. How strange to be carried so late in life and toward nothing that he truly knew, freed, it seemed, from his erotic crudeness, his facile scorn and his chagrined laugh— not a fact, but a chance, something like the afternoon light on high trees, quite useless and thrilling. How strange to be living and to be grown and to be carried. (pp. 203-204)

Once the opportunity to escape from "his shroud" arrives, Farragut, who had the foresight to take along a razor blade, begins the slow process of cutting the canvas. "He would settle for the stamina of love, a presence he felt like the beginnings of some stair" (p. 205). The blade slips and cuts his fingers and his thigh, and though "he could feel the wetness of the blood, . . . this seemed to have happened to someone else" (p. 203). Soon he is able to step "out of his grave" and into freedom, and the exchange is completed.

Farragut's progress of escape is Dante-esque, a leave-taking from hell, followed by a journey through purgatory into paradise. Once on the street he admires "the uniform darkness of the houses" where "no lights of sickness, worry or love" burn (p. 206). Then he hears piano music, "some beginner's piece" that someone is playing in the dark (p. 206). He passes by a dump and inhales its air, "although it was no more than the bitterness of an extinguished fire" (p. 207). If he had looked up he would have seen clouds hurrying past a nearly full moon that might have reminded him

'not of fleeing hordes but of advancing ranks and throngs, an army more
swift than bellicose. . . . But he saw nothing of what was going on in
heaven because his fear of falling kept his eyes on the sidewalk . . ."
(p. 207).

Then way ahead of him and on the right he saw a rectangle of
pure white light and he knew he had the strength to reach this though
the blood in his boot now made a noise. It was a laundromat. . . . The
doors to most of the machines hung open like the doors to ovens.
Opposite were the bull's-eye windows of drying machines and in two
he could see clothes tossed and falling, always falling—falling heed-
lessly, it seemed, like falling souls or angels if their fall had ever been
heedless. He stood at the window, this escaped and bloody convict,
watching these strangers wait for their clothes to be clean.
(pp. 207-208)

The images emphasized in these passages are those of an apocalyptic
vision: Gehenna, the advancing hordes in the heavens, the beckoning
pure white light, the knot of people waiting for their clothes to be washed
clean again. Throughout, the accent is on "fear of falling," falling, and
on strangeness and strangers.

Then under a street light Farragut spots another stranger who "could
be an agent from the Department of Correction . . . or given his luck so
far, an agent from heaven" (p. 208). (Recall the twin aspects of Judgment
Day.) The stranger possesses "an electric heater with a golden bowl shaped
like the sun and a sky-blue motorcycle helmet" (p. 208; cf. Eccl. 12:6;
Rev. 16:1f.; 21:9f.). Farragut was convicted; this man has been evicted.
The stranger asks, " 'You wouldn't want to share a place with me, would
you, if I found something beautiful?' " To which Farragut replies,
" 'Maybe' " (p. 209). They get on a bus together, and "the brightly lighted
bus had the same kind and number of people—for all he knew, the same
people—that he had seen in the laundromat" (pp. 209-210).

The stranger pays Farragut's bus fare, and then a second symbolic
action follows, reminiscent of the Sermon on the Mount (Matt. 5:40)
and especially of the lines from the Last Judgment: "I was a stranger and
you never made me welcome, naked, and you never clothed me, sick and
in prison and you never visited me" (Matt. 25:43f.). The stranger notices
that it is raining and that Farragut has no raincoat, so he gives him one
of his own coats. Farragut tries it on, and the stranger pronounces it "a
perfect fit" (p. 210). This is the second exchange with another person
that effects Farragut's "miraculous" escape, his transformation from death
to new life. The novel ends amid baptismal rain, and its closing line is
an echoing of Paul's words to the Philippians (4:4f.), words which Charles
Wesley appropriated in his "Hymn for Our Lord's Resurrection."

Farragut walked to the front of the bus and got off at the next stop. Stepping from the bus onto the street, he saw that he had lost his fear of falling and all other fears of that nature. He held his head high, his back straight, and walked along nicely. Rejoice, he thought, rejoice.   (p. 211)

When I have a little vexation, it grows in five minutes into a theme for Sophocles.

John Keats

Step outside the narrow borders of what men call reality, and you step into chaos . . . or imagination.

Ralph Ellison

To begin with, I was alienated by your swift declension through the loss of guilt as a useful emotion to the contemporary universality of paranoia. What can you be speaking of? The appeal to a sense of original sin remains in my experience universal.

*John Cheever in an Open Letter
to Elizabeth Hardwick*

Life is made up of marble and mud. . . . What is called poetic insight is the gift of discerning in this sphere of strangely mingled elements, the beauty and the majesty which are compelled to assume a garb so sordid.

Nathaniel Hawthorne

The easiest way to parse the world is through mythology.

John Cheever

The leveling process is the victory of the abstract over the individual. The leveling process in modern times corresponds, on reflection, to fate in antiquity.

Sören Kierkegaard

8: The Stories
of John Cheever

The publication of *The Stories of John Cheever* in 1978 alerted American readers to the fact that an obscured, rather than hidden, national treasure had long existed in their midst. The collection garnered all the major literary awards of the year, mirroring its initial ecstatic reception by countless reviewers. On rereading these reviews, one cannot but come away with the impression that even the most hard headed, if not slightly jaded, reviewers had experienced the surprise of consternated delight. Paul Gray specifically addressed this reaction, noting that "one of the surprises . . . is that the stories are almost better than people remember. Never before has it been possible to see so much of his short work so steadily and so whole. . . . It charts one of the most important bodies of work in contemporary letters."[1] John Leonard was more specific still:

> It would be meaningless and impudent to commend one or another story in a volume that is not merely the publishing event of the "season" but a grand occasion in English literature. For whatever the opinion is worth, John Cheever is my favorite writer.[2]

Richard Locke's enthusiasm was genuine but qualified by what he perceived as Cheever's limitations "in subject, theme, setting, emotional range, diversity of literary effect, intellectual play and psychological subtlety or depth." Locke's objections thereafter were too general or historical in vantage point—one might say tendentious—to be entirely clear as criticism. But at the close of his review a reader finally realized that Locke was rehearsing, instead, the more familiar objections made to Cheever's previous novels. Thus his review ended in a confusion of generous and niggardly perceptions, a giving with one hand and a taking away with the other, though concluding at last with a gesture of gratitude:

1. Paul Gray, "Inescapable Conclusions," *Time*, October 16, 1978, p. 122.
2. John Leonard, *New York Times*, November 7, 1978, p. 43.

. . . Cheever's largest gift [is] the power to present a sensuous (especially a visual) detail that effortlesly carries intense emotional and symbolic force. . . . A novel requires a more architectonic imagination, a less purely visual and anecdotal sensibility than Cheever's. A story is a peep through a window, a novel sees the whole town. A story is a song or a snapshot; a novel is an opera or a movie. A novel can wrap you in its toils, take over your life, but a story can go straight to your heart in an instant. With this book Cheever has given us all a heartfelt gift.[3]

To my mind, such strained and inelegant metaphors admirably demonstrate the viscous soup that intelligent people who champion the distinction between story and novel over-much are compelled to stir in defense of categorical prejudices. Nonetheless, I cite Locke's exiguous reservations for positive purposes, because John Irving, a working novelist himself, registered an entirely opposite reaction. Irving said in his glowing review:

Since I'm a novelist—whose taste is solidly with the novel—I must add that this collection of craft and feeling *reads* like a novel. There is not only the wonder of finishing one good story after another, there is that cumulative weight, that sense of deepening, that I have formerly associated only with the consecutiveness of a true (and truly narrative) novel. Although I'd read many of these stories before, reading them consecutively was a compelling experience. Cheever never repeats himself tediously, but he does repeat himself in ways we come to anticipate and love. . . . Sixteen of *The Stories of John Cheever* moved me as if they had been incredibly lovely and compressed novels. At least 50 stories are stories you'll want to read again, and all 61 have something good enough in them to make you laugh or cry.[4]

Shortly after these reviews appeared, Cheever—keenly aware of Locke's objections and ones similar to them—wrote an essay for *Newsweek* entitled "Why I Write Short Stories." In it he remarked,

The novel, in all its greatness, demands at least some passing notice of the classical unities, preserving that mysterious link between esthetics and moral fitness; but to have this unyielding antiquity exclude the newness in our ways of life would be regrettable. . . . We are not a nomadic people, but there is more than a hint of this in the spirit of our great country—and the short story is the literature of the nomad.[5]

3. Richard Locke, "Visions of Order and Domestic Disarray," *New York Times Book Review*, December 3, 1978, p. 78.
4. John Irving, "Facts of Living," *Saturday Review*, September 30, 1978, pp. 45-46.
5. John Cheever, "Why I Write Short Stories," *Newsweek*, October 30, 1978, pp. 24-25.

Then, in typical Cheever fashion, he attempted to close the question concerning all such academic distinctions (slyly opening it at the same time) by recounting—what else—a story. He imagined himself looking from a window in suburbia onto a neighbor's yard where there hang "enough seasoning marijuana to stone a regiment."

> Is forgetfulness some part of the mysteriousness of life? If I speak to Mr. Hartshore about his cannabis crop, will he tell me that the greatness of Chinese civilization stood foursquare on the fantasies of opium? But it is not I who will speak to Mr. Hartshore. It will be Charley Dilworth, a very abstemious man who lives in the house next door. He has a No Smoking sign on his front lawn and his passionate feelings about marijuana have been intelligently channeled into a sort of reverse blackmail.
>
> I hear them litigating late one Saturday afternoon when I have come back from playing touch football with my sons. The light is going. It is autumn. Charlie's voice is loud and clear and can be heard by anyone interested. "You keep your dogs off my lawn, you cook your steaks in the house, you keep your record player down, you keep your swimming-pool filter off in the evenings and you keep your window shades drawn. Otherwise, I'll report your drug crop to the police and with my wife's uncle sitting as judge this month you'll get at least six months in the can for criminal possession."
>
> They part. Night falls. Here and there a housewife, apprehending the first frost, takes in her house plants while from an Elizabethan, a Nantucket, and a Frank Lloyd Wright chimney comes the marvelous fragrance of wood smoke. You can't put this scene in a novel.

The esthetical issues remain unresolved, of course, but perhaps Cheever's acknowledged attitude is best. Who cares, he implies, since literature, like heaven, is a mansion with many rooms, each set aside for heart's desire? In several stories, he expresses his own limited personal goals in light of such brilliant variety. For example, in "A Vision of the World," the narrator tells us: "What I wanted to identify then was not a chain of facts but an essence—something like that indecipherable collision of contingencies that can produce exaltation or despair. What I wanted to do was grant my dreams, in so incoherent a world their legitimacy."[6] In "The Brigadier and the Golf Widow," he observes, "We travel with such velocity these days that the most we can do is to remember a few place names. The freight of metaphysical speculation will have to catch up with us by slow train, if it catches up with us at all" (p. 510).

Cheever's own charming preface to *The Stories* supports these insertions in a most personal way. He admits that the collection declares "a

6. John Cheever, *The Stories of John Cheever* (New York: Knopf, 1978), p. 515. Hereafter references to the collection will be included in the text.

aked history of one's struggle to receive an education in economics and
ove":

> Here is the last of that generation of chain smokers who woke the
> world in the morning with their coughing, who used to get stoned at
> cocktail parties and perform obsolete dance steps like "the Cleveland
> Chicken," sail for Europe on ships, who were truly nostalgic for love
> and happiness, and whose gods were as ancient as yours and mine,
> whoever you are. The constants that I look for in this sometimes dated
> paraphernalia are a love of light and a determination to trace some
> moral chain of being. Calvin played no part at all in my religious
> education, but this presence seemed to abide in the barns of my child-
> hood and to have left me with some undue bitterness.   (pp. vii-viii)

The preface's perspective is historical, personal, and apparently partisan,
shaped with wry modesty: by contrast, the stories end up being the opposite. The majority are impossible to date through internal evidence; the
problems they engage are perennial; and the dramatic instances, those
"collisions of contingencies," are "indecipherable" precisely because of
their universality. In an excellent extended review, Richard Schickel distinguished those properties of a Cheever story that allow us to share in
a personal vision and recognize the communal revealed in the particular:

> The perception is that the world is infinitely more variable, far richer
> in wonders—sudden calamities and equally sudden graces—than we
> are brought up to believe it is. Or than most of us like to admit as
> adults with a vested interest in preserving the illusion of a certain
> existential logic in our lives, a sense of the past leading intelligibly to
> the present, the present sensibly predicting the future. The tension
> derives from balancing his tragic sense of life with his equally strong
> appreciation of our sheer circumstantial craziness, which he feels re-
> deems us by reminding us of life's infinite and infinitely unpredictable
> possibilities.[7]

Schickel accents the extraordinary balance between light and dark in
Cheever's fiction, his ability to protect himself from that univocal embrace
of the dark that leads to ironic excess, even cyncism:

> Like any honest observer, he cannot escape recognition of the fact
> that when life is not banal it is often tragic. But he also sees, as few
> serious writers of his time have, that there is something more to be
> considered—those grace notes and epiphanies, those misunderstand-
> ings and fancies, those strange persistences of tradition, of communal

7. Richard Schickel, "The Cheever Chronicle," *Horizon*, 21 (September 1978),
28.

and family ties, of sexual need, that keep people going through the bad and barren patches.

Schickel's reading is extremely perceptive, although he omits mention of the two radical factors, inseparable within Cheever's personality, that generate such remarkable balance: his religious sensibility and his sense of humor. Cheever, first and foremost, is a believer in the first article of the Creed; this is his tonic key in terms of which all harmonies and disharmonies are heard, especially grace notes. His comic vision is at one with the first wonder expressed in the Creed. In his essay "Comedy," Christopher Fry spoke to the wedding of wonder, belief, and humor "Comedy is an escape, not from truth but from despair; a narrow escape into faith. It believes in a universal cause of delight, even though knowledge of the cause is always twitched away from under us, which leaves us to rest on our own buoyancy."[8] Any reader who tackles the task of reading all of these stories consecutively gradually finds that a movement of deepening consciousness is taking place—that reconciliation between men and men, men and their fates is deemed truly possible, though difficult that, as Schickel puts it, "there is less iron in his ironies, more forgiveness and that there resides a conviction that losses do not necessarily make us lost." After reading the whole collection, one comes away from it struggling to articulate this complex response. Once again, Fry's words possibly serve best, for we have grown aware of truth that

> Somehow the characters have to unmortify themselves: to affirm life and assimilate death and persevere in joy. Their hearts must be as determined as the phoenix; what burns must also light and renew: not by a vulnerable optimism but a hard-won maturity of delight, by the intuition of comedy, an active patience declaring the solvency of good.

A READING

For the sake of clarity, I will divide consideration of the stories into four main categories according to their generic locales: the urban or New York stories; the exurban or summer vacation stories; the suburban stories; and the expatriate or foreign stories, generally centered in Italy. A fifth category, that of reminiscence or story-essay, might be welcome as well, but I make only brief references to the stories that fit this description. (These include "Percy," "The Jewels of the Cabots," "Another Story," "Reunion," "A Miscellany of Characters," and "Three Stories.") Any division is arbitrary and inadequate, of course, but I choose these because the place

8. Christopher Fry, "Comedy," in Comedy: Meaning and Form, ed. Robert W. Corrigan (San Francisco: Chandler, 1965), p. 15.

where a Cheever character lives is itself revelatory, i.e., revealing of choice, morality, tradition or its absence, security and/or disjunction in his or her life.

On the other hand, place, though revelatory, is not so important as it might seem. Part of Cheever's genius lies in his conviction that no matter where his characters dwell, they inhabit a transfigurable world, a world where the demonic and the angelic are both eager for unexpected entry, where people apparently unheroic can suddenly metamorphose into nymphs and satyrs and splendid gods and goddesses. The themes in tension that I noted earlier persist throughout all the stories: newness and nostalgia, memory and forgetting, home and displacement, voyage and stasis, confinement and freedom, love and venery, enlargement and diminishment, the demonic and its opposites. The difference in location, therefore, effects a difference in emphasis or variation; the particular ambience evokes a specific heightening of perception or dramatizes a distinctive blindness, perhaps, but the themes engaged—all centering on the mystery of the solitary self in the midst of a variable world—provide a consistent subtext that unites these stories beyond local habitations and names. It is this accumulative thematic unity, I think, that creates what Irving describes as the "feel" of a novel in these stories.

The Urban or New York Stories

The major thematic accents of these earlier, New York stories are those of strangeness and displacement, of physical and moral imprisonment, and of divorce, both possible and actual, as symbolic of these themes. It is significant that the main characters are seldom New York natives; instead, they are visitors or new arrivals or reluctant settlers—displaced persons all. (Cheever composed all of these stories while living at 400 East 59th Street in an apartment overlooking the Manhattan exit and the entrance to the Queensborough Bridge, and the emotions recorded reflect his vantage point from an aerie nest.)

The city itself takes on the symbolic stature of a mysterious stranger, a hovering presence that intrudes and departs at will, at certain times a faceless bystander and at others the seeming agent of accident, chance, chaos, and revelation. Its residents are in the embrace of the stranger who occasionally reveals his face in a chance meeting. In "The Season of Divorce" we hear:

> A blind man asks you to help him across the street, and as you are
> about to leave him, he seizes your arm and regales you with a passionate
> account of his cruel and ungrateful children; or the elevator man who
> is taking you up to a party turns to you suddenly and says that his
> grandson has infantile paralysis. The city is full of accidental revela-

tion, half-heard cries for help, and strangers who will tell you everything at the first suspicion of sympathy. . . .   (p. 140)

Some stories are shaped around classical myths to dramatize this alien
remoteness which is so close. The undistinguished story "Torch Song" is
of interest only because it updates the dual character of the enticing
devouring female in terms of the Aphrodite-Persephone myths, characteristic of the city itself. "The Pot of Gold" is an ironic variant on the
Argonaut saga in which a Jason and a Medea, in pursuit of the golden
fleece, discover their mutual love, a more unexpected treasure. In the
story we learn of the fate of their companions on this urban voyage:

> The guests at the party were the survivors of a group that had coalesced
> ten years before, and if anyone had called the roll of the earliest parties
> in the same room, like the retreat ceremony of a breached and deci-
> mated regiment, "Missing. . . . Missing. . . . Missing" would have
> been answered for the squad that had gone into Westchester; "Missing.
> . . . Missing. . . . Missing" would have been spoken for the platoon
> that divorce, drink, nervous disorders, and adversity had slain or
> wounded.   (pp. 113-114)

The story closes with the husband discovering what he had over-
looked, not really missed—his wife's love: "Here it was, here it all was,
and the shine of the gold seemed to him then to be all around her arms"
(p. 117).

There is one marvelous scene that redeems a similar, though overly
sentimental and obvious, odyssey recounted in "O City of Broken Dreams."
The story records the efforts of a budding playwright, Evarts Malloy, and
his simple wife Alice as they arrive in the city, anxious for success and
conquest. The Malloys are country bumpkins, and when they attend the
Murchison's party they are impolitely ignored by apparently urban sophisticates. An opportunity arises for Alice to sing, however—a sardonic
offer—and Alice stands in the center of the room to warble "Annie
Laurie." The event is depicted as simultaneously comic and poignant;
moreover, Cheever artfully varies the perspective on the scene, moving
from the principals to the party crowd and back again. He further reinforces the contrast between sophisticate and bumpkin by first modifying
it, reminding us that these sophisticates are as uprooted and displaced and
homesick as Alice is:

> Her voice was well pitched, her figure was stern and touching, and she
> sang for those people in obedience to her mannerly heart. When
> [Evarts, her husband] had overcome his own bewilderment, he noticed
> the respect and attention the Murchisons' guests were giving her music.

Many of them had come from towns as small as Wentworth; they were good-hearted people, and the simple air, rendered in Alice's fearless voice, reminded them of their beginnings.   (p. 49)

But this sentimental union in memory of past and present is suddenly de-sentimentalized, and those words "obedience," "mannerly heart," and "beginnings" take on a further meaning. For we learn that long ago Alice's voice teacher

> had taught her to close [the song] with a piece of business that brought her success as a child, as a girl, as a high-school senior. . . . She . . . taught [her] on the closing line, 'Lay me doun and dee,' to fall in a heap on the floor. She fell less precipitously now that she had got older, but she still fell, and Evarts could see that night, by her serene face, that a fall was in her plans.   (p. 49)

Fearful and consternated, Evarts turns his back to her, and by doing so suggests that he too has become citified at least momentarily; thus a breach between Wentworth and the big city is confirmed through gesture. The guests' reaction re-establishes the contrast between bumpkin and sophisticate, rooted in a transition irrecoverable:

> Alice took a quick breath and attacked the last verse. Evarts had begun to sweat so freely that the brine got into his eyes. "I'll lay me doun and dee," he heard her sing; he heard the loud crash as she hit the floor; he heard the screams of helpless laughter, the tobacco coughs, and the oaths of a woman who laughed so hard she broke her pearl bib. The Murchisons' guests seemed bewitched. They wept, they shook, they stooped, they slapped one another on the back, and walked, like the demented, in circles.   (p. 49)

Being "out of place" and truly displaced are not quite the same thing; but here one is a dramatic instance of the other. Evarts turns around and helps his wife to her feet and to the hall. She asks, " 'Didn't they like my song?' " He replies, " 'It doesn't matter, my darling, it doesn't matter, it doesn't matter' " (p. 50). His answer is both correct and incorrect, and it capsulates well the peculiar power of the scene.

These New York stories are tales of outsiders, and their condition and circumstance are reinforced by the narrator's voice, the voice of one who is himself an outsider. All of these stories are recounted in the third person—the chatty, first-person Cheever narrator appears in the suburban stories and thereafter—and the perspective is a combination of the knowing and the quizzical, the sympathetic and the satiric. The stresses on strangers and strangeness, then, find their artistic parallel in the narrator's own perspective *as* stranger. This feature makes these stories especially reminiscent of Nathaniel Hawthorne's tales and stories; in them the issue of "correct" interpretation and the possibility of an erroneous assessment is a theme interwoven with the narrator's stance as an emotionally curious, intellectually detached investigator. Most of Cheever's later stories will abandon this vantage point, but the tone and familiar themes will be retained. In these later stories the narrator is not so much a stranger as he is a "newcomer" in the face of surprising, often bizarre events.

Several critics have noted the affinity between Cheever's and Hawthorne's fiction.[9] This opens up an especially fruitful field of study, most notably of the allegorical and mythic techniques as well as the moral and imagistic balance of light and darkness they employ. Cheever continually seeks what Hawthorne described as his goal in the preface to *The Scarlet Letter*, "a neutral territory, somewhere between the real world and fairyland, where the Actual and the Imaginary may meet, and each imbue itself with the nature of the other . . . [where] Ghosts might enter . . . without affrighting us." In Cheever's case, this effort becomes even more pronounced in his later stories; in the early stories the affinity is strongest in the area of narrative tone. In his superb study, *Form and Fable in American Fiction*, Daniel Hoffman aptly describes Hawthorne's stylistic tone. With certain adjustments, one could substitute Cheever's name for his as descriptive of the inchoative qualities of these urban stories and as indicative of the ambiguous power of his more developed work. Hoffman says of Hawthorne's writing:

> Its salient feature is the skeptical offering of the multiple meanings, each borne aloft by the clause of a rather formal periodic sentence. The tone of this style is curiously both detached and committed, both amused and serious, both dubious and affirmative. Its commitment, seriousness, and affirmation, however, all point to something other than the literal content of its assertions; toward *that* the style indicates detachment, amused tolerance, dubiety. . . . What it does affirm is, as one would expect of Hawthorne, a multiple truth larger than either of the partial truths offered by its alternatives: the world of fact *is* an hieroglyph of the spirit, and the language of the spirit is beyond the capacity of either unassisted belief or unassisted reason to read aright. Perhaps its reading requires the collaboration of both the intellect and the passions.[10]

9. Elizabeth Hardwick, among others, has noted the Hawthornian properties in Cheever's work. I have not advanced along this avenue very far, because Prof. Samuel Coale, an expert in Cheever, is devoting a full chapter to the influence of Hawthorne and the American Romantic tradition on Cheever in his study to be published next year. I have already benefited greatly from Coale's insights regarding this connection, and I await his fuller and better informed treatment.

10. Daniel Hoffman, *Form and Fable in American Fiction* (New York: Norton, 1961), pp. 173-174.

Cheever's finest early New York story, "Clancy in the Tower of Babel," is also the finest illustration of this combination of qualities. Superficially it resembles "The Superintendent" and "Christmas Is a Sad Season for the Poor," but it is eminently superior to them. It is composed entirely of narrative and dialogue without any essay-like digressions, and the perspective is that of "limited privileged" access to Clancy's thoughts. The title insinuates the theme: in Babel, confusion of tongues mirrors man's fate, and yet, though we do not speak the same language and misunderstanding is inevitable, our feelings—ironically, because we cannot articulate them—are the basis for a common ground for at least a mute sharing.

We are told immediately that James and Nora Clancy, both Irish immigrants, are "cleanly and decent people," that their "home farms had been orderly places" enjoying "the grace of a tradition," and that "their simple country ways were so deeply ingrained that twenty years in the New World had had little effect on them" (p. 118). On hearing this, a reader familiar with earlier stories expects a satiric barb at the ready, but no, the description is accurate and straightforward, and the irony is elsewhere. Clancy is an energetic, immensely loyal elevator operator, and his occupation implicitly entails that union of metaphors—involving travel, imprisonment, elevation and descent, and passenger transit—exploited in the story. Clancy regards most of the tenants "with an indiscriminate benevolence" (p. 119), but his charitable concerns are fixed on Mr. Rowantree, a bachelor tenant, who seems to have no friends or guests. Curious, Clancy visits Rowantree's antique store, and is mystified; he "had never seen so much junk" and feels that "Mr. Rowantree was wasting his time" (p. 120). But, we are told, "it was more than the confusion and the waste that troubled him; it was the feeling that he was surrounded by the symbols of frustration and that all the china youths and maidens in their attitudes of love were the company of bitterness" (pp. 120-121).

This recording of Clancy's impressions is an excellent example of the Hawthorne-like narrative tone, which challenges us to respond in multiple ways. Is Clancy's reaction wrong or right or both? What is the narrator's own attitude? Where is the stress: on Clancy's uncultured perplexity, and so merely funny; or on his moral and emotional intuitions, and so possibly insightful?

Rowantree's commitment to the immemorial *objets d'art* of pagan antiquity is immediately contrasted with Clancy's doting love for his teenage son, John, an affection representative to him of newness, hope, and a different embrace of immortality beyond the palpable. Clancy would often visit his son's room just to look at "the wonderful boy" while he slept.

It was sinful, Clancy knew, to confuse the immortality of the Holy
Spirit and earthly love, but when he realized that John was his flesh
and blood, that the young man's face was *his* face improved with mobility and thought, and that when he, Clancy, was dead, some habit
or taste of his would live on in the young man, he felt that there was
no pain in death.   (p. 121)

The compatibility in contrast between the two men is dramatized
further when Mr. Rowantree arrives at his elevator the next day, together
with a homosexual companion named Bobbie whom Clancy initially mistakes for a young man. But "the young man was not a young man. . . .
He was as old as Mr. Rowantree, he was nearly as old as Clancy" (p. 122).
Clancy refuses to take them up in his elevator car, for "the idea of Bobbie's
being in the Building was a painful one for him to take, and he felt as if
it contested his own simple view of life" (p. 122). The superintendent
later calls Clancy aside, tells him that Rowantree wants him fired, and
warns him to mind his own business.

The next week is Holy Week, and on Monday Clancy joins "his
bitterness at having to live in Sodom to the deep and general grief he
always felt at the commencement of those events that would end on
Golgotha" (p. 123). With an almost liturgical rightness, the day is gloomy
and sad. On one of his descents in the elevator, Clancy smells gas, "the
odor of winter, sickness, need, and death" (p. 123). He traces it to Rowantree's door; with a master key he enters the apartment and finds
Rowantree on his knees with his head in the oven crying, " 'Bobbie's
gone, Clancy' " (p. 124). Clancy turns off the gas and goes downstairs to
turn off Rowantree's gas source; he returns to discover Rowantree with
his head in the oven again and shouts, " 'You're wasting your time,
Mr. Rowantree!' " (p. 124), echoing his pronouncement earlier in the
antique shop.

After work, Clancy walks home and the weather fits his mood:

The sky was black. It was raining soot and ashes. Sodom, he thought,
the city undeserving of clemency, the unredeemable place, and, raising
his eyes to watch the rain and the ashes fall through the air, he felt
a great despair. . . . He longed for the simple life of Ireland and the
City of God, but he felt that he had been contaminated by the stink
of gas.   (p. 124)

That evening he learns that Bobbie has returned and all is well, except
that Rowantree tried again to get him fired. On hearing this, Clancy feels
sick; the next day his condition worsens, and he ends up going to a
hospital. Frank Quinn, the doorman of the building, visits the hospital
and gives Clancy a narrow manila envelope filled with money, a gift from

the tenants. Clancy is shocked to learn that it was Rowantree who collected these gifts, going from floor to floor and apartment to apartment
in tears. And suddenly Clancy has a vision of his own funeral. It takes
place before a church altar amid sanctuary lights; the handful of mourners
are all from Limerick (near his hometown in Ireland)—once fellow passengers with him "on the boat." Hearing the music of the bells and the
priest's voice, he sees Rowantree and Bobbie in a back pew. "They were
crying and crying. They were crying harder than Nora" (p. 126).

Disturbed by the vision and its implications, Clancy abruptly leaves
the hospital despite protestations and returns home. He immediately calls
the superintendent, telling him he will report to work in the morning.
That night, intent on returning to the Tower of Babel, he first confronts
the puzzling mysteries to which he has been exposed: "Why should a man
fall in love with a monster? Why should a man try to kill himself? Why
should a man try to get a man fired and then collect money for him with
tears in eyes, and then perhaps, a week later, try to get him fired again?"
(p. 126). All of these seem "perversions" to Clancy's uncomplicated mind,
and thus, as he prepares to face them in his tower again, he attempts to
choose the words he will use to address Rowantree. " 'It's my suggestion,
Mr. Rowantree,' he would say, 'that the next time you want to kill your-
self, you get a rope or a gun. It's my suggestion, Mr. Rowantree,' he would
say, 'that you go to a good doctor and get your head examined' " (p. 126).

The next and final paragraph is arguably the best in all of Cheever's
fiction. The story closes, in contrast with Clancy's efforts to articulate
common-sense judgment, with a series of brief, muted epiphanies, revelations of the extraordinary amid the ordinary. The drab city itself is
redeemed for Clancy by his realization that it was built by and for common
men like himself, and thus not so strange at all. His wife's beauty and his
son's exceptional talents, he guesses, would be missed by some critical
stranger, an outsider intent only on the apparent. How could Clancy tell
such a man of such elusive personal truths as those he knows? So his
epiphanies, bred in silence, end that way as well. Clancy, the most common of common men, now perceives the mysterious communality of all
human affection, the ineffableness of love and desire in a world that seems
only squalid to strangers, intent on judgment and defects:

> The spring wind, the south wind that in the city smells of drains,
> was blowing. Clancy's window looked out onto an expanse of clothes-
> lines and ailanthus trees, yards that were used as dumps, and the naked
> backs of tenements, with their lighted and unlighted windows. The
> symmetry, the reality of the scene heartened Clancy, as if it conformed
> to something good in himself. Men with common minds like his had
> built these houses. Nora brought him a glass of beer and sat near the

window. He put an arm around her waist. She was in her slip, because of the heat. Her hair was held down with pins. She appeared to Clancy to be one of the glorious beauties of his day, but a stranger, he guessed, might notice the tear in her slip and that her body was bent and heavy. A picture of John hung on the wall. Clancy was struck with the strength and intelligence of his son's face, but he guessed that a stranger might notice the boy's glasses and his bad complexion. And then, thinking of Nora and John and that this half blindness was all that he knew himself of mortal love, he decided not to say anything to Mr. Rowantree. They would pass in silence.   (pp. 126-127)

Cheever's most famous and most anthologized New York story, "The Enormous Radio," develops toward the opposite realization: the mysterious communality of evil rather than of love. The opening sentence alerts the reader to this theme of communality and typicalness with its accent on "average" and the like, suggesting also that the Westcotts are abstract representatives: "Jim and Irene Westcott were the kind of people who seem to strike that satisfactory average of income, endeavor, and respectability that is reached by the statistical reports in college alumni bulletins" (p. 33). The more detailed description of them that follows reinforces this impression, reaching an ironic climax with the observation that they differed from the mean standard "only in an interest they shared in serious music" (p. 33), itself an ominous foreboding.

When the Westcotts' old radio, "sensitive, unpredictable, and beyond repair" (p. 33) gives out, Jim buys a new one. Irene is struck immediately by "the physical ugliness of the large gumwood cabinet" (p. 33); it seems to her that "the new radio stood among her intimate possessions like an aggressive intruder" (p. 34). The "malevolent green light" emanating from the dials so disturbs her that she tries to conceal the cabinet behind a sofa; yet we learn that "as soon as she had made her peace with the radio, the interference began" (p. 34). When she turns on a Mozart quintet, demonic and eternal images characterize its sound: "a crackling sound like the noise of a burning powder fuse" and "a rustling that reminded Irene unpleasantly of the sea" (p. 34). At first in union with Mozart's melody, she hears the dialing and ringing of phones, the noise of the elevator, the buzz of razors and mixers, and "the lamentation of a vacuum cleaner," for "the powerful and ugly instrument" enjoys a "mistaken sensitivity to discord" (p. 34).

The next day, the random and intrusive sounds of an impersonal city become more intense and particularized; she and her husband overhear bits and pieces of their neighbors' lives: the "Missouri Waltz," marital arguments, complaints and demands, the chatter of a cocktail party—all in contrast to the innocent sing-song of a nursery rhyme, repeated by a nurse, that celebrates innocence and quaint romance. A second contrast lies in their juxtaposition with the music specifically chosen by the Westcotts: a Chopin prelude with its "passionate and melancholy music" (p. 35). Though initially fearful that they, too, might be overheard, the Westcotts cannot resist listening. A share in such god-like omnipresence is too tempting, as Irene's comment betrays: " 'Isn't this too divine? Try something else. See if you can get those people in 18-C' " (p. 37). Thereafter, their dials capture a cross-section of commonplace moments: a boring monologue, a quarrel, a home movie travelogue, and finally a snippet indicative of mortal sorrow in which a sick woman confides to her husband, " 'There are about fifteen or twenty minutes in the week when I feel like myself. . . . I just don't feel like myself, Charlie' " (p. 37).

Irene is by turns exhilarated and depressed; her once "simple and sheltered" life is now complex and opened. She now knows her neighbors well enough for censure but not well enough for compassion and sympathy. Cheever's brilliance is especially manifest throughout in his perfect ear for snatches of human speech, each of which crystallizes what the reader intuits is evidence of a moral, psychological circumstance. Furthermore, Cheever notes that "as the afternoon waned, the conversations increased in intensity" (p. 38), a development corresponding with the natural and mythic cycle of darkness and cold that humans re-enact.

A few days after they get the radio, the Westcotts go out for dinner; it is a clear, warm evening, brilliant with light. On the way they hear a Salvation Army band playing "Jesus Is Sweeter"; Irene listens raptly and says, " 'They're really such nice people, aren't they? . . . so much nicer than a lot of the people we know' " (p. 39). Later, on the way home from the dinner party, Irene gazes up at the spring stars and quotes Portia's lines from *The Merchant of Venice*: "How far that little candle throws its beams,/So shines a good deed in a naughty world" (v, i, 90f.). The quote here functions as an obvious ironic counterpoint to the theme; less obviously, the context of Portia's remark is also significant. Shortly before she utters it, Lorenzo has addressed his beloved Jessica in words even more appropriate:

> The man that hath no music in himself,
> Nor is not moved with concord of sweet sounds,
> Is fit for treasons, stratagems, and spoils;
> The motions of his spirit are dull as night,
> And his affections dark as Erebus:
> Let no such man be trusted.   (V, i, 83)

Given the story's rich beginnings, I find its ending a disappointment. The reader has followed Irene's own subtle transformation, an alteration caused by her reluctant assimilation of the sadness, evil, and discord she

has overheard. Her transition from naive innocence to experience is affecting, as is her gradual horror at the possibility that her own private
vagaries can be recorded. Suddenly, however, the tale confronts us with
another irony (and one never artistically planted in the story): that she
is and has been a fraud, a thief, a cruel, unfeeling woman who coolly had
an abortion. The turnabout is both too neat and too dramatically implausible—an opinion that, I suspect, Cheever came to share. But he
used this sudden development to heighten the force of the final paragraph,
which records a chilling moment of tension and hope, and then ends with
a series of abstract bulletins of distant disasters that counterpoint the
Westcotts' "private" predicament and the abstract summary provided in
the opening paragraph:

> Irene stood for a minute before the hideous cabinet, disgraced and
> sickened, but she held her hand on the switch before she extinguished
> the music and the voices, hoping that the instrument might speak to
> her kindly. . . . The voice on the radio was suave and non-committal.
> "An early-morning railroad disaster in Tokyo," the loudspeaker said,
> "killed twenty-nine people. A fire in a Catholic hospital near Buffalo
> for the care of blind children was extinguished early this morning by
> nuns. The temperature is forty-seven. The humidity is eighty-
> nine."   (p. 41)

Cheever's last, properly New York story, "The Bus to St. James's"—
which John Irving described well "as the saddest love affair you'll ever
read about"—dramatizes, instead, the momentum of mysterious attrac-
tion. If the perception of evil reminds us of our solidarity with the race,
so much the more does the prompting of love, which generates the realization that union is not only possible but, as it were, foreordained. In
one marvelously tender scene in which the two lovers meet surreptitiously
in an out-of-the-way restaurant, Cheever cleverly insinuates the ironic
truth that from the outside, from a stranger's perspective, any sharing in
unspoken love is difficult to differentiate in its deportment from a sharing
in sadness. We hear: "For a while neither of them spoke. A stranger,
noticing them in the restaurant, might have thought that they were a pair
of old friends who had met to discuss a misfortune" (p. 279). The description that follows compounds each of these ironies, and in its way is
the moral reversal of the transmutations effected through "The Enormous
Radio":

> For lovers, touch is metamorphosis. All the parts of their bodies
> seem to change, and they seem to become something different and
> better. That part of their experience that is distinct and separate, the
> totality of the years before they met, is changed, is redirected toward
> this moment. They feel they have reached an identical point of inten-

sity, an ecstasy of rightness that they command in every part, and any recollection that occurs to them takes on this final clarity, whether it be a sweep hand on an airport clock, a Chicago railroad station on Christmas Eve, or anchoring a yawl in a strange harbor while all along the stormy coast strangers are blowing their horns for the yacht-club tender, or running a ski trail at that hour when, although the sun is still in the sky, the north face of every mountain lies in the dark. (p. 279)

The Exurban or Vacation Stories

Cheever's characters begin vacations with eagerness and romanticize them in memory, for they represent escape, sanctuary, newness, a recovery of roots. Yet in fleeing the impersonal stranger that is the City, they encounter another, since their moral baggage accompanies them. All efforts at disconnection stand exposed in reverse; past and present, willy-nilly, ever interconnect. "The Seaside Houses," which I analyzed earlier, expresses this ambivalence in its opening paragraph:

> The journey to the sea has its ceremonious excitements, it has gone on for so many years now, and there is the sense that we are, as in our dreams we have always known ourselves to be, migrants and wanderers—travelers, at least, with a traveler's acuteness of feeling. . . . But as strong as or stronger than this pleasant sense of beginnings is the sense of having stepped into the midst of someone else's life. All my dealings are with agents, and I have never known the people from whom we have rented, but their ability to leave behind them a sense of physical and emotional presences is amazing. . . . Sometimes there is in the long hallway a benignness, a purity and clearness of feeling to which we all respond . . . and we rent their happiness as we rent their beach and their catboat. Sometimes the climate of the place seems mysterious, and remains a mystery until we leave in August. . . . We bring in our things, wandering, it seems, through the dense histories of strangers. (p. 482)

Haunted houses and dense histories are the common themes of these stories. Efforts at escape effect ironic returns; the insular locales exaggerate the truth that no man is an island; and "family" magnifies what is often denied but is too familiar. "Goodbye, My Brother," addressed earlier, is the best—one might say the quintessential—Cheever vacation story, and "The Seaside Houses" is a close second. Another, "The Day the Pig Fell into the Well," more structurally ambitious and lengthier, is similar in theme. The narrative begins in jaunty fashion and in what seems a celebratory spirit:

In the summer, when the Nudd family gathered at Whitebeach Camp, in the Adirondacks, there was always a night when one of them would ask, "Remember the day the pig fell into the well?" Then, as if the opening note of the sextet had been sounded, the others would all rush in to take their familiar parts, like those families who sing Gilbert and Sullivan, and the recital would go on for an hour or more. The perfect days—and there had been hundreds of them—seemed to have passed into their consciousness without a memory and they returned to this chronicle of small disasters as if it were the genesis of summer.   (p. 219)

This opening paragraph is leisurely and homey, and suggests the time-less quality of the family's experience. Before the reader can pause to ponder why a disaster, rather than a "perfect day," becomes their song in harmony, the narrator in the next three paragraphs rushes on, reproducing in an objective voice the competing voices as they would narrate the "facts" connected with that special day. Like all such efforts, the effect is a jumble of detail, important and unimportant, a backing up and filling in of facts—mystifying to a stranger. Next the narrator allows each of the principals to offer his or her own version or modification of the event. Because of sudden time shifts and digressions, the reader grasps—indistinctly at first and then more clearly—that the period covered is actually fifteen years, and that the pig story is the objective correlative for the weaving of another tale, more individualistic and difficult to share.

The pig's drowning is in fact the emotional point of reference for romance, misunderstanding, divorce, and even the denial of death. We learn that within a year the pig story had taken on special weight, "and already in this short time alterations had been made in its form" (p. 222). Gradually, even factual mistakes are excused and incorporated if they reflect well on some favorite or less well on an enemy. The pig story has become the equivalent of a sacred ritual, a memorial service evoking and re-establishing community. By contrast, we learn that in the interim one of the Nudds' sons, Hartley, had been killed in the war, and that this family so intent on ritual has neglected to hold a memorial service for him. Three years later, one is held at the Episcopal chapel, but "Mrs. Nudd derived no comfort whatever from the reading of the prayers. She had no more faith in the power of God than she had in the magic of the evening star. Nothing was accomplished by the service so far as she was concerned" (p. 231).

This reaction takes on special poignancy at the story's close, when all the surviving principals are reunited fifteen years after the big day.

That late in the season, the light went quickly. It was sunny one minute and dark the next. . . . For a while it seemed unimaginable that anything could lie beyond the mountains, that this was not the end of the world. The wall of pure and brassy light seemed to beat up from infinity. Then the stars came out, the earth rumbled downward, the illusion of an abyss was lost. Mrs. Nudd looked around her, and the time and the place seemed strangely important. This is not an imitation, she thought, this is not the product of custom, this is the unique place, the unique air, where my children have spent the best of themselves. The realization that none of them had done well made her sink back in her chair. She squinted the tears out of her eyes. What had made the summer always an island, she thought; what had made it such a small island? What mistakes had they made? . . . Why should these good and gentle people who surrounded her seem like the figures in a tragedy?

"Remember the day the pig fell into the well?" she asked.
                                                      (pp. 234-235)

The ritual begins once more, and the family members "all waited graciously for their turn" (p. 235). The story is an illusory emblem of happiness and distinction and has taken on a liturgical significance for each of them, being as it is a record of aspiration, sharing, and linkage. But the reader realizes, as they do not, that the mundane drama of the event has been unknowingly elevated and transformed, that all of them, by concentrating on their respective roles, by repeating and yet reshaping the telling, have valiantly attempted to convert it into consequence. Unwittingly, they have fashioned a false tradition about that special day, hoping that in fact its recollection indicates that they were once a happy, united family and continue to be. Ironically, this tale of disaster does unite them, but its mythic truth is more powerful than they know. Cheever shows great restraint in exposing the sadder ironies involved, and his story about the story ends gently and subtly—and so more affectingly—on its last powerful line:

The story restored Mrs. Nudd and made her feel that all was well. It had exhilarated the rest, and, talking loudly and laughing, they went into the house. Mr. Nudd lighted a fire and sat down to play checkers with Joan. Mrs. Nudd passed a box of stale candy. It had begun to blow outside, and the house creaked gently, like a hull when the wind takes up the sail. The room with the people in it looked enduring and secure, although in the morning they would all be gone.   (p. 235)

Three other less distinguished stories—"The Hartleys," "The Summer Farmer," and "The Common Day"—are shaped around similar themes: repetition as a delusive armor against inevitable change; pastoral escape issuing in unwanted emotional and moral collision; the paradox of the permanent peeping out beneath the ephemeral. Occasionally, individual

scenes capsulate wonderfully this complex of moral and emotional reaction, although the story as a whole might be a bit pat and contrived. In
"The Summer Farmer," for example, we enter a brief evening scene at a
summer house in northern New England after (the central character) Paul
Hollis's sister Ellen has been drinking and has "talked uninterruptedly
about the past and, particularly, about Father—Father this and Father
that" (p. 84). The description of Nature in the story belies her enthusiasm, and the overheard song (with Babylon representing their urban
home) is ironically one with the questioning and multiple character of
memory and of the legacies and losses from childhood.

> A northwest wind had driven the thundershower out of the county
> and left in the air a poignant chill, and when they went out on the
> piazza after dinner to watch the sun go down, there were a hundred
> clouds in the west—clouds of gold, clouds of silver, clouds like bone
> and tinder and filth under the bed. "It's so *good* for me to be up here,"
> Ellen said. "It does so much for me." She sat on the rail against the
> light, and Paul couldn't see her face. "I can't find Father's binoculars,"
> she went on, "and his golf clubs have disappeared." From an open
> window of the children's room, Paul heard his daughter singing, "How
> many miles is it to Babylon? Three score miles and ten. Can we get
> there by candlelight? . . ." Immense tenderness and contentment fell
> to him with her voice from the open window.
>   It was so good for them all, as Ellen said; it did so much for them.
> It was a phrase Paul had heard spoken on that piazza since his memory
> had become retentive. Ellen was the mote on that perfect evening.
> There was something wrong, some half-known evil in her worship of
> the bucolic scene—some measure of her inadequacy and, he supposed,
> of his.   (pp. 84-85)

As this passage exemplifies, the recurring subject in all of Cheever's
vacation stories (seven in all, with "The Chaste Clarissa" merely an extended joke upending the confusion between reality and illusion) is that
of memory and forgetting and the losses that inevitably attach to both.
The locales, owing to the very nature of their impermanent character,
generate a somewhat specific brand of homesickness and nostalgia.
Cheever's later stories incorporate these themes and extend their implications—even more artfully, I would say—and wed them with other
moods and tenses and equally challenging thematic concerns.

The Suburban Stories

"The suburban stories" is an umbrella term to cover the tales told of
relocated urbanities who dwell in places like Shady Hill, Bullet Park,
Maple Dell, and Proxmire Manor, a train ride away from New York. Its

characters are commuters whose lives are divided between business and life, work and play, people who are not so much uprooted as transplanted, for whom transfers and mobility are a way of life. Their condition and circumstance inevitably disclose a universal truth about the human comedy, for what they do becomes emblematic of who they are, as occasionally they realize. Being commuters, they seem especially subject to sudden mutations: unsought transformations and metamorphoses; rapid transits of a spiritual and emotional and moral kind; delayed arrivals and departures that upset all psychological schedules. As commuters, they grow more aware than most people of the illusions linked with timetables. The trains they take imprison them, as does their ideal of the single-generation nuclear family. Separation is synonymous with their vocation; just as their days are split between home and work, so are their nights—even play becomes a form of work, another instance of separation, another challenge to achievement. They chose their suburbs as safe sanctuaries, but they find themselves unexpectedly disarmed and easy prey for less palpable, existential dangers. They have fled the ominous Stranger that is the City, created new neighborhoods, substituted neighborliness for charity, made normality the ideal—and yet demonic intrusions, uninvited guests, and nocturnal visitors in dreams haunt their houses and populate their gardens.

This thumbnail summary of mine sounds faintly pompous and patronizing—and woefully abstract. Cheever writes of such things, of course, but hardly in the way I have. Instead, he creates an inhabitable world, free of easy censure, a moral universe both as typical and as specific as the finely textured biblical and classical cosmos that mirrors the seemingly mundane behavior of his characters. Like his readers, they too are creatures with fitful impulses; they too can be smug and so mistaken about the "evils" of suburbia. This point is deftly made early in the stories; the opening paragraph of "The Trouble of Marcie Flint," for example, puts us on guard:

> "This is being written aboard the S.S. *Augustus*, three days at sea. My suitcase is full of peanut butter, and I am a fugitive from the suburbs of all large cities. What holes! The suburbs, I mean. God preserve me from the lovely ladies taking in their asters and their roses at dusk lest the frost kill them, and from ladies with their heads whirling with civic zeal. I'm off to Torino, where the girls love peanut butter and the world is a man's castle and . . ." There was absolutely nothing wrong with the suburb (Shady Hill) from which Charles Flint was fleeing, his age is immaterial, and he was no stranger to Torino, having been there for three months recently on business.   (p. 289)

The last sentence undercuts all smug cynicisms of a sociological sort and makes Mr. Flint a more "immaterial" universal figure than he or we readily acknowledge. A paragraph later we are told that "like all bitter men, Flint knew less than half the story and was more interested in unloading his own peppery feelings than in learning the truth" (p. 289). The irony of the story that follows is that it is but a dramatization of that sentence. Marcie, the wife left behind, with her "great stores of feminine sweetness and gallantry" (p. 289), in fact enjoys a far more eventful life in the interim than the fugitive Charles, bored to tears onboard a ship in mid-passage. The "truth" involved, we eventually learn, is a small truth, but as Cheever is wont to remind us, small truths are just as truthful as large ones. In the middle of the story, we hear the narrator's plaintive voice:

> [Maple Dell] was the kind of place where the houses stand cheek by jowl, all of them white frame, all of them built twenty years ago, and parked beside each was a car that seemed more substantial than the house itself, as if this were a fragment of some nomadic culture. And it was a kind of spawning ground, a place for bearing and raising the young and for nothing else—for who would ever come back to Maple Dell? Who, in the darkest night, would ever think with longing of the three upstairs bedrooms and the leaky toilet and the sour-smelling halls? Who would ever come back to the little living room where you couldn't swing a cat around without knocking down the colored photograph of Mount Rainier? Who would ever come back to the chair that bit you in the bum and the obsolete TV set and the bent ashtray with its pressed-steel statue of naked woman doing a scarf dance?   (pp. 291-292)

Who? Charles Flint, that's who. All of these precise details, noted here with a jaundiced eye, are at the story's close parodied by Flint's sentimental reveries rooted in the ordinary. His journal ends, after "he sees a vision of his family running toward him up some steps—crumbling stone, wild pinks, lizards, and their much-loved faces," on a note of knightly gallantry: " 'I will gentle Marcie—sweet Marcie, dear Marcie, Marcie my love. I will shelter her with the curve of my body from all the harms of the dark' " (p. 301).

Cheever himself obviously found the world of suburbia the opposite of stultifying. In the fall of 1951 he and his family moved out of New York City and settled up the Hudson in Scarborough, New York, on the estate of Frank A. Vanderlip, about a half-hour drive from the city. Later, in a memoir article in *Esquire*, he recalled the reasons for the abrupt transition.

> I could see the landscape of my children's youth destroyed before my eyes. . . . That was the winter we never had enough money. . . . In March one of the obligations I couldn't—or at least neglected to—

meet was the electric bill and our lights were turned off. The children took their baths by candlelight and, while they enjoyed this turn of events, the effect of the dark apartment on my feelings was somber. We simply didn't have the scratch.[11]

In an earlier article, he had described his family's new residence on the Scarborough estate: "The lathes were sold after [the owner's] death and the place was turned into a guesthouse, which we rent from the chatelaine. The drains are often clogged, the heating plant is infirm, and the roof leaks, and because of these considerations we pay a modest rent."[12]

In 1961, with a bit more "scratch" the Cheevers moved a few miles north to Ossining, New York (in 1956-57 they lived in Italy) and into a lovely old house, built in 1799, beautifully terraced and wooded and set back from the main road. This move and the earlier one were beneficent to Cheever's imagination, for at the ripe young age of thirty-nine, after twenty-one years of being a professional writer, he finally discovered the least likely but most fertile landscapes for his fancies, and out of them he created Cheever country. As I mentioned in the chapter on style, the year 1951 is, in its way, a year of demarcation in Cheever's corpus; at that time he found not only a new song but a truer and more flexible singing voice as well.

After at least two literary generations and countless imitators, we tend to forget how original Cheever's stories were in the early 1950's. These stories concern what was then a new class in America: a middle class that worked in the city and lived in the country, one with few ties (beyond visits) with the preceding generation and yet one feverently devoted to the next generation—a middle class in more ways than one. American fiction before this era had concentrated its attention either on the rich or the pioneer or the rural folk or the struggling urban lower classes. The middle class were hardly neglected, of course, but in fiction their milieu was not distinctive—theirs was no "special" or recognizable place with its own ambience. Thus they were found in cities (as in John Marquand's novels) or in towns (as in Sinclair Lewis's satiric fiction), a rung possibly higher or lower than that of others but situated on the same ladder. Cheever was the first to give this new class a distinctive voice, one congruent with their own new and complex circumstance.

This accomplishment alone ought to establish Cheever's lasting importance in the history and development of American fiction. But a historical perspective, if urged too strongly, implies a narrowness not there.

11. John Cheever, "Moving Out," *Esquire*, 54 (July 1960), 67.
12. John Cheever, "The Journal of a Writer with One Hole in his Sock," *The Reporter*, December 29, 1955, p. 25.

The fact is that *at least* six of these suburban stories rank with the finest achievements in our literature, and as long as men and women can read our language, they will endure. (By my count, these include "The Country Husband," "The Swimmer," "The Death of Justina," "The Brigadier and the Golf Widow," "The Housebreaker of Shady Hill," and "O Youth and Beauty!". Persuasive argument could coax me to expand the list.) There are approximately twenty-six suburban stories, and all, unlike the urban or expatriate stories, are outstanding. Though the six stories mentioned constitute an estimable touchstone, the others are deemed the lesser only by comparative standards like unity or energy or imaginative power. Gems are so strewn about throughout them that a like vignette or perception in another writer's work would make that story richly memorable.

For example, in "The Sorrows of Gin," a tale told from the vantage point of an eight-year-old girl named Amy, we hear this:

> She imagined that the people who traveled on the locals were engaged on errands that were more urgent and sinister than commuting. Except when there was a heavy fog or a snowstorm, the club car that her father traveled on seemed to have the gloss and the monotony of the rest of his life. The locals that ran at odd hours belonged to a world of deeper contrasts, where she would like to live.   (p. 201)

Amy's recorded awareness, so affixed to adventure and coming as it does so early in the story, disarms the reader until the story's end, when one realizes that this seemingly child-like fancy capsulates the story's theme and a more universal truth. Amy, dismayed by her parents' behavior and the sorrows that gin generates, decides to run away. Her father is alerted and rushes to the train station to bring her home. Ostensibly a dense, preoccupied adult, briefly he, too, shares Amy's emotion and intuition; yet as an adult he also knows that locals and expresses are not so different as one would hope. The last paragraph reads with doubled ironies, for, as readers, we have shared Amy's perspective thus far; now we realize that the "sorrows" of gin are more inclusive:

> It was dark by the time Mr. Lawton got down to the station. He saw his daughter through the station window. The girl sitting on the bench, the rich names on her paper suitcase, touched him as it was in her power to touch him only when she seemed helpless or when she was very sick. Someone had walked over his grave! He shivered with longing, he felt his skin coarsen as when, driving home late and alone, a shower of leaves on the wind crossed the beam of his headlights, liberating him for a second at the most from the literal symbols of his life—the buttonless shirts, the vouchers and bank statements, the order blanks, and the empty glasses. He seemed to listen—God knows for what. . . . Then, as it was with the leaves, the power of her figure

to trouble him was ended; his gooseflesh vanished. He was himself. Oh, why should she want to run away? Travel—and who knew better than a man who spent three days of every fortnight on the road—was a world of overheated plane cabins and repetitious magazines, where even the coffee, even the champagne, tasted of plastics. How could he teach her that home sweet home was the best place of all? . (p. 209)

"The Sorrows of Gin" links cocktails with travel in a more symbolic sense; the story "Just One More Time" unites them explicitly as indicative of an identification badge or a way of life:

[The Beers] were the kind of people that you met continually at railroad stations and cocktail parties. I mean Sunday-night railroad stations. . . . And in some ways the cocktail parties where your paths crossed were not so different, after all, from the depots, junctions, and boat trains where you met. They were the kind of party where the company is never very numerous and the liquor is never very good— parties where, as you drink and talk, you feel a palpable lassitude overtaking any natural social ardor, as if the ties of family, society, school, and place that held the group together were dissolving like the ice in your drink. But the atmosphere is not so much one of social dissolution as of social change, realignment—in effect, the atmosphere of travel. The guests seem to be gathered in a boat shed or at a railroad junction, waiting for the boat or the train to depart. (pp. 248-249)

This story about the resilient, omnipresent Beers and its ironic cousin, "The Worm in the Apple," are upbeat tales about enviable types who do not seem to need any real destination to ever arrive at the ready. Both are extended jokes on Cheever's part, mini-meditations on people who appear born without the freight of original sin. Dull they might be, and yet. . . .

"The Wrysons" is a delightful variation on this theme of the ignorant, and consequently surprised, outsider. The story is shaped around two motifs, "strangeness" and "oddity" (not the same things, we learn), and the fun increases for the reader only as his sympathy concomitantly intensifies. We learn immediately, right from the opening sentence, that the Wrysons are people very much concerned with "the appearance of things":

The Wrysons wanted things in the suburb of Shady Hill to remain exactly as they were. Their dread of change—of irregularity of any sort—was acute, and when the Larkin estate was sold for the old people's rest home, the Wrysons went to the Village Council meeting and demanded to know what sort of old people these old people were going to be. . . . They seemed to sense that there was a stranger at the gates—unwashed, tirelessly scheming, foreign, the father of disorderly children who would ruin their rose garden and depreciate their real-estate investment, a man with a beard, a garlic breath, and a book.   (p. 319)

Irene Wryson "was both shy and contentious—especially contentious on the subject of upzoning," while her husband Donald "had a laugh like a jackass"; the two were easily alarmed by divorce reports and quack grass (p. 319). The narrator candidly agrees that both were "odd," but then goes on to qualify his meaning, attempting valiantly to put that adjective in its more proper perspective when discussing Shady Hill:

They were not as odd as poor, dizzy Flossie Dolmetch, who was caught forging drug prescriptions and was discovered to have been under the influence of morphine for three years. They were not as odd as Caruthers Mason, with his collection of two thousand lewd photographs, or as odd as Mrs. Temon, who, with those two lovely children in the next room—But why go on? They were odd.   (pp. 320)

Irene's oddity centered on a dream that some enemy or American pilot had exploded a hydrogen bomb. Her actual perturbation was caused by the fact that "she could not relate [the dream] to her garden . . . or her comfortable way of life" (p. 320), i.e., her Edenic sanctuary, and that in the dream she could view hundreds, thousands of city refugees in boats of every description streaming up the river, closing in on Shady Hill. "She cried, in her dream, to see this inhumanity as the world was ending. She cried, and she went on watching, as if some truth was being revealed to her—as if she had always known this to be the human condition . . ." (p. 320). Later in her dream, she saw herself with her daughter at the medicine cabinet ("the one place in the house that the Wrysons . . . had not put in order"), looking for the bottle marked "Poison"; on finding it, she gave her daughter a pill and put a pill to her own lips, but at that moment the bathroom ceiling collapsed in a deluge and she dropped it. "She groped around in the water for the poison, but it was lost, and the dream usually ended in this way. And how could she lean across the breakfast table and explain her pallor to her husky husband with this detailed vision of the end of the world? He would have laughed his jackass laugh" (p. 321).

Irene's oddity is linked with a dream of doom; Donald's oddity is linked with nostalgia. When he was a child, lonely and insecure, his mother had taught him how to bake a Lady Baltimore cake; thus, as an adult, whenever misery or consternation struck him, he would bake a cake and so revive his mother's ghost and the security he once shared with her. We are told,

. . . during the eight or nine years he had been married to Irene he must have baked eight or nine cakes. He took extraordinary precautions, and she knew nothing of this. She believed him to be a complete stranger to the kitchen. And how could he at the breakfast table—all two hundred and sixteen pounds of him—explain that he looked sleepy because he had been up until three baking a Lady Baltimore cake, which he had hidden in the garage? (p. 322)

After recounting what he labels "unpleasant facts" about "these not attractive people" (p. 322), the narrator offers us two alternate endings for the story. The first relates a death amid disaster for the Wrysons and a "sad tale" for their surviving daughter, as if the narrator intuits what a callous reader might *wish* had happened. "But this did not happen," he tells us, "and if it had, it would have thrown no light on what we know" (p. 323).

More light is thrown by the second ending, ostensibly an account of what "really" happened. One night Irene has her dream about the bomb and suddenly wakes to smell a sweetness in the air she associates with atomic ash. She follows the sweetness and the smoke to its source in the kitchen, where her husband has burned his cake. They confront each other in consternation. Their story seemingly ends as it began, but a subtle shift has taken place—their momentary realization of shared ignorance and mutual, though unarticulated, fears suggests at least the beginnings of the most elusive, disordered kind of human understanding, especially for the reader.

She turned off the oven, and opened the window to let out the smell of smoke and let in the smell of nicotiana and other night flowers. She may have hesitated for a moment, for what would the stranger at the gates—that intruder with his beard and his book—have made of this couple, in their nightclothes, in the smoke-filled kitchen at half past four in the morning? Some comprehension—perhaps momentary—of the complexity of life must have come to them, but it was only momentary. There were no further explanations. He threw the cake, which was burned to a cinder, into the garbage, and they turned out the lights and climbed the stairs, more mystified by life than ever, and more interested than ever in a good appearance. (p. 324)

The consequent fruit of the Tree of the Knowledge of Good and Evil is comprised of two rich legacies for mankind: fear of death and sexual confusion. Furthermore, as this story illustrates, a little knowledge seems a dangerous thing, so often repressed or more often yoked to an unsettling ignorance. The urban stories take the communality of evil and its opposite for granted (the ominous presence of the City is its symbolic embodiment); but in Cheever's suburban stories the effects of original sin are denied, and thus ignorance is more often a mode of willful ignoring. "The Wrysons" comically dramatizes this effort to deny death; the hilarious "The Brigadier and the Golf Widow" does the same thing but also links it with the tree's second legacy: sexual confusion.

The story begins with the narrator looking out onto the garden next door, where the Pasterns have built a bomb shelter surrounded by homey, amusing statuary. He conjectures that "Mrs. Pastern set out the statuary to soften its meaning," and goes on to tell us that "sitting on her terrace, sitting in her parlor, sitting anywhere, she ground an ax of self-esteem," and that "a stranger watching her board a train might have guessed that Mr. Pastern was dead, but Mr. Pastern was far from dead" (p. 498). In fact, we learn that at that moment,

> he was marching up and down the locker room of the Grassy Brae Golf
> Club shouting, "Bomb Cuba! Bomb Berlin! Let's throw a little nuclear
> hardware at them and show them who's boss." He was brigadier of the
> club's locker-room light infantry, and at one time or another declared
> war on Russia, Czechoslovakia, Yugoslavia, and China.   (p. 498)

Thus the comic connotations of the story's quaint title are established immediately; as the story progresses, other, more dire meanings attach to it.

The action proper begins with a tour for charity. Mrs. Pastern collects donations for infectious hepatitis, a disease which is her special province— "Mrs. Balcolm worked for the brain; Mrs. Ten Eyke did mental health" (p. 499). Unable to visit all the prospective donors on her list, she asks her husband Charlie to finish her rounds that evening while she cooks dinner. He does so, and in the process meets Mrs. Flannagan, "a plump woman with red hair" who is arranging flowers in her hallway, and who "seemed to be one of those women who cling to the manners and graces of a pretty child of eight" (p. 500). Their encounter propels Charlie into that mysterious middle distance between innocence and experience. Mrs. Flannagan, supposedly without cash and unable to find her checkbook, invites him in for a drink (they consume six in all), and her behavior is a combination of the child-like ways of pretended innocence and of that evident experience which generates the radical need for such pretension. As they drink, she confides that she "would rather live in danger than die of loneliness and boredom" (p. 500). Touched by her adventuresome spirit and especially by her plumpness ("why did he, at this time of life, seem almost ready to sell his soul for plumpness?"), Charlie suggests "that they go upstairs and look for her checkbook there" (p. 501).

When Charlie finally returns from his mission, it is after eleven. He resumes his brigadier bravado while watching the news on TV, but that evening he is strangely troubled. His garden world seems altered. In bed he tries to play nine imaginary holes of golf, "but the green of the links seemed faded"; he gets up and looks out the window, and "in the starlight he could see the trees stripped of their leaves" (p. 501). Leaves and foilage now remind him only of losses, so that when he thinks of Mrs. Flannagan, his anxiety is lessened. "There are, he thought, so few true means of forgetfulness in this life that why should he shun the medicine even when the medicine seemed, as it did, a little crude?" (p. 502).

Charlie's musings on knowledge and forgetfulness, disease and medicine—and later a brigadier's victory and defeat—shape the story that follows. We learn, for example, that a "new conquest always had a wonderful effect on Charlie" (p. 502). He becomes magnanimous toward all creatures, great and small, exhibiting the nobler restraints of an occupation force. When his relationship with Mrs. Flannagan experiences setbacks, those, too, are described in martial imagery: "There is something universal about being stood up in a city restaurant between one and two— a spiritual no-man's-land, whose blasted trees, entrenchments, and ratholes we all share, disarmed by the gullibility of our hearts" (p. 503). Though Charlie is nonplussed by Mrs. Flannagan's behavior, his militaristic heart melts easily when he contemplates her efforts at innocence and moral self-esteem:

> Sometimes, driving through a New Hampshire mill town late in the day, he thought, you will see in some alley or driveway, down by the river, a child dressed in a tablecloth, sitting on a broken stool, waving her scepter over a kingdom of weeds and cinders and a few skinny chickens. It is the purity and the irony of their pride that touches one; and he felt that way about Mrs. Flannagan.   (p. 503)

To my knowledge, no other writer but Cheever would insert this sentimental reverie, recalled in such precise detail, so suggestive as it is of regal instincts conjoined with actual powerlessness, and then upend the imagery and expose its soft, gooey center of virile sentiment in the conversation that follows. Our brigadier enters Mrs. Flannagan's home by the back door, "and in her company he felt as if he had just worked his shoulders free of a heavy pack" (p. 503). Just as he is ready to grind his own axe of self-esteem, she puts him off, telling him, " 'I want my favor first' " (p. 504). What follows is likely the finest extended comic exchange in Cheever's fiction; their conversation is wonderfully childish, a concatenation of secrets, guesses, and promises, as well as a series of sallies marked by unsuspected reconnoitering, probes, retreats, and a surprise attack on our brigadier.

"What is it?"

"Guess."

"I can't give you money. I'm not rich, you know."

"Oh, I wouldn't think of taking money." She was indignant.

"Then what is it?"

"Something you wear."

"But my watch is worthless, my cuff links are brass."

"Something else."

"But what?"

"I won't tell you unless you promise to give it to me."

"I can't make a promise until I know what it is you want."

"It's something very small."

"How small?"

"Tiny. Weeny."

"Please tell me what it is." Then he seized her in his arms, and this was the moment he felt most like himself: solemn, virile, wise, and imperturbable.

"I won't tell you unless you promise."

"But I can't promise."

"Then go away," she said. "Go away and never, never, come back."

She was too childish to give the command much force, and yet it was not wasted on him. . . .

"Please tell me."

"Promise."

"I promise."

"I want, she said, "a key to your bomb shelter."

The demand struck at him like a sledge-hammer blow, and suddenly he felt in all his parts the enormous weight of chagrin. All his gentle speculations on her person—the mill-town girl ruling her chickens—backfired bitterly.   (p. 504)

The scene has the resonance of classical farce, so reminiscent of the traditional encounter of *miles gloriosus* and a seemingly slavish trickster. Beyond these pagan reminiscences, however, is the insinuation of the primordial biblical encounter between the sexes—already planted and later developed in its imagery of the garden and the fall:

The demand abraded his lust, but only for a moment, for now she was back in his arms, marching [!] her fingers up and down his rib cage, saying, "Creepy, creepy, creepy mouse, come to live in Charlie's house." His need for her was crippling; it seemed like a cruel blow at the back of his knees. And yet in some chamber of his thick head he could see the foolishness and the obsolescence of his hankering skin. But how could he reform his bone and muscle to suit this new world. . . ? Her front was round, fragrant, and soft, and he took the key off its ring

. . . a genuine talisman of salvation, a defense against the end of the world—and dropped it into the neck of her dress.   (pp. 504-505)

The old Adam forsook the Tree of Life for the other; here a new Adam does the same, and in the act "knows" immediately "in some chamber of his thick head the foolishness and the obsolesence of his hankering skin" (p. 504), knows he is helpless in this "new world" aborning. The bishop's visit to the Pasterns' garden is a comic reminder of the Lord's arrival after the fall in Eden, and His noting Adam and Eve's nakedness and other defects. In this case, Mrs. Pastern feels she has been "betrayed by her ducks and gnomes" (p. 506), her intended camouflage only exposing her to the bishop. He asks to visit the shelter, and on seeing it, observes wryly, " 'It is an unfortunate characteristic of ecclesiastical architecture . . . that the basement or cellar is confined to a small space under the chancel. This gives us very little room for the salvation of the faithful—a characteristic, I should perhaps add, of our denomination' " (p. 507).

Although the bishop makes no specific or personal request, his visit troubles Mrs. Pastern, and impious thoughts seize her mind: "She had believed all her life in the holiness of the priesthood, and if this belief was genuine, why hadn't she offered the bishop the safety of her shelter at once? But if he believed in the resurrection of the dead and the life of the world to come, why was a shelter anything that he might need?" (p. 507). The role of a modern Mrs. Noah is not an easy one. Shortly after the bishop leaves, a gossipy neighbor calls to tell her that Mrs. Flannagan has showed her the key to the bomb shelter, and Mrs. Pastern realizes that her husband "would betray her in their plans for the end of the world" (p. 508). Nature conspires with her disposition and it begins to rain; she cannot flee because of the judgments she and her husband have made:

Outside, the sky darkened, the wind changed, it began to rain. What could she do? She couldn't go back to Mother. Mother didn't have a shelter. . . . And then she remembered the night—the night of judgment—when they had agreed to let Aunt Ida and Uncle Ralph burn, when she had sacrificed her three-year-old niece and he his five-year-old nephew; when they had conspired like murderers and had decided to deny mercy even to his old mother.   (p. 508)

When her husband comes home, she confronts him with the news, and he drives to Mrs. Flannagan's to find out "the truth." She greets him in the peignoir he bought for her, and he soon realizes that she will never admit the truth, for "like most incurable fibbers, she had an extravagant regard for the truth, which she expressed by sending up signals meant to

indicate that she was lying" (p. 509). Charlie pours himself a whiskey
and then goes to use the bathroom, where he finds himself "face to fac
with an absolutely naked stranger" (p. 509). Mrs. Flannagan's explanatio
is at first childish and then reflects a comic confirmation of the Pastern'
own plots for their shelter: "It was she who broke the silence. 'I do no
know who he is, and I have been trying to make him go away. . . . It i
my house, after all, and I did not invite you into it . . .' " (p. 509).

Charlie drives home in the rain; when he lets himself into the house
he notices the smell of cooking, and thinks that "these signs and odor
must have been one of the first signs of life on the planet, and might b
one of the last" (p. 509). When he sees the evening paper, he become
his former self just for a moment, shouting, " 'Throw a little nuclea
hardware at them!' " but then he falls back into his chair and asks softly
" 'Dear Jesus, when will it ever end?' " (p. 509). His wife overhears hin
and takes the muted cosmic question as a statement, saying, " 'I've beer
waiting for you to say that. . . . You *want* the world to end, don't you
Don't you, Charlie, don't you?' " (p. 510).

Her question hangs in ironic suspension, for their story ends abruptly
Cheever added a lengthy coda that the editors at the *New Yorker* wante
to delete; he protested vigorously, claiming it was integral, and so i
remains.[13] The coda consists of a letter written by the narrator's mother
which fills in the facts about the Pasterns. Within six weeks they wer
barred from Shady Hill, as if by the gleaming swords of the cherubim
forced to travel endlessly until finally their house was sold and Charli
was imprisoned for being unable to redeem his debts. Her account end
with a touching vignette: Mrs. Flannagan, also driven out, returns on
day during "the miracle of a snowstorm" that "covered everything quickl
like a spread of light" (p. 510), and walks back to the Pasterns' lawn an
stands before the bomb shelter, just looking at it. The narrator's mothe
writes, "I don't know what in the world she was thinking of but the shelte
looks a little like a tomb, you know, and she looked like a mourne
standing there with the snow falling on her head and shoulders . . .'
(p. 511).

Thus this Eden-Apocalypse story ends on a note of ignorance an
with poignant irony. At the story's start, the garden with its bomb shelte
and surrounding statuary resembled an impregnable shrine, and the nar
rator's complaint about "what would the dead [nineteenth-century writers]
have done" about it puzzled us as well. It ends with a visitation or pil
grimage, equally puzzling in its motivation to outsiders, a quasi-religiou

---

13. Private conversation with John Cheever, April 27, 1980.

rek to what had been a symbol of salvation but became the catalytic
gent of dispersal.

The exurban story "A Vision of the World" is also shaped around the
iden-Apocalypse motif, but includes a comic insinuation about the perplexity that follows revelation. It opens with an ordinary man spading his
garden in complacent contentment at a seaside cottage. To his surprise
he discovers a personal note buried in a shoe-polish can which reads:
'I, Nils Jugstrum, promise myself that if I am not a member of the Gory
Brook Country Club by the time I am twenty-five years old I will hang
myself' " (p. 512). The Saturday gardener is briefly shaken, but the sky
s blue and the smell of grass fills the air, both reminders of "those over-
ures and promises of love we know when we are young" (p. 512).

Amid such peaceable thoughts, however, he notices black ants con-
quering red ants and carrying off their corpses, a robin being pursued by
blue jays, a cat "scouting a sparrow," and finally a copperhead shedding
ts winter skin. He tells us, "What I experienced was not fright or dread;
t was shock at my unpreparedness for this branch of death. Here was
ethal venom, as much a part of the earth as the running water in the
brook, but I seemed to have no space for it in my considerations"
p. 512-513). He returns to the house to get his gun; his gun-shy dog sees
t and its reaction brings his other dog. Both dogs become the objective
correlative of his own humanly mixed feelings on encountering the snake
n his peaceful garden:

> At the sight of the gun she began to bark and whimper, torn unmer-
> cifully by her instincts and anxieties. Her barking brought the second
> dog, a natural hunter, bounding down the stairs, ready to retrieve a
> rabbit or a bird, and, followed by two dogs, one barking in joy and the
> other in horror, I returned to the garden in time to see the viper
> disappear into a stone wall.   (p. 513)

The narrator tells us that his wife is sad because she often feels like
a character in a television situation comedy who can be turned off. He
then confides that his "wife is often sad because her sadness is not a sad
sadness, sorry because her sorrow is not a crushing sorrow," and that he
would leave her but, "I could not bring myself to leave my lawns and
gardens" or "divorce myself from the serpentine brick walk I have laid";
he finally admits that "while my chains are forged of turf and house paint,
they will still bind me until I die" (p. 514). That evening he and his wife
go to the Gory Brook Country Club for a dance. While there, the narrator
observes: "We seemed to be dancing on the grave of social coherence. But
while the scene was plainly revolutionary, where was the new day, the
world to come?" (p. 514).

The day's discoveries and such reflections upset his normal composure, and for a time even his dream-life goes unexpectedly awry. (Earlier he observed, "It pleased me to think that our external life has the quality o a dream and that in our dreams we find the virtues of conservatism," and "What I wanted to do was to grant my dreams, in so incoherent a world their legitimacy.") In the Bible, dreams are often unexpected media of revelation, the opposite of complacent conservatism; the challenge is that of truthful interpretation, and this becomes the narrator's lot. He has a series of dreams, the first involving an exotic island in the sun, where he pronounces a phrase ("Porpozec ciebie. . . .") from the native language and is complimented. In the second dream he stands at a window of a cottage in Nantucket:

> Then I saw a single figure coming down the beach. It seemed to be a priest or a bishop. He carried a crozier, aand wore the miter, cope, soutane, chasuble, and alb for high votive Mass. . . . He saw me at my window, raised his hand, and called. "Porpozec ciebie nie prosze dorzanin albo zyolpocz ciwego." (p. 516)

In the third dream he is on the winning team in a football game, and hears the same phrase used, unaccountably, as a cheer.

The untranslatable phrase triggers "the excitement of discovery" in the narrator, but it dismays his wife when he repeats it for her, and she recommends a vacation. He flies to Florida, and that night dreams of a pretty woman kneeling in a field of wheat. She seems to him more real than the concrete objects of his waking life, and, when she speaks to him, she repeats the strange phrase. His story ends with the phrase's meaning still enigmatic. Nonetheless, the disquiet and peculiar serenity it evokes become allied with a revelation that nature provides. It is important to recall that the Book of Revelation in the Bible ends with the images of the tree and the waters of life being restored (Rev. 22:1-2), symbolically reversing the loss of the tree and the fountain of life in the Garden of Eden. (The tree of life is often associated, as it is here, with the palm tree—in Greek called *phoinix*—from which dates hung.) This tale, in comic fashion, recapitulates the beginning, the sad interim, and the end of Revelation, with its emphasis on the restoration of love and virtue and dry bones and peace and nature itself. The narrator's last lines record an apocalyptic vision:

> Then either I awake in despair or am waked by the sound of rain on the palms. I think of some farmer, who, hearing the noise of rain, will stretch his lame bones and smile, feeling that the rain is falling into his lettuce and his cabbages, his hay and his oats, his parsnips and his corn. I think of some plumber who, waked by the rain, will smile at a vision of the world in which all the drains are miraculously cleansed

and free. Right-angle drains, crooked drains, root-choked and rusty drains all gurgle and discharge their waters into the sea. I think that the rain will wake some old lady, who will wonder if she left her copy of *Dombey and Son* in the garden. Her shawl? Did she cover the chairs? And I know that the sound of the rain will wake some lovers, and that its sound will seem to be a part of that force that has thrust them into one another's arms. Then I sit up in bed and exclaim aloud to myself, "Valor! Love! Virtue! Compassion! Splendor! Kindness! Wisdom! Beauty!" The words seem to have the colors of the earth, and as I recite them I feel my hopefulness mount until I am contented and at peace with the night.   (p. 517)

Modulations on the biblical theme of Revelation also occur in "The Angel of the Bridge" and "The Scarlet Moving Van," the one benign, the other somewhat sinister. "The Angel of the Bridge" is a spiritual and psychological parable recounted by an apparently naive but gracious narrator. He begins by telling us about his mother who has a phobia about dying in an airplane and offers the reason: "she does not relish change" (p. 491). He himself finds flying exhilarating, and describes the peculiar excitement he felt when he flew West on a dark night: the obscure "hoop of light" he saw seemed like "the emergence of a new world, a gentle hint at my own obsolescence, the lateness of my time of life, and my inability to understand the things I often see" (p. 491). Soon after he learns that his brother also has a phobia—he calls it a family eccentricity—about elevators, because his brother fears the buildings that they're in will fall down. Our eminently sane and sober narrator finds this terribly funny, but he cannot resist a speculation: ". . . I wondered how many of the men waiting with him to cross the street made their way as he did through a ruin of absurd delusions, in which the street might appear to be a torrent and the approaching cab driven by the angel of death" (p. 492).

He soon finds out. One evening, while returning from a visit with his brother in New Jersey, he runs into a thunderstorm as he drives across the George Washington Bridge. The wind is so strong that he is unnerved: "It seemed to me that I could feel the huge structure swing. . . . I could see no signs of a collapse, and yet I was convinced that in another minute the bridge would split in two and hurl the long lines of Sunday traffic into the dark water below us. This imagined disaster was terrifying" (p. 493). The experience so upsets him that eventually he goes to see his doctor, who is scornful, and then a psychiatrist, who tells him that his "fear of bridges was the surface manifestation of a deep-seated anxiety" and that he should go into analysis (p. 494). Rejecting this advice, he flees to Las Vegas, where outside his hotel window he sees a huge statue of a woman, revolving slowly in a beam of light outside a nightclub; even when the

lights are turned off, she continues to turn ceaselessly. He feels an odd
kinship with her and her plight of restless movement. As he continues
to observe the life outside the window, he sees a drunken woman nearly
fall twice, and a sudden fight at a stoplight. "The fight, like the hoop of
light I had seen from the plane, seemed like the sign of a new world, but
in this case an emergence of brutality and chaos" (p. 494). (In the beginning of the Book of Genesis the first of God's creations is light amidst
the formless void of chaos; in the Book of Revelation the apocalyptic
collision between light and chaos occurs again before the renewal of creation and a new beginning. In the interim, human history—restlessness,
change, falls and recoveries, warfare—reflects man's middle position between light and chaos.)

The narrator's normal serenity is upset; he attempts to make reasonable his phobia through the jargon-laden explanations of pop psychology,
but he cannot, for his condition seems more radical and so beyond any
diagnostic explications. In myth the image of a bridge always suggests the
dangerous passage one must make, and it recurs in many ancient initiatory
and funereal rites, in which it symbolizes the point of ontological transition between one mode of being and another. In Scripture the primary
symbol for such passage is the Exodus, the Israelites crossing amid the
dark waters and the wind (suggested by the images used to describe the
storm on the bridge) from bondage to a new land. Later the Exodus motif
(as in the sacrament of baptism) will be emblematic of the movement
of initiation, pilgrimage, seeming death, and the passage to "faith" and
renewal. The Perilous Bridge, like the Narrow Gate, is an elaboration of
this motif: to cross it means one has arrived at the place of restoration,
the Promised Land, Paradise, where, though one is radically changed (a
new being), he has in fact become more truly himself.[14]

On the Sunday that the narrator takes his daughter back to school
his fear intensifies. Though he gets across the bridge on the way there,
he is paralyzed on the way home: he cannot summon the courage to enter
beyond the bridge's approach over the Hudson. He stops his car, feeling
that "everything that I loved—blue-sky courage, lustiness, the natural
grasp of things . . . would never come back" (p. 497). Unexpectedly, a
young girl carrying a suitcase "and—believe me—a small harp" (p. 497)
gets into his car, presuming he has stopped for her. She tells him she is
a folksinger and sings him a simple folk ballad, one with paradisaical lyrics
celebrating a vision of the world—free from even its most minor flaws:
" 'I gave my love a cherry that had no stone. . . . I gave my love a

---

14. Mircea Eliade, *The Sacred and the Profane* (New York: Harcourt Brace Harvest
Book, 1957), pp. 180ff.

hicken that had no bone/I told my love a story that had no end/I gave
~y love a baby with no cryin' " (p. 497).

In the Book of Exodus it is the angel of the Lord that leads Israel
~hrough the Red Sea unscathed (Ex. 14:19; Num. 20:16). Here the girl
~ads the narrator out of his fear:

> She sang me across a bridge that seemed to be an astonishingly sensible,
> durable, and even beautiful construction . . . and the water of the
> Hudson below us was charming and tranquil. It all came back—blue-
> sky courage, the high spirits of lustiness, an ecstatic sereneness. . .
> and I drove on toward the city through a world that, having been
> restored to me, seemed marvelous and fair.   (p. 497)

"The Scarlet Moving Van" records a similar pattern but almost com-
~letely in reverse. The story begins with a first-person lamentation:
'Goodbye to the mortal boredom of distributing a skinny chicken to a
~amily of seven and all the other rites of the hill towns" (p. 359). The
~eremiad-like tone is appropriate, for the story that follows concerns wan-
~lering and eventual exile after the collapse of social fidelities. It opens
~vith the invasion of the scarlet moving van into the village. "The gilt
~nd scarlet of the van, bright even in the twilight, was an inspired attempt
~o disguise the true sorrowfulness of wandering" (p. 359). The colors, gold
~nd scarlet, remind us of the colors proper to Apollo and Dionysus, and
~uit the character of Gee-Gee, who, along with his wife Peaches, is mov-
~ng into the neighborhood. We are told that Gee-Gee had been a hand-
~ome man, though his yellow curls are now thin, and his "face seemed
~oth angelic and menacing" (p. 360). That night their new neighbors,
~he Folkestones, invite the couple over for a drink, and they stay late.
Suddenly Gee-Gee interrupts the party conversation and pronounces,
" 'God, but you're stuffy people' " (p. 360). This upsets the other guests
and his wife, but he assures her cryptically, " 'I have to teach them,
honey. . . . They've got to learn' " (p. 361). He then proceeds to take
off almost all of his clothes. Peaches apologizes for his behavior, explaining
that this has been Gee-Gee's behavior pattern for quite some time, and
that they have been forced to leave communities eight times in the past
eight years. This was not always so, she insists. " 'They called him the
Greek God at college. That's why he's called Gee-Gee. . . . Oh, I wish
he'd come back. I wish he'd be the way he was' " (p. 361).

Ironically, Gee-Gee does "come back" several mornings later, and his
personality is winning and genial, so like Apollo's return each day. We
are told that "in the morning light and surrounded by new friends, he
seemed to challenge the memory [of his churlish conduct]" (p. 361). Yet
at subsequent parties he appears transformed again, singing dirty songs,
dancing jigs or flings in his underwear. The central character, Charlie

Folkestone, is "greatly troubled at the spectacle of someone falling s
swiftly from grace" (p. 362), and especially troubled by what Gee-Ge
considers his prophetic message. At one such party a climax is reache
after Gee-Gee again pulls one of his stunts, and the passage that follov
it, beginning with the phrase " 'Oh, Jesus,' " insinuates in what first seen
a startlingly inappropriate manner the likeness of Gee-Gee's "teaching
to the prophetic mission of Jesus:

> "Will you do anything to help yourself?" [Charlie asked].
> "I have to teach them." Then he threw back his head and sobbed,
> "Oh, Jesus ..."
> Charlie turned away. It seemed, at that instant, that Gee-Gee had
> heard, from some wilderness of his own, the noise of a distant horn
> that prophesied the manner and the hour of his death. . . . Folkestone
> felt an upheaval in his spirit. He felt he understood the drunken man's
> message; he had always sensed it. It was at the bottom of their friend-
> ship. Gee-Gee was an advocate for the lame, the diseased, the poor,
> for those who through no fault of their own live out their lives in
> misery and pain. To the happy and the wellborn and the rich he had
> this to say—that for all their affection, their comforts, and their priv-
> ileges, they would not be spared the pangs of anger and lust and the
> agonies of death. . . . He spoke from some vision of the suffering in
> life, but was it necessary to suffer oneself in order to accept his message?
> It seemed so.   (p. 363)

But prophets are without honor in their own country, and Gee-Ge
is expelled from the community. Charlie learns that he has broken hi
hip right before Christmas, so one afternoon he stops in to visit Gee-Ge
in his new neighborhood, a development "like a penal colony" (p. 364)
He greets Gee-Gee, who is riding in a child's wagon, alone and drunk
As they drink, Charlie, concerned about Gee-Gee's carelessness witl
cigarettes, worries about his burning to death. But Gee-Gee assures him
" 'Don't worry about me. . . . I have my guardian angel' " (p. 365)
Though still worried ("How could he openly abandon a friend—a neigh
bor, at least—to the peril of death?"), Charlie leaves him and drive
home in a snowstorm. When he is finally secure at home, he receives ar
urgent call from Gee-Gee: he has fallen out of the wagon, he is helpless
can Charlie come back and help him? But Charlie does not. Gee-Gee':
message about the lame, the diseased, the poor has gone unheeded. "Ther
the image of Gee-Gee returned, crushing in its misery, and [Charlie]
remembered Peaches standing in the hallway at the Watermans' calling,
'Come back! Come back!' " (p. 367).

But Charlie does not come back. In Scripture angels are the ministers
of God's judgment (Matt. 13:41, 49); here Charlie's own decision dooms

im. No longer a sheep but a goat, a fish and darnel fit for rejection, he ecomes the counterpart of Gee-Gee's Dionysian night-side, obsessed with rink and sexual suspicion—and yet he has no prophetic message save hat of selfish suffering. "In the end, he lost his job, and they had to nove, and began their wanderings, like Gee-Gee and Peaches, in the carlet-and-gold van" (p. 368).

This ambiguous fable about guilt, knowledge, and suffering ends with curious coda. We learn that Gee-Gee actually survived his crisis without tress. "That boozy guardian angel, her hair disheveled and the strings of er harp broken, still seemed to hover over where he lay" (p. 369; cf. Matt. 26:43). The fire department came to his aid, and, in fact, one ireman remained as a companion to him, eating and drinking, until Peaches returned. Gee-Gee's story ends on a cyclical note—a restoration omewhat different from that of "The Angel of the Bridge"—for he re-covers and resumes his "disorderly life," and he and his family "had to nove at the end of the year, and, like the Folkestones, vanished from he hill towns" (p. 369). And we presume that Gee-Gee continued to proclaim his puzzling message elsewhere.

Two other, more excellent stories, "O Youth and Beauty!" and "Just Tell Me Who It Was," are like these, superficially diverse and yet reverse counterparts of each other. "O Youth and Beauty!", in fact, might be a more apt title for the latter story. Both are composed from the point of view of a chatty, amicable neighbor, describing the absurd events and psychology of a "fall" others have undergone. Youth and age, innocence and experience, desire and decrepitude are the themes of both stories; yet one has a comic upward tilt and the other a tragic downward tilt.

The Pyms, husband Will and wife Maria, are at the center of "Just Tell Me Who It Was." Will is a "self-made man" with "hardly a trace of the anxieties" of a man born in poverty, one who "had been able to make something plausible and coherent in spite of his mean beginnings" (p. 370). Given such a description, readers familiar with Cheever perk up at these lines, ready for the whammy on Will. But it does not come in the way we expect. Instead, we learn that Will is "a cheerful, heavy man with a round face that looked exactly like a pudding. Everyone was glad to see him, as one is glad to see, at the end of a meal, the appearance of a bland, fragrant, and nourishing dish made of fresh eggs, nutmeg, and country cream" (p. 370).

Evidently Will is an Everyman of "some" substance; it is his wife Maria, years younger than he, who provides his life with some distinc-tiveness. "She sometimes called him Daddy. Will was so proud of her and spoke so extravagantly of her beauty and her wit that when people first met her they were always disappointed" (p. 371). One day both of them take a walk in the woods with their children. It is early spring, a season pulsating with the aroma of beginnings, an Edenic atmosphere at that hour "when the dark of the woods and the cold and damp from any nearby pond or brook are suddenly felt, when you realize that the world was lighted, until a minute ago, merely by the sun's fire, and that your clothes are thin" (p. 372).

The circumstance suggests both the idyllic and the ominous, but Will entertains only thoughts of Paradise. In a romantic gesture, Will carves his and Maria's initials in the bark of a tree to express his love. Yet although he does not so intend it, the gesture and the scene are resonances of the postlapsarian fate of the original Adam: the consequences of his action (reason and sensuality) reflect the twin fruits of the tree of the knowledge of good and evil. "It was Maria's youth and beauty that had informed his senses and left his mind so open that the earth seemed spread out before his eyes like a broad map of reason and sensuality" (p. 372).

This symbolic cluster and ironic tension quicken in the events that follow. On a night soon after, we discover Maria "tying apple blossoms to branches," a task given her as a member of the decorations committee for the Apple Blossom Fete; the result is that in their living room "was the beginning of a forest of flowering branches" (p. 373). When Will asks her what her costume for the event is like, she models it—a surprise—for him: "She was wearing gold slippers, pink tights, and a light velvet bodice cut low enough to show the division of her breasts" (p. 374). Will's reaction is instantaneous:

> A terrible sadness came over Will. The tight costume—he had to polish his eyeglasses to see it better—displayed all the beauty he worshipped, and it also expressed her perfect innocence of the wickedness of the world. The sight filled poor Will with lust and dismay. . . . He thought that she looked like a child—a maiden, at least—approaching some obscene doom. In her sweet and gentle face and her half-naked bosom he saw all the sadness of life. (p. 374)

At first Will tells her she can't wear the costume, but her tears and protests wear him down: "How—even when they were in grave danger— could he refuse innocence and beauty?" (p. 374).

The night of the dance Maria presents him with another surprise, her choice of his costume, although its symbolic appropriateness escapes them both.

> It was a suit of chain mail with a helmet. Will was pleased with the costume, because it was a disguise. . . . [Maria] cut some ostrich feathers off an old hat and stuck them gaily into his helmet. Will went toward a mirror to see himself, but just as he got there, the visor slammed shut, and he couldn't get it to stay open. (p. 375)

Thus begarbed—the one half-blind, the other naked to their ene-mies—the couple goes off to the dance. There they are separated, for Will dances clumsily in his mail and cannot catch up to Maria as she whirls about like the belle of the ball. He asks the orchestra to play "I Could Write a Book," because it was "their music," and he is certain that, on hearing it, she will leave her partner and look for him. But Maria does not search him out, and, discouraged, Will goes home alone. Maria stays through the last dance, and although her virtue remains intact, other losses have dogged her steps. The narrator records her sensations of de-pletion, and some of the passage's poignancy arises from its understated allusions to the biblical Apocalypse: the dragon-Leviathan who breathes fire and eats virgins; the spilled wine, suggestive of the great harlot and the cup of God's anger (Rev. 14:8; 17:4); the sweeping of the remnants of evil into the Abyss; and, finally, the restoration of the trees of life and the light of the morning (Rev. 22):

> She had lost her pocketbook. Her tights had been torn by the scales of a dragon. The smell of spilled wine came from her clothes. The sweetness of the air and the fineness of the light touched her. The party seemed like gibberish. . . . The hundreds of apple blossoms that she had tied to branches and that had looked, at a distance, so like real blossoms would soon be swept into the ash can.
>
> The trees of Shady Hill were filled with birds. . . . The pristine light and the loud singing reminded her of some ideal—some simple way of life, in which she dried her hands on an apron and Will came home from the sea—that she had betrayed. She did not know where she had failed, but the gentle morning light illuminated her failure pitilessly.   (pp. 376-377)

When she returns home in tears, Will's suspicions are aroused, and he searches his memory for hints of infidelity. Now his memories are negatively colored: her taking a bath and wearing a new dress just to go to the movies; her unexpectedly enthusiastic imitation of a strip-teaser at the Women's Club revue for charity months ago; his glimpse of someone who looked like her with another man on a Manhattan street. Her sense of guilt and his suspicion are rooted in differing aspects of ignorance, alternative instances of human separateness. The day after the dance Will takes his children for a walk in the woods, and, Adam-like, "he lectured them, as he always did, on the names of trees" (p. 379). His children now seem "like live symbols of his trouble," and "when he passed the tree where he had carved their initials, he thought of the stupendous wicked-ness of the world" (p. 379).

That evening Maria encourages Will to go alone to the Townsends' party with ironic reasoning: " 'There'll be a lot of gossip about the dance, and you can hear it all, and then you can come home and tell me all about it' " (p. 379). Mission to-be-accomplished. Will goes to the party and confronts a chain of evidence he cannot gather in: a maid tells him "a pair of gold slippers and a blue lace girdle" were found in the parking lot after the dance; he spots a cuckolded husband and senses a counterpart; the Chesneys invite him to a lecture to be held " 'on marriage problems—extramarital affairs, that sort of thing' "; the rector of Christ Church solicitously tells him, " 'I want you to feel free to come to my study, Will, and talk to me if anything is troubling you' "; an upstanding banker, a priggish pillar of community order, is anxious to discuss "the immorality at the party" (p. 381).

Will is depressed and decides to leave—and Cheever's comic sense is especially impressive at this point. Most writers would rest content after interweaving so deftly these revelatory and non-revelatory snatches of conversation, but Cheever pushes beyond these accomplishments. For, as Will starts to leave, he accidentally runs into two women who are, in differing ways, mirrors of his own condition as well as its augmenters. The first is Mrs. Walpole, who gaily greets him with the line, " 'I see that your wife hasn't recovered sufficiently to face the public today' " (p. 381). The narrator then comments:

> A peculiar fate seems to overtake homely women at the ends of parties—and journeys, too. Their curls and their ribbons come undone, particles of food cling to their teeth, their glasses steam, and the wide smile with which they planned to charm the world lapses into a look of habitual discontent and bitterness. Mrs. Walpole had got herself up bravely for the Townsends' party, but time itself—she was drinking sherry—had destroyed the impression she intended to make. Someone seemed to have sat on her hat, her voice was strident, and the camellia pinned to her shoulder had died.   (pp. 381-382)

After this brush with Mrs. Walpole, Will runs into Helen Bulstrode, a lonely lush whose husband "was pleasant, wealthy, and forbearing" (p. 382). She suddenly speaks to Will copiously in French; he fails to understand her, and this so angers her that she shouts after him as he leaves.

The next evening a neighbor named Edith Hastings comes on an errand for her husband. She wants to know if Will is interested in buying some apple trees. When Will hesitates, she assures him there is no hurry: " 'I mean, there isn't any special time for planting apple trees, is there? And, speaking of apple trees, how was the fete?' " (p. 384). For the reader, this casual juxtaposition creates delight, but for Will the association implies something else, and he asks her sharply, " 'Is that what you came here to talk about?' " He accuses her of being party to filthy gossip, and offends her and upsets his wife. Contrite, he says to Maria later, " 'Who was it, Mummy? Just tell me who it was and I'll forget about it' " (p. 384).

The next day, on awakening in the guest room, Will has a vision of the villain. The truth stands revealed: it must be Henry Bulstrode—this would explain his wife's mystifying spiel of drunken French two nights ago. Righteous and manly once more, Will goes to the train station, spies Bulstrode, walks over to him and, "without any warning at all" (p. 385), knocks him down. A commotion ensues and then subsides. Will is himself again—in fact, he feels better. In myth the quest for youth or immortality is often prominently associated with a tree with golden fruit that is guarded by a dragon or monster. The one who would gather the fruits of the tree must confront the monster and slay him (as the emissary angel does in the Apocalypse); only then will the mystery of restoration, renewal, youth, the wedding of love with mercy, the glimpse of an emerald rainbow encircling a bejeweled throne (Rev. 4:4) be revealed. The fact that Will's exhilaration is based on a comic mistake should not distract us unduly; for all that, his new vision that closes the story is nothing less then, well, beatific:

> The amazing thing was how well Will felt when he boarded the train. Now his fruitful life with Maria would be resumed. They would walk on Sunday afternoons again, and play word games by the open fire again, and weed the roses again, and love one another under the sounds of the rain again, and hear the singing of the crows; and he would buy her a present that afternoon as a signal of love and forgiveness. He would buy her pearls or gold or sapphires—something expensive; emeralds maybe; something no young man could afford. (p. 385)

If this story is a farcical fable with an ambiguous ending, "O Youth and Beauty!" is its amplification. Cash Bentley's former talent and continual passion for jumping hurdles provides not only the symbolic center but becomes, with its rhythm of ups and downs, the formal shape of the story as well. The accent on monotony and repetition, along with the insinuation of track metaphors like "tag end," "track of time," "go here and go there," "preliminaries," "race," and "obstacles," is sounded from the opening paragraph. The story opens with one of Cheever's most famous sentences. It is a periodic sentence in the classical Latin tradition, and its very structure, though a parody, hints at tradition and timelessness and a humorous yoking of Cicero's O tempora! O mores! and his Numquam se minus otiosum esse quam cum otiosus ("O times! O customs!" and "Never less idle than when wholly idle"):

At the tag end of nearly every long, large Saturday-night party in the suburb of Shady Hill, when almost everybody who was going to play golf or tennis in the morning had gone home hours ago and the ten or twelve people remaining seemed powerless to bring the evening to an end although the gin and whiskey were running low, and here and there a woman who was sitting out her husband would have begun to drink milk; when everybody had lost track of time, and the baby-sitters who were waiting at home for these diehards would have long since stretched out on the sofa and fallen into a deep sleep, to dream about cooking-contest prizes, ocean voyages, and romance; when the bellicose drunk, the crapshooter, the pianist, and the woman faced with the expiration of her hopes had all expressed themselves; when every proposal—to go to the Farquarsons' for breakfast, to go swimming, to go and wake up the Townsends, to go here and go there—died as soon as it was made, then Trace Bearden would begin to chide Cash Bentley about his age and thinning hair. The chiding was preliminary to moving the living-room furniture . . . and when they had finished, you wouldn't know the place. Then if the host had a revolver, he would be asked to produce it. Cash would take off his shoes and assume a starting crouch behind a sofa. Trace would fire the weapon out of an open window, and if you were new to the community and had not understood what the preparations were about, you would then realize that you were watching a hurdle race. Over the sofa went Cash, over the tables, over the fire screen and the woodbox. It was not exactly a race, since Cash ran it alone, but it was extraordinary to see this man of forty surmount so many obstacles so gracefully. There was not a piece of furniture in Shady Hill that Cash could not take in his stride. The race ended with cheers, and presently the party would break up.   (p. 210)

Those last three sentences, here recounted with an awe-struck tonality, become in an ironic reversal the kernel of the story that follows. Seemingly enthusiastic, the chant-like recitation of events, punctuated by temporal conjunctions like "when" and "then," later reminds the reader instead—as the story develops—of the cadences of Koheleth in the biblical book of Ecclesiastes, and of his comments that "God has put eternity in man's mind" and yet "there is nothing new under the sun." Cheever's remarkable gift for specificity distracts, and the personal address ("you who are new to all this) disarms us, muting the scene's poetic universality.

Immediately Cheever alters his style to describe in extensive detail an average day in the life of Cash's wife, Louise. Hers is a life "exacting and monotonous," and their marital life together (as the cliché "they had their ups and downs" reveals) is the same (p. 211). Their every day is like Saturday night: a series of secular rituals, of less-than-earnest resolve, eminently predictable (Cheever unites his summary by stressing the word "would" throughout), of slips and bumps and returns on the track. "But these quarrels and reunions, like the hurdle race, didn't seem to lose their interest through repetition" (p. 213). We also learn of a mutuality: if Cash's fixation is on youth, Louise's fixation is on youth and beauty— concerns, ironically, more subjective than objective. In anticipating a party, she would ready herself with painstaking care:

> Louise Bentley put herself through preparations nearly as arduous as the Monday wash. She rested for an hour, by the clock, with her feet high in the air, her chin in a sling, and her eyes bathed in some astringent solution. The clay packs, the too tight girdle, and the pluck- ing and curling and painting that went on were all aimed at rejuven- ation. . . . But she was a lovely woman, and all the cosmetics that she had struggled with seemed, like her veil, to be drawn transparently over a face where mature beauty and a capacity for wit and passion were undisguisable. (p. 313)

That spring the Bentleys attend an anniversary party held in their honor; the late-hour rite and rote take place again, but this time Cash falls and breaks his leg. His fracture ushers in images and perceptions of a broken world for Cash, a universe of brittle fragments that possibly include him: "He, or everything around him, seemed subtly to have changed for the worse. Even his senses seemed to conspire to damage the ingenuous world that he had enjoyed for so many years" (p. 214). Inti- mations of mortality begin to visit his life: he opens the icebox at home and notices the rank smell of spoiled meat; in the attic, while looking for his varsity sweater, he breaks a spider web that covers his mouth "as if a hand had been put over it" (p. 214). Then Thanatos and Eros merge oddly in his instinctual life: one night he spots an old whore, "so sluttish and ugly that she looked like a cartoon of Death," and yet "his lips swelled, his breathing quickened, and he experienced all the other symp- toms of erotic excitement"; a few nights later his wife brings some faded roses in from the garden that "smelled more of earth than anything else . . . a putrid, compelling smell" (p. 214).

Then Cheever artfully contrasts Cash's plight with his neighbors' un- mixed enthusiasm for the summer, for the embrace of the earth and its scents, as they get off the train on a summer night "in a bath of placid golden light" (p. 215). The scene is Edenesque; all are enthralled by the beauty of Demeter, Mother Earth, while Cash is smitten by her daughter Persephone.

> Up on the hill, the ladies say to one another, "Smell the grass! Smell the trees!". . . On Alewives Lane sprinklers continue to play after dark. You can smell the water. The air seems as fragrant as it is dark—

it is a delicious element to walk through—and most of the windows on Alewives Lane are open to it. . . . Last night's stars seem to have drawn to themselves a new range of galaxies, and the night sky is not dark at all, except where there is a tear in the membrane of light.
(p. 215)

Cash meanwhile, is entertaining other, no less "elementary" sensations as he sits at home and watches a young people's party in the neighbor's garden behind his house. To his eyes the party and its setting seem prelapsarian:

There is nothing on their minds but the passing summer nights. Taxes and the elastic in underpants—all the unbeautiful facts of life that threaten to crush the breath out of Cash—have not touched a single figure in this garden. . . . He feels as if the figures in the next yard are the specters from some party in that past where all his tastes and desires lie, and from which he has been cruelly removed. He feels like a ghost of the summer evening.   (p. 216)

Cash's own post-lapsarian, ghostly reflections are suddenly interrupted by the arrival of friends, who invite him and his wife to the club for a drink. The couples go, and there find people their own age at the bar, but Cash instead goes into the ballroom and cuts in on a young couple dancing. The girl is dismayed not only by his vehemence but by his "ancient two-step," and signals "a boy" for deliverance (p. 216). Cash, now cut out and despondent, resolves to attempt his hurdling feat right there in the club. "All his grace and strength seemed to have returned to him" (p. 217), and he completes his obstacle course to noisy applause, though he groans and falls shortly after his victory.

Cash is resurrected, and it is appropriate that his story ends on a Sunday. He and his family go off to church, where "Cash sang, prayed, and got to his knees, but the most he ever felt in Church was that he stood outside the realm of God's infinite mercy, and, to tell the truth, he no more believed in the Father, the Son, and the Holy Ghost than does my bull terrier" (p. 217). That night, depressed by the "suburban Sunday-night blues," he runs the ritual circuit of drinking parties in the neighborhood. In the meantime, his wife is religiously performing a different symbolic action, though with similar intent: "Louise was upstairs, cutting out of the current copy of Life those scenes of mayhem, disaster, and violent death that she felt might corrupt the children" (p. 218). When Cash arrives home, he begins to move the living-room furniture. Then he calls Louise to come downstairs, and when she does, hands her the starting pistol. On her first pull of the trigger nothing happens, because the safety is on. Cash, impatient, urges her to release it, and hurdles the sofa without waiting for her. The results are starkly recorded: "The pistol went off and Louise got him in midair. She shot him dead" (p. 218). The story's ending is a shock, but one the reader has been subtly prepared for. In a way, Cash's fate—death in mid-air—seems on reflection a parody of William Butler Yeats's poem "An Irish Airman Foresees His Death":

I balanced all, brought all to mind,
The years to come seemed waste of breath,
A waste of breath the years behind
In balance with this life, this death.

"The Housebreaker of Shady Hill" records a similar running of an obstacle course, but in it the apocalyptic ending is a revelation of merciful judgment rather than of destruction and final catastrophe. Johnny Hake's personal story begins with a lengthy "genesis" account of his life: his job working for a "patriarchal" firm run by an old man in whose presence he "behaved . . . as if he had shaped me out of clay with his own hands and breathed the fire of life into me"(p. 253); his freely chosen expulsion from the job; his guilt about his rejection of his querulous mother and yet his simultaneous desire "to do it all over again in some emotional Arcadia, and have us both behave differently" (p. 257); his homesickness for "countries I've never seen," and his longing "to be what I couldn't be" (p. 257).

The turning point arrives as he looks down into his garden and, because he is almost destitute, resolves to steal from a neighbor, for it seems "money had it all over love" (p. 257). His housebreaking caper is successful, but he is consumed by guilt. Like Cash Bentley after his "fall," Hake feels that the external world is suddenly transformed. In Cash's case, such alternation followed a physical fracture; here it follows an "infraction." Hake also realizes that he is an active participant in the communality of evil, and he begins to translate the most casual language into the criminal: "It was only 'steal' and all its allied nouns, verbs, and adverbs that had the power to tyrannize over my nervous system, as if I had evolved, unconsciously, some doctrine wherein the act of theft took precedence over all the other sins in the Decalogue and was a sign of moral death" (p. 261). He sees dishonest counterparts everywhere, "and all the arches and spires of St. Patrick's only reminded me of poor boxes" (p. 262). Not unlike Cash and his sensations of fracture, Hake feels separated from the world of goodness, from those "people who stitched up the big holes in the world that were made by men like me" (p. 363).

The first climax occurs when Hake attends the Communion service at his church on Sunday morning, and realizes he is in "no condition" to help take up the collection. The sense of solidarity and the familiar consoling sounds and smells of divine worship now make him dizzy. "Then I heard, in the baseboard on my right, a rat's tooth working like an auger in the hard oak. 'Holy, Holy, Holy,' I said very loudly, hoping to frighten the rat. 'Lord God of Hosts, Heaven and earth are FULL of Thy Glory!' " (p. 263). Thus, distracted by one sign, he misses another, and he neglects to share in the Communion sacrament.

Later that day he rakes leaves in his garden, for "what could be more contrite than cleaning the lawn of the autumn's dark rubbish under the streaked, pale skies of spring?" (p. 264). Yet his anguish persists; "seeing a bare dogwood tree in the starlight, I thought, How sad everything is!" (p. 265). After he behaves rudely at the family celebration of his birthday, he and his wife argue, and she, contending that his recent behavior has been "hideous," encourages him to leave. He packs a bag in a fit of anger and goes to the train station, but then begins marching home—met, halfway there, by his wife. Several evenings later he plans to rob his neighbors, the Pewters, but as he walks to their home, "there was a harsh stirring in all the trees and gardens, like a draft on a bed of fire, and I wondered what it was until I felt the rain on my hands and face, and then I began to laugh" (p. 268). The biblical images of wind, fire, and water are those associated with the visitation of a revelatory presence. Here the apocalyptic water and fire transmit not destruction but renewal and laughter. Hake's disordered world is now reordered and restored, and he realizes "how I had been given the gifts of life so long as I possessed them, and I possessed them then—the tie between the wet grass roots and the hair that grew out of my body, the thrill of my mortality that I had known on summer nights . . ." (p. 268). That night he had a dream about another kind of recovery, a pleasant one of the sort Cash Bentley would have envied:

> I dreamed I was sailing a boat on the Mediterranean. I saw some worn marble steps leading down into the water and the water itself—blue, saline, and dirty. I stepped the mast, hoisted the sail, and put my hand on the tiller. But why, I wondered as I sailed away, should I seem to be only seventeen years old? But you can't have everything.
>
> It is not, as somebody once wrote, the smell of corn bread that calls us back from death; it is the lights and signs of love and friendship.   (p. 268)

As these stories illustrate, the rectilinear narratives and cyclic, symbolic patterns of the Bible often provide a subtext in Cheever's fiction, even when the story is primarily comic in perspective. As I have indicated, one significant pattern that animates Cheever's first four novels is his playful variation on the Cain and Abel myth. Two of his later stories

("Goodbye, My Brother" and "The Lowboy") exploit this theme explicitly; more often he creates counterparts to his main character who function
in similar fashion. But it is important to recall Cheever's own remarks on
the composition of "Goodbye, My Brother": he said he wrote this tale of
fraternal conflict because "there was some ambiguity in my indignation,"
and that the two brothers represent the two halves of John Cheever as
he alternately "rejoiced and brooded during a summer on Martha's Vineyard."[15] Fraternal tension, then, is an attempt to objectify in dramatic
terms the subjective splits, the polar tensions, and the spiritual, emotional
divisions within the *individual* self. Employment of the Cain-and-Abel
pattern, so symbolic of man's alternating impulses toward love and death,
informs these stories with a universal character.

Cheever has said that "the easiest way to parse the world is through
mythology." Allusions to classical myth function much like biblical allusions—and sometimes they overlap, as they do in Cheever's stories.
Odysseus in "The Swimmer," Venus in "The Country Husband," satyrs
in "Brimmer," an Aphrodite-like chimera in "The Chimera," Diana and
Helen in "Goodbye, My Brother," Artemis in "Artemis, the Honest Well
Digger," Hecate in "The Music Teacher," Actaeon, Orpheus, Hermes,
Nerissa, and Venus in "Metamorphoses," and many more—all are dramatic allusions offered to universalize (not heroicize) the diverse tensions
in moral experience. Myth also takes for granted the mysterious in life,
and mythic tales, precisely because of their rich ambiguity and multiform
character, challenge rationalistic presuppositions about order in our world.
(By contrast, Cheever's wonderful story "The Geometry of Love" parodies
this misconception. Its hero, Charlie Mallory, an engineer who has encountered a series of mystifying disorders in his life, tries to use Euclidean
geometry to resolve the problems of love and the eternal verities. Logic,
order, and coherence are his goals, and for a while he succeeds. Unfortunately, chaos obtrudes from the most unlikely places; still, he pushes
on with Euclid as his savior. Eventually, his embrace of abstractions is
reversed, and the external world begins first to diminish and then to
vanish before his eyes. The mysteries of love, pain, and death elude all
simple, geometric analogies.)

"The Country Husband" is a long story, so rich in incident and in
emotional colorations that it reads more like a novella, and the classical
allusions studded throughout give it the contour of an abbreviated comic
epic as well. Its hero, Francis Weed, is an Aeneas manqué, torn between
duty and death; like Aeneas, he discovers he is a son of Venus. Weed's

Aeneid begins with an escape from a Troy-like destruction and recounts his many wanderings in quest of a peaceable home. Despised and pursued by Juno (the goddess of marriage), haunted by memories of his mother and his past, he dallies with Dido, visits the underworld, fights off Harpies, has a battle with a young Turnus, and consults a Sybil (the modern version—a psychiatrist). And his journey ends not in a new city but in the restoration of the old city, Olympus-like in its sportiveness and tranquillity—Jupiter's realm.

The story opens with the description of a near-disaster, and, throughout it, Cheever in a casual way points up symbolic details that will become correlatives for the story's theme. We meet Francis Weed high in an airplane amid such dense clouds that "nothing could be seen of the earth" (p. 325). The weather is heavy, and the man beside him sneaks a drink from a flask; Francis smiles at him, but the man looks away—"he wasn't sharing his pain killer with anyone" (p. 325). Suddenly the plane begins "to drop and flounder wildly"; the storm's violence "divided [Weed's] attention," and "inside, the shaded lights, the stuffiness, and the window curtains gave the cabin an atmosphere of intense and misplaced domesticity" (p. 325). We are told that "all but the children saw in their minds the spreading wings of the Angel of Death," while up front, incongruously, the pilot sings a nursery rhyme faintly: " 'I've got sixpence, jolly, jolly sixpence. I've got sixpence to last me all my life . . .' " (p. 325). The plane crashes in a cornfield, an emergency door is opened, "letting in the sweet noise of their continuing mortality—the idle splash and smell of a heavy rain," and passengers flee while "praying that the thread would hold" (p. 325).

Thus the story starts with a miraculous deliverance and a return to earth. The original Aeneas, after a similar deliverance, could console his companions with the words *Forsam et haec olim meminisse juvabit* ("Perhaps some day it will be a joy to remember these events"). Francis feels that way himself, but unfortunately there is no Dido immediately present who is willing to listen. He returns home on a "day in late September, as fragrant and shapely as an apple," and steps into his living room, which is spacious "and divided like Gaul into three parts" (p. 326). Barbarians who need taming—three of his four children—inhabit it. As he attempts to recount the marvels he has undergone, no one hears him, for "tonight the children are absorbed in their own antagonisms" (p. 327). His wife Julia is serene, oblivious, and above the fray, and summons them to dinner. "This simple announcement, like the war cries of the Scottish chieftains, only refreshes the ferocity of the combatants" (p. 327). Francis goes upstairs to tell his oldest daughter about his adventure, only to find her absorbed in a *True Romance* magazine; "she doesn't understand about the plane crash, because there wasn't a drop of rain in Shady Hill" (p. 328).

Dinner itself is a Trojan War, complete with hectoring; Francis tries valiantly to narrate his epic escape, but his wife interrupts with her own tale, one more appropriate to the Trojan women left behind: "She paints with lightning strokes the panorama of drudgery in which her youth, her beauty, and her wit have been lost. Francis says that he must be understood; he was nearly killed in an airplane crash, and he doesn't like to come home every night to a battlefield" (p. 328). Juno, the goddess of marriage, is a most capricious deity.

What follows involves a characteristic Cheever technique: contrasting a scene of conflict with a perception of a seemingly Arcadian landscape. Francis, driven from the battlefield, escapes to his garden to absorb the sights and sounds of tranquillity. As he enters the scene, knighthood seems in flower again, and the music is extremely romantic. Old Mr. Nixon shouts at the squirrels attacking his bird-feeder, " 'Varmints! Rascals! Avaunt and quit my sight!' " (p. 328). A neighbor plays the "Moonlight Sonata" out of tempo and with much *rubato*, "like an outpouring of tearful petulance, lonesomeness, and self-pity—of everything it was Beethoven's greatness not to know" (p. 329). Yet Francis realizes that the music rings out "like an appeal for love, for tenderness, aimed at some lovely housemaid . . ." (p. 329). These two observations reflect what will soon be Francis's own fate. So, too, does the arrival of a neighbor's pet retriever, Jupiter, carrying "the remains of a felt hat in his mouth" (p. 329). Francis calls " 'here, Jupiter, here, Jupiter,' " but this dog, endowed with the name of the supreme deity who is the originator of all change and the guardian of order (and the consoler of Venus in the *Aeneid*), prances off in another direction.

The evening after the plane crash the Weeds attend a neighbor's party, and Francis notices the new maid passing drinks and vaguely remembers her. "He had not developed his memory as a sentimental faculty. Wood smoke, lilac, and other such perfumes did not stir him, and his memory was something like his appendix—a vestigial repository" (p. 330). But after probing his memory, he locates her in an incident he witnessed during the war: she was a young girl, publicly chastised in a French village square, for living with a German during the Occupation. Ritualistically, a man shaved her hair and the crowd jeered as she undressed herself. "The jeering ended gradually, put down by the recognition of their common humanity. One woman spat on her, but some inviolable grandeur in her nakedness lasted through the ordeal" (p. 331). Before this moment, Francis was anxious, though unable, to tell his exotic tale of the plane crash; now, privy to another, he refuses to tell anyone. "And if he had told the story now, at the dinner table, it would have been a social as well as a human error. The people in the Farquarsons' living room seemed united in their tacit claim that there had been no past, no war—that there was no danger or trouble in the world" (p. 331).

Recollections of nakedness and survival then oddly affect him: "the encounter [with the scorned woman] left Francis feeling languid; it had opened his memory and his senses, and left them dilated" (p. 331). Dilation of the senses accompanies him home; on arriving he becomes smitten with the baby sitter, Anne Murchison. Cupid's errant arrow stings him at once, and he feels "a pang of recognition as strange, deep, and wonderful as anything in his life" (p. 331). He drives Anne home, and as he enters her street, "he seemed, in turning into it, to have come into the deepest part of some submerged memory" (p. 332). After he returns home, the girl's presence fills his mind, and his thoughts remind us of the imagery and sensations of the opening scene in the garden, for she fills "chamber after chamber with her light, her perfume, and the music of her voice" (p. 333). Francis' "vestigial repository" is stirred, and his memory-life weds with his imagination. He dreams that he is "crossing the Atlantic with her on the old *Mauretania* and, later, living with her in Paris" (p. 333). When he wakes from the dream, he gets up and smokes a cigarette at the open window. We then hear this remarkable passage, an entry into his imaginative life in its quest for serenity, adventure, ardor and beauty, sexual conquest, and repose:

> Getting back into bed, he cast around in his mind for something he desired to do that would injure no one, and he thought of skiing. Up through the dimness of his mind rose the image of a mountain deep in snow. It was late in the day. Wherever his eyes looked, he saw broad and heartening things. Over his shoulder, there was a snow-filled valley, rising into wooded hills where the trees dimmed the whiteness like a sparse coat of hair. . . . The light on the trails was blue, and it was harder than it had been a minute or two earlier to pick the turns, harder to judge—now that the snow was all deep blue—the crust, the ice, the bare spots, and the deep piles of dry powder. Down the mountain he swung, matching his speed against the contours of a slope that had been formed in the first ice age, seeking with ardor some simplicity of feeling and circumstance.   (p. 333)

The next morning Francis arrives at the station just as his train is pulling out, "and the longing he felt for the coaches as they drew stubbornly away from him reminded him of the humors of love" (p. 333). Not only is his memory-life resurrected, but all his ordinary sensations are dilated as well, since "the image of the girl seemed to put him into a relationship to the world that was mysterious and enthralling" (p. 333).

In the *Aeneid* Aeneas recognizes his mother, Venus, as she is *avertens*, turning to leave him; Francis spots her as she speeds by in an express train: "Then he saw an extraordinary thing; at one of the bedroom windows sat an unclothed woman of exceptional beauty, combing her golden hair. She passed like an apparition through Shady Hill, combing and combing her hair, and Francis followed her with his eyes until she was out of sight" (p. 334).

But this vision is immediately interrupted by a local Harpy, Mrs. Wrightson, and he insults her though vengeance will be hers later. As she limps away from him, his vision of Venus and his memory of the girl rejuvenate his spirits, and he "wanted to sport in the green woods, scratch where he itched, and drink from the same cup" (p. 335). Nonetheless, his free-spirited, satyr-like impulses are dampened by thoughts of a possible statutory rape charge, and he suddenly recalls another, less lucky figure in the epic of Troy: "On the letterhead of his firm there was a drawing of the Laocoön, and the figure of the priest and his sons in the coils of the snake appeared to him to have the deepest meaning" (p. 335). Then, walking down Fifth Avenue, he passes the statue of Atlas and thinks "of the strenuousness of containing his physicalness within the patterns he had chosen" (p. 335).

That evening he arrives home, discovers Anne in the hall, and smothers her with kisses. She struggles, but not for long, "because just then little Gertrude Flannery appeared from somewhere and said, 'Oh, Mr. Weed . . .' " (p. 335). Gertrude is one of Cheever's most wonderful minor character creations. She is an omnipresent spirit, symbolic of the ubiquitous vagaries of conscience and fidelity. In this *Aeneid* her role is an admixture of the Greek spy Sinon, the gods' messenger Iris, who can fly to the very ends of the earth and the underworld, and especially, as here, Mercury, who warned Aeneas that he should not dally with Dido.

> Gertrude was a stray. She had been born with a taste for exploration. . . . Garrulous, skinny, and unwashed, she drifted from house to house around the Blenhollow neighborhood, forming and breaking alliances based on an attachment to babies, animals, children her own age, adolescents, and sometimes adults. Opening your front door in the morning, you would find Gertrude sitting on your stoop. Going into the bathroom to shave, you would find Gertrude using the toilet. . . . She was helpful, pervasive, honest, hungry, and loyal. She never went home of her own choice. When the time to go arrived, she was indifferent to all its signs. "Go home, Gertrude," people could be heard saying in one house or another, night after night. "Go home, Gertrude. It's time for you to go home now, Gertrude." "You had better go home and get your supper, Gertrude." "I told you to go home twenty minutes

ago, Gertrude." "Your mother will be worrying about you, Gertrude."
"Go home, Gertrude, go home."   (p. 336)

The fun of the refrain is reinforced by the fact that "Go home, Gertrude,
go home" is precisely what the shaken Francis says as he gives her a
quarter and begs for her silence. As the days go by, "the abyss between
his fantasy and the practical world" yawns so wide that he begins writing
unrestrained love letters to Anne, using phrases like "heavenly bliss" and
"love nest" (p. 337).

One night Clayton Thomas, the young son of a friend, arrives at the
Weed's house for a short visit. Clayton is awkward, "tall and homely,"
with horn-rimmed glasses and a deep voice (p. 338). Offhandedly and
with smug self-regard, he mentions that he and Anne Murchison are
engaged to be married, that both have so much in common that " 'we
sent out the same Christmas card last year without planning it, and we
both have an allergy to tomatoes, and our eyebrows grow together in the
middle' " (p. 339). On hearing this revelation, Francis suffers a crash
more formidable and frightening than the one he survived. This time,
however, he is not totally speechless. After the young man leaves his
house, Francis tells his wife that "Clayton was lazy, irresponsible, affected,
and smelly" (p. 339). Days go by before he can work his revenge, but
then a friend calls up to request a job recommendation for Clayton.
Francis is disingenuous about his personal regrets, informing the caller
that Clayton is a "worthless" kid, a dangerous type, and, moreover, " 'I'd
feel obliged to warn people against him. He's a thief . . .' " (p. 343). In
the meantime he has also had a bitter fight with his wife, who castigated
him for having insulted Mrs. Wrightson at the train station.

Aeneas is no longer *pius*. Stricken by the wickedness of his deed,
Francis wonders, after reflecting on the recent odd chain of events, "how
he could have avoided arriving at just where he was" (p. 344). The winds
of Aeolus, at Juno's behest, have shipwrecked him here, between a rock
and a hard place. Distressed, he decides to consult with a Sybil, and so
must also enter the Underworld of the psychiatrist's office.

> The scene for his *miserere mei Deus* was, like the waiting room of so
> many doctors' offices, a crude token gesture toward the sweets of do-
> mestic bliss: a place arranged with antiques, coffee tables, potted plants,
> and etchings of snow-covered bridges and geese in flight, although
> there were no children, no marriage bed, no stove, even, in this trav-
> esty of a house . . . where the curtained windows looked straight onto
> a dark air shaft.   (p. 344)

When Francis gives his name to the secretary, a lurking policeman rushes
to arrest him, thinking he is the man who has been threatening the

doctor's life. But Rhadamanthys, judge of the Underworld, exonerates him, and he is allowed to enter the psychiatrist's den. The first words he blurts out are a funny and touching summary of his misshapen epic; with tears in his eyes, he says hoarsely, " 'I'm in love, Dr. Herzog' " (p. 345).

Cheever appends a coda to the story: a glimpse of Shady Hill a week or ten days later. We see—not so much Aeneas's new race and new nation, although something like it—but the Fields of the Blest in eternal suspension. Our tour is cinematic, beginning with close-ups and then edging out to offer us a cosmic view. Early images and characters return, as if to take their gracious bows, and yet we sense they are now immortals, liberated, at least momentarily, from the endless cycle of birth, love, and death. We hear: "The village hangs, morally and economically, from a thread; but it hangs by its thread in the evening light" (p. 345). A neighbor plays his version of the "Moonlight Sonata"; a housemaid is writing a letter to Arthur Godfrey; Francis Weed, now *homo faber*, is building a coffee table. His Sybil recommended this as therapy for survival, and he "finds some true consolation in the simple arithmetic involved and in the holy smell of new wood" (p. 345). Meanwhile, upstairs, his son, in the spirit of modern adventure, puts on his space suit with its magic cape, climbs onto his bed, and "spreads his arms and flies the short distance to the floor, landing with a thump" (p. 345)—and the gesture and the sound remind us of his father.

The camera then moves outdoors for a panoramic view. Repetition, romance, folly, pretense, and retrieval all characterize this pastoral Olympus where immortals sport and Jupiter reigns. Each detail builds toward the majestic final sentence, which functions like a freeze frame in cinema, reminding us of Hannibal crossing the Alps to avenge the memory of Dido:

> "Go home, Gertrude, go home," Mrs. Masterson says. "I told you to go home an hour ago, Gertrude. It's way past your suppertime, and your mother will be worried. Go home!" A door on the Babcocks' terrace flies open, and out comes Mrs. Babcock without any clothes on, pursued by a naked husband. . . . Over the terrace they go and in at the kitchen door, as passionate and handsome a nymph and satyr as you will find on any wall in Venice. Cutting the last of the roses in her garden, Julia hears old Mr. Nixon shouting at the squirrels in his bird-feeding station. "Rapscallions! Varmints! Avaunt and quit my sight!" A miserable cat wanders into the garden, sunk in physical and spiritual discomfort. Tied to its head is a small straw hat—a doll's hat—and it is securely buttoned into a doll's dress, from the skirts of which protrudes its long, hairy tail. As it walks, it shakes its feet, as if it had fallen into water.

"Here, pussy, pussy, pussy!" Julia calls.

"Here, pussy, here, poor pussy!" But the cat gives her a skeptical look and stumbles away in its skirts. The last to come is Jupiter. He prances through the tomato vines, holding in his generous mouth the remains of an evening slipper. Then it is dark; it is a night where kings in golden suits ride elephants over the mountains.   (pp. 345-346)

If "The Country Husband" is Cheever's *Aeneid*, "The Swimmer" is his *Odyssey*, a surrealistic epic, deftly shortened, of a man condemned to wandering and eager to return home. Along the way he enjoys the hospitality of Alcinous, visits the land of the Lotus-eaters, who live on the fruit of forgetfulness, outwits (or so he thinks) the one-eyed Cyclops, dallies with Calypso and Circe, and attempts passage between Scylla and Charybdis and thinks he survives; and when he arrives home he is not recognized.

Neddy Merrill's odyssey begins on a midsummer Sunday at the edge of a neighbor's pool. "In the west there was a massive stand of cumulus cloud so like a city seen from a distance—from the bow of an approaching ship—that it might have had a name" (p. 603). We learn that he "had slid down his banister that morning and given the bronze backside of Aphrodite on the hall table a smack" (p. 603). (Recall that Aphrodite was the champion of the Trojans and Odysseus was a wily Greek; this goddess does not suffer indignities gladly or without reprisal.) Neddy decides to tackle a heroic challenge: he will swim home, a trip of eight miles, by way of the archipelago of swimming pools owned by his friends, an Aegean sea with Ithaca his destination. Neddy "had a vague and modest idea of himself as a legendary figure," and "making his way home by an uncommon route gave him the feeling that he was a pilgrim, an explorer, a man with a destiny . . ." (pp. 603-604). He is, but chance can be malign and history indifferent, as his journey reveals. His summery feelings expand as he travels by water through the pools of the Grahams, the Hammers, the Lears, and the Howlands, and stops at the Bunkers for a drink. "Oh, how bonny and lush were the banks of the Lucinda River!" (p. 605). (He has named his epic waterway in honor of his wife, his Penelope.) He hears thunder in the distance but even the prospect of a storm elates him: "Why did he love storms . . . why did the first watery notes of a storm have for him the unmistakable sound of good news, cheer, glad tidings?" (p. 606).

But a subtle change in circumstance and in perception takes place while he waits out the storm in the Levy's gazebo: "The rain had cooled the air and he shivered. The force of the wind had stripped a maple of its red and yellow leaves and scattered them over the grass and the water. Since it was midsummer the tree must be blighted, and yet he felt a peculiar sadness at this sign of autumn" (p. 606). He then visits the Welchers, and he finds their pool dry. This upsets him, because it does not square with his interior map, and he tries to recall when and if the Welchers had gone away. "Was his memory failing or had he so disciplined it in the repression of unpleasant facts that he had damaged his sense of the truth?" (p. 607). This is the narrator's first explicitly ominous intrusion, arousing the reader's suspicions about the nature of this journey, a trip Neddy undertakes because of his imaginative and adventuresome spirit.

But he pushes on and tries to traverse the gap between Scylla and Charybdis—the deadly traffic on Route 424. Barefoot and almost naked, he is the subject of ridicule, and finds himself "unprepared" for this phase of his journey, despite once anticipating it. "Why, believing as he did, that all human obduracy was susceptible to common sense, was he unable to turn back?" (p. 607). He cannot recollect even the places and events of his morning, for "in the space of an hour, more or less, he had covered a distance that made his return impossible" (p. 607). He finally succeeds in crossing the highway divider and soon reaches the pool at the Recreation Center, an Odysseus in the Underworld, a place rank and foul, filled with harsh, shrill sounds. He remembers the clear, sapphire water of the Bunkers' pool with nostalgic longing, and he "thought that he might contaminate himself . . . by swimming in this murk, but he reminded himself that he was an explorer, a pilgrim, and that this was merely a stagnant bend in the Lucinda River" (p. 608).

He next visits the Hallorans, a couple naked like Nausicaa and her maidens on the shore, and he notices that their beech hedge is yellow. Mrs. Halloran addresses him "with an unseasonable melancholy," saying, " 'We've been terribly sorry to hear about all your misfortunes, Neddy' " (p. 609). He does not understand her remark, and as he puts on his trunks, he finds them loose and wonders "if, during the space of an afternoon, he could have lost some weight" (p. 609). He suddenly feels cold and tired, sees leaves falling, and smells wood smoke—unseasonable reactions and signs. When he stops in for a drink with the Sachses, Helen Sachs tells him there's nothing to drink in the house—and hasn't been since Eric's operation, three years ago. Disconcerted, Neddy goes on to the Biswangers' pool, where a party is in progress. The Biswangers are the Cyclopses of Bullet Park, social boors whom everyone patronizes; nonetheless, Neddy is desperate for a drink of revival and starts for their bar. But Grace Biswanger calls him a gate crasher, and even the bartender is rude to him.

He swims the length of their pool and moves on to the next one, which belongs to his former mistress, Shirley Adams. Neddy is convinced that his brief stay with Circe will be curative:

> Love—sexual roughhouse in fact—was the supreme elixir, the pain killer, the brightly colored pill that would put the spring back into his step, the joy of life in his heart. They had had an affair last week, last month, last year. He couldn't remember. . . . She was there, her hair the color of brass, but her figure, at the edge of the lighted, cerulean water, excited in him no profound memories.   (p. 611)

She spurns his advances, so he dives into her pool, but loses strength unexpectedly, and has to paddle to the ladder.

> Going out onto the dark lawn he smelled chrysanthemums or marigolds—some stubborn autumnal fragrance—on the night air, strong as gas. Looking overhead he saw that the stars had come out, but why should he seem to see Andromeda, Cepheus, and Cassiopeia? What had become of the constellations of midsummer? He began to cry.
>   (p. 611)

Even the stars, reliable guides for all voyagers, have betrayed him, and his emotional direction meets a detour. But one pool remains—the Gilmartins'. "Here, for the first time in his life, he did not dive but went down the steps into the icy water and swam a hobbled sidestroke . . . stopping again and again with his hand on the curb to rest" (p. 612). Neddy, now exhausted, has accomplished his goal, but he is so stupefied "that his triumph [seems] vague" as he walks toward his house. Once there, he finds it plunged into darkness, with its doors locked and the knobs rusted. "He shouted, pounded on the door, tried to force it with his shoulder, and then, looking in at the windows, saw that the place was empty" (p. 612).

The fact that "The Swimmer" is so cleverly constructed should not distract one from its other merits. Its structure is reminiscent of other literary successes: a dark version in miniature of James Joyce's *Ulysses*, of Tennyson's "Enoch Arden" and "Ulysses," or of those tales that concentrate in an imaginative instant the passing of a lifetime, like Ambrose Bierce's "An Occurence at Owl Creek Bridge" and William Golding's *Pincher Martin*. But, in addition, this story is a meditation on time, the discrepancy between "human" time, so subjective and yoked with the vagaries of memory, and "natural" time, so independent and objective and inevitable. Here, Neddy's progressive weariness is emblematic of his physical aging—of which he has been oblivious—as well as of the psychological fatigue brought about by denial and untruth. The extraordinary accuracy of realistic detail is lulling at first—Bullet Park with its snobbery and smugness is rendered with exactness; only gradually does the reader realize that this is a surrealistic fable, the record of a journey in a mind's life, at once as instantaneous and crowded as a dream. Elsewhere in his fiction Cheever employs these techniques, but nowhere except in "The Swimmer" does he concentrate them in such rigorous combination.

The Expatriate Stories

In "The Bella Lingua" the Cheever narrator defines for us the difference between a traveler and an expatriate:

> For the tourist, the whole experience of traveling through a strange country is on the verge of the past tense. Even as the days are spent, these *were* the days in Rome, and everything—the sightseeing, souvenirs, photographs, and presents—is commemorative. . . . But for the expatriate there is no past tense . . . and he lives in a continuous and unrelenting present. Instead of accumulating memories, the expatriate is offered the challenge of learning a language and understanding a people.   (p. 302)

Cheever's expatriate stories grew out of his experience of living in Italy for a year after completing *The Wapshot Chronicle*. These stories (there are approximately nine) contain many of the themes and shapes of his other stories, but the emphasis on a stranger's perspective, that of the ignorant outsider, comes to the fore. In his domestic stories he dramatizes the absurd cross-purposes possible in ordinary conversation; in these stories language itself is a mine field, potentially explosive, separating both enemy from friend and friend from friend. In Italy, furthermore, language is a vehicle for mystification:

> Arrangements in Rome are so complicated that lucidity and skepticism give way when we try to follow the description of a scene in court, a lease, a lunch, or anything else. Each fact or detail breeds more questions than it answers, and in the end we lose sight of the truth, as we were meant to do. Here comes Cardinal Micara with the True Finger of Doubting Thomas—that much is clear—but is the man beside us in church asleep or dead, and what are all the elephants doing in the Piazza Venezia?   (p. 204)

Questions, secrets, and incongruities characterize this group of stories. The last line of the opening paragraph of "The Duchess," with its appropriate song title, provides a fine summary: "We live in a world where the banks of even the most remote trout streams are beaten smooth by the boots of fishermen, and the music that drifts down from the medieval walls into the garden where we sit is an old recording of Vivienne Segal singing 'Bewitched, Bothered and Bewildered' . . ." (p. 347).

That said, it is regrettable to add that the majority of these stories are inferior products amid Cheever's rich harvest. Each contains some bright and glowing passages, but often the imaginative or emotional energy we associate with Cheever is absent. "The Golden Age," a story about a television writer considered a poet in Italy, is an account tilted toward a one-joke surprise. "Brimmer," a tale told by a priggish bore, is more vitally charged and ironic throughout, but it has a similar shape and tilt. "Montraldo" is a rambling, disjointed, and curiously unfresh series of diary-like entries of an American thief who has fled to Italy. "Clementina" is a straightforward narrative, written with a wry eye, about expatriation in reverse. Clementina is an Italian maid-servant hired by American expatriates in Italy; she returns to America with them and realizes that "in leaving one world and coming to another she had lost both" (p. 446). Her story provides Cheever with the opportunity to satirize, from the vantage point of a gentle soul, American customs or the lack thereof, and it closes with one of his most striking sentences—as he records one of Clementina's most private, native memories amidst the incongruous setting of a Baltimore racetrack:

> . . . although the race was beginning, she saw instead the white snow and the wolves of Nascosta, the pack coming up the Via Cavour and crossing the piazza as if they were bent on some errand of that darkness that she knew to lie at the heart of life, and, remembering the cold on her skin and the whiteness of the snow and the stealth of the wolves, she wondered why the good God has opened up so many choices and made life so strange and diverse.   (p. 451)

On reading these lesser expatriate tales, one senses that what Wilfred Sheed called Cheever's "mega-faculty," that inextricable union of memory and imagination, functioned best on native soil. Perhaps Italy already possessed such a "fabulous" dimension, a demonic/angelic ambivalence, a skein of skeletal traditions, that there was little he could personally invest in order to vitalize it dramatically. Certainly its language and Roman Catholic/residually pagan ambience tend to resist being captured even by the lyrical sonorities of the Book of Common Prayer and Solomon's Song of Songs—and these sonorities are his. Many writers (and even more visitors) have observed that Italy frustrates transformation, and this appears to have been Cheever's fate. Friends and acquaintances of his are unanimous in declaring that any experience he has undergone— if it is not incorporated into and transformed by his imagination—ceases to exist for him. Memory unadorned or never animated by the efforts of invention and embellishment is as dead as the past. A clue that he was well aware of this himself is found in the lengthy story "Boy in Rome," published in Esquire in February 1960. It is the story of a teen-aged American boy living in Rome who is nostalgic to return to the idyllic Nantucket island of his memory. He becomes involved in a complicated scheme to smuggle a painting into the States, but the scheme is aborted, and he remains stranded in Italy. The story is heavily plotted, a first-person narrative written in the meandrous style of a teen-ager. Just as the reader himself becomes a bit impatient at the mounting tedium and sentimentality, he is shocked by this interruption:

> (But I am not a boy in Rome but a grown man in the old prison and river town of Ossining, swatting hornets on this autumn afternoon with a rolled-up newspaper. . . . Why should I exchange this scene for the dark streets around the Pantheon? Why, never having received from my parents anything but affection and understanding, should I invent a grotesque old man, a foreign grave, and a foolish mother? . . . But my father taught me, while we hoed the beans, that I should complete for better or worse whatever I had begun and so we go back to the scene where he leaves the train in Naples.)   (p. 465)

Though a striking exception, this exasperated interlude is revealing. Fortunately, Cheever's inspiration does not flag so noticeably elsewhere in these stories. In fact, two of them, though slight, are fun. "The Bella Lingua" is a nonchalant, anecdotal narrative, tracing the befuddlement of several American expatriates in a series of vignettes that illustrate that misunderstanding and ignorance have deeper roots in the human soul than the mere distractions of cultural differences would lead us to think. Near the story's close, one character (thus far, relatively silent) makes explicit this tale's theme and one of Cheever's central subjects when she says,

> "Homesickness is nothing. . . . Fifty percent of the people in the world are homesick all the time. . . . When you're in one place and long to be in another, it isn't as simple as taking a boat. You don't really long for another country. You long for something in yourself that you don't have, or haven't been able to find."   (p. 317)

"The Duchess" is an updated fairy-tale, with an oddly nineteenth-century flavor, about a Roman noblewoman who, like Penelope, frustrates the attentions of a stream of round-heeled suitors of royal blood as she patiently awaits the moment to claim the stuffy commoner who is her heart's desire.

The one precious gem in this group of stories is "The World of Apples." If a critic were pressed to single out *the* representative story of Cheever's latter years, he would very likely choose this one. Its style is both simple and sonorous; its narrative line is linear, dramatic, and unadorned; and the tale's emotional power creeps up imperceptibly on the reader, building up as it does only on what is recorded objectively—details glimpsed in action, observation, dreams, and memories—a record whose music edges gently from monaural to stereo to multitrack and on into reverent silence. In addition, the story is a distillation of Cheever's familiar themes (the seeming polarity between flesh and spirit, memory and forgetting, the two faces of Nature), as well as personal manifesto, a private summing-up of a career bent on meeting the challenges of language as it valiantly approximates human truth. Like much of Cheever's work, it is also the record of a spiritual journey, a pilgrim's crisis both foolish and noble, where even detours mark an encounter with the mysterious, and where the destination arrived at seems more mysterious still.

The title "The World of Apples" is ambiguously Edenesque, a reminder of the pre-lapsarian, paradisaical world where such trees flourished without contamination, and also of the fruit plucked that undid us and issued in the wormier world of apples in which we live. The human heart dwells in both worlds of apples, and neither youth nor age nor honors nor disgrace can alter that—nor can a Romantic hope in the power of poetry.

The story's central character is Asa Bascomb, a Robert Frost-like poet and aged widower. We meet him alone, swatting flies, an eighty-two-year-old American living in Italy, muttering morosely that he has not won the Nobel Prize. Bascomb, we learn, "was known vaguely as the Cézanne of poets," but this association mistakenly arose "because the title of his most popular work was *The World of Apples*—poetry in which his admirers found the pungency, diversity, color, and nostalgia of the apples of the northern New England he had not seen for forty years" (p. 613).

Asa lives in a villa at the base of Monte Carbone (the charcoal mountain), and "he had in his garden many fountains, fed by the springs on the summit" (p. 614). Every morning he works, and every afternoon he climbs the precipitous stairs to the village up above. "The beauties of the place were various and gloomy. He would always be a stranger there, but his strangeness seemed to him to be some metaphor involving time as if, climbing the strange stairs past the strange walls, he climbed through hours, months, years, and decades" (p. 614). Though an expatriate, he is popular with the villagers, and two or three times a week "some pilgrims would find their way to the villa" and ask him to autograph their copies of *The World of Apples*.

The narrator intrudes a bit to inform us that Bascomb was long associated with four contemporary poets, each of whom came to a sad end. One shot himself, another drowned himself, the third hanged himself, and the last died of delirium tremens. Asa, however, well acquainted with suicidal temptations, takes vigorous precautions against them. "He had seen in Z—the closest of the four—some inalienable link between his prodigious imagination and his prodigious gifts for self-destruction, but Bascomb in his stubborn, countrified way was determined to break or ignore this link—to overthrow Marsyas and Orpheus" (p. 615). So far he has avoided the fate of Marsyas, the satyr who challenged Apollo in a poetry contest and literally lost his skin, and the fate of Orpheus, a poet capable of enchanting the Underworld itself but incapable of disciplining his passion for Eurydice enough to resist looking back, and so lost her forever. Instead Asa has chose another mode of looking back—that of memory—so that "his work seemed to be an act of recollection" (p. 615). In his poetic compositions, "it was definitely his memory that was called into play—his memory of sensation, landscapes, faces, and the immense vocabulary of his own language. . . . He did not seem to choose his words at all but to recall them from the billions of sounds that he had heard since he first understood speech" (p. 615).

Memory for him has thus become a precious instrument "to give his life usefulness" (p. 615), and lately he has grown worried about whether his memory is failing. To combat this possibility he taxes his memory to recall verb conjugations, the principals in the Crimean War, the lines of the great poets before him, and the routes through cities. Lord Byron's first name eludes him in maddening fashion, but he excuses this lapse and seems content.

One day in spring he and an admirer visit Monte Felici (the happy mount), where "all that remained of the abandoned town on the summit were two churches or cathedrals of uncommon splendor" (p. 616).

> Bascomb loved these. They stood in fields of flowering weeds, their wall paintings still brilliant, their facades decorated with griffins, swans, and lions with the faces and parts of men and women, skewered dragons, winged serpents, and other marvels of metamorphoses. These vast and fanciful houses of God reminded Bascomb of the boundlessness of the human imagination and he felt lighthearted and enthusiastic. (pp. 616-617)

Asa's expatriate heart is thus stirred by the wedding of opposites that Italy declares: the Christian and the pagan, the spiritual and the sensual, the past revered as a relic and yet ornamented with heathen beastly shapes.

But another "marvel of metamorphosis" soon takes place within him. Shortly thereafter he enters the woods to relieve himself and stumbles upon a couple making love; their image so haunts him that the "struggling couple seemed to have dimmed his memories of the cathedrals" (p. 617). Back at his villa some nuns arrive in quest of his autograph.

> They paid him the usual compliments—he had created a universe that seemed to welcome man; he had divined the voice of moral beauty in a rain wind—but all that he could think of was the stranger's back.

It seemed to have more zeal and meaning than his celebrated search for truth. It seemed to dominate all that he had seen that day—the castles, clouds, cathedrals, mountains, and fields of flowers. When the nuns left he looked up to the mountains to raise his spirits but the mountains looked then like the breasts of women. His mind had become unclean.　　　　　　　　　　　　　　　　　　　　(p. 617)

At night he is visited by obscene dreams and on awakening is assaulted by venereal images. "The welcoming universe, the rain wind that sounded through the world of apples had vanished. Filth was his destiny, his best self, and he began with relish a long ballad called The Fart That Saved Athens" (p. 617). His memory-life is now narrowed, and, despite interruptions by admiring pilgrims seeking his autograph, he spends the next several days composing pornographic pieces, beginning with parodies of the great pagan classics and descending gradually to those imitative of the most base and common kind. On the second day of this debauch he leaves his study only to be confronted by fourteen university students, who chant, like exorcists, "The Orchards of Heaven"—the opening sonnet of *The World of Apples*—but to no avail, for the blue sky now seems empty of meaning. "While he tackled his indecent projects with ardor he finished them with boredom and shame. The pornographer's course seems inflexible and he found himself repeating that tedious body of work that is circulated by the immature and the obsessed" (p. 618).

True to Cheever's usual comic structure, our perplexed hero flees from his crisis by traveling to Rome, only to confront, unexpectedly, counterparts of himself. Entering a public toilet he "found himself face to face with a male whore, displaying his wares" (p. 618). Bascomb's interpretive reaction is itself metamorphic: "The man's face was idiotic—doped, drugged, and ugly—and yet, standing in his unsavory orisons, he seemed to old Bascomb angelic, armed with a flaming sword that might conquer banality and smash the glass of custom" (p. 618). He then visits an art gallery where the painter or photographer "seemed to be suffering from the same infection as [he was], only in a more acute form" (p. 618). His imaginative world suddenly transformed, he wonders "if there was a universality to this venereal dusk that had settled over his spirit. Had the world, as well as he, lost its way?" (p. 618). He enters a concert hall to cleanse his impressions, and yet while the soprano sings *Die Liebhaber der Brücken*, he "began the disgusting and unfortunate habit of imagining that he was disrobing her" (p. 619). Even Art, so splendid in its objectivity and rooted—as it is claimed—in disinterest, provides no respite for him.

Disconsolate, Bascomb returns home and takes from his bookcase the great ribald Latin classics of the pre-Christian era by Petronius and Juvenal, pacesetters for his new-found craft, exemplars of a tradition and, possibly, inspirations. When he reads them, his reaction moves first from envy of their unfettered, pre-Christian world to reflections on an apocalyptic, angelic crown that he oddly desires, and then on to a curious connection of the two seemingly opposed world views; all the while he recalls images from his memory-life about the central, though mixed, realities that continue to engage his heart. The passage is one of Cheever's finest in its probing of psychological truth, and illustrates well Auden's remark that "no artist . . . can feel comfortable as a Christian; every artist who happens also to be a Christian wishes he could be a polytheist."[16]

Here were candid and innocent accounts of sexual merriment. There was nowhere that sense of wickedness he experienced when he burned his work in the stove each afternoon. Was it simply that his world was that much older, its social responsibilities that much more grueling, and that lewdness was the only answer to an increase of anxiety? What was it that he had lost? It seemed then to be a sense of pride, an aureole of lightness and valor, a kind of crown. He seemed to hold the crown up to scrutiny and what did he find? Was it merely some ancient fear of Daddy's razor strap and Mummy's scowl, some childish subservience to the bullying world? . . . He seemed to hold the crown, hold it up into the light; it seemed made of light and what it seemed to mean was the genuine and tonic taste of exaltation and grief. The limericks he had just completed were innocent, factual, and merry. They were also obscene, but when had the facts of life become obscene and what were the realities of this virtue he so painfully stripped from himself each morning? They seemed to be the realities of anxiety and love: Amelia standing in the diagonal beam of light, the stormy night his son was born, the day his daughter married. One could disparage them as homely but they were the best he knew of life—anxiety and love—and worlds away from the limerick on his desk. . . .   (pp. 619-620)

The questions posed are those neither Freud nor Puritanism has answered satisfactorily. Asa's renewal occurs through neither of these avenues but through a more mysterious kind of retrieval—the evoking of memories of his wife and children at random moments. The mysteries of love and anxiety are not solved but merely demonstrated there, and yet the story's first turning point has been reached.

The second turning point occurs immediately after. Asa's cook tells him of the sacred angel of Monte Giordano (the Mountain of the River Jordan) that can " 'cleanse the thoughts of a man's heart' " because it is " 'made of olivewood from the Mount of Olives, and was carved by one of the saints himself' " (p. 620). Asa resolves to make a pilgrimage to Monte Giordano and "for some reason [carries] a seashell." His choice is

16. W. H. Auden, *The Dyer's Hand* (New York: Vintage, 1968), p. 456.

significant, for a seashell, because of its resemblance to the genital organs of a woman, is a traditional symbol of the magical powers of fecundity, birth, and regeneration. In pagan literature, Aphrodite, the goddess of love, is born from a marine conch; in Christianity, scallop shells symbolized the hoped-for Resurrection in Roman funeral rites.[17] Bascomb also carries his Lermontov medal, a gift to him from the Russians, intending it as a gift to the sacred angel—a link between the modern and the ancient world.

Formerly the goal for other pilgrims, Bascomb now sets out as a pilgrim himself. On the way he stretches out on the grass and falls asleep, and dreams a homeland dream of mixed memories: an old truck with four flat tires standing in a field of buttercups; a child with a paper crown and a bath towel for a mantle hurrying round the corner of a white house; an old man feeding a bone to a stray dog; "autumn leaves [smoldering] in a bathtub with lion's feet" (p. 621). Thunder wakes him and he walks on, joined by a dog who, unaccountably, is afraid of thunder. But Bascomb, because he is a man and so endowed with memory of thunder and its benign effects, is elated. "Then the wind picked up the branches of the trees and he lifted his old nose to smell the rain, minutes before it fell. It was the smell of damp country churches, the spare rooms of old houses, earth closets, bathing suits put out to dry—so keen an odor of joy that he sniffed noisily" (p. 621).

Bascomb seeks shelter from the rain, and once again, as a traveler, he meets a counterpart, here a vision of his more serene self. An old man invites him into his lean-to. Bascomb finds him "enviably untroubled"; he is convinced that the man "would never be forced to make a pilgrimage with a seashell in his pocket," and that, unlike the poet Yeats, "he did not ask his soul to clap hands and sing, and yet he seemed to have reached an organic peace of mind that Bascomb coveted" (p. 621). When the storm is over, the poet thanks his protector and leaves; on his way again he walks, "like all the rest of us, in some memory of prowess—love or football, Amelia, or a good dropkick" (p. 621).

Finally arriving at the church of the sacred angel at dusk, Bascomb finds it locked. He seeks out the priest and finds him "in a vineyard, burning prunings" (p. 622), as in the parable of the darnels in Matthew 13. Bascomb explains that he wishes to donate a gift to the angel and shows the priest the gold medal. A comic exchange follows, for the priest not only suspects that the medal's gold is false but notices the lettering in Russian, and so judges it communist-tainted and unsuitable. But "at

17. Mircea Eliade, *Images and Symbols* (New York: Sheed & Ward, 1969 ed.), pp. 125-150.

that moment the clouds parted and a single ray of light came into the vineyard, lighting the medal. It was a sign. The priest drew a cross in the air and they started back to the church" (p. 622).

Earlier, in the opening of the chapter on Style, I quoted the funny and touching descriptive paragraph that follows. In the story's context, it takes on an affecting verve and warmth and unites dramatically each of Bascomb's passions: for poetry and literature, for the sacred relics of human life, for illumination, deliverance, and benediction:

> It was an old, small, poor country church. The angel was in a chapel on the left, which the priest lighted. The image, buried in jewelry, stood in an iron cage with a padlocked door. The priest opened this and Bascomb placed his Lermontov medal at the angel's feet. Then he got to his knees and said loudly: "God bless Walt Whitman. God bless Hart Crane. God bless Dylan Thomas. God bless William Faulkner, Scott Fitzgerald, and especially Ernest Hemingway." The priest locked up the sacred relic and they left the church together. There was a café on the square where he got some supper and rented a bed. This was a strange engine of brass with brass angels at the four corners, but they seemed to possess some brassy blessedness since he dreamed of peace and woke in the middle of the night finding in himself that radiance he had known when he was younger. Something seemed to shine in his mind and limbs and lights and vitals and he fell asleep again and slept until morning.   (p. 622)

The images are those of apocalyptic deliverance: a redemptive gift, angels at four corners, dreams of peace, an awakening into youthful renewal, followed by the perception of light and the sleep of the just. After this climax, a coda is appended to the story—Cheever's technique for thematic amplification—that recounts the events of the following day.

Bascomb begins his pilgrimage home, and his journey opens with another apocalyptic sensation, for he hears "the trumpeting of a waterfall" (p. 622). In an attempt to find its source, he recovers his roots. On entering the woods (recall a similar, upsetting entry earlier), he discovers that it is a "natural fall," and "it reminded him of a fall at the edge of the farm in Vermont where he had been raised" (p. 622), the setting of inspiration for The World of Apples. He recalls that, as a young boy, he had visited it on a Sunday afternoon and had watched "an old man unlace his shoes and undress himself with the haste of a lover" (p. 622). After wetting his hands and arms and shoulders, the old man "had stepped into the torrent, bellowing with joy" (p. 622). Only after he had dried himself, dressed, and left, did Bascomb realize that the man was his father.

This memory of a joyful bath bestirs him, now an old man himself, to imitate his father. Although "knowing that a mossy stone or the force of the water could be the end of him he stepped naked into the torrent, bellowing like his father. He could stand the cold for only a minute but when he stepped away from the water he seemed at last to be himself" (p. 623).

Like so many Cheever stories, this one ends with a symbolic baptism and epiphany, while the setting suggests the situation of a fall and a cleansing inexorably linked, as they inevitably are in the world of apples. Furthermore, Bascomb's immersion is a symbolic action leading to re-creation in its varied, multiple senses: a recovery of the deepest roots of ancestral memory—the source of his "poetry"—and a restoration of his spiritual self through fleshly and naked surrender to the natural world, a world that he had transformed and that now is transforming him. As Proverbs 25:25 puts it, "As cold water to the thirsty soul, so is good news from a far country."

Ironically, Bascomb has put off, in Saint Paul's sense, the old man in spirit, and so a pilgrimage ends, fittingly, where it started. His story closes with a sentence that is an appropriate summary of Cheever's own career in his later years: "His return to Monte Carbone was triumphant and in the morning light he began a long poem on the inalienable dignity of light and air that, while it would not get him the Nobel Prize, would grace the last months of his life" (p. 623).

There's been too much criticism of the middle class way of life. Life can be as good and rich there as anyplace else. I am not out to be a social critic . . . nor a defender of suburbia. It goes without saying that the people in my stories and the things that happen to them could take place anywhere.

John Cheever

When a writer calls his work a romance, he wishes to claim a certain latitude, both as to its fashion and material, which he would not have felt himself entitled to assume had he professed to be writing a novel.

Nathaniel Hawthorne

It requires moral courage to grieve; it requires religious courage to rejoice.

Sören Kierkegaard

Mostly, we authors must repeat ourselves—that's the truth. We have two or three great moving experiences in our lives— experiences so great and moving that it doesn't seem at the time that anyone else has been caught up and pounded and dazzled and astonished and beaten and broken and rescued and illuminated and rewarded and humbled in just that way ever before.

F. Scott Fitzgerald

If I am overflowing with life, am rich in experience for which I lack expression, then nature will be my language full of poetry—all nature will be fable, and every natural phenomenon be a myth.

Henry David Thoreau

9: Oh What a Paradise It Seems

When John Cheever's latest novel, *Oh What a Paradise It Seems*, appeared in March 1982, it was the subject of universal critical praise. Gone were the usual reviewer's misgivings about digressiveness, the narrator's quirkiness, structural incoherence, and the like that marked Cheever criticism in the past. Nor were there any complaints about its brevity of one hundred pages; instead, reviewers to a person marveled at how much Cheever accomplished in a small space, at his ability to make a short piece of fiction feel like a big one.

Critical unanimity fragmented only on the question of what to label the work. Robert M. Adams chose the category *nouvelle*, citing Henry James: "It would almost seem that the old master had Mr. Cheever in his mind's eye when he wrote of 'the only compactness that has a charm, the only spareness that has a force, the only simplicity that has a grace—those, in each order, that produce a *rich* effect.' "[1] Adams noted the inadequacy of the category and went on to call the book a "poetic narrative," hinting "at a parable without ever taking on the symmetry of one," touching "on melodrama, but glancingly," at times possessing "the frame of an idyll." John Updike offered the opinion that the book "is too darting, too gaudy in its deployment of artifice and aside, too disarmingly personal in its voice, to be saddled with the label of novel or novella; it is a parable and a tall tale—both subgenres squarely within the Judaeo-Christian tradition, North American branch."[2] Like Updike, most reviewers favored "parable" with a dash of difference; Cheever himself called it "an ecological romance," and perhaps that expresses its mixture of qualities best. In romance the basic plot structure is one of quest and adventure, undertaken by a single knight; a heroine appears, and the two engage in a courtly version of love; challenges with monsters, dragons, and such are met; marvelous and supernatural intrusions occur that are

---

1. Robert M. Adams, "Chance Taker," *New York Review of Books*, April 29, 1982, p. 8.
2. John Updike, "On Such a Beautiful Green Little Planet," *New Yorker*, April 5, 1982, p. 189.

not deemed astonishing; while throughout the chivalric ideals of valor, sacrifice, mercy, honor, and duty characterize its spirit and perspective.

The story of *Oh What a Paradise It Seems* is extremely short by usual supermarket standards, and its plot is quite simple. The main character is not so much a character as it is, like so many of Cheever's creations, a place animated by bright and fallen spirits: Beasley's Pond. The pond is the centerpiece of emotional concern, and, like Camelot or Charlemagne's France, it becomes the occasion for a host of excursions and digressions that inch us into a comically fabulous romance. First we meet Lemuel Sears, a man "old enough to remember when the horizons of his country were dominated by the beautiful and lachrymose wine-glass elm tree and when most of the bathtubs one stepped into had lions' claws."[3] Sears, who lives in New York City, decides one Sunday in January to go skating. He arranges to visit his oldest daughter in her suburban town of Janice, and then goes off to Beasley's Pond nearby to skate—an experience that delights him. But when he returns weeks later he is appalled to find that this pond where both mobility and permanence are celebrated has been rezoned as a dump site in preparation for a war memorial. He hires a lawyer to investigate the project, and when the lawyer is ominously killed, he seeks out an environmentalist named Horace Chisholm to pursue the matter.

Gradually we readers learn, as Sears and others do, that the town's politicians, in cahoots with organized crime, have decided to use the pond as a dump for financial gain. The subsequent story recounts all the serious and eccentric efforts of a mixed cast of characters to save Beasley's Pond. Besides Sears and Chisholm, these people include a housewife, Betsy Logan, who poisons the teriyaki sauce in a supermarket to convince authorities to stop poisoning Beasley's Pond. Her near-lethal act succeeds, and the story ends happily with the restoration of the pond.

A second strand of events, signifying Sears's pursuit of another kind of restoration, proceeds in tandem with the central plot. He falls desperately in love with Renée Herndon, a real-estate agent, a character as appealing as she is capricious. Although a woman of pronounced sensuality, she spends several evenings a week at abstinence meetings held in various basements. Neither Sears nor we ever discover the precise purpose of these meetings, whether they are organized for the conquest of weight, alcohol, or tobacco; they remain as mysterious as the woman herself is. When Renée leaves him, Sears undergoes the "Balkans of the spirit" (p. 43) and briefly takes up with a male elevator operator; ashamed

---

3. John Cheever, *Oh What a Paradise It Seems* (New York: Knopf, 1982), p. 5. Hereafter references to the novel will be included in the text.

and confused, he consults with a psychiatrist, who tells him he is a hopeless neurotic, having "invented some ghostly surrogate of a lost school friend or a male relation from your early youth" (p. 60). Finding himself at an emotional dead end, Sears devotes all his energies to the recovery of Beasley's Pond, so that when its story ends happily, his does as well.

A plot summary, however, tends to conceal the many other rich dimensions of the novel. Foremost among these is the spiritual, religious dimension. As Joshua Gilder pointed out in a fine essay, "If in fact [Cheever's characters] sometimes appear to be teetering on the edge of a spiritual abyss, this, to Cheever, is the universal human condition. The author shares an identity with his characters, not in an autobiographical sense, but in a Christian one."[4] The title of Gilder's essay was appropriate: "John Cheever's Affirmation of Faith." In her review Ann Hulbert concurred:

> The religious outlines of Cheever's moral world stand out clearly now, bounding the suburban lawns and homesick heroes of the fiction he has been writing for four decades. As the title of his last volume of selected stories, The World of Apples (1974), suggests, Cheever's short fiction has portrayed a fallen world, where man's body daily betrays his spirit. In his last novel, Falconer (1977), he followed a man accused of fratricide into the hell of prison. Now Cheever is in pursuit of paradise.[5]

John Leonard also agreed but expressed the idea differently: "[Cheever] mobilizes language in the service of decencies and intuitions that are no longer sanctioned on any altar or practiced in any politics. His stories are brilliant prayers on behalf of 'the perfumes of life: seawater, the smoke of burning hemlock, and the breasts of women.' "[6] John Updike stressed this effort at spiritual evocation in the light of America's nineteenth-century literary tradition:

> Ever more boldly the celebrant of the grand poetry of life, Cheever, once a taut and mordant chronicler of urban and suburban disappointments, now speaks in the granular, cranky, impulsive, confessional style of our native wise men and exhorters since Emerson. The pitch of his final page is positively transcendental. . . . Cheever's instinctive belief in the purity and glory of Creation brings with it an inevitable sensitivity to corruption; like Hawthorne, he is the poet of the poisoned. . . . Nature stamps Man at every moment, and litters our lives

4. Joshua Gilder, "John Cheever's Affirmation of Faith," Saturday Review, March 1982, p. 18.

5. Ann Hulbert, "Lonely Nomads," New Republic, March 31, 1982, p. 42.

6. John Leonard, "Cheever Country," New York Times Book Review, March 7, 1982, p. 26.

with clues to the supernatural. . . . Were Cheever, cosmopolitan as
he has become, less a New Englander than he is, with the breath of
Thoreau and Emily Dickinson in his own lovely quick light phrasing,
he might fail to convince us that a real glory shines through his transparent inventions.[7]

Yet he does. Each of these reviewers in differing ways recognizes that
salvage and salvation are at the heart of this story. A convinced believer
in the slippages and slides of human errancy (original sin), Cheever is
even more resolute about the first article of the Creed, "I believe in God
the Father Almighty, Maker of heaven and earth." (The Creed opens the
Anglican morning service, and Cheever admitted that he usually shouted
these particular words rather loudly.) These two truths—the Maker and
His makings along with man's making and unmakings—are the recurring
themes of his work. Cheever knows well that we live in a world that
seldom admits to such basic beliefs. Denial of the one would lead us to
pretend that our inherited world is ugly, but *we* are potentially beautiful
if only . . . and suddenly our if's multiply, for they depend on our dis-
connecting all our human linkages with parentage, the race, our own
personal history, severing our ties with all the mysterious elements that
make us who we are. The other denial of makings, that of Creation itself,
is more subtle and even more egoistic, perhaps, because if we do not care
whether something like Beasley's Pond, a mountain, a tree, or a garden
in all its awesome objectivity should *last* without us, then we grow blind
to the grander mystery of all created life itself, expressed so simply in the
Creed.

This is the basic dramatic conflict throughout the story, and varied
efforts to save Beasley's Pond also function as a metaphor for something
more elusive still—the quest for spiritual salvation, achieved only by
embracing the world and what transcends it. In an interview Cheever
remarked of the character Sears: "I think if he wishes to discover any
purity in himself, he's not going to find it in himself; he's going to find
it in some larger sphere—of which he, of course, is a part."[8] Thus, in
this story, as in most of Cheever's fiction, every gesture, every sensation—
even puzzlement—can be emblematic of a spiritual discovery: "A trout
stream in a forest, a traverse of potable water, seemed for Sears to be the
bridge that spans the mysterious abyss between our spiritual and our carnal
selves" (p. 85).

Cheever's use of language throughout the story supports these themes,
for it is so often psalm-like in its confession of perplexity and weakness,

7. Updike, "On Such a Beautiful Green Little Planet," pp. 192-193.
8. John Cheever in Gilder, "John Cheever's Affirmation of Faith," p. 18.

by turns worshipful and irritated, suppliant and celebratory. As John Leonard observed accurately, "He isn't just waiting for grace; he seeks to invoke it. . . ."[9] He went on to add, "The heart is a compass; there is inside our mess of memory and desire a moral pole toward which the knowing needle swings and points."

All of this might suggest the somber or the excessively sober. But not so. To my mind no other current writer enjoys simultaneously such a vivid sense of transcendence and an equally vivid sense of humor, or glides so easily from the sublime to the ridiculous and back. This story is composed of eleven brief chapters, but it is so enriched with memorable incidents— some hilarious, others melancholy—that, on finishing it, a reader recalls a novel that *must* have been three times its length. The reason is that no incident stands by itself; it is always allied with random memories, austere or oddball reflections, and overheard drama, while throughout the story everyone is like Beasley's Pond itself: both fragile and worthy of redemption.

A READING

The title, *Oh What a Paradise It Seems*, challenges us to remember the twin paradises, the one lost and the other sought, the one revealed to us in memory and nostalgia and the other in aspiration and hope. Who else but Cheever would be bold enough to offer such a title and then sly enough to add "seems," eliciting our imaginative complicity? The word "seems" is the story's central linguistic motif, repeated with variations on almost every page. The word is multi-suggestive, and Cheever exploits each of its connotations expertly. "Seems" might imply the discrepancy between appearance and reality, between illusion and fact, between aspiration and frustration. Then again, it can suggest a more positive discrepancy: that between the superficial and the genuine, between the outer and the inner, between an aspect or glimmer and the truth itself. Its usage deliberately frustrates any exact designation—which is precisely Cheever's intent.

Earlier I noted Cheever's flexible use of "as if" throughout his fiction. In this novel "seemed" replaces "as if" but functions in similar fashion. The word is employed to stimulate the reader's imagination and elicit a fellow feeling with the imaginative efforts of the characters and the narrator. Far from being a murky or frail word in the context, it is an invitation to share impressions and insights. Cheever also employs other variants, such as "guessed," "imagined," "might," and "would," especially in describing spiritual sensations. As in the past, all of these variants on

9. Leonard, "Cheever Country," p. 26.

the word "seems" provide the sinews of his fiction and account for its remarkable ambiguity. To be precious, one might say that the extremes of human truth—issuing in smiles or sadness—arrive at the "seams" of Cheever's work; more properly, they conjoin at the "seems" where all loving connections, like jokes and compassion, meet.

Allied with this device is the striking absence of specification in the novel. The time period of the plot action is indefinite, accentuated by the narrator's refrain, "At the time of which I am writing. . . ." The location of Beasley's Pond is never clarified, though it is the central subject, nor is the country in Eastern Europe that Sears recalls. This nonspecification extends to subordinate characters like Renée and Eduardo, the elevator operator. As Robert M. Adams noted, "There's an enormous, charming, unreliable vacancy in and around [them]," a casualness of entrance and exit by these characters so that a speedy reader skating blithely on the surface might miss the thinness of the ice that supports him. Adams then develops this important point:

> The tendency of the solid surfaces to tail off into vagueness counterpoints the way people in the story change their minds abruptly and without explanation, the way crucial developments are determined by coincidence. . . .
>
> That's what you call spacing it, and it's spaced out still further by the narrator's occasional erratic interventions, leisurely and free-floating. The sense of psychic distance, inconsequence, open possibility is enhanced by the vaudeville of Cheever's style, his skill at seeming to tell a simple unpretentious story absolutely straight, while introducing patterns of sidestep and evasion. Seeming is the theme of the book, apparent giving and real taking away.[10]

These shifts are evident from the novel's opening page. The opening (and closing) line reminds us of a fairy tale, set within an idyllic nineteenth-century village, where, Camelot-like, nothing is extreme about the weather or the circumstance, a most congenial spot for happy-ever-aftering.

> This is a story to be read in bed in an old house on a rainy night. The dogs are asleep and the saddle horses—Dombey and Trey—can be heard in their stalls across the dirt road beyond the orchard. The rain is gentle and needed but not needed with any desperation. The water tables are equitable, the nearby river is plentiful, the gardens and orchards—it is at a turning of the season—are irrigated ideally. Almost all the lights are out in the little village by the waterfall where the mill, so many years ago, used to produce gingham. (p. 3)

10. Adams, "Chance Taker," p. 8.

The narrative voice is beguiling, companionable yet formal, as balanced and decorous as that of a tour guide. We are assured, "You might think of it as a sleepy village, out of touch with a changing world, but in the weekly newspaper Unidentified Flying Objects are reported with great frequency. . . . They have been seen by substantial members of the population, such as the vice-president of the bank and the wife of the chief of police" (p. 3).

An ominous—perhaps even satiric?—note has been struck, but the narrator appears oblivious as he continues his tour. He points out the many village dogs, all mongrels, and observes, with seeming pride,

> These mixtures of blood—this newness of blood, you might say—had made them a highly spirited pack, and they hurried through the empty streets, late it seemed for some important meal, assignation or meeting, quite unfamiliar with the loneliness from which some of the population seemed to suffer. The town was named Janice after the mill owner's first wife.   (p. 4)

Deftly, in fewer than thirty-five lines, Cheever has established the polite, meandrous, vaguely apologetic (though not obtuse) tone of our narrator, a man of chatty propriety, fond of history but not its captive. More subtly, he has introduced in a casual way his story's major themes and images: rain and water, the concepts of need and plenty, of equitableness and the ideal, the images of light and "a turning of the season" and of objects beyond space witnessed to. The dogs, too, are representative of their owners: new blood, late for urgent business, though unacquainted with human loneliness—or so "it seemed."

Finally, we arrive at Beasley's Pond, "shaped like a bent arm, with heavily forested shores" (p. 4). Then we are told, with a sly foreshadowing,

> Here were water and greenery, and if one were a nineteenth-century painter one would put into the foreground a lovely woman on a mule, bent a little over the child she held and accompanied by a man with a staff. This would enable the artist to label the painting "Flight into Egypt," although all he had meant to commemorate was his bewildering pleasure in a fine landscape on a summer's day.   (pp. 4-5)

Our tour takes place in summer, but the story proper begins in winter with a quote from William Butler Yeats's "Sailing to Byzantium": "An aged man is but a paltry thing, a tattered coat upon a stick, unless . . ." (p. 5). In the poem Yeats desired to be a golden bird set upon a golden bough; here Lemuel Sears, "an old man but not yet infirm" (p. 5), is instead exhilarated by the sight of a cardinal on East 78th Street in New York City, and decides to go skating. He calls his daughter in Janice to make arrangements; father and daughter enjoy "a highly practical relationship, characterized principally by skepticism" (p. 5).

While Sears skates, skepticism and its manifold opposites are re-introduced. He happily remembers an English paleontologist who claimed that the skate was the instrument whereby *Homo sapiens* outstripped Neanderthal man "in the contest for supremacy" (p. 7). Yet despite the fact that this thesis "was all a fabrication" and later exposed, "Sears found the poetry of his ideas abiding because the fleetness he felt on skates seemed to have the depth of an ancient experience" (p. 7). A young girl, one of the few others skating, expresses her delight, saying, " 'Isn't it heavenly? I love it, I like it, I like it, I love it,' " evoking erotic memories within Sears of a girl he can bearly remember:

> The pleasure of fleetness seemed, as she had said, divine. Swinging down a long stretch of black ice gave Sears a sense of homecoming. At long last, at the end of a cold, long journey, he was returning to a place where his name was known and loved and lamps burned in the rooms and fires in the hearth. It seemed to Sears that all the skaters moved over the ice with the happy conviction that they were on their way home. Home might be an empty room and an empty bed to many of them, including Sears, but swinging over the black ice convinced Sears that he was on his way home. Someone more skeptical might point out that this illuminated how ephemeral is our illusion of homecoming. (pp. 7-8)

This passage is characteristic of Cheever and especially characteristic of this novel. The accent on "seemed," on the discrepancy between "sensible" skepticism and comforting illusion, undercuts any obvious irony. In its place we are induced to contemplate the mysterious adventure of homecoming, of arrival and returns to clean, well-lighted places of welcome, those imaginable regions the heart seeks but where all easy ironies evaporate. The following week Sears returns to the pond to skate; more people are there than previously, and the non-skeptical tone is reinforced through the emphasis on up and down, a communal falling and recovery: ". . . most of the population, like Sears, simply went up and down, up and down, completely absorbed in the illusion that fleetness and grace were in their possession and had only to be revealed. Sears fell once or twice but then so did almost everyone else" (p. 8). Expectancy, hope, and renewal accelerate as shadows arrive. Sears notices that the "voices, considering the imminence of night, had an extraordinary lightness," and that "he and his companions on the ice seemed to enjoy that extraordinary preoccupation with innocence that absorbs people on a beach before the fall of darkness"(pp. 8-9).

But the vibrant words "extraordinary," "absorption," "grace," and "lightness" are upended by what follows. When Sears returns weeks later he discovers that the pond is being used as a dump, and he sees "the shell of a ten-year-old automobile and a little closer to him a dead dog."

> Here was the discharge of a society that was inclined to nomadism without having lessened its passion for portables. Most wandering people evolve a culture of tents and saddles and migratory herds, but here was a wandering people with a passion for gigantic bedsteads and massive refrigerators. It was a clash between their mobility—their driftingness—and their love of permanence that had discharged its chaos into Beasley's Pond.   (p. 9)

Abruptly, nomadism has replaced homecoming, and chaos has supplanted innocence and peace. Sears is especially disturbed because so many of the items now dumped were once gifts, tokens of affection meant to celebrate erotic mysteries. "To see these souvenirs of our early loves spread-eagled, rusted and upended by the force with which they were cast off can be a profoundly melancholy experience" (p. 9).

Alert readers will note this offhand reflection actually signals the transition to the second chapter, in which Sears takes up with a real-estate agent named Renée Herndon. Immediately, the sight of "these souvenirs of our early loves" is contrasted with the "infinitely greater" memory capacity of the mechanical computer. Our narrator disarmingly suggests that Sears's exposure "to the computer memory with its supernatural command of facts and its supernatural lack of discernment . . . may have heightened his concern with sentimental matters . . ." (p. 10). But before we can dwell on the odd use of "supernatural" and the tentative phrase "may have," we are rushed into another sentimental encounter.

Sears meets Renée while standing in a cashier's line in a bank. People who choose to stand in line either are challenging automation or are lonely, in search of human contact; they are "of that generation who imagined there to be a line at the gates of heaven " (p. 11). When Sears sees Renée ahead of him, he is smitten immediately; with Beasley's Pond polluted, he begins pursuit of a naiad, a water nymph and guardian of fresh ponds and springs. Throughout the story, Renée's behavior is decidedly erratic, but she is meant to be a figure more symbolic than realistic. As a naiad-like creature, she is associated with water; water, as I noted, is always an ambiguous symbol either of birth and fertility or of death and destruction—as capricious as Nature itself.

Furthermore, and perhaps more pertinently, Carl Jung in his study of male psychology regards the nymph as an instance of a male's encounter with his *anima* image, i.e., the unconscious feminine aspect of his own personality.[11] In Jungian psychology, a male's psychic maturation takes place only after a series of encounters with the four progressive stages of that *anima* image. The lowest stage entails his confrontation with an Eve or Earth figure, the feminine under its purely biological aspect. The image of a water nymph reflects this relatively undeveloped stage in the process of a male's individuation, and so she inevitably represents the fragmentary within him: temptation, transitoriness, multiplicity, and dissolution.[12] Sears's initial emotions upon seeing Renée correspond to Jung's insights:

> [Sears] thought that perhaps it was nostalgia that made her countenance such a forceful experience for him. It could have been that he was growing old and feared the end of love. . . . When in the movies he saw a man and woman kiss ardently he would wonder if this was a country which tomorrow or the day after he would be expected to leave. (p. 11)

This erotic perception is immediately followed by a dream-like reverie, a series of conversions linked with memory and the exploration of the mystery of the self, the self as associated throughout with natural images. The descriptive language is at once definite and imprecise; the repetition of the words "could" and "seemed," together with "but" and "and yet," indicate that a personal *image,* of the *self* rather than of another, is sought after. In addition, as if to moderate any extreme solemnity, Cheever

---

11. See Carl G. Jung, "From the Psychology of Transference," *Basic Writings of C. G. Jung* (New York: Random House, 1959), pp. 403-404; and Carl G. Jung, *Man and His Symbols* (New York: Dell, 1964), pp. 186ff. For the material on nymphs, see Carl G. Jung, *Psychology and Alchemy, Collected Works* 12-13 (Princeton: Princeton Univ. Press, 1967).

12. I have been sorely tempted to offer a mythic interpretation of the whole structure of the novel. It seems clear to me at least that Sears's alienation from the once pure, now polluted pond represents *psychologically* (and so mythically) man's separation from nature because of human consciousness—and hence the stress on ignorance. *Spiritually* it represents a "fall," i.e., man's post-Eden exclusion from paradise; as the Genesis account suggests, his sexual alienation and confusion is a dramatic instance of this. Also, in biblical fashion, the novel both begins and ends in "seeming" paradise, and the pattern in between dramatizes man's rather errant pursuits of felicity.

I did not take this approach, however, because I felt I had overdone such mythic interpretation in my study of John Updike. Not only is once enough, but I feel this story does not require such explication. But had I taken this route, I would have relied heavily on the brilliant studies of M. H. Abrams, *Natural Supernaturalism: Tradition and Revolution in Romantic Literature* (New York: Norton, 1971); Northrop Frye, *A Study of English Romanticism* (New York: Random House, 1968); R. W. B. Lewis, *The American Adam* (Chicago: Univ. of Chicago Press, 1955); Daniel Hoffman, *Form and Fable in American Fiction* (New York: Norton, 1961); and Thomas Weiskel, *The Romantic Sublime: Studies in the Structure and Psychology of Transference* (Baltimore: Johns Hopkins Univ. Press, 1976).

sprinkles the passage with erotically comical images to highlight Sears's dreamy turmoil:

> Her looks aroused the most forthright and robust memories: the flag being raised at the ballpark before the first pitch while a baritone sang the National Anthem. This was an exaggeration, but the memories her appearance summoned involved only brightness. Her hair was a modest yellow. . . . In her rather small features he saw nothing at all like a mountain range and yet here was very definitely a declaration of paradise, either mountainous or maritime, depending upon one's tastes. He might have been regarding some great beach on another day of the week, but today he seemed to see the mountains, seemed disposed to raise his eyes, his head, and brace his shoulders as we do when, driving along some ghastly gambling-house strip, we see snow-covered mountains and feel how enduring is their challenge and their beauty. The components of his life seemed to present the need for a bridge and she and he seemed competent to build one that morning in the bank. . . . She could have been the winsome girl on the oleo-margarine package or the Oriental dancer on his father's cigar box who used to stir his little prick when he was about nine.   (pp. 11-12)

All of these, save the last, are familiar symbols in Cheever's fiction, emblematic of mystery and aspiration. Immediately there follows another symbol, more pronounced and structurally integrated than in his previous work: "The music that filled the air of the bank at that hour was a Brandenburg Concerto, played as ragtime."

> He imagined the smoothness of her naked back . . . so like a promised land. He wanted her as a lover, of course, and he felt that a profound and gratifying erotic consummation is a glimpse at another's immortal soul as one's own immortal soul is shown. . . . He stepped out of line, tapped her lightly on the shoulder and said: "I wonder if you can tell me what the music is that they're playing. You look to me as if you understood music."
> "You don't understand the first thing about women," she said.   (pp. 12-13)

Renée's first words soon become a refrain she repeats throughout their affair, essential to the musical (and thematic) shape of the novel. Elsewhere, overheard music punctuates various encounters, highlighting comic incongruity. Without being excessively fanciful, one might even say that the very structure of the novel itself is "a Brandenburg Concerto, played as ragtime." Or, better, a Bach fugue within one. Like a fugue, *Oh What a Paradise It Seems* is a contrapuntal composition. Central to this musical form is the "subject" (here the novel's title states it); in the first exposition of the subject (the paradise of Beasley's Pond) the orchestral voices enter, stating the subject in turn, then relinquishing it to take up the counter-subject (the paradisaical potential of erotic love). After this initial ex-position, any number of "episodes" in which the subject is ostensibly absent may follow, or else the subject might be modified by inversion or augmentation or diminution. The delight of fugal composition lies in the flexibility possible *within* the form and in the artist's skill at achieving, after seeming randomness, a complex climax wherein, for example, the subjects mirror each other in polyphonic fashion at the end—all of which takes place in *Oh What a Paradise It Seems*. "Ragtime" in this context refers more properly to the modern instruments used and the syncopation employed to dramatize the apparent improvisation at work.

Sears and Renée's first date contrasts with their bank encounter. Then Sears was tugged toward paradisaical transports; now he arrives in an in-fernal region: "The offices where she worked struck him as being char-acterized by a kind of netherness. They were on the nether floor of a nether building in a nether neighborhood . . ." (p. 13). As in the polluted pond, there is evidence only of portability, mobility, and impermanence. Because Sears has feigned interest in finding a new apartment, Renée shows him a dispiriting apartment, "a sort of nomadic hideout" (p. 15) characterized by its uniformity, sameness, and loneliness. Both are dis-appointed, and they make a second date, arranging to meet at St. Anselm's Presbyterian Church a few days later. Upon arriving, Sears is consternated to find her at a closed meeting—"members only," a sign announces. Curious, his imagination stirred, he glances inside the meeting room, expecting, perhaps, something infernal, but views instead its opposite: a scene penetential and apocalyptic in its universality. "He was at once struck by his incompetence at judging the gathering. Not even in times of war . . . had he seen so mixed a gathering. It was a group, he thought, in which there was nowhere the force of selection" (p. 17).

Sears is puzzled by the meeting's purpose. Some regret and effort at abstinence is communally shared, but he cannot discover its focus. His ignorance prompts him to imaginative effort as he overhears the group recite something in unison:

He guessed from the eagerness and clarity in their voices that it could not be an occult mantra. It was difficult to imagine what it could be. The cadence had for Sears the familiarity of church scripture and might have been the Lord's Prayer or the Twenty-third Psalm, but there was some sameness to the cadence in the seventeenth-century translations of scripture and unless he was told he would never know what they were chanting. (p. 19)

The sounds are too elusive for his comprehension, and the fact of his ignorance about the mysterious is reinforced when Renée emerges and

then tells him again, " 'You don't understand the first thing about women.' "
At their next meeting such a confusion is shared through symbolic action.
Renée takes him to an apartment for rent, and when she cannot find the
key that will open a promising locked door within it, she begins to sob.
The occasion stirs a memory within Sears involving Estelle, his second
wife, an incident nebulous and inexact that occurred in "some" airport—
"London, he guessed." After the bag clearance, she had attempted to
open a door with a "No Admittance" sign; she had pounded on the locked
door in frustration and, like Renée, began inexplicably to cry. This confluence of memory and renewed event reminds Sears of his most fundamental ignorance of the mystery of womankind, and of the truth that
compassion itself is the generous gesture that encloses ignorance:

> He felt then for his wife how much he loved her and how abso-
> lutely ignorant he was of the commandment that ruled her life. She
> seemed, pounding on the door in the London dawn, to have come
> from a creation about which he knew nothing although they had slept
> in each other's arms for years. His feeling for Renée was confused and
> profound and when she began to cry he took her in his arms, not to
> solace her for the locked door of course but to comfort her for Arthur
> [her former husband] and every other disappointment in her
> life.   (pp. 22-23)

The third chapter at first seems like a mere "episode" establishing a
tenuous plot connection. Nonetheless, fugue-like, it cues our memory to
previous themes. We are introduced to the neighborhood of Salazzo the
barber, a housing development deeply rooted in "seems":

> The architecture was all happy ending—all greeting card—that is, it
> seemed to have been evolved by a people who were exiles or refugees
> and who thought obsessively of returning. . . . [These houses] were
> nostalgic for the recent past or the efficient simplicities of some future,
> but they all expressed, very powerfully, a sense of endings and returns.
> Anything about these houses that seemed artificial or vulgar was
> justified by the fact that they were meant to represent serene
> retirement.   (p. 25)

The narrator's tone of demure apology extends to his own imaginative
exertions into the world of "seems": "It is with the most genuine reluctance that I describe the house [Salazzo] returned to and the asininity of
the game show that his wife and two daughters were watching on television" (p. 25). Despite the narrator's seeming reluctance, the scene he
describes is both hilarious and poignant. Salazzo, plagued by bills and a
lack of customers, arrives home only to have his wife announce that
" 'there's nothing to eat in the house except dog food,' " so he decides,

under the circumstances, that their dog, Buster, " 'is going to be the first sacrifice we make' " (p. 26). A sacrificial intent issues in the oddest of noble responses, one worthy of a knight errant but perhaps unexpected in a community of free-spirited dogs: The narrator intrudes:

> We know very little about the canine intelligence and nothing at all about the canine sense of eternity, but Buster seemed to understand what was expected of him and to welcome the chance to play a useful role in the life of the family even if it cost him his own life. . . . Sammy led the old dog out into the backyard and asked him to sit down a little to the right of the charcoal brazier. He then backed away a few yards and shot him through the heart.   (pp. 26-27)

Out of chaos comes order—and not for the last time—but an order of a perverse kind. Salazzo's wife, Maria, disconsolate at her husband's desperation, visits Uncle Luigi, who sets Sammy up as the money collector for the dumping of fill in Beasley's Pond. All then seems serene, except that their next-door neighbor, Betsy Logan, witnessed the dog's murder.

The fourth chapter returns briefly to the Renée-Sears relationship, one continued in many a church basement. Seeming, imagination, ignorance, and confusion stalk Sears's steps more keenly. He grows increasingly puzzled at these mysterious meetings: "But since abstinence, continence, some intangible moral value was at the bottom of this group, how could he have expected anything but a disparate gathering? The life of the spirit had no part, it seemed, in the establishment of caste" (p. 32).

Sears feels vaguely of them, for "he didn't suppose that he could scorn men and women who must be looking for something better. That things had been better was the music, the reprise of his days" (p. 33). Still, he is not one with them. He surmises that these people would agree with his conservative prejudices about the past, but "he would not dream of abdicating his airs and pretenses for their company" (p. 33).

And yet dreams, though unasked for, do occur. On a rainy night Sears, apparently so divorced from others, feels strangely allied with nature and its promptings. The passage describing this alliance artfully unites the images of water and renewal, music and love, and darkness and tender passion that we have seen—all circumscribed once again by the verb "seemed":

> That was a rainy night. It would be very unlike Sears to ally the sound of rain to his limited knowledge of love but there was, in fact, some alliance. It seemed that the most he knew of love had been revealed to him while he heard the music of rain. . . . The importance of rain is agricultural and plenty may have been involved, since plenteousness is one aspect of love. Darkness to some degree belongs to

rain and darkness to some degree belongs to love. In countless beds he
had numbered his blessings while he heard the rain on the roof. . . .
(pp. 33-34)

Meanwhile, by contrast, nature and its music produces an opposite
effect on Betsy Logan. The Salazzos have purchased a set of wind chimes,
and at night their music wakes her. "The wind chimes seemed to speak
to her although she wanted nothing to do with them . . . telling their
dumb, continuous story in a language she could not understand"
(pp. 35-36). Frustrated, she finally summons the courage to complain to
Mrs. Salazzo, asking her to turn them off during the night. Misunderstanding the point, Mrs. Salazzo replies, " 'You must be going crazy. You
think I can turn off the wind?' " (p. 37).

This comic juxtaposition within the fourth chapter illustrates again
Cheever's instinct and talent for moderating romantic sentiment about
Nature with another perspective. The fifth chapter recapitulates the associations of music and Nature from a further, even more explicitly comical perspective.

We learn that Renée "was the kind of woman who, as soon as she
entered her apartment, turned on first the lights and then the record
player. . . . [Sears] knew from experience that silence—the absence of
music—was for some men and women as suspect as darkness" (p. 39).
Just as the music of the wind chimes disconcerts Betsy, Renée's practice
disconcerts Sears—though in parody of keen musical responsiveness:

> One night when they were making love the record player was perform-
> ing a romantic piano concerto that closed with a long chain of per-
> cussive, false and volcanic climaxes. Every time the pianist seemed
> about to ascend his final peak he would fall away from the summit into
> a whole spectrum of lower octaves and start his ascent once more, as
> would Sears. Finally Renée asked, "Aren't you ever going to come?"
> "Not until the pianist does," said Sears. This was quite true and they
> concluded their performances simultaneously. He never knew whether
> or not she had understood him.   (p. 39)

That last line is a comic reversal of Renée's refrain, "You don't understand the first thing about women." Their reciprocal ignorance grows
throughout their relationship. Sears is grateful to her for reinstating him
within the country of love, although they are incompatible in other ways.
She renews within him a sense of natural potency and linkage with the
human race. When Sears is getting ready to see Renée after a week's
abstinence, the narrator invites us to watch him as he puts his genitals
in his trousers:

. . . he seemed to enjoy something very like authority, as if this most commonplace organ, possessed by absolutely every other man on the planet, were some singular treasure, such as the pen that was used for signing the Treaty of Versailles, robbing Bulgaria of Macedonia, giving her Aegean coast to Greece. . . . Sears seemed to think he was handling history.   (p. 41)

This comic conceit is itself reversed when Renée abruptly leaves him without explanation. "Now there are, it seemed to Sears, some Balkans of the spirit, where the villages are lit by fire and the bears weigh upwards of seven hundred pounds, and to which he now found himself quite helplessly being transported" (p. 43). The Treaty of Versailles quite arbitrarily created the Balkan states; equally arbitrarily, Renée's precipitateness creates another:

He seemed to have reached his Balkans by plane. The plane was large and he traveled first class, but he found himself in some airport where no one could tell him when his plane would depart and no one anyhow could speak any language that he knew. His grief was more the grief of a traveler than a lover.   (pp. 44-45)

Sears's sudden, incongruous homosexual relationship with the elevator operator in Renée's apartment building derives its meaning from this metaphoric context, as does the emphasis on "seeming": "The stranger's embrace seemed to comprehend that newfound province of loneliness that had frightened Sears. He seemed to know all about that mountainous city where there was no beauty and no coffee and where a homely waitress wiped a rubber plant's leaves with an untruthful newspaper" (p. 45). Displacement and sharing now collide in surprise: "Sears's next stop, of course, was a psychiatrist " (p. 45).

Sears's session with Dr. Palmer, "a homosexual spinster," in Chapter Seven is another wonderful example of Cheever's hilarious treatment of psychiatrists, one worthy of Peter DeVries or Woody Allen at their most madcap. Cheever elucidated his own bias by saying, "I am inclined to deal with them lightly in my fiction. Psychoanalysis runs counter to fiction with the idea that everything is symptomatic. Fiction is not about what's symptomatic, it's about what's astonishing in life. Fiction is meant to illuminate."[13] In the novel he insinuates this conviction more drolly.

At the time of which I'm writing, vogues in healing were changing swiftly. . . . The conviction that one could master the mysteriousness of life through the interpretation of dreams and an exhaustive analysis of one's early life was perhaps the most prevalent form of belief in the

13. Gilder, "John Cheever's Affirmation of Faith," p. 19.

Western World. This stood, of course, four-square upon the ruins of the legitimate confessional and the reformation of the roles played by parents in one's coming of age.   (p. 51)

Sears tells the doctor, " 'There seem to be contrary polarities in my constitution. I think my sexual conduct moral only in that it reflects on my concept of love' " (p. 53). The emotional power of this scene with the psychiatrist comes not from the deliberately banal dialogue but, as in so much of Cheever's fiction, from what is vaguely overheard and vaguely remembered as a counterpoint to it. While they talk, for example, Sears hears from the window "the loud, cheerful voice of a man calling some other man to throw him a ball. It was a voice from the playing field but the depth of his longing and nostalgia was not only for his youth but for the robustness, simplicity and beauty that life could possess . . ." (pp. 53-54). His efforts to confess these feelings to the doctor, in fact, betray "a sincere attempt to recapture this simplicity and usefulness" (p. 54), an adumbration of his later efforts to save Beasley's Pond. Here they immediately trigger memories of his two wives. He remembers that when he met his first wife, "beloved Amelia," he "felt at once that he had known her in some other life. . . . When she lay dying in his arms, twenty years later, his grief was unassuageable but there was a sense that she was returning to some stratum of existence where they had first met and where they would meet again" (p. 55).

Thoughts of his second wife, Estelle, become intertwined with his memory of a meeting with a blind prophetess named Gallia in Eastern Europe. Gallia was famous there for her formidable oracular powers, most recently for prophesying that "uranium prices would fall" (p. 56), and everyone spoke of her in hushed, reverent tones. Sears once went to see her (she lived in a cave within a volcano), accompanied by an interpreter struck almost speechless in anticipation of this grave encounter:

> She asked to feel something of his and he gave her his wallet. She fingered the wallet and began to smile. Then she began to laugh. So did Sears. She returned the wallet to him and said something to his interpreter. "I have no idea what she means," said the interpreter, "but what she said was 'La grand poésie de la vie.' " The prophetess stood and so did Sears. They were both laughing. Then she held out her arms and he embraced her. They parted, laughing.   (p. 58)

Mystery and laughter ever conjoin to fashion the human truth, and what else can we call it but the majestic poetry of life? Unfortunately, this "cheerful brush with a prophet was no help at all in Sears's understanding of Estelle" (p. 58). His second wife fancied herself equipped with "supernatural insights" into the future, although "Sears could not remember her having prophesied any triumphs of the spirit" (p. 59). Her talent sadly eluded her one evening when she crossed the train tracks on an unsafe wooden walk:

> She had started across the walk when a young man shouted: "Hey, lady, that ain't safe. A train is coming." "Who *do* you think you are speaking to?" she exclaimed, believing in introductions and other courtesies. "I happen to *know* the future." She stepped straight into the path of the Trenton Express and nothing was found of her but a scrap of veiling and a high-heeled shoe. (p. 60)

This farcical episode demonstrates comically the illusion of any human assurance about the future, and counterpoints the psychiatrist's efforts to ferret out the truth by exploring the past. Past, present, and future are equally mysterious, and Sears's ignorance is all-embracing. Gallia alone was cryptically correct when she said, "La grand poésie de la vie," and, as Cheever himself noted, Sears will not discover the purity he seeks within himself but only within a larger sphere, that connected with Beasley's Pond.

So, too, will Betsy Logan, whose story runs parallel to the tale of Sears. In Chapter Six we meet her in the Buy Brite supermarket, wheeling her cart "through a paradise of groceries" (p. 46). Like Sears's experience while skating, her deportment in the supermarket partakes of an ancient, primitive experience which the narrator describes:

> It is because our fortresses were meant to be impregnable that the fortresses of the ancient world have outlasted the marketplaces of the past, leaving the impression that fear and bellicosity were the keystones of our earliest communities, when in fact those crossroads where men met to barter fish for baskets, greens for meat and gold for brides were the places where we first grew to know and communicate with one another. Some part of Betsy's excitement at Buy Brite may have been due to the fact that she was participating in the one of the earliest rites of our civilization. (p. 46)

This quaint digression by the narrator, with its hint of civility and companionableness, is upended by the battle in Buy Brite soon to follow. Cheever reinforces the comic contrast further by noting the baroque music piped into the supermarket:

> This music had been chosen by a nephew of one of the majority stockholders, who seemed to think that there would be some enjoyable irony between eighteenth-century music and the tumult of a contemporary shopping center. . . . There is no irony, of course. The capital of Brandenburg was a market village and on a summer's day when the doors of the cathedral stood open the great concertos must have been

heard by the grocers and merchants. Betsy pushed her cart toward the express lane to the music that has contributed more, perhaps, than any other voice to our concept of nobility. Betsy pushed her cart toward lane 9—the express lane.   (pp. 47-48)

Alas, despite this idyllic suggestiveness, Betsy discovers Maria Salazzo ahead of her in the express lane, her cart loaded with the week's groceries she has chosen, drunk with the power that newfound money affords one. The two women engage in a verbal battle about Maria's right to use the express lane, Betsy complaining, " 'It is everybody's business. It's just like driving on the right-hand side of the road. There are a few basic rules or the business of life comes to a standstill' " (p. 50). These words trigger action: each woman dumps the groceries from the other's cart. Finally Maria, as "passionate as if she felt herself to be a figure in some ancient patriotic or religious contest, came at Betsy, swinging" (p. 50). The ancient civilities and aspects of social sharing are thus reversed, and the precarious human balance they support is briefly revealed as lopsided by an equally "ancient contest."

This disruptive interlude prepares us for the efforts at social recovery that begin in the ninth chapter. Throughout this study I have stressed that Cheever is fond of creating counterparts to dramatize "the polarities of the human constitution." In Chapter Nine, we discover two characters, Betsy Logan and Horace Chisholm, who are counterparts of Sears; like him, both are in search of spiritual purity and natural simplicity and find these only in the mystery of social sharing.

We meet Betsy again with her husband and two children on a lovely summer's day at the beach. Betsy's ambivalent emotional exhilaration there recapitulates Sears's experience while skating during the winter, for "the brine and the blue sky and the sand all seemed most natural to her as if this were her home" (p. 71). The fall of darkness moves her as it did Sears earlier; she is affected, too, by the ritual of leaving the beach:

> While she gathered up the towels and the sandwich papers and Binxie's diapers she remembered watching on TV when an astronaut went into space. After the countdown the camera had shown all the people along the beach packing up their sandwich baskets and their towels and their folding furniture and going back to the parking lot, and she remembered that this had moved her more deeply than the thought of a man walking around on the moon.   (pp. 71-72)

Betsy's memories and reveries of elation are quite specific, but her intimations of sadness and separation are not. When she thinks about the people who left the beach earlier, it seems to her that "they had received some urgent message to leave and that the beach was their home and that on leaving the beach they would be like the evacuees of war . . . who have to travel for years, perhaps for a lifetime, seeking a new home" (p. 72). Though happy as she drives her family back home, Betsy begins to "wonder—foolishly, she well knew—if modern life with its emphasis on highways had not robbed men and women of some intrinsic beauty that the world possessed. . ." (p. 73).

This vague sense of loss is particularized immediately when she and her husband inadvertently leave their baby, little Binxie, on the side of the highway. Fortunately, her counterpart, the environmentalist Horace Chisholm, is driving in their direction and sharing the same thoughts. Chisholm provides an excellent example of the way in which Cheever is able to create a subordinate character in a few short pages who can elicit our sympathy and interest and also personify the dramatic and thematic collisions in the story. Chisholm's reflections, and especially his spiritual instincts, capsulate all the emotional tensions that the other major characters have undergone.

Our introduction to Chisholm also deftly repeats the images proper to Betsy's own reflections. We hear that Chisholm feels that environmental hazards had "summoned him imperatively to do what he could to correct this threat to life on the planet," and that "the diminished responsibilities of our society—its wanderings, its dependence on acceleration, its parasitic nature—deeply troubled him" (p. 75). Though a homeless man himself, divorced and isolated, Chisholm—like Betsy and Sears—resists dwelling on the negatively mysterious; instead, absences and deprivations prompt him toward positive aspiration and a mysterious hopefulness, despite a brief visit to the Balkans of the spirit:

> He seemed to be searching for the memory of some place, some evidence of the fact that he had been once able to put himself into a supremely creative touch with his world and his kind. He longed for this as if it were some country which he had been forced to leave. . . . He felt so lonely that when the car ahead of him signaled for an exit he felt as if he had been touched tenderly on the shoulder by some stranger in some place like a crowded airport, and he wanted to put on his parking lights or signal back in some way. . . . In a lonely fantasy of nomadism he imagined a world where men and women communicated mostly with one another by signal lights and where he proposed marriage to some stranger because she turned on her parking lights an hour before dusk, disclosing a supple and romantic nature. (p. 76)

Seldom has Cheever expressed so succinctly and simply the central themes that pervade his fiction. Nostalgia and aspiration, the human demand for signals of affection, the need for imaginative projection and fantasy, the possibility of the wedding of strangers, of true marriage in its broadest sense as a responsiveness to the humanly companionable gestures of kindness and compassion—all of these generate the power of "la grand poésie de la vie."

All this is reinforced further by Chisholm's grappling with a mystery starker still, one transcending all physical bonds. The repetition of the word "seemed" in the following passage, augmented by emotional perplexity, suggests a more radical spiritual deprivation that is beyond articulation.

> His physical reality and the reality of the car he was driving were unassailable, but his spiritual reality seemed to be vanishing in a way that he had never before experienced. He even seemed to have lost the power to regret his past and its adventures. . . . He seemed about to become a cipher. The pain, perhaps the most galling he had ever known, lacked any of the attributes of pain, any of its traditional bloodiness.
>
> Then he seemed lost. He was lost. He had lost his crown, his kingdom, his heirs and armies, his court, his harem, his queen and his fleet. He had, of course, never possessed any of these. He was not in any way emotionally dishonest and so why should he feel as if he had been cruelly and physically stripped of what he had never claimed to possess? He seemed to have been hurled bodily from the sanctuary of some church, although he had never committed himself to anything that could be called serious prayer.   (p. 77)

Chisholm's spiritual crisis, characterized by a sense of loss and displacement, issues in the marvelous discovery of the baby in the blue baby carrier by the side of the road. This discovery is surprising but not totally unexpected, for Chisholm finds the baby only because he is on a nostalgic search for wild blackberries, symbolic to him of innocence and his youthful home. Furthermore, it is the "brightness and blueness [of the carrier that] seemed to declare that it was worth his attention"—images of light and the ethereal sky—and when he finds the child he exclaims, " 'You must be Moses, you must be King of the Jews' " (p. 78).

Chisholm's exclamation is not so far-fetched as it appears, for discovery of the baby effects a spiritual exodus for him, leading him forth from social isolation and egocentric enslavement. Immediately on seeing the abandoned child, he imagines its mother's tragedy and is moved to sympathy. He then feels himself "distinguished" and is deliriously happy to be "transporting a pleasant baby" (p. 78); at the police station he rejoices at seeing the baby and his father reunited and realizes that "continuity had seemed to be what he sought that afternoon when he had felt so painfully lost"(p. 80). Out of gratitude Betsy's husband Henry invites

Chisholm for dinner the following night. At the end of the evening Betsy says to him, " 'We don't know how to thank you for saving Binxie's life,' " and he replies, " 'Do whatever you can to save Beasley's Pond' " (p. 81)— and the human connection of shared responsibility for what transcends us as individuals, for continuity amid loss thus becomes dramatically established.

The next chapter echoes the very same themes and images from Sears's point of view, this time building to a musical climax incorporating all the sounds we have heard. Sears has gone out to inspect Beasley's Pond and is dismayed to see that "where the water was clear one saw trails of vileness like the paraphernalia of witchcraft" (p. 84). But this confrontation with the diabolical and the corrupt in its trickling increment spurs him toward an entirely different, explicitly religious vision, for Sears himself has now become a seer, gradually moving from his typical ignorance toward insight into the mystery of the first creation:

> The illusion of eternal purity the stream possessed, its music and the greenery of its banks, reminded Sears of pictures he had seen of paradise. The sacred grove was no legitimate part of his thinking, but the whiteness of falling water, the variety of its sounds, the serenity of the pools he saw corresponded to a memory as deep as any he possessed. He had on his knees in countless cavernous and ill-ventilated Episcopal churches praised the beginning of things. He had heard this described in Revelation as a sea of crystal and living creatures filled with eyes, but it seemed that he had never believed it to be anything but a fountainhead. (p. 84)

This passage artfully recapitulates the thematic and imagistic thrusts of the novel, a story concerned with beginnings and endings, with genesis and revelation, with heard and imagined music, with decay and infirmity contrasted with purity and restoration. Furthermore, the reader soon realizes that at issue is not a sentimental homesickness that aging inevitably generates within man but a more profound and older spiritual mystery: nostalgia for the source of one's very existence that predates that corruption sin brings which so diminishes the greener energies of memory and hope, signified by the word "seems" and the baptismal sound of water:

> When he was young, brooks had seemed to speak to him in the tongues of men and angels. Now . . . the sound of water seemed to be the language of his nativity, some tongue he had spoken before his birth. Soft and loud, high and low, the sound of water reminded him of eavesdropping in some other room than where the party was. (p. 85)

Contrast is provided by the events of the town board meeting, which farcically demonstrate the opposite: the corruption of language and the absence of light. When the mayor reads Sears's impassioned letter (titled "Is Nothing Sacred?") that he wrote to a newspaper, the gentle nostalgia expressed in it sounds eccentric and absurd to knowing ears, and the issue of Beasley's Pond seems closed.

"Seems," however, is the operative word. After Chisholm's murder, Betsy recalls his request that she do whatever she can to save the pond, and she does so. She returns to the Buy Brite supermarket (where love music is playing) with a bottle of teriyaki sauce dosed with ant poison and a note reading, "Stop poisoning Beasley's Pond or I will poison the food in all 28 Buy Brites." Her plan is to put the bottle with the others like it in the "Oriental corner," and it is significant that in order to do so she must first search diligently for the proper aisle and section. Having found it at long last, she places the bottle with its message on the shelf and returns home. We then learn that she is very much like Sears and Chisholm: "Her love for Henry and the children was quite complete, it seemed happily to transcend her mortality, and yet beyond this lay some unrequited melancholy or ardor. She was one of those women whose nostalgia for a destiny, a calling, would outlast all sorts of satiation. It seemed incurable" (p. 95).

Betsy's scheme finally succeeds, and the dumping at Beasley's Pond ceases. The "resurrection" of the pond has thus been effected, and the story ends as it began—as a tour, this time conducted by Sears in the proud, though technical, language of restoration and purity. The fugue-like story closes with its contrapuntal subjects in harmonious union, for we learn that "Sears spoke with an enthusiasm that sprang from the fact that he had found some sameness in the search for love and the search for potable water. The clearness of Beasley's Pond seemed to have scoured his consciousness of the belief that his own lewdness was a profound contamination" (p. 99). His former ignorance now is enlarged, embracing the mystery of creation itself, of which he is a part; now his human lack of knowledge transcends mere ignorance and touches on mystery, and issues in an instinctive humility and praise for our multiple "worlds":

> What moved him was a sense of those worlds around us, our knowledge however imperfect of their nature, our sense of their possessing some grain of our past and of our lives to come. It was that most powerful sense of our being alive on the planet. It was that most powerful sense of how singular, in the vastness of creation, is the richness of our opportunity. The sense of that hour was of an exquisite privilege, the great benefice of living here and renewing ourselves with love. What a paradise it seemed! (p. 100)

Fiction is experimentation; when it ceases to be that, it ceases to be fiction. One never puts down a sentence without a feeling that it has never been put down before in such a way, and perhaps even the substance of the sentence has never been felt. Every sentence is an innovation.

John Cheever

His best poems are the poetry of a man fully human—of someone sympathetic, magnanimous, both brightly and deeply intelligent; the poems see, feel, and think with equal success; they treat with mastery that part of existence which allows of mastery, and experience the rest of it with awe or sadness or delight. Minds of this quality of genius, of this breadth and delicacy of understanding, are a link between us and the past, since they are, for us, the past made living; and they are our surest link with the future, since they are that part of us which the future will know.

Randall Jarrell,
"Reflections on Wallace Stevens"

Radiance and light, I suppose, originate with fire. I suppose it's one of the oldest memories man has. In my church, the mass ends, of course, not with a prayer, not with an amen. It ends with the acolyte extinguishing the candles. . . . Light, fire— these have always meant the possible greatness of man.

John Cheever

Epilogue

Not unlike a Cheever novel, this study inevitably ends where it began. *Oh What a Paradise It Seems* was Cheever's fond farewell to the mysterious and varied radiances of the created world and also a graceful gesture of thanks to his readers, with whom he had shared so much sadness and merriment. Shortly after his death a memorial service in his honor was held at Trinity Episcopal Church in Ossining, and that generous valedictory spirit was re-enacted and reciprocated. Even the readings from the Book of Common Prayer, which the congregation read in unison, seemed appropriately Cheeveresque: "I have lifted up mine eyes unto the hills: from whence came my help. My help cometh from the Lord: which hath made heaven and earth" (Ps. 121); "Out of the deep have I called unto thee, O Lord: Lord, hear my voice" (Ps. 130); and "I heard a voice from heaven saying unto me: Write . . ." (Rev. 14:13).

The novelist Saul Bellow, who had been the closest of friends to John Cheever for almost forty years, addressed the congregation before the service started. Bellow began by affectionately recalling their long relationship, one deeply rooted in "human essences" despite their ethnic, regional, religious, and temperamental differences; he then ended by commenting on Cheever the writer with this eloquent, restrained tone of thanksgiving:

> [Cheever's] intention was, however, not only to find evidence of a moral life in a disorderly society but also to give us the poetry of the bewildering and stupendously dream-like world in which we find ourselves. There are few people around who set themselves such a task, who put their souls to work in such a way. . . . Those who choose such an enterprise, who engage in such a struggle, make all the interest of life for us. The life John led leaves us in his debt, we are his debtors, and we are indebted to him even for the quality of the pain we feel at his death.

Burton Benjamin, a senior executive producer at CBS News and another close friend of Cheever's for over thirty years, followed Bellow to the pulpit. He did not speak of things literary but of "John the friend, who could captivate a child with a smile and a story, who could come into your house and suddenly the sun was shining." Benjamin then offered the congregation a series of brief, personal memories, and the friends and family gathered there laughed with warm reminiscence at each anecdote. He closed by saying:

> Last Sunday the Ossining paper called and asked my wife: Did she have a comment about John? "All I can say," Aline said, "is that it's as if the heart of Ossining were gone."
>
> Yes—and in another sense, no. It has not gone. John is with us today. He will be with us tomorrow. And not only in those lovely, sensitive and brilliantly crafted words he left us and the world. For those fortunate few who knew him, his heart beats on. Forever.

The day before this memorial service in Ossining, John Cheever was buried in the Cheever family plot in the cemetery in Norwell, Massachusetts. His family had asked John Updike to deliver the eulogy at the graveside, and Updike graciously agreed to do so. I would like to quote the full text of his superlative tribute, because it traces warmly the rhythms of Cheever's life and work and also so ably summarizes the spirit of his achievement that it is, effectively, like an epitome of all my own, often tendentious, efforts at understanding Cheever throughout this study.

*   *   *

Friends and kin are gathered here in sorrow to bury John Cheever. We will miss him, as husband, father, uncle, companion, colleague, and exemplar. America will miss him, the leading fabulist of his generation and a cultural presence of an artistic certainty and a personal gallantry rare in any generation. Let me speak first of his certainty: he wrote prose fiction in a manner more common with poets and their poetry, as a kind of dictation, that flowed, when it did, effortless and compact. His swift rich style never rested to belabor the obvious or to preen, always outracing expectation and keeping the thread between reader and writer taut. I remember how, in the mid-seventies when John and I both lived solitary lives in Boston at opposite ends of the Back Bay, I would visit his apartment on Bay State Road and see in his typewriter, in a room that betrayed few other signs of habitation, a page containing some sentences about the main entrance to an institution called Falconer, an entrance crowned by an escutcheon representing Liberty, Justice, and Government. Liberty, one sentence firmly stated, "wore a mobcap and carried a pike." My visits occurred not much oftener than once a month, and from month to month the page in the typewriter never advanced. In April, as I remember, his health and his creativity in severe peril, he fled that apartment and his teaching post at Boston University and returned to the New York area and gave up alcohol. Time passed, John held to his vows and regained much of his health, and the novel *Falconer* appeared, to triumphant reviews and sales. I bought it, and on the first page read those very sentences which I had seen so long stalled in his typewriter on Bay State Road. I don't know that he changed a word, just carried the novel onward to its conclusion. That magic certainty of his prose, a cause for delight and envy for those others of us who try to write, was there in his earliest short stories and there in his last. His wonderful certainty can be observed, too, in his artistic career as a whole: no poems, little criticism, hardly any journalism exist in his published production; he was a teller of tales purely, and that purity contributed to the esteem in which he was held. His best self was the self in print; his readers had to do no editing of one who so scrupulously and instinctively edited himself.

His gallantry, if no other instance could be cited, was beyond all praise and admiration demonstrated in the style of his last, fatally stricken year. It was a summer ago that John and Mary entertained me and my wife at lunch in Ossining; his pain was such that he had no appetite, yet he insisted on sitting with us throughout the meal, courtly and witty, and took us then on a brief excursion to his favorite local sight, the Croton Dam. How much he loved water, light, and all the literally priceless blessings that Nature lavishes down upon our preoccupied and hastening lives! How much *joie de vivre* co-exists in his fiction with the tragic shadows, with his biting sociology and his sensitivity to human waste, unfulfillment, and cruelty. Though I had known John as a reader knows a writer since my teens, and we met at ceremonies from time to time, I saw a lot of him only on two extended occasions: in Boston in the mid-seventies and in Russia in 1964. It was in Russia, strange to say, that he seemed happier and more at home. His exceedingly quick humor and brisk apprehension lit up the potentially glum Soviet surroundings and made those weeks of touring catacombs and classrooms and speaking to wary clusters of writers and students as gay as an April in Paris. The Russians were drawn to his courage and ebullience and became more themselves in his presence. John was a great spirit, and these connoisseurs of the spirit knew it, and loved him.

So, too, we here loved him, each in his and her own way, each with our own witness of his certainty and gallantry. In our loss let us console ourselves with the lasting radiance of his work and with the special triumph of his last seven years, when in a willed act of rebirth he came back from a precarious state to write again, and to win greater financial and critical success than he had known before. He became, as writers evidently must in this age, a television and platform personality, without sacrificing a jot of his wit, mettle, and natural succinctness. He saw his collected short stories, that for four decades had held the astonishing mirror up to *New Yorker* subscribers, become a resounding best-seller and win a Pulitzer Prize. He saw his stories and a play performed on television, and wrote an enchanting farewell to our seeming earthly paradise. He saw his daughter publish two novels and his wife publish a lovely book of poems; all around him, there was singing. He enjoyed the honor and conviviality of the literary community of which he was a notably generous member, especially in his encouragement of younger writers. He read, and swam, and walked through landscapes and cityscapes with strenuous enjoyment, exercising what he called "a love of light and a determination to trace some moral chain of being." His religious faith, mysterious as all faiths are, must help account for his artistic integrity and his air of artistic freedom. He enjoyed, at the end, national fame, without seeming to have sought it. He took all worldly honors, one was sure, with a grain of salt, having located, early in his life, the private place of satisfactions, the secret pride and strength. His span of life, no more and no less than the biblically allotted span of three score and ten, fills me with pleasure in its contemplation, and gratitude. I feel lucky to have known John. I think all who knew him were lucky. There was something about him intensely graceful—full of grace—that made life seem a treasure. So it was. So it is.

Index